Windows on Justice in Northern Iberia 800–1000

Although it has a rich historiography, and from the late ninth century is rich in textual evidence, northern Iberia has barely featured in the great debates of early medieval European history of recent generations. Lying beyond the Frankish world, Spanish and Portuguese experience has seemed irrelevant to the Carolingian Empire and the political fragmentation (or realignment) that followed it. But Spain and Portugal shared the late Roman heritage which influenced much of western Europe in the early middle ages and by the tenth century records and practice in the Christian North still shared features with parts farther east.

What is interesting, in the wider European context, is that some of the so-called characteristics of the Carolingian world – the public court, collective judgment – are as characteristic of the Iberian world. The suggestion that they disappeared in the Frankish world, to be replaced by 'private' mechanisms, has played a major role in debates about the changing nature of power in the central middle ages: what happened in judicial courts has been central to the grand narratives of Duby and successive historians, for they are a powerful lens into the very real issues of politics and power.

Looking at the practice of judicial courts in Europe west of Frankia allows us to think again about the nature of the public; identifying all the records of that practice allows us to adjust the balance between monastic and lay activity. What these show is that peasants, like other lay people, used the courts to seek redress and gain advantages. Records were not entirely framed nor practice entirely dominated by ecclesiastical interests.

Wendy Davies, FBA, is Professor Emerita of History at University College London, UK.

Windows on Justice in Northern Iberia 800–1000

Wendy Davies

Routledge
Taylor & Francis Group
LONDON AND NEW YORK

First published 2016 by Routledge

2 Park Square, Milton Park, Abingdon, Oxfordshire OX14 4RN
52 Vanderbilt Avenue, New York, NY 10017

Routledge is an imprint of the Taylor & Francis Group, an informa business

First issued in paperback 2019

British Library Cataloguing in Publication Data
A catalogue record for this book is available from the British Library

Library of Congress Cataloging-in-Publication Data
Names: Davies, Wendy, 1942– author.
Title: Windows on justice in northern Iberia, 800–1000 / by Wendy Davies.
Description: Abingdon, Oxon, England : Ashgate, 2016. | Includes bibliographical references and index.
Identifiers: LCCN LCCN 2015027230 | ISBN 9781409464730 (hardcover : alkaline paper) | ISBN 9781409464747 (ebook) | ISBN 9781409464754 (ePub)
Subjects: LCSH: Law, Medieval. | Justice, Administration of—Spain—History. | Justice, Administration of—Portugal—History. | Justice, Administration of—Iberian Peninsula—History. | Iberian Peninsula—History.
Classification: LCC KJ147.D38 2016 | DDC 349.4609/021—dc23
LC record available at http://lccn.loc.gov/2015027230

ISBN: 978-1-4094-6473-0 (hbk)
ISBN: 978-0-367-88232-7 (pbk)

Typeset in Bembo
by Apex CoVantage, LLC

Contents

Illustrations

Figures

Table

Conventions

For abbreviations of works referred to in this book, please see the Bibliography. In quoting from Latin texts, I follow the punctuation and capitalization of the editions quoted unless otherwise indicated. However, I have used *u* consistently, rather than *v*, regardless of the usage of the edition quoted. I have kept name forms as spelled therein when quoting texts, but have used modern forms in discussion and translations where there is a commonly used form. For those unfamiliar with Latin of this period and area, note that orthography is extremely unstable and that grammar does not follow classical norms; I have not attempted any corrections or 'improvements'. My translations are very free; they are not intended to be literal (unless indicated); rather, they are intended to make sense in modern English.

Since the period covered by this book is 800–1000, my comments relate to charters of the period before 1000 unless otherwise specified. Hence, if, for example, I say there are no occurrences in Samos charters, I mean that there are none in Samos charters dated before 1000.

I have categorized people as high aristocrats, aristocrats, middle-range people or peasants. By this I mean to differentiate the exceptionally wealthy propertied person (high aristocrat) from the person of lesser means who nevertheless still lived entirely off income from his or her lands and who operated on a regional stage (aristocrat); by 'middle-range' I mean the person of some property, but without the scale or spread of interests of aristocrats – more like the country gentleman of modern history; and by peasant I mean someone who laboured on the land, whether richer or poorer, tenant or small-scale proprietor. This is basically a categorization by scales of property interests and of personal mobility. Of course, we cannot always be sure of the social status of individuals in these texts. However, I have taken to be peasants those who were associated with very small units of property, of low value, within a small area (usually that of a single community), who did not themselves travel far, and whose disputes – if they were involved in them – were of a petty kind. They contrast strongly with aristocrats, who had large, scattered estates (sometimes many) and who can be seen to have travelled considerable distances. Middle-range people do not seem to have laboured, but interacted at local level rather than on a wider field – in practice, not so very different from rich peasants. (Identification by patronymic very often indicates an aristocrat, but does not have to do so – there are many cases of Celanova texts referring to peasant and dependent cultivators by patronymic; the point of using the patronymic was to differentiate the person indicated from others with the same name).

In describing payments arising from judicial process, I have used 'fee', 'fine' or 'compensation' if the nature of the payment is clear and unambiguously differentiated. In this I understand 'fee' to be payment for a service, to the person providing the service, with no necessary implication of blame; I understand 'fine' to be a penalty for an offence or a failing, payable to an authority, and it does carry an implication of blame; I understand 'compensation' also to be a penalty, with implication of blame, but it is functionally different from 'fine' in that it was paid to an injured party rather than to an authority. Even in modern English usage these categories can overlap – for example, payment of court costs can be required of a losing party, the costs in effect becoming a penalty. In texts relating to the early middle ages, ambiguity and overlap is even more common. In Iberian judicial texts, the nature of a payment is often ambiguous, although very occasionally a text like Lor34 specifies that a payment is a fee for holding a court and for providing a resolution to a dispute. The person to whom the payment should be made can be ambiguous too, although there are often indications of this; where there is an indication, payment is most often destined for an authority. Such authorities were very rarely the state, although a small group of sanction formulas specifies payments due to a king; authorities were mostly court holders, of various kinds. Most of the sanctions attached to charters specify penalties, but some do not specify who should receive them, although both court holders and successful litigants feature; it is often implied, however, that the beneficiary of the transaction recorded in the charter should receive the penalty payment if the transaction were to be disrupted.[1] Compensation to an injured party is only rarely specified, but occasionally it happened.[2] The technical term *iudicatum* found in these texts usually refers to payment to a court holder (occasionally to a judge); while in origin this may well have been a fee in respect of holding the court – that is, court costs – in effect it operated as a penalty. The same applies to the *saionicum*, the fee paid to a legal officer. Very occasionally distribution of payments between court holder, judge and officer is specified, but usually there is no such indication.[3]

In view of this plethora of ambiguities, where a text is unclear or ambiguous about the nature of the payment, I have used the word 'fine' as a general term for all such payments; and for the purposes of classification of texts, I have used the term Fine for all documents recording such payments.[4]

It is conventional to refer to charters as originals, copies, pseudo-originals and *falsos* or fabrications. It has very reasonably been pointed out that, in dealing with early medieval texts, we can rarely know with complete certainty whether

1 For example, Cel72, Sob98, Li89; see ch. 4, pp. 106–11, 117–19, for sanction formulas.
2 See ch. 1, pp. 30–1.
3 See ch. 1, p. 31.
4 See Chapter 2.

a charter on a single sheet is an original or not; and indeed the idea that there would always have been a single original is in itself questionable.[5] However, the modern editors of many excellent editions have used the conventional terms, and I have therefore followed their usage unless otherwise indicated. By 'original', therefore, I mean a charter on a single sheet of parchment which has no obvious anachronisms in its physical characteristics or in its wording, and which is consistent with a record produced at the time stated, in the name of the principal actor, by the named scribe, if one is recorded. By 'pseudo-original' I mean a charter on a single sheet whose physical characteristics were intended to suggest production at the time stated, but which was created at a later time. By *falso* or 'fabrication' I mean a charter designed to deceive, which does not necessarily attempt reproduction of appropriate physical characteristics.

Authenticity is a different issue. Charters of this area at this period do not use authentication techniques, such as seals or signatures, and in the absence of those we have no means of authentication. Further, without corroborative evidence, we have no means of knowing whether the information conveyed by a charter is 'true': an original can intentionally or unintentionally misrepresent circumstances, and is in any case likely to have some element of bias; equally, a fabrication can provide some useful information about perspectives and about the time of its production, and in some circumstances can reproduce elements of earlier texts. I treat the information provided by originals as credible unless there is good reason to do otherwise, and that provided by pseudo-originals and fabrications as useful for some purposes. Copies can be contemporary or later, sometimes centuries later. There is no intrinsic reason why a copy should be any less credible than an original; I therefore treat the information provided by copies as credible unless there are clear anachronisms.

5 For a succinct discussion of the problems, see Brigitte Bedos-Rezak, 'Towards an archaeology of the medieval charter: Textual production and reproduction in northern French *chartriers*', in Adam J. Kosto and Anders Winroth (eds), *Charters, Cartularies, and Archives: The Preservation and Transmission of Documents in the Medieval West* (Toronto, 2002), pp. 43–60; and for a longer discussion, see Olivier Guyotjeannin and Laurent Morelle, 'Tradition et réception de l'acte médiéval: Jalons pour un bilan des recherches', *Archiv für Diplomatik*, 53 (2007), pp. 367–403, especially pp. 372–89.

Acknowledgements

I am indebted to many people for assistance during preparation of this book. I owe thanks to the British Academy and to the Leverhulme Trust for, respectively, a grant and an Emeritus Fellowship that made archive work possible; to the Pierpont Morgan Library for the cover illustration and Figure 7.2; to the Archivo Histórico Nacional for permission to print Figures 3.8 and 6.1; to the Archivo de la catedral de León and the cathedral chapter for permission for Figures 3.1, 3.2, 3.3, 3.4, 3.5, 3.6, 3.7 and 7.3; to the Archivo histórico diocesano de León for permission for Figure 2.4; to the Archivo de la catedral de Oviedo and the cathedral chapter for permission for Figures 0.1 and 0.2, and to the Archivo de la catedral de Lugo and cathedral chapter for permission to reprint Figures 5.2 and 8.3.

I am also particularly grateful to the archivists of León cathedral, Oviedo cathedral, the diocese of León, the diocese of Santiago de Compostela, the university of Santiago, the monastery of San Pelayo in Oviedo and the Spanish National Archive for their very considerable assistance when I was carrying out archive work; to Ainoa Castro for copies of her own photographs and advice on the palaeography of particular charters; to the librarians of the Bodleian Library, Oxford on many occasions, and to Roger Wright for frequent advice on the development of the language.

Isabel Alfonso, Álvaro Carvajal Castro, Julio Escalona, Jinty Nelson, André Marques and Chris Wickham very kindly read my whole manuscript in draft form, and Miguel Calleja, Julia Crick, David Ganz, Eduardo Manzano, Rob Portass and Bernhard Zeller read parts of it. Their comments were invaluable, although, of course, I alone am responsible for the final words.

Antonio Uriarte González of the Consejo Superior Investigaciones Científicas, Madrid, was assiduous, responsive and imaginative in preparing the maps; Álvaro Carvajal, David Peterson, José Carlos Sánchez Pardo and André Marques provided considerable assistance in identifying locations for the maps, and Julio Escalona was immensely helpful in providing practical assistance to complete the figures and much else. I am exceptionally grateful to them all.

Since this book went to press I have benefitted greatly from reading Graham Barrett, 'The Written and the World in Early Medieval Iberia', University of Oxford D. Phil. thesis, 2015.

Prologue

In the archive of Oviedo cathedral there still survives a very unusual charter relating the settlement of a tenth-century dispute. This is kept in a folder, with other early charters, in a chest in the centre of the reading room, and it is now classified as ACO B.1.11.[1] This text gives some detail about a judicial hearing concerning a monastery at Gordón, which lies on the southern side of the Cantabrian Mountains on the route from the tenth-century royal centre, León, to an earlier centre at Oviedo. The case was heard in 953, in Gordón, before the judges Teodoredo (Theodore) and Felix. What had happened was that a man called Victino had offered Brother Pedro land on which to build a monastery; once the monastery had been built, Victino (with the support of his family) had taken it over together with its appurtenant land, as well as another church Pedro had inherited and a vineyard he had received from Abbot Severo and a woman called Gogina. At the hearing three witnesses swore a formal oath on behalf of Brother Pedro – by Almighty God the Father, who made heaven and earth, the sea and all things in it, by the twelve prophets and twelve apostles and four gospels, and by the relics of the holy virgin Mary, mother of our Lord Jesus Christ, and the relics of Santa Marina, in whose place this oath was sworn – and an innocent (Fredenando) went to the ordeal of hot water, emerging with undamaged hand on the third day after the ordeal; finally Vilifredo (Victino's spokesman) agreed to assign the property to Pedro; a later endorsement, apparently added in 981, confirms that the judgment against Victino was correct. Several different sets of named people witnessed different parts of the procedure, and the hearing and final handover were managed by the *saio* (a legal officer) called Karoso. An endorsement on the back of the charter reads *condiciones de erias* – 'oath concerning Herias' – a place that lies on the same route from León to Oviedo, but north of Gordón; it is mentioned towards the end of the text, when Pedro and Vilifredo promise the *saio* they will go to Herias for the formal handover of the property.

1 Published as OvC26. I am extremely grateful to the cathedral chapter and to the archivist, Don Agustín Hevia Ballina, for permission to view the charter, and to Miguel Calleja for his considerable assistance on those occasions. For the text, see below, pp. 60–3.

Figure 0.1 ACO B.1.11: Archivo Capitular de Oviedo. Catedral de Oviedo, Sección Pergaminos: Serie B, Carpeta 1, no. 11

Source: Reproduced by permission of Cabildo Metropolitano de Oviedo, SICBM de Oviedo.

The unusual things about this record are these: it is an extremely large document, apparently original, written on a single sheet of parchment, 541 mm × 372 mm; the form of the record, which essentially consists of a short introduction, a statement of the claim, the oath and a series of witness lists, does not match that of other accounts of judicial proceedings,[2] and its content is exceptionally repetitive, Brother Pedro's accusation being repeated three times in almost identical words, although there are some gaps and inconsistencies in the story told, the verb shifts between first and third person and present and past tense, and the syntax of some parts appears unfathomable.[3] For example, the role of Sister Gogina is extremely unclear – initially she was one of those who advised Victino to proceed against Pedro, but later she is held to have been one of the donors of the vineyard to Pedro in the first place. There are also three churches mentioned in the context of one or more meetings – Santa María, Santa Marina and San Martín – and relics of both María and Marina are noted; this is, of course, possible, but it looks as if some element of confusion has crept in, since at first Santa Marina and later Santa María are cited as the location of Severo's confirmation of Pedro's ownership before judges – in the repeated passages.

2 See below, pp. 26–32.
3 See below, pp. 150–51.

The layout of the charter is also very unusual: the main text occupies the top three-fifths of the parchment and the third, righthand, column of three columns below the top three-fifths; all of this is written in a single hand; witnesses are in two columns in the remaining space, to the left of this third column, and the endorsement of 28 years later lies at the bottom of the lefthand column. Two long chrismons (in the main hand) run down the lefthand sides of columns one and three. The column of text, at bottom right (column three), actually records, quasi verbatim, two sets of witnesses of the ordeal as well as some of the key declarations of the procedure, in three successive commitments by the principal actors Pedro and Vilifredo to appear before the judges on a given day, to accept the agreement and to accompany the *saio* for the formal concluding transfer of the property. It thereby constitutes a kind of special witness/confirmer section, together with an appendix of key commitments. It is perfectly clear that this appendix was intentional, since a single chrismon (in the original hand) runs down the lefthand side of this column and the different parts of the appendix are signalled by the positioning of the 'bows' on the chrismon, respectively four for the witness section, two for the first commitment, and one each for the second and third (see Figure 0.2).[4] The two lefthand columns below the main text contain the subscriptions and in some cases *signa* (marks) of further witnesses, including the king, members of the royal family, court officers and prominent bishops. The main hand is unusual for this period in its use of an open 'a', although this is not unknown in tenth-century charters. The names and *signa* of the king and high-status witnesses are in several different hands, different inks and at varying orientations; some of them overlap the righthand column, indicating that they were added after the main text was written. So, while at first sight one might well doubt that this was really a record made in 953, the fact that these high-status subscriptions include a 'standard' judge's *signum* and the 'correct' *signum* for the bishop of León of the time, and the further fact that the 981 endorsement was clearly added after the first column of high-status witnesses, does make it likely that this was a record made some time in the tenth century.

The charter nevertheless remains problematic and raises many issues. Firstly, there are material questions: is the exceptional size significant (it is far bigger than most records of disputes), and what is the significance of its very unusual layout? Secondly, there is its form: again, this is very unlike that of most dispute records; how can this be explained, and is there any particular value in the appendix of three separate commitments by the major parties and in the fact that the charter contains six different witness lists (the formal witnesses of the sworn oath, those present at the oath, those present when the innocent entered the ordeal, those who saw him emerge from the ordeal with clean hand, the high-status witnesses, the witnesses of the 981 endorsement)? Can the text be

4 See further below, pp. 73–4, 87, for chrismons and for the 'bows'.

Figure 0.2 ACO B.1.11, lower righthand side

credible as a record of judicial proceedings? The threefold repetition of the main accusation, with its errors and inconsistencies and variations, must have been copied from a written text, given the way it varies.[5] What, if anything, does it tell us about the process of creating records of judicial proceedings?[6] What, if anything, does it tell us about what happened in the course of judicial proceedings? Are the events it relates credible? Could we really believe that the king of León and a host of the highest aristocrats were present at this rural dispute (although it was near a royal *castellum*, a fort where the king imprisoned rebels in 944)?[7] Is it possible that what we are glimpsing are the ramifications of a family dispute over property? Gogina seems to be someone's sister, and she is both the benefactor of Pedro and one of those who advised Victino

5 See the Appendix to the Coda.

6 See the treatment of this text by Roger Collins, '"Sicut lex Gothorum continet": Law and charters in ninth- and tenth-century León and Catalonia', *English Historical Review*, 100 (1985), pp. 489–512, at pp. 498–501; but also that of Justiniano Rodríguez, *Ordoño III* (León, 1982), pp. 171–8, who deals at length with some of the problems; and see my further comment on this below, pp. 51, 146–7.

7 Li44 (918); Justo Pérez de Urbel, *Sampiro. Su crónica y la monarquía leonesa en el siglo X* (Madrid, 1952), ch. 23.

to withdraw property from Pedro, while Victino was advised by other family members, including his wife and sisters. What kind of people were the actors, the judges, the legal officer who received the commitments, the many witnesses? Were local people involved at all in the process of settling the dispute? And if it is at all credible, what does this property dispute have to do with the high politics of the kingdom of León?

This book is about these issues. It is about the structure, form and language of dispute records in northern Iberia in the ninth and tenth centuries, and about the materiality of the texts that survive on single sheets. It is about the people who took practical roles in court cases, and about those who chose to use courts to settle their differences. It is about the role of the local, and the relationship between local process and the world of kings and aristocrats. And it is about distinctiveness: were these practices peculiar to northern Iberia, or echoed in western Europe beyond the Pyrenees? I shall return to the particular problems posed by ACO B.1.11 and the monastery of Gordón as the book proceeds. For some solutions, turn to Chapters 2 and 5.

1 Orientation

Time and territory

This book is about that part of the early middle ages for which we have localizable evidence of good quality, and plenty of it. That means, in practice, the ninth and tenth centuries. The very early middle ages, the Visigothic period, is well documented, but its texts come from the high culture of kings and prominent clerics; the material written on slate in the sixth and seventh centuries certainly comes from a more local culture, but most of it comes from a limited area of the central *meseta*.[1] Hardly anything at all has survived from the eighth century, creating a complicating and often frustrating hiatus. The mid-ninth century is therefore the time when we can begin to investigate practice, rather than prescription, in a wide range of different locations.[2]

Iberia is a huge peninsula, with a wide range of different landscapes and different climates. It is a land of raised plateaux, punctuated by high mountain ranges; in the north these ranges are broken by the two great river systems of the Duero and the Ebro (see Figure 1.1). Much of the Duero basin lies on the vast plateau of the *meseta*, which is hot and arid in summer, although it is crossed by long river valleys running south to the Duero from the Cantabrian Mountains; the basin is bounded on the south by the Central System of mountains. To the north of the Cantabrian Mountains is a narrow coastal strip, its cramped settlements looking out to sea, traditionally an area of retreat from disturbances on the *meseta*. To the west, across the León Mountains, lies Galicia, a land of high rainfall which makes it wet and green for much of the year; Portugal, for the most part south of the Duero, lies to the south of Galicia; however, in early medieval political terms what we now call northern Portugal belonged with Galicia. To the east of the *meseta* lie the high sierras of the Iberian System bordering the Ebro valley and the region of La Rioja, while beyond them are the forests and hills of the Basque Country, Navarre and Aragón, until the

1 See n. 86 below for Visigothic legal texts; for slates, see Isabel Velázquez Soriano, *Las Pizarras Visigodas (Entre el latín y su disgregación. La lengua hablada en Hispania, siglos VI–VIII)* (Salamanca, 2004).

2 See further below, pp. 10–17, for available texts.

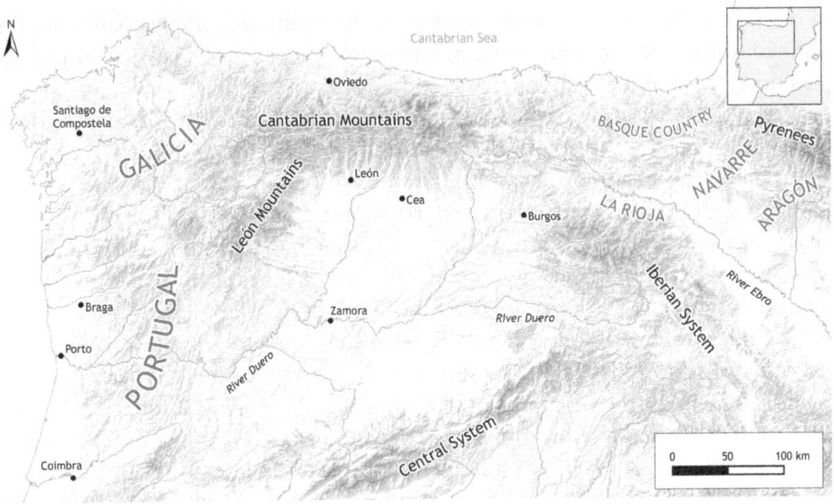

Figure 1.1 Principal relief features of Iberia

land merges into the foothills of the Pyrenees. This is a diverse land, varying from mountainous regions that are largely unsuitable for cultivation, although farmed in parts, to a hot plateau that requires careful agricultural management. However, northern Iberia had predominantly mixed farming in the early middle ages – arable and pastoral, orchards and vineyards. It was an overwhelmingly rural economy, and urban development was late by western European standards. León was clearly a fully functioning urban centre in the tenth century; there are hints of the beginnings of urban development at Burgos, in Castile; there were clearly nucleations at Coimbra, Zamora, Oviedo and Santiago de Compostela, the latter probably already of significant size in the tenth century, and all were ecclesiastical centres; the marketplace of Cea was a noted place of exchange; although the evidence is very weak, there must have been the beginnings of urban development at Braga; and one would expect the port of Porto to have had some commercial functions by the late tenth century. But that is all, and – although we should expect archaeology to provide more evidence in the next few decades – most of these cases offer limited evidence at the moment.[3] Given

3 Juan Antonio Quirós Castillo and Belén Bengoetxea Rementeria, *Arqueología (III) (Arqueología Postclásica)* (Madrid, 2006), pp. 336–44, provides a useful survey of the consequences of the absence of well-stratified archaeological sequences. For León, see Claudio Sánchez-Albornoz, *Estampas de la vida en León durante el siglo X* (Madrid, 1924), and Carlos Estepa Díez, *Estructura social de la ciudad de León (siglos XI–XIII)* (León, 1977); for Zamora, see Cel430 (951), Cel428 (983), and Iñaki Martín Viso, *Fragmentos del Leviatán. La articulación política del espacio zamorano en la alta edad media* (Zamora, 2002), especially pp. 67–104; for Santiago, see Fernando López Alsina, *La ciudad de Santiago de Compostela en la alta edad media* (Santiago de Compostela, 1988).

these diverse landscapes, and the very rural economy, one might expect significant regional difference in social practice; whether or not that was in fact the case in respect of judicial practice is to be seen.

Iberia was politically fragmented in these later centuries of the early middle ages, and much of the peninsula was dominated by the Muslim Caliphate of al-Andalus, the successor of the Emirate established in the early eighth century, with a partly Arabic, partly Berber, partly continuing Latin culture.[4] The ninth and tenth centuries have traditionally been associated with the beginning of the so-called Reconquista, a time when kings of northern Spain began to recover control of some territory from the Muslim states of the south.[5] While a historiographical framework dominated by an unrelieved picture of ever-expanding reconquest is nowadays very questionable, it is certainly the case that northern kings were involved in campaigning southwards in this period and Muslim expeditions penetrated into the far north of their territory;[6] rulership therefore had a practical military dimension, although government was relatively limited. Kings had significant personal properties, however, from which they appear to have derived the greater part of their income.[7]

There were essentially two Christian kingdoms in this period, although political geography was much more unstable than the traditional picture of unitary Spanish political development towards the Castile and Aragón of the late middle ages might suggest, and although some of the powerful regional aristocracies added complexity to political trends (see Figure 1.2). Firstly there was the kingdom of Pamplona or Navarre, about which we know relatively little in the ninth and tenth centuries, although its kings seem to have acquired considerable power by the late tenth century and were to become very significant in the eleventh. Its base lay in the mountains which are the western extension of

4 Hugh Kennedy, *Muslim Spain and Portugal: A Political History of al-Andalus* (London, 1996); Eduardo Manzano Moreno, *Conquistadores, emires y califas, Los omeyas y la formación de al-Andalus* (Barcelona, 2006); for Berbers, see Pedro Chalmeta Gendrón, *Invasión e islamización: la sumisión de Hispania y la formación de al-Andalus* (Madrid, 1994), and cf. David Peterson, *Frontera y lengua en el alto Ebro, siglos VIII–XI* (Logroño, 2009), pp. 106–48.

5 For broad general surveys, see, for example, in English, Roger Collins, 'The Spanish kingdoms', in Timothy Reuter (ed.), *The New Cambridge Medieval History, Volume III: c.900–c.1024* (Cambridge, 1999), pp. 670–91, and in Spanish, Amancio Isla Frez, *La alta edad media. Siglos VIII–XI* (Madrid, 2002).

6 The issues are many, but centre on whether or not large parts of the north had been depopulated as a consequence of Muslim conquest, on whether 'repopulation' was part of the northern kings' recovery strategy, and on whether, therefore, colonizers came as free settlers, bringing an unusual spirit of freedom to peasant communities. See Claudio Sánchez-Albornoz, 'Pequeños propietarios libres en el reino Asturleonés. Su realidad histórica', in *Agricoltura e mondo rurale in occidente nell'alto medioevo*, Settimane di studio del centro italiano di studi sull'alto medioevo, 13 (1966), pp. 183–222, and see further n. 38 below.

7 For a recent appreciation of how kings built up their properties and their political capacity in the tenth century, see Álvaro Carvajal Castro, 'La construcción de la monarquía asturleonesa en la meseta del Duero. Estudio de los procesos de integración territorial (s. IX–XI)' (Universidad de Salamanca, Tesis Doctoral, 2013).

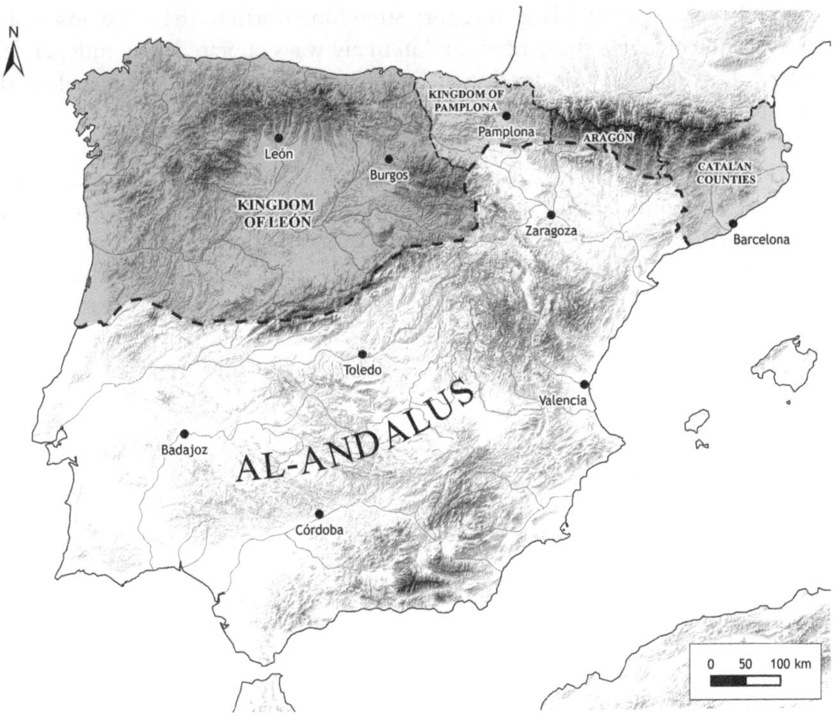

Figure 1.2 Iberia *c.* 950

the Pyrenees, although tenth-century kings had interests in the Ebro valley to the south and in effect incorporated the region of Aragón to the east.[8] Secondly, there was the kingdom of Asturias-León, about which we know much more. The latter had its origins in the very far north, with a royal base at Oviedo, north of the Cantabrian Mountains, for most of the ninth century; the royal base moved to the old Roman city of León around 910. Within the kingdom of León it is useful to think of four distinct zones: the north, including the long Liébana valley, which lay on the northern edge of the Cantabrian Mountains (within the modern autonomous regions of Asturias and Cantabria); Galicia in the west, which had its own distinctively regional aristocracy and occasionally a separate king in the tenth century, although it is debatable how far a separate political identity was sustained;[9] León itself and the *meseta* that surrounded it, and lastly Castile, on the eastern edge of the *meseta*, between the León heartland to the west and the Pamplona kingdom and Muslim Ebro valley to the east – by

8 See Juan José Larrea, *La Navarre du IVe au XIIe siècle* (Paris and Brussels, 1998).

9 See Amancio Isla Frez, *La sociedad gallega en la alta edad media* (Madrid, 1992), pp. 177–97; Robert Portass, 'All quiet on the western front: Royal politics in Galicia from *c.* 800 to *c.* 950', *Early Medieval Europe*, 21 (2013), pp. 283–306. See further below, pp. 206–9.

the mid-tenth century a large territory, stretching north to the sea, whose count grew in power across the century and in many ways operated as an independent ruler.[10] Portugal did not develop an independent political identity before the later eleventh century.

Beyond the scope of this book, in the far north east, in the Pyrenees and their southern and western hinterland, lay Catalonia, subject to Frankish expeditions in the late eighth century and established as a 'march' or border zone of the Carolingian Empire in the early ninth.[11] Initially comprising seven counties, more were added before the more prominent counts began to absorb the lesser counties; nevertheless, the counts continued to look to the north-east, towards the Frankish state, for more than a century. In the later tenth century one count, the count of Barcelona, emerged predominant, and the Frankish orientation began to dissolve.[12]

Written sources

At the moment there is little relevant archaeological evidence and the texts available for the study of judicial practice in ninth- and tenth-century northern Iberia are overwhelmingly charters – records of the transfer of property rights. There is little in the way of letters or tracts or narrative sources,[13] although there

10 Justo Pérez de Urbel, *Historia del condado de Castilla* (3 vols, Madrid, 1945), is the classic treatment; Gonzalo Martínez Díez, *El condado de Castilla (711–1038): la historia frente a la leyenda* (2 vols, Valladolid, 2005). See further below, pp. 20–6, on counts.

11 Catalonia does not form part of the subject matter of this book since, although it shared many features of judicial practice, it was in many ways different from the rest of northern Iberia in the early middle ages and had a close association with Frankish culture. See the comments of Adam J. Kosto, *Making Agreements in Medieval Catalonia: Power, Order, and the Written Word, 1000–1200* (Cambridge, 2001), pp. 5–6. However, see below, ch. 9, for some important points of comparison.

12 The classic study of Catalonia in this period is Pierre Bonnassie, *La Catalogne du milieu du Xe à la fin du XIe siècle: croissance et mutations d'une société* (2 vols, Toulouse, 1975–76); see also his shorter assessment, Pierre Bonnassie, *La Catalogne au tournant de l'an mil. Croissance et mutations d'une société* (Paris, 1990). More recently, see Jonathan Jarrett, *Rulers and Ruled in Frontier Catalonia, 880–1010: Pathways of Power* (Woodbridge, 2010), and, emphasizing Frankish connections, Josep María Salrach, *Justícia i poder a Catalunya abans de l'any mil* (Vic, 2013).

13 There is a Hispanic Passionary, which is a compilation of the *passiones* of Roman, Visigothic and Mozarab martyrs in Spain, begun in the seventh century and reaching its definitive form in the eleventh; the few items which could be of tenth-century origin (most are much earlier) probably derive from Mozarabic contexts in southern Iberia; for detailed descriptions of the contents, and a survey of arguments for dating, see María Adelaida Andrés Sanz, Carmen Codoñer, Salvador Iranzo Abellán, José Carlos Martín and David Paniagua, *La Hispania visigótica y mozárabe. Dos épocas en su literatura* (Salamanca, 2010), pp. 336–59. There are two short tenth-century *Vitae*: the exceptionally brief so-called Life of Abbot Salvo of Albelda, of *c.* 976, is published by Charles J. Bishko, 'Salvus of Albelda and frontier monasticism in tenth-century Navarre', *Speculum*, 23 (1948), pp. 559–90, at pp. 575–6; see also Andrés Sanz et al., *La Hispania*, p. 364. For the *Vita Froilanis*, see José Carlos Martín, 'La *Vita Froilanis episcopi Legionensis* (BHL 3180) (s. X): introducción, edición crítica y particularidades lingüísticas', in Monique Goullet (ed.), *Parva pro magnis munera. Études de littérature tardo-antique et médiévale offertes à François Dolbeau par ses élèves* (Turnhout, 2009), pp. 561–84. See also Andrés Sanz et al., *La Hispania visigótica,*

are chronicles from the late ninth century as well as the chronicle written by Sampiro in the very early eleventh and some tenth-century annals;[14] these are important works, but they are relatively brief and are concerned with the deeds of kings; they include little that bears on judicial process. However, there is a large corpus of liturgical material, of some relevance. The surviving liturgical *ordines* are of the eleventh century; this material is Mozarabic (that is, from the increasingly Arabized Christian communities of the south), and was ultimately of Visigothic origin; doubtless it underwent some changes between the sixth and seventh centuries and our surviving material of the eleventh century, but much of what we find in eleventh-century manuscripts must have been known in some parts of the north in the ninth and tenth centuries, and it may well have coloured the way that some charters were written.[15]

Although there are relatively few surviving new literary compositions of the ninth and tenth centuries, it was during the tenth century that many of the great Spanish manuscripts were written. The contents of these manuscripts were in large part devotional and in large part copies of much earlier works, especially of the late antique period: bibles, psalters, liturgical texts; monastic rules; Saints' Lives and Passions; patristic works, especially those of Gregory the Great and Cassian, and of the Spaniards Isidore and Ildephonsus; the Commentary on the Apocalypse by Beatus of the Liébana; and, rather surprisingly, several works of the Carolingian Smaragdus of Saint-Mihiel.[16] But there was also work which might best be described as academic, like the large glossaries from San Millán de la Cogolla;[17] and like the great collection of the Codex Albeldense, of 974–76, ultimately from the monastery of Albelda, which includes the Visigothic laws

pp. 269–96, for the corpus of ninth-century Cordoban letters (and other material) from southern Iberia, and Manuel Cecilio Díaz y Díaz, *Index Scriptorum Latinorum Medii Aevi Hispanorum* (Madrid, 1959), pp. 119–64, for other works, comments and notes written in the ninth and tenth centuries.

14 Sampiro's chronicle, together with notes and critical study, is published in Justo Pérez de Urbel, *Sampiro. Su crónica y la monarquía leonesa en el siglo X* (Madrid, 1952), at pp 273–346. The ninth-century chronicles are published in *Crónicas Asturianas*, ed. and trans. Juan Gil Fernández, José L. Moralejo and Juan Ignacio Ruiz de la Peña (Oviedo, 1985). For the Castilian annals, see José Carlos Martín, 'Los *Annales Castellani Antiquiores* y *Annales Castellani Recentiores*: edición y traducción anotada', *Territorio, Sociedad y Poder*, 4 (2009), pp. 203–26.

15 *Liber Ordinum Episcopal (Cod. Silos, Arch. Monástico, 4)*, ed. José Janini (Silos, 1991); *Liber Ordinum Sacerdotal (Cod. Silos, Arch. Monástico, 3)*, ed. José Janini (Silos, 1981). See my further comment in Wendy Davies, 'Local priests in northern Iberia', in Steffen Patzold and Carine van Rhijn (eds), *Men in the Middle: Local Priests in Early Medieval Europe* (Berlin, forthcoming), and see below, pp. 118–19.

16 For description and contents of the manuscripts, see Agustín Millares Carlo, *Corpus de códices visigóticos*, prep. Manuel Cecilio Díaz y Díaz, Anscari M. Mundó, José Manuel Ruiz Asencio, Blas Casado Quintanilla and Enrique Lecuona Ribot (2 vols, Las Palmas de Gran Canaria, 1999). For more detailed discussion, see Manuel Cecilio Díaz y Díaz, *Códices visigóticos en la monarquía leonesa* (León, 1983), and Claudio García Turza (co-ord.), *Los manuscritos visigóticos: estudio paleográfico y codicológico. I. Códices riojanos datados* (Logroño, 2002).

17 For example, Madrid, Real Academia de la Historia, Codex Emilianense 46, of 964; Millares Carlo, *Corpus*, no. 197.

and canons, the Life of Abbot Salvo of Albelda, who died in 962, and the so-called Chronicle of Albelda, one of the late ninth-century chronicles.[18] These works comes from prominent monastic centres, as do manuscripts from Cardeña, Santo Domingo de Silos and León.

Surviving charters of this period are written in Latin and number about 2,700 from the whole of northern Iberia, excluding Catalonia; they are overwhelmingly of the tenth century, but there is a handful from the Visigothic period, about twenty from the eighth century and a little over 200 from the ninth century. About two-thirds of them survive in cartulary copies and one-third on single sheets of parchment; many of the latter are 'originals', but some are contemporary or later copies and some are falsifications. The distinction between copy and original is important, for whereas an original will indicate scribal practice of the time that the record was made, it is always possible that a copy has been updated or otherwise edited – as some clearly were; some cartulary copyists changed spelling and grammar to more classical forms, as well as adding new material.[19]

For the most part the charters record gifts and sales, but records of disputes sometimes precede details of gifts, as explanatory background. The charter collections also include full or partial accounts of particular dispute cases, detached from any record of gift, in addition to the gift charters with extended narratives. These come from localities across northern Spain and Portugal, although there are relatively few from Navarre and Aragón. The biggest collections of pre-eleventh-century charters are from the monastery of Celanova in Galicia, in an important cartulary including 223 records, in twelfth-century hands, three different collections having been brought together in one cartulary;[20] the episcopal collections from León, including 591 records, from cartularies and on single sheets, many of which are originals;[21] the monastery of Sahagún on the *meseta*, including 372 records in an early twelfth-century cartulary and on single sheets,[22] and the monastery of Cardeña in Castile, with a late eleventh-century cartulary including the majority of the 212 pre-1000 records.[23] Not quite so

18 Biblioteca de El Escorial, MS. d.I.2; Millares Carlo, *Corpus*, no. 49. Manuel Cecilio Díaz y Díaz, *Libros y librerías en la Rioja altomedieval* (Logroño, 1979), p. 64. The Chronicle is almost certainly of Oviedo, not Albelda, origin.

19 See above, pp. x–xi, for a note on the terminology of original and copy.

20 *O Tombo de Celanova: Estudio introductorio, edición e índices (ss. IX–XII)*, ed. José Miguel Andrade Cernadas, with Marta Díaz Tie and Francisco Javier Pérez Rodríguez (2 vols, Santiago de Compostela, 1995); charters are hereafter cited by number as Cel1, Cel2 etc. Some charters are long, composite records of several (sometimes many) transactions, for which see below, pp. 69–72.

21 *Colección documental del archivo de la catedral de León (775–1230), I (775–952)*, ed. Emilio Sáez (León, 1987); *II (953–985)*, ed. Emilio Sáez and Carlos Sáez (León, 1990); *III (986–1031)*, ed. José Manuel Ruiz Asencio (León, 1987); charters are hereafter cited as Li1, Li2, Lii259, Liii512 etc.

22 *Colección diplomática del monasterio de Sahagún (857–1230), I (siglos IX y X)*, ed. José María Mínguez Fernández (León, 1976); charters are hereafter cited as S1, S2 etc.

23 *Colección documental del monasterio de San Pedro de Cardeña*, ed. Gonzalo Martínez Díez (Burgos, 1998), an edition which includes a few charters from sources other than the cartulary; charters are hereafter cited as C1, C2 etc.

large but still substantial are two twelfth-century Galician cartulary collections from the monastery of Sobrado de los Monjes, 45 km north-east of Santiago de Compostela, and a cartulary of *c.* 1200 and a handful of single sheets from that of San Julián at Samos, 65 km to the south east of Sobrado, in the western foothills of the Cantabrian mountains; they include 117 and 73 records respectively;[24] as also an early twelfth-century collection in a late twelfth-century cartulary, ultimately from several different sources, from San Millán de la Cogolla in the rich agricultural lands of La Rioja, to the east (118 records, some of which are composite, detailing many more transactions).[25] The corpus of charters from Portugal is also significant, and includes 236 records on single sheets and in cartularies, from different sources. This material is most easily accessible in a mid-nineteenth-century collection, although that collection does not include all charters that are now known and although there are more recent editions of Braga, Coimbra and Lorvão charters (the latter from an important cartulary, begun in the early twelfth century); there are 12 unpublished charters.[26] There are also several series of charters in favour of the church of Santiago de Compostela, of which the 58 of Tumbo A (a cartulary begun in the second quarter of the twelfth century) are especially relevant for present purposes; and there are smaller but significant collections (from single sheets and cartularies) from north-west Galicia – notably from the monasteries of San Lorenzo de Carboeiro, San Martín Pinario, San Payo de Antealtares, all of which are most easily accessed in the recent *La Coruña* collection, altogether 60 records, some of which are severely damaged and some false.[27] There would appear to be in the order of 70 charters from before 1000 from the bishopric of Lugo; there are some surviving single sheets, preserved both in the Lugo cathedral archive and

24 *Tumbos del monasterio de Sobrado de los Monjes*, ed. Pilar Loscertales de García de Valdeavellano (2 vols, Madrid, 1976), hereafter cited as Sob1, Sob2 etc.; *El Tumbo de San Julián de Samos (siglos VIII–XII)*, ed. Manuel Lucas Álvarez (Santiago de Compostela, 1986), hereafter cited as Sam1, Sam2, etc.

25 *Cartulario de San Millán de la Cogolla*, ed. Antonio Ubieto Arteta (Valencia, 1976), hereafter cited as SM1, SM2 etc. Now available in an online edition, 'Becerro Galicano de San Millán de la Cogolla' (2013): http://www.ehu.es/galicano/?l=es, hereafter cited as BG1, BG2 etc., which is based on Fernando García Andreva, *El becerro galicano de San Millán de la Cogolla. Edición y estudio* (Logroño, 2010).

26 *Portugaliae Monumenta Historica a saeculo octavo post Christum usque ad quintumdecimum, Diplomata et Chartae*, ed. Alexandre Herculano de Carvalho e Araujo and Joaquim José da Silva Mendes Leal (vol. 1 of 1 vol. only, Lisbon, 1867–73), hereafter cited as PMH DC 1, PMH DC 2 etc.; *Liber fidei sanctae bracarensis ecclesiae*, ed. Avelino de Jesus da Costa (3 vols, Braga, 1965, 1978, 1990); *Livro Preto. Cartulário da Sé de Coimbra*, ed. Manuel Augusto Rodrigues (Coimbra, 1999); *Liber testamentorum coenobii Laurbanensis* (2 vols, León, 2008), hereafter cited as Lor1, Lor2 etc. Very grateful thanks are due to André Marques, who supplied the numbers and allowed me access to his inventory of all ninth- to eleventh-century Portuguese charters.

27 *La documentación del Tumbo A de la catedral de Santiago de Compostela: estudio y edición*, ed. Manuel Lucas Álvarez (León, 1997), hereafter cited as SantA1, SantA2 etc.; *La Coruña. Fondo Antiguo (788–1065)*, ed. Carlos Sáez and María del Val González de la Peña (2 vols, Alcalá, 2003–2004), hereafter cited as LaC1, LaC2 etc.

in the National Archive in Madrid, some of which are published in scattered locations, but some of which remain unpublished; there are also many copies, both on single sheets and in cartularies.[28] The recent publication of transcripts made by Cañizares del Rey in the mid-twentieth century includes transcripts which can be inaccurate, but in the absence of an edition of modern standards, I have used the work, as I have also occasionally used the recent publication of the earliest, thirteenth-century, cartulary, *Tumbo Viejo*, which includes many of the most infamous *falsos* of the early middle ages.[29]

There are also some smaller collections which are important, especially those from the monastery of Santo Toribio on the edge of the Liébana valley in the far north, in an early fourteenth-century cartulary which includes a significant proportion of ninth-century charters (77 from before 1000); from the cathedral of Oviedo and the monastery of San Pelayo beside it (with a high proportion of single sheets in both collections, 34 and 26 records respectively); 49 records from Otero de las Dueñas on the northern edge of the *meseta* – very important because virtually all of its pre-eleventh-century charters are original single sheets from lay archives, and 47 records from Valpuesta in Castile (in two cartularies, of which the earlier includes folios written in tenth-century hands).[30] There are in addition some charters in cartularies from Arlanza, also in Castile; some from Albelda, within the orbit of both Castile and Navarre, and some from San Juan de la Peña, farther east in Aragón (comparative numbers for Arlanza are 25, Albelda 29, San Juan 32, though the latter include many

28 I have cited most of these by archive number, ACLu and AHN. Nearly all of the published editions are listed in Ainoa Castro, *Colección diplomática altomedieval de Galicia I: Documentación editada en escritura visigótica (662–1234)* (A Coruña, 2011), and it is to be hoped that Dr Castro will complete publication of the unpublished charters in the near future. Her volume does not include AHN 1325A–6 and AHN 1325A–9, both of which were published by Claudio Sánchez-Albornoz, 'Documentos para el estudio del procedimiento judicial en el reino asturleonés', in *Homenaje a Don Agustín Millares Carlo* (2 vols, Gran Canaria, 1975), vol. 2, pp. 146–7, 152–3, nor the charter on the dorse of AHN 1325A–4, which is published by Antonio López Ferreiro, *Colección diplomática de Galicia histórica* (Santiago de Compostela, 1901), pp. 394–5. It is impossible to assess total numbers of Lugo charters from a distance, but Cañizares del Rey (see n. 29 below) has 70 charters from before the year 1000 – a number which includes some *falsos*.

29 Ventura Cañizares del Rey, *Colección Diplomática (569–1463)*, ed. Manuel Rodríguez Sánchez and Óscar González Murado (Lugo, 2012), hereafter cited as Cañ1, Cañ2 etc.; *Tumbo Viejo de Lugo (transcripción completa)*, ed. and trans. José Luis López Sangil and Manuel Vidán Torreira, *Estudios Mindonienses*, 27 (2011), pp. 11–373, hereafter cited as TV1, TV2 etc. I am extremely grateful to Ainoa Castro for allowing me to see some of her own transcripts.

30 *Cartulario de Santo Toribio de Liébana*, ed. Luis Sánchez Belda (Madrid, 1948), hereafter cited as T1, T2 etc.; *Colección diplomática del monasterio de San Vicente de Oviedo (años 781–1200)*, ed. Pedro Floriano Llorente (Oviedo, 1968), hereafter cited as Ov1, Ov2 etc.; *Colección de documentos de la catedral de Oviedo*, ed. Santos García Larragueta (Oviedo, 1962), hereafter cited as OvC1, OvC2 etc.; *Colección documental del monasterio de Santa María de Otero de las Dueñas (854–1108)*, ed. José Antonio Fernández Flórez and Marta Herrero de la Fuente (León, 1999), hereafter cited as OD1, OD2 etc.; *Los becerros gótico y galicano de Valpuesta*, ed. José Manuel Ruiz Asencio, Irene Ruiz Albi, Mauricio Herrero Jiménez (2 vols, Burgos, 2010), hereafter cited as V1, V2 etc.

falsos).[31] And finally, there are very small numbers of ninth- or tenth-century charters in collections which are mainly of eleventh-century or later material; these include 8 charters from Oña in Castile, 13 (mostly suspect) from Leire in Navarre, 7 from Santa María del Puerto in Cantabria; from the *meseta*, 30 from Eslonza (including a number of tenth-century charters on single sheets), 10 from Castañeda, 18 from Dueñas and 13 from San Pedro de Montes, as well as the very substantial collection of 186 records from Astorga (largely inaccessible because the majority of charters in the published edition are calendared rather than published in full).[32] There is one rather doubtful charter on a single sheet from Jaca in the western Pyrenees.[33] There remain small numbers from further scattered collections which do not supply material relevant for present purposes.

Although the collection and preservation of charters and cartularies was largely undertaken by ecclesiastical bodies, in the middle ages and later, the beneficiaries of transactions were not necessarily ecclesiastical: many charters record transactions between lay parties, for example gifts and payments from peasants to aristocrats or sales between peasants.[34] These records ended up in church collections because they were the former title deeds of property that ultimately was given to churches (for example, Peasant A sold land to Peasant B, who had a record made, and later Peasant B's son gave that land to the local church, together with existing records). There were also some lay archives; it is clear that lay people with significant property holdings also made a point of keeping records in the tenth century, although these are less likely

31 *Cartulario de Albelda*, ed. Antonio Ubieto Arteta (València, 1960), hereafter cited as A1, A2 etc.; *Cartulario de San Pedro de Arlanza, antiguo monasterio benedictino*, ed. Luciano Serrano (Madrid, 1925), hereafter cited as Ar1, Ar2 etc.; *Cartulario de San Juan de la Peña*, ed. Antonio Ubieto Arteta (2 vols, València, 1962–63), charters (in vol. 1) hereafter cited as SJP1, SJP2 etc.

32 *Colección diplomática de San Salvador de Oña*, ed. Juan del Alamo, vol. 1 (Madrid, 1950), hereafter cited as Oña 1 etc.; *Documentación medieval de Leire (siglos IX a XII)*, ed. Ángel J. Martín Duque (Pamplona, 1983); 'Cartulario de la iglesia de Santa María del Puerto (Santoña)', ed. Manuel Serrano y Sanz, *Boletín de la Real Academia Historia*, 73 (1928), pp. 420–42, hereafter cited as SMdelP1, SMdelP2 etc.; *Colección documental del monasterio de San Pedro de Eslonza (912–1300)*, vol. 1, ed. José Manuel Ruiz Asencio and Irene Ruiz Albi (León, 2007), hereafter cited as E1, E2 etc.; *El Tumbo del monasterio de San Martín de Castañeda*, ed. Ángel Rodríguez González (León, 1973), hereafter cited as Cast1, Cast2 etc.; *El monasterio de San Isidro de Dueñas en la edad media*, ed. Carlos M. Reglero de la Fuente (León, 2005); *Tumbo Viejo de San Pedro de Montes*, ed. Augusto Quintana Prieto (León, 1971); *Colección documental de la catedral de Astorga (646–1126)*, vol. 1, ed. Gregoria Cavero Domínguez and Encarnación Martín López (León, 1999), hereafter cited as Ast1, Ast2 etc.

33 Roger Collins, 'Visigothic law and regional custom in disputes in early medieval Spain', in Wendy Davies and Paul Fouracre (eds), *The Settlement of Disputes in Early Medieval Europe* (Cambridge, 1986), pp. 85–104 and 252–7, at pp. 255–6, hereafter cited as Jaca. Collins treats this charter as original, but some features (e.g. *bonos barones senes*) seem unlikely to derive from mid-tenth-century drafting.

34 For detailed discussion of types of record, see Wendy Davies, *Acts of Giving: Individual, Community, and Church in Tenth-century Christian Spain* (Oxford, 2007), pp. 88–96, 110–12, 135–8.

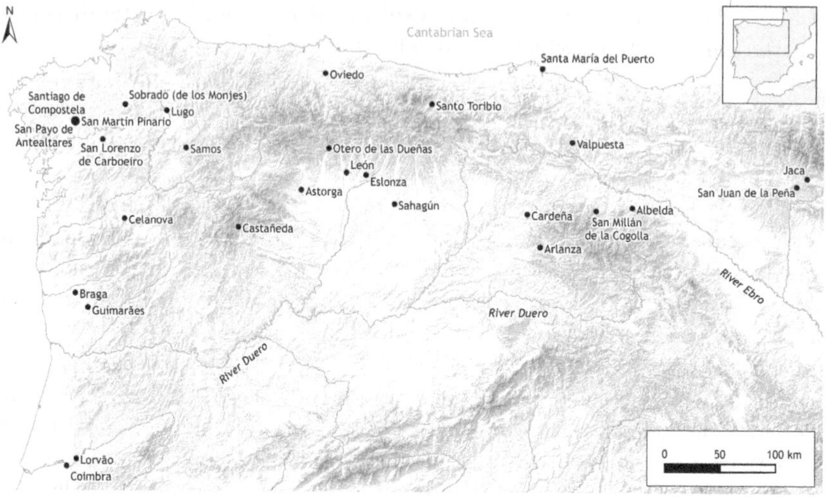

Figure 1.3 Provenance of principal charter collections

to have survived than the church collections.[35] Hence, a large collection of single sheets, like that in León cathedral archive, includes cathedral charters, charters from several monasteries in León, and also many charters recording transactions between lay persons of property that subsequently ended up in church hands. Cartulary copyists also sometimes copied records of transactions between lay parties, which means that we are not dependent on the survival of single sheets for knowledge of lay transactions.[36] The fact that lay people used, and kept, documents detailing their transactions is exceptionally important for any analysis of practice.

Now, charters were drawn up in different ways; some were dictated by a redactor (a composer or author) to a person who wrote what he heard dictated; but some were composed and physically written by a single person; sometimes we can differentiate these functions, but often we cannot. Where we have sufficient knowledge, I shall refer to the former as redactors and to those who did the physical writing as writers; where we do not know, I shall call them scribes. There were several different kinds of scribe, whose practice could vary substantially: scribes working for royal households (although there was not as yet any formal chancery), highly experienced scribes in the scriptoria of great monasteries and cathedrals, functional scribes in aristocratic households, idiosyncratic scribes in lay religious households and scribes based at local churches. Indeed,

35 See Warren C. Brown, Marios Costambeys, Matthew Innes and Adam J. Kosto (eds), *Documentary Culture and the Laity in the Early Middle Ages* (Cambridge, 2013).

36 See below, ch. 3, for material characteristics of charters, and ch. 4, for charter writing.

some charters were written by local priests or minor clerics for local people, and some were explicitly written at local churches.[37]

Modern writing

The past century of historical writing in Spain has been dominated by the idea of Muslim conquest in 711 and its various perceived consequences. Prominent among these perceptions is the view that this conquest was overturned across many centuries by a long struggle between Christians and Muslims, the so-called Reconquest, the final conquest of the Muslims coming in 1492.[38] While it is perfectly clear that in the long term a Muslim Caliphate was replaced by a Christian kingdom, scholars nowadays acknowledge that there was much more interaction between north and south than traditionally allowed, and that in the later ninth and tenth centuries there were plenty of political, economic and cultural contacts between them. It remains conventional, however, to situate the origins of the central medieval aristocracy of northern Iberia in the resumption of political control of the *meseta*.[39] In considering internal social and political change within the Christian kingdoms, most Spanish historians of the later twentieth century accepted a basic principle of feudal development.[40] In other words, they accepted the emergence of a world characterized by the domination of private lords over the persons, labour and surplus of a largely servile peasant population, and by the fragmentation of the public power of the state and its dispersal among the greater private lords. The development of private lordly power has been crucial to the historiography of the past two

37 On this, see Davies, *Acts of Giving*, pp. 93–109, and Wendy Davies, 'Local priests and the writing of charters in northern Iberia in the tenth century', in Julio Escalona and Hélène Sirantoine (eds), *Chartes et cartulaires comme instruments de pouvoir. Espagne et Occident chrétien (VIIIe–XIIe siècles)* (Toulouse, 2013), pp. 29–43.

38 The bibliography is enormous, but the work of Claudio Sánchez-Albornoz has been central to this historiography. See Claudio Sánchez-Albornoz, 'Las behetrías: la encomendación en Asturias, León y Castilla', *Anuario de Historia del Derecho Español*, 1 (1924), pp. 158–336 (reprinted in his *Viejos y nuevos estudios sobre las instituciones medievales españolas* (3 vols, Madrid, 1976–80), vol. 1, pp. 15–191), and Claudio Sánchez-Albornoz, *Despoblación y repoblación del valle del Duero* (Buenos Aires, 1966), to name two key works. See also Ramón Menéndez Pidal, 'Repoblación y tradición en la cuenca del Duero', in Manuel Alvar, Antonio María Badía Margarit, Rafael de Balbín and Luís Felipe Lindley Cintra (eds), *Enciclopedia Lingüística Hispánica* (2 vols, Madrid, 1960–67), vol. 1, pp. xxix–lvii. There is a useful, brief recent survey by Julio Escalona Monge, 'Mapping scale change: Hierarchization and fission in Castilian rural communities during the tenth and eleventh centuries', in Wendy Davies, Guy Halsall and Andrew Reynolds (eds), *People and Space in the Middle Ages, 300–1300* (Turnhout, 2006), pp. 143–66, at pp. 143–9.

39 See Pascual Martínez Sopena, *La Tierra de Campos Occidental. Poblamiento, poder y comunidad del siglo X al XIII* (Valladolid, 1985), pp. 329–30; Vicente Ángel Álvarez Palenzuela, 'La nobleza del reino de León en la alta edad media', in *El reino de León en la alta edad media, VII, Estudios* (León, 1995), pp. 149–329, at pp. 160–83.

40 The essential work is Abilio Barbero and Marcelo Vigil, *La formación del feudalismo en la Península Ibérica* (Barcelona, 1978).

generations. Most scholars identified the central middle ages as the key period of feudalization, charting the development at different rates within a tenth- to twelfth-century bracket, although often quite late in the bracket, and pointing to differences between the Spanish development and that of the classical Frankish model.[41] Although younger scholars are beginning to adopt different approaches, the language of feudalism is still embedded in much history writing.[42]

This prevailing discourse is important for understanding the context in which judicial practice has been discussed in Spain, particularly during the last forty years. Both earlier and recent work have used judicial texts to illuminate the nature and development of political power.[43] If political power was fragmented and privatized, was justice also privatized in the courts held by lords, as suggested for other parts of western Europe?[44] Now, one particularly dominant theme of the literature is that power and judicial functions were delegated by kings to aristocrats.[45] How can these quite contrary notions – royal delegation of judicial functions as against the private appropriation of such functions – be reconciled? And if peasants were dominated by private lords, did this impact upon their access to justice? There is a significant literature on peasant resistance,[46] as also on collective responsibility and collective action at local level, including in the context of judicial action.[47]

41 See especially Carlos Estepa Díez, 'Formación y consolidación del feudalismo en Castilla y León', in *En torno al feudalismo hispánico. I congreso de estudios medievales* (Ávila, 1989), pp. 157–256; Reyna Pastor, 'Sur la genèse du féodalisme en Castille et dans le León, Xe–XIIe siècles. Point de départ pour une histoire comparative', in Hartmut Atsma and André Burguière (eds), *Marc Bloch aujourd'hui. Histoire comparée et sciences sociales* (Paris, 1990), pp. 259–70; Josep M. Salrach, 'Les féodalités méridionales: des Alpes à la Galice', in Eric Bournazel and Jean-Pierre Poly (eds), *Les féodalités* (Paris, 1998), pp. 313–88. For a useful survey of approaches, see José Ángel García de Cortázar, 'La formación de la sociedad feudal en el cuadrante noroccidental de la península ibérica en los siglos VIII a XII', *Initium*, 4 (1999), pp. 57–121, especially pp. 69–75. Cf. Julio Escalona Monge, 'De "señores y campesinos" a "poderes feudales y comunidades". Elementos para definir la articulación entre territorio y clases sociales en la alta edad media castellana', in Ignacio Álvarez Borge (ed.), *Comunidades locales y poderes feudales en la edad media* (Logroño, 2001), pp. 115–55.

42 New approaches: Carvajal Castro, 'La construcción de la monarquía asturleonesa en la meseta del Duero'; Robert Portass, *Society, Community and Power in Early Medieval Christian Spain* (Woodbridge, forthcoming); Simon Barton and Robert Portass (eds), *Beyond the Reconquista: Essays on the Politics, Society and Culture of Medieval Iberia, 800–1200* (Liverpool, forthcoming).

43 See, for example, Alfonso Prieto Prieto, 'La potestad judicial de los reyes de León', in *El reino de León en la alta edad media, II: Ordenamiento jurídico del reino* (León, 1992), pp. 519–64.

44 See, for example, Guy Bois, *The Transformation of the Year One Thousand: The Village of Lournand from Antiquity to Feudalism*, trans. Jean Birrell (Manchester, 1992 [first published 1989]), especially pp. 65–8; but see further below, pp. 202–3, on privatization, and pp. 251–2, for some comparison.

45 See further below, pp. 22–5.

46 Reyna Pastor, *Resistencias y luchas campesinas en la época del crecimiento y consolidación de la formación feudal. Castilla y León, siglos X–XIII* (2nd edn, Madrid, 1990 [1st edn 1980]).

47 Claudio Sánchez-Albornoz, 'El régimen de la tierra en el reino asturleonés hace mil años', in *Viejos y nuevos estudios*, vol. 3, pp. 1,313–521, at pp. 1,447–75; Pastor, *Resistencias y luchas campesinas*, pp. 54, 78–80. See further below, pp. 219–26.

Law and justice have long been discussed by Spanish medieval and legal historians, regularly since the beginnings of the annual journal *Anuario de Historia del Derecho Español* in 1924, founded by Sánchez-Albornoz. Much of this has been undertaken in the context of legal history, with a keen interest in establishing the nature of law and the ways in which it changed. Since legal texts were copied in the tenth century and were cited in charters, all of this work remains relevant; it includes papers of continuing importance, such as the 1924 classic paper of Sánchez-Albornoz on the *behetrías*;[48] the work of Arvizu y Galarraga and Rubio on testamentary disposition; that of García Gallo on the *fuero* of León, and that of Martínez Díez on institutions.[49] Valdeavellano's many contributions include seminal papers on the alienability of property and on guaranteeing transactions.[50]

This legalistic approach of much of the twentieth century has given way in the last generation to a greater concern with what actually happened at a judicial assembly, and increasingly with the political context and social meaning of judicial process.[51] Important papers on procedure, for example by Prieto Morera, Martínez Díez and Martínez Sopena, mean that we now have a good idea of the mechanics of procedure.[52] Nearly thirty years ago, Roger Collins wrote two agenda-setting papers (in English) on the texts generated by judicial process, as well as on process itself.[53] José María Mínguez set Spanish justice within the prevailing context of feudalization, while Isabel Alfonso has published a series of papers – on dispute resolution, judicial rhetoric, penalties

48 Sánchez-Albornoz, 'Las behetrías'.

49 Fernando de Arvizu y Galarraga, *La disposición 'mortis causa' en el derecho español de la alta edad media* (Pamplona, 1977); José-Antonio Rubio, '"Donationes post obitum" y "donationes reservato usufructu" en la alta edad media de León y Castilla', *Anuario de Historia del Derecho Español*, 9 (1932), pp. 1–32; Alfonso García-Gallo, 'El fuero de León. Su historia, textos y redacciones', *Anuario de Historia del Derecho Español*, 39 (1969), pp. 5–171; Gonzalo Martínez Díez, 'Las instituciones del reino astur a través de los diplomas (718–910)', *Anuario de Historia del Derecho Español*, 35 (1965), pp. 59–167.

50 Luis García de Valdeavellano, 'La cuota de libre disposición en el derecho hereditario de León y Castilla en la alta edad media (Notas y documentos)', *Anuario de Historia del Derecho Español*, 9 (1932), pp. 129–76; Luis García de Valdeavellano, 'Escodriñamiento y otorificación. Contribución al estudio de la reivindicación mobiliaria en el derecho español medieval', in *Centenario de la ley del notariado* (2 vols, Madrid, 1965), vol. 2, pp. 125–335.

51 Cf. Barbero and Vigil, *La formación del feudalismo*, pp. 362–80.

52 Agustín Prieto Morera, 'El proceso en el reino de León a la luz de los diplomas', in *El reino de León en la alta edad media, II: Ordenamiento jurídico del reino* (León, 1992), pp. 381–518; Gonzalo Martínez Díez, 'Terminología jurídica en la documentación del reino de León. Siglos IX–XI', in *Orígenes de las lenguas romances en el reino de León, siglos IX–XII* (2 vols, León, 2004), vol. 1, pp. 229–72; Pascual Martínez Sopena, 'La justicia en la época asturleonesa: entre el *Liber* y los mediadores sociales', in Ana Rodríguez (ed.), *El lugar del campesino. En torno a la obra de Reyna Pastor* (València, 2007), pp. 239–60. See further below, pp. 26–32, and also my comments in Wendy Davies, 'Settling disputes in early medieval Spain and Portugal: A contrast with Wales and Brittany?', in Ralph A. Griffiths and Phillipp R. Schofield (eds), *Wales and the Welsh in the Middle Ages: Essays Presented to J. Beverley Smith* (Cardiff, 2011), pp. 89–107.

53 Roger Collins, '"Sicut lex Gothorum continet": Law and charters in ninth- and tenth-century León and Catalonia', *English Historical Review*, 100 (1985), pp. 489–512; Collins, 'Visigothic law and regional custom'; see further below, pp. 47 n39, 51 n56, on these papers.

and more – which enormously increase our understanding of the political relationships surrounding the use of courts.[54] Professor Alfonso is leading a major project on judicial practice in the central middle ages, 'Procesos judiciales en los reinos del norte peninsular (ss. IX–XI)', which has established a comprehensive database of relevant material, publicly accessible from 2016; the results of this project will become increasingly available.

There has therefore been some lively and productive attention to judicial court procedure and politics in the early middle ages, building on the long tradition of legal history. It has clarified procedure and brought political context to the fore. But there has been a strong tendency to treat texts recording judicial process, especially the detailed texts of court cases, as objective reporting – as if they were modern court records; there has been relatively little analysis of the texts, nor assessment of the circumstances that produced them, nor differentiation between the several kinds of text and their evidential value.[55] That is what this book sets out to do. Further, work to date, like work on the aristocracy or peasantry, has tended to deal within a tenth- to twelfth- or thirteenth-century time bracket, focusing on the eleventh and twelfth centuries, with a backward glance at the tenth century. The eleventh century was a time of considerable economic change and a time of rapidly shifting political context – as the territory of kingdoms expanded and changed shape, new families came into high politics and the great aristocratic families embedded. In this book, I am primarily interested in what was happening before those changes, and in whether or not the system as we see it in the tenth century had any relationship with a more distant past.

Counts

Although the designation 'count' is familiar in western Europe, the term 'count', *comes*, is problematic in many ninth- and tenth-century contexts. Since it has

54 José María Mínguez, 'Justicia y poder en el marco de la feudalización de la sociedad leonesa', in *La giustizia nell'alto medioevo*, Settimane di studio del centro italiano di studi sull'alto medioevo, 44 (1997), vol. 1, pp. 491–546. Isabel Alfonso Antón, 'Resolución de disputas y prácticas judiciales en el Burgos medieval', in Juan José García González, Francisco Javier Peña Pérez and Luis Martínez García (eds), *Burgos en la plena edad media* (Burgos, 1994), pp. 211–43; Isabel Alfonso, 'Litigios por la tierra y "malfetrías" entre la nobleza medieval castellano-leonesa', *Hispania*, 57/3 (1997), pp. 917–55; Isabel Alfonso, 'Judicial rhetoric and political legitimation in medieval León-Castile', in Isabel Alfonso, Hugh Kennedy and Julio Escalona (eds), *Building Legitimacy: Political Discourses and Forms of Legitimacy in Medieval Societies* (Leiden, 2004), pp. 51–87; Isabel Alfonso Antón, 'Memoria e identidad en las pesquisas judiciales en el área castellano-leonesa medieval', in José Antonio Jara Fuente, Georges Martín and Isabel Alfonso Antón (eds), *Construir la identidad en la edad media. Poder y memoria en la Castilla de los siglos VII a XV* (Cuenca, 2010), pp. 249–79. Note also Josep María Salrach, 'Prácticas judiciales, transformación social y acción política en Cataluña (siglos IX–XIII)', *Hispania*, 57/3 (1997), pp. 1,009–48, which includes useful comment on practice in the whole of northern Iberia.

55 Isabel Alfonso has assessed Sahagún texts in her 'El formato de la información judicial en la alta edad media peninsular', in Julio Escalona and Hélène Sirantoine (eds), *Chartes et cartulaires comme instruments de pouvoir. Espagne et Occident chrétien (VIIIe–XIIe siècles)* (Toulouse, 2013), pp. 191–218; the PRJ database differentiates between types of dispute text.

a major bearing on our interpretation of the politics of justice, the problem needs some direct treatment at this early stage. We will need to consider to what extent counts monopolized court holding and to what extent they (and other court holders) had authority to hold courts delegated downwards from kings.

Individuals who are characteristically referred to as 'counts' in the secondary literature are often not called 'count' in the early medieval texts in which they feature, although some editors have added the title 'count' in their summaries of charters.[56] This is partly a consequence of the weight of later retrospective reflection. Already in the twelfth century there was some tendency for revisions of earlier charters to add comital titles: so, for example, the witness list of San Rosendo's 942 endowment of Celanova in the Celanova cartulary has 12 people labelled *comes et dux* and 13 people labelled *comes* alone;[57] and there is a tendency for *falsos*, like those attributed to ninth-century kings, to include the designation *comes* in witness lists.[58] It is also the case that credible twelfth-century charters are much more likely to cite comital titles themselves, like, for example, the groups of counts in the witness lists of mid-twelfth-century royal grants to Santiago.[59] This therefore raises a question of whether far fewer people were called 'count' in the later ninth and tenth centuries than we tend to assume, as also whether cartulary compilers in the twelfth century added comital titles to original charters when they copied them. Although conventionally called 'count' by modern writers, Hermenegildo of Sobrado is never referred to as 'count' in any of the many charters detailing his holding of judicial courts in the first half of the tenth century, even though these are cartulary copies (but the cartulary compiler did once call him 'count' in the title he added to a charter);[60] while it is possible to construct an argument about his countship from family relationships, from references to counties in the Sobrado cartulary

56 For example, Lor33 (928), OvC33 (991).

57 Cel2; the form of the witness list of this charter is not credible as a record written in 942; it is completely inconsistent with other records from that time and place (although the text could certainly reflect Rosendo's endowment and the list might just reflect those present). Cf. the listing of counts in some suspect or reworked Sahagún charters, e.g. S98, S99, S168; José Antonio Fernández Flórez, 'El fondo documental del monasterio de Sahagún y sus *scriptores* (siglos IX–X)', in Juan Ignacio Ruiz de la Peña Solar (ed.), *El monacato en los reinos de León y Castilla (Siglos VII–XIII). X Congreso de Estudios Medievales, 2005* (Ávila, 2007), pp. 125–46, at pp. 111, 119, 120.

58 For example, Flor19 (804), which has five; Flor45 (841), which has four; Flor153 (896), which has four, localized; cf. TV80 (910), in which counts commit to restore buildings in Lugo.

59 SantA102 (1137), SantA103 (1140), SantA107 (1141 or 1143), for example, from Tumbo A; cf. the doubtful SantA18 (899); cf. also E170 (1192), on a single sheet. See the comments of Carlos Estepa Díez, 'Los confirmantes en los diplomas de Alfonso VIII (1158–1214)', in Julio Escalona and Hélène Sirantoine (eds), *Chartes et cartulaires comme instruments de pouvoir. Espagne et Occident chrétien (VIIIe–XIIe siècles)* (Toulouse, 2013), pp. 45–69, for construction of witness lists in the later twelfth century.

60 Sob21 (931), Sob23 (949), Sob24 (931), Sob29 (931), Sob31 (951) etc.; nor do the sanctions of these judicial texts mention a *comes* – rather, penalties are due to *uobis*. Sob85 (929) for the title; and Sob129 (942) has a general reference to *comites* in the text; differently, Sob43 (818) has a much-discussed *comes*. See also n. 66 below for Hermenegildo.

and from earlier and later history, that is not quite the same. There is nothing in texts of the first half of the tenth century, when he was active, to link Hermenegildo's court holding with countship. Flaino Muñoz is a subtly different but still comparable case: while he is not referred to as 'count' in many of the (original) charters in which he is named as court holder, he is so termed from 995;[61] it is as if he acquired a title during the course of his activity.

This problem has been flagged by Pascual Martínez Sopena, but although counts have attracted a very large historiography, I am not aware that anyone has confronted the problem head-on.[62] The historiography is dominated on the one hand by the search for the origins of the major comital families of the eleventh, twelfth and thirteenth centuries, and on the other by the development of the county of Castile, given its importance to the subsequent development of the Crown of Castile, the kingdom encompassing the greater part of Spain after 1230.[63]

As indicated above, there has been a strong emphasis in much twentieth-century writing on the fact that authority, including judicial authority, was delegated from kings.[64] Claudio Sánchez-Albornoz, as ever influential, argued that territories called *commissos*, *comitatos* and *mandationes* (terms he viewed as interchangeable) were established by kings as a basis of administration, and that people were appointed by kings to exercise the office of count.[65] Charters of the later tenth century in the monastery of Sobrado's cartulary have played a major part in the argument for delegation in suggesting that kings confirmed the authority of that monastery to act in the manner that counts had acted in the past.[66] However, in the later twentieth century and the past decade there

61 OD38, OD39, OD43 (997); but not OD26 (986), OD27 (987), OD31 (991), OD32 (992), OD33 (992), OD34 (993); all of these appear to be original charters on single sheets.

62 Pascual Martínez Sopena, 'El conde Rodrigo de León y los suyos. Herencia y expectativa de poder entre los siglos X y XII', in Reyna Pastor (comp.), *Relaciones de poder, de producción y parentesco en la edad media y moderna* (Madrid, 1990), pp. 51–84, at p. 56 (citing the case of Flaino Muñoz); Pascual Martínez Sopena, 'Reyes y nobles en León (ca. 860–1160)', in José María Fernández Catón (coord.), *Monarquía y sociedad en el reino de León. De Alfonso III a Alfonso VII* (2 vols, León, 2007), vol. 1, pp. 149–200, at p. 183.

63 For early counts of Castile, see Carlos Estepa Díez, 'La Castilla primitiva (750–931): condes, territorios y villas', *Territorio, Sociedad y Poder*, 2 (2009), pp. 261–78.

64 See, for example, Luis García de Valdeavellano, *Curso de historia de las instituciones españolas. De los orígenes al final de la edad media* (Madrid, 1968), pp. 501–3; Mariel Pérez, '*Rebelles, infideles, traditores*. Insumisión política y poder aristocrático en el reino de León', *Historia, instituciones, documentos*, 38 (2011), pp. 361–82, at pp. 378–9.

65 Sánchez-Albornoz, 'El régimen', pp. 1,352–63; '*Homines mandationis* y *iuniores*', in *Viejos y nuevos estudios*, vol. 1, pp. 365–577, at pp. 443–74.

66 Particularly Sob106 (958), confirmation of Sobrado's *comissum* of Présaras, *secundum regiam consuetudinem comitibus solebat mandare*, by King Ordoño IV; Sob107 (968), confirmation of Sobrado's control of (specified) *comitatos* by the six-year-old King Ramiro III; Sob108 (978), confirmation of Sobrado's *mandationes* and the *comisso* of Présaras by Ramiro III, claiming that Hermenegildo, *comes*, and his family had first obtained these powers. These are all cartulary copies. Clearly someone in the Sobrado orbit made the equation *comisso/comitatus/mandatio* and associated counts with their direction, but we do not know at what point after 952 that was.

has been some tendency to modify this argument by allowing for a background of territorial chiefdoms, whose chiefs exercised control of this or that territory before the reach of kings was consolidated;[67] for longer continuities and the development of hereditary interests in some parts;[68] for the acquisition of earlier family interests by ecclesiastical bodies,[69] and for some element of privatization of authority.[70] All of this is genuinely difficult to assess because of the need to work from later copies of supposedly earlier texts, because of the rewriting of some earlier texts in the interests of powers claimed in the eleventh and twelfth centuries, and because of the paucity of eighth- and early ninth-century material.

But we might say this.[71] The late ninth-century Asturian chronicles do name a few counts, as does Sampiro in the early eleventh century when reflecting on the tenth-century past, although not many are named in either case.[72] Turning to charters, if we confine observations in the first instance to charters preserved on single sheets, then we can note that there are considerably more references to counts in the later tenth century than earlier;[73] that it is rare for anyone to be designated 'count' in a witness list, although it does occur, somewhat erratically, and when this happens there is rarely more than one person so termed;[74] that there are occasional references to named counts in the main text of charters (though not in the witness lists of those charters), particularly in judicial contexts, but also sometimes in the names of topographical features and boundary points;[75] that there are occasional text references to unnamed counts gathered together at meetings;[76] that there are occasional references to unnamed counts

67 See especially Carlos Estepa Díez, 'Configuración y primera expansión del reino astur. Siglos VIII y IX', in Francisco Javier Lomas and Federico Devís (eds), *De Constantino a Carlomagno. Disidentes, heterodoxos, marginados* (Cádiz, 1992), pp. 179–95; cf. Ignacio Álvarez Borge, 'Estructuras de poder en Castilla en la alta edad media: señores, siervos, vasallos', in *Señores, siervos, vasallos en la alta edad media. XXVIII Semana de estudios medievales, Estella, 16 a 20 de julio de 2001* (Pamplona, 2002), pp. 269–308, at p. 289; Iñaki Martín Viso, 'Poder político y estructura social en la Castilla altomedieval: el condado de Lantarón (siglos VIII–XI)', in José Ignacio de la Iglesia Duarte (co-ord.), *Los espacios de poder en la España medieval. XII semana de estudios medievales Nájera 2001* (Logroño, 2002), pp. 533–52, at pp. 535–6.

68 Ermelindo Portela Silva, 'Galicia y la monarquía leonesa', in *El reino de León en la alta edad media, VII, Estudios* (León, 1995), pp. 9–70, at pp. 29–30.

69 Isla Frez, *La sociedad gallega*, pp. 146–51.

70 Pérez, '*Rebelles, infideles, traditores*', pp. 378–9.

71 For reasons of balance, I cannot deal with all the issues here, but hope to do so at greater length in the forthcoming Barton and Portass (eds), *Beyond the Reconquista*.

72 *Crónicas Asturianas*, ed. and trans. Gil Fernández, Moralejo and Ruiz de la Peña, pp. 176, 178, 180, of counts of Galicia, Álava and Castile; Pérez de Urbel, *Sampiro*, pp. 316, 333, 335, of counts of Burgos especially.

73 For example, on Sahagún single sheets, only 23 per cent of tenth-century references to counts are pre-950.

74 For example, Li45 (918), Lii295 (956), S221 (964) – *comitissa*.

75 For example, Oña3 (944), LaC50 (947), Lii290 (955), Cañ41 (959), AHN 1325A–9 (973) – all judicial; Li51 (920), bounds – *de Ueremudo comite*.

76 For example, Jaca (958, though questionable that this is an unaltered record of 958), Lii410 (968), S284 (976) – an eleventh- or twelfth-century copy.

in sanctions, either prohibiting the intrusion of a count or specifying penalties due to a count (although there are considerably more references of this type in cartulary copies),[77] and that in some areas – but by no means all – counts feature in the *regnante* type of dating clause (that is, 'at the time when King X was ruling and Y was count in Z').[78] The latter feature (which is particularly characteristic of cartulary copies, but does occur on single sheets too) is very regionally limited: it is a predominantly eastern, especially Castilian, characteristic.[79] There are a number of indications that Castilian practice, as also the prominence of counts of Castile, was distinctive: the countship of Fernán González, for example, was noted from some considerable distance, particularly when no others were noted.[80]

These observations suggest that there were indeed some people referred to as 'count' from the time of our earliest surviving charters; since *comite/comice* is the commonest form of reference, even where one might expect nominative or accusative cases, we must presume this was how the word was normally used: a count was a *comite* rather than a *comes*.[81] The redactors of charters tended to associate these counts with authority and with ruling; hence the *regnante* clauses, the judicial hearings before (*ante*) this or that count, and their military leadership in the chronicles. However, there is little in early charters (that is charters from before 950) to indicate the source of that authority,[82] and most people termed 'count' behaved like members of a landed aristocracy, and hence

77 For example, Lii508 (985), S355 (997); note the comital prohibition in the false S70 (938).

78 V10 (911), *comite Gundesalbo Telluz in Lantarone*; V11 (919), *comite Munnio Uigilazi in Alaba* (both of these Valpuesta charters are in a cartulary, but in that part written by an early tenth-century scribe); S52 (933), *Fredenando Gontesalbes comite in Kastela*; S136 (952), *comite nostro Adefonso in Leuanensem*; Lii478 (980), *domna Tota cometissa iudicante ciui Domnas*.

79 Although the witness list of Sam217 (973) has *tenente Lemos et Sarriam comite Domno Fernando*; this is a cartulary copy, but it is so distinctive in the Samos collection that it must reflect the wording of an original. For a thorough treatment of the Castilian *regnante* clauses, see Julio Escalona, 'In the name of a distant king: Representing royal authority in the county of Castile, ca. 900–1038', in *Early Medieval Europe*, 24 (2016), pp. 74–102.

80 For example, in the Galician Cel426 (951).

81 *Gundesindus Froiani et comyti*, where the *y* is a subsequent insert, top of first column of witness list, Li93 (932); *noster comite Assuri Fredenandiz*, Oña3 (944); *ante comite domno Gundessaluus*, LaC50 (947); *ad comite Gundesaluo*, LaC65 (pre-962); *ad Comitem Gudesteo Hordoniz . . . ille comite . . . ipse comite*, Cañ41 (959). There are many more examples in cartulary copies: *Ego comite Gisuadus*, E7 (928); *ad lege ubi fuisset ille comite et suos iudices*, PMH DC 183 (999). I am grateful to Roger Wright for advising that, in accordance with normal rules for forming romance words, it was the accusative form *comitem* that survived in speech and (losing final *m*) gave rise to Modern Spanish *conde*, and therefore that the form *comite* must indeed reflect speech.

82 Nothing in charters on single sheets; but the Celanova cartulary has royal delegation of the *commisso* of Quiroga to Gutier Menéndez in 929 and that of Caldelas (and other areas) to Fruela Gutiérriz, under his mother's guidance, in 942 (Cel207, Cel499); in neither case was the beneficiary described as count of those areas, and Gutier in practice operated over a much wider area, as did Fruela's mother, his wife; we have no record of either man holding a judicial court, although Gutier appeared with the king in Lugo to hear the early stages of the Odoíno dispute over Santa Comba, Cel265 (before 982, probably in 932).

of long-established families. From the mid-tenth century there are some credible charters indicating royal delegation of limited spheres of authority (particularly over people rather than over territories) to individuals, although these were rarely counts, and more often clerics.[83] Royal capacity to command was clearly developing in the later tenth century, and even more so in the eleventh century;[84] and at roughly the same time use of the term 'count' was clearly increasing. However, these two trends do not map neatly on to each other, and they appear to represent different processes – on the one hand development and delegation of royal authority to appropriate people, and on the other increasing use of an honorific title for top people. As for the ninth and earlier tenth centuries, clearly a small number of people were referred to as 'count', often 'our count', *noster comite*, but the designation is rare; most of these people can be seen holding judicial courts; there is nothing which directly supports the notion that they acquired this power by any act of royal delegation; and, significantly, it is perfectly clear that other people held courts too.[85] Counts certainly held judicial courts, but you did not have to be a count to do so. It would therefore appear that in the ninth and tenth centuries, a few individuals could be termed 'count', individuals who were authority figures, with substantial landed property. We do not know why or whence the label had come; however, given widespread knowledge of some Visigothic law and given the notable frequency of references to *comites* in that corpus of law, especially in judicial contexts, it is easy to understand how the word *comes* could have come to describe authority figures.[86] There is little to suggest that every part of northern Iberia was within the sphere of some count; rather, there was an irregular and incomplete patchwork of a count here, a count there, with some very marked regional differences.

83 For example, Ordoño III gave the bishop of León, *ad inperandum*, the castle of San Salvador *qum mandationibus suis uel homines ei deseruientes*, Lii300 (951–6), an original charter; the monk Zuleiman, mayordomo of Queen Teresa, mother of Ramiro III, held *mandationes* in several places, for which he answered to the queen, Liii560 (pre-994), also an original charter. Carlos Estepa Díez, 'Poder y propiedad feudales en el período astur: las mandaciones de los Flaínez en la montaña leonesa', in *Miscel·lània en homenatge al P. Agustí Altisent* (Tarragona, 1991), pp. 285–327, remains the best treatment of *mandationes*; he clearly demonstrates that by the 1020s holding a *mandatio* brought with it the power to hold a court, ibid., p. 318.

84 Cf. OD56 (1001) and OD70 (1006), both of which explicitly indicate that Pedro Flaínez, son of Flaino Muñoz, held the *mandación* of Valdoré and that Pedro had control over the movement of the population; however, he is not referred to as 'count' in either charter. OD99 (1014) is explicit that Pedro held the *mandación* of Lorma, and in this text he is called 'count', in the forms *comes* and *comite* (five times). These charters are originals. There is, however, no explicit reference to delegation of the authority he held until 1019, when royal delegation is explicit (OD116).

85 On this latter point, see further below, pp. 157–8, 190–5, 225.

86 This does not have to imply continuity or memory of Visigothic *comites*, for there was clearly some knowledge of Visigothic law texts in ninth and tenth centuries (on which, see below, pp. 26–7). *Leges Visigothorum*, ed. Karl Zeumer, MGH Leges nationum Germanicarum, sectio I.1 (Hanover, 1902), pp. 33–456: pp. 78, 157, 288, 314, 378, for example.

In view of this, in what follows I shall refer to individuals as counts if they are so termed in the texts in which they feature (in charters both on single sheets and in cartulary copies), but I will not make an assumption of countship if the texts are silent on this point. And I will not assume that power to hold a court had been delegated unless the point is made explicitly.

The essentials of judicial court procedure

Although assemblies which dealt with judicial business will sometimes have handled other business too, particularly in the case of kings' courts, it is perfectly clear that across northern Iberia in the ninth and tenth centuries public meetings were convened for the specific purpose of doing judicial business. I shall refer to them as 'courts' since this word conveys this meaning in modern English; in the Latin texts, if a word was used for the court it tended to be *iudicium*, literally 'judgment'.[87] While there are many things we do not know about these assemblies, we do know that some judges had expert knowledge, and that there were dedicated legal officers and elements of a standard procedure. In what follows, I shall summarize those elements of procedure on which there is general agreement.

For some of the judges, expertise included knowledge of a corpus of written law. Some records of court cases in northern Iberia refer to an existing, ancient body of law; this was written in Latin in a prescriptive style and derived from the Visigothic state of the sixth and seventh centuries; it is often referred to as the book, *Liber*, or as the judges' law, *Forum iudicum*, but also more simply as *lex gotica.*[88] Reference to the law in ninth- and tenth-century texts can be extremely vague – with comments like 'as *lex gotica* provides' – but sometimes book, title and chapter of the law are identified, and sometimes there is a direct quotation from it. In a property dispute between the aristocrat Velasco Hánniz and the monastery of Abellar, heard before the bishop of León in August 952, the record quotes book IV, title 2, chapter 19 on freedom of alienation of property for those without children, grandchildren or nephews and nieces (*filios aut nepotes uel pronepotes*) and also book V, title 2, chapter 6 on *post-mortem* donation;[89] by contrast, the record of a case about the adultery of a woman with her father-in-law remarks less precisely that the *Liber* judged that she should be handed over into servitude (although she subsequently made a payment instead);[90] even the long inventories of property acquired by Celanova's

87 Though I note that Niermeyer, citing Frankish sources, gives 'judicial assembly' as the primary meaning. For all the things that courts do besides adjudication, cf. Marc Galanter, 'Justice in many rooms: Courts, private ordering, and indigenous law', *Journal of Legal Pluralism and Unofficial Law*, 19 (1981), pp. 1–47, at p. 3.

88 *Forum iudicum*: see *Leges Visigothorum*; for the ecclesiastical corpus: *Concilios visigóticos e hispano-romanos*, ed. José Vives, with Tomás Marín Martínez and Gonzalo Martínez Díez (Barcelona, 1963).

89 Li256. The former law text is ch. 20 of Zeumer's edition.

90 Liii561 (994): 'et fuimus ad Librum et iudicauit ut tradissent me seruire sicut alia ancilla origenale'.

officer Cresconio in the late tenth century note that some property received in lieu of a judicial fine was acquired because *lex gotica* had determined the fine.[91] Now, such quotations and citations can abbreviate or massage the text of *Lex Visigothorum* as it was established in the early twentieth century, and while certain passages are often cited, many are never cited at all. There are therefore issues about how much of the corpus was known in the early middle ages and issues over how much of the law cited was the Visigothic law of the sixth and seventh centuries and how much had been changed to suit recent or contemporary purpose; there are also issues about the practical application of the law.[92] These issues are intensified by the apparent break in the transmission of law texts in north-west Iberia, for all the early (seventh- to ninth-century) manuscripts of the law are Catalan or Septimanian, including two Carolingian copies of a Septimanian text; there are no early manuscripts from the kingdom of Asturias-León, the earliest being the late tenth-century Riojan collections noted above.[93] Despite these problems, reference to written prescription was clearly a norm, and it is perfectly clear that this ancient law was regarded as authoritative.

The matters handled by judicial courts ranged from petty and substantial property disputes to theft, arson, wounding, rape and homicide.[94] The key person in the management of a court case was a legal officer called a *saio* – a man who could initiate a court case on receipt of a complaint, who supervised the taking of oaths, who formally conveyed property that had to be transferred as the result of a judgment or an agreement, and who can sometimes be seen taking a fee for his services (*saionicum*).[95] There were usually different procedural stages in the course of hearing a case, which could last across several occasions and be heard in different locations; these locations included recognized meeting places, royal and aristocratic households, disputed land and churches. In a record of an assault and wounding case in 946, on the *meseta*, the priest Berulf gave notice to the *saio* on 26 March that he had a case against a man called Matheo, who had invaded the land of the church of San Esteban and wounded its men, to the value of 72 *solidi*, the *solidus* being a notional unit of account,

91 Cel368 (at pp. 525 and 531): 'et habui ipso modio de triigo ad pariare per sententia secundum mihi lex gotica ordinat'.

92 The best discussion of the issues is by Aquilino Iglesia Ferreirós, 'La creación del derecho en Cataluña', *Anuario de Historia del Derecho Español*, 47 (1977), pp. 99–423; the article deals specifically with Catalonia, but its extremely subtle treatment of the difference between quoting, abbreviating and modifying the law in Catalan charters has relevance for the whole of northern Iberia. It includes a comprehensive list of citations of the law in Catalan charters from the ninth to the mid-thirteenth century. See now also Barrett (above, p. xii).

93 See pp. 11–12; see Manuel Cecilio Díaz y Díaz, 'La Lex Visigothorum y sus manuscritos. Un Ensayo de reinterpretación', *Anuario de Historia del Derecho Español*, 46 (1976), pp. 163–224. See below, pp. 236–7, for *Lex Romana Visigothorum*.

94 See below, pp. 198–203, 228–30, for particular cases; and for a summary Davies, 'Settling disputes in early medieval Spain and Portugal', pp. 90–93.

95 See further below, pp. 164–8.

not a coin;[96] Matheo agreed to appear to hear the charge, on pain of 100 *solidi* if he defaulted; there follows the verbatim evidence of two witnesses on behalf of Berulf; then come the formal *conditiones sacramentorum*, a record of the oaths of these witnesses. This is followed by Matheo's confession and his witnessed agreement to restore the land to Berulf the following Saturday, on pain of 100 *solidi*; and finally a further witnessed agreement, on 7 May, that Matheo and family would pay a fine of 200 *solidi* in the event of any further incursions. There are at least three, and perhaps more, separate meetings here within a six-week period; there are oaths and witnessed agreements, as well as witness evidence: two different sets of witnesses are recorded for this one case, in addition to the witnesses who gave evidence. Recalling the record of ACO B.1.11 with which I began, the six different sets of witnesses of that case, of which two were subsequent to the main hearings, imply at least three separate meetings, as is in any case clear from the text and from the three different commitments to the *saio* that were made by the principal actors.[97]

Taking evidence from witnesses was one method of progressing a case, and it was also common for all or for a subset of witnesses to take an oath about their evidence; this was recorded as the *conditiones sacramentorum*, as in the Berulf case above. Usually it was the judges who decided which party's witnesses should swear – being given the chance to take the oath was in effect an indicator of success. So, in a Portuguese case of 999 between a layman and the monastery of Guimarães over ownership of a farm, the *saio* heard the opening statements of each party and then required both sides to appear with five witnesses each on an appointed date, at an appointed place, Pedralva.[98] There, unusually, each set of five gave evidence. Then the *saio* sent everyone to the count's court, where the judges read all the documents, 'understood everything' and found that the monastery's representative had the truth. They then ruled that the monastery's five witnesses should take the oath.[99] Here written evidence was provided as well as oral, but the written word did not necessarily override other evidence here as elsewhere, for documents could be pronounced false;[100] indeed, it was the oath about documents that clinched the Guimarães case, not the documents themselves.

Taking a solemn oath was common in Spain and Portugal, although the function of the oath can look ambiguous to us now.[101] The oath was very frequently a confirmation, or test, of witness evidence, and rarely seems to have

96 Li192. No coin was minted in northern Iberia at this period, although silver was clearly used by weight in some parts; see Wendy Davies, 'Sale, price and valuation in Galicia and Castile-León in the tenth century', *Early Medieval Europe*, 11 (2002), pp. 149–74.

97 See above, pp. 1–4.

98 PMH DC 183.

99 See further below, pp. 211–13, on witnesses.

100 C55 (945) – in which a false charter was burned; cf. Oña3 (944), and Lii410 (968), in which the authenticity of a charter was questioned. See also Alfonso, 'Judicial rhetoric and political legitimation', pp. 80–1.

101 Cf. the comments of Alfonso, 'Resolución de disputas y prácticas judiciales', p. 217.

been 'oath-helping' (compurgation) in the strict sense. (An oath-helper, the supporter of an accused person, essentially swore to the reliability and good character of the accused rather than to the particular facts of a case; sworn witnesses did the latter, although in practice it is often difficult to differentiate between the two in early medieval contexts.[102]) The record of a judicial decision in favour of two brothers over water rights relating to a mill in the River Tirón comes close, however, to the classic model of oath-helping: the brothers brought 12 witnesses to the court and three *fiadores*; the witnesses testified and the *fiadores* swore oaths; the best explanation is that the latter swore to the truthfulness of the brothers.[103]

Cases could also be determined by an ordeal, an appeal that the judgment of God be revealed through an innocent person: an innocent was usually taken to the ordeal, with trusted men appointed to witness it; come the appointed day, people gathered at a designated church; the innocent removed hot stones from boiling water and his or her hand was bound; three or four days later the hand was unwrapped, in front of witnesses (as in the Gordón case of ACO B.1.11); if the hand was unharmed, as certified by the appointed witnesses, the case was in theory settled.[104] Use of the ordeal is not evidenced very often in this material, and it appears to have been invoked when there was an element of doubt, particularly where there was reason to doubt the honesty of some actors. In these cases, the ordeal was intended as a test of the quality of the sworn evidence – proof that the oath was good. As a procedure, this is extremely unusual; its use to test witnesses is surprising: in Catalonia, for example, the ordeal was reserved for the accused.[105]

Many cases end with a confession, though not all. Confession is in part just a convention of the record-making tradition, particularly when a text ends with an 'acknowledgment' of fault and with a statement that 'truth' was thereby revealed. However, there appears to have been a standard ritual of confession

102 See further below, pp. 242–3.

103 SM27 (940) = BG391; *fiadores* could designate sureties here, given that the word *fiador* is sometimes used for this function (for example, Cel368, T66); however, *fidiator* is more common and there is no reference in this text to an earlier transaction which had been guaranteed; in the context oath-helping seems more likely. Cel144 (n.d.) seems to refer to an oath-helping case: a late tenth-century list of persons attached to Celanova refers to a woman whose father had denied paternity – the man he accused took an oath with 12 others in order to clear himself.

104 Settled in favour of those who had taken the oath (as in ACO B.1.11), but in many cases confession comes before the final stage; in at least two cases, although the oath-taker appears to have won, this was later questioned (SantA24, Cañ41).

105 Cf. Collins, 'Visigothic law and regional custom', p. 87. Appearance of this practice in some texts of Visigothic law is a ninth- or tenth-century addition; see Salrach, 'Prácticas judiciales, transformación social y acción política', p. 1,020, and see further below, pp. 136–9. Whether or not use of the ordeal was always a straightforward proof is arguable; see Stephen D. White, 'Proposing the ordeal and avoiding it: Strategy and power in western French litigation, 1050–1110', in Thomas Noël Bisson (ed.), *Cultures of Power: Lordship, Status, and Process in Twelfth-century Europe* (Philadelphia, PA, 1995), pp. 89–123, who argues that its use was strategic, to 'gain a tactical advantage', pp. 91–2, 99–101, 122. See further below, pp. 243–5.

used in court, which is not recorded in the same way as these acknowledgements, and there is no reason to suppose that all noted confessions were simply a formulaic way of concluding a record.[106]

Decisions were characteristically made by judges in court cases, often termed *iudices*, and they characteristically, although not invariably, worked in panels of several individuals. Some of them clearly had expertise in law, although most members of a judging panel did not do so. The decisions they made tended to be about procedure, and particularly what should happen next in the conduct of the case, rather than a final right or wrong, though the latter does sometimes occur; so, for example, it was the judges who decided how many witnesses were needed or which party should take the oath, and it was the judges who tramped the countryside looking for the markers of a disputed boundary.[107] Although one of the expert judges sometimes appears to have presided over a hearing, more usually there was a court holder who took the chair. This court holder could be the king or a count, or other lay person or a cleric; it is quite clear that some monasteries held courts in their capacity as major landowners.[108] He (or occasionally she) can quite often be seen taking a fee in respect of his or her holding of the court, the *iudicatum*, and we have many references to property which had been handed over *in iudicato* – that is, handed over as a court fee or fine – without any detail of the preceding case.[109] (In what follows, I treat all references to *iudicatum* as evidence that a fee had been paid, and therefore that a court session had been held.)

As for penalties: the ordeal was a test not a penalty. If a person lost a property dispute, the usual outcome was restitution of the property to the declared owner, with no necessary penalty, but with heavy sanctions if there should be a further attempt to gain the property. 'Criminal' cases were different. For wounding, penalties were assessed in *solidi* or in cattle. The manner of reference implies that these were compensatory payments, presumably assessed in accordance with the scale of the injury, and payable to the injured person. On the other hand, for rape, arson, siege and theft, penalties were levied that were payable to the court holder; in other words, they were in effect fines.[110] In extreme

106 See further below, pp. 44–8, 126–30.

107 See below, pp. 160–2, and Wendy Davies, 'Judges and judging: Truth and justice in northern Iberia on the eve of the millennium', *Journal of Medieval History*, 36/3 (2010), pp. 193–203.

108 See below, pp. 157–8, 186–90, on monastic court holders, and in general Wendy Davies, 'Holding court: Judicial presidency in Brittany, Wales and northern Iberia in the early middle ages', in Fiona Edmonds and Paul Russell (eds), *Tome: Studies in Medieval Celtic History and Law in Honour of Thomas Charles-Edwards* (Woodbridge, 2011), pp. 145–54.

109 Cf. Martínez Díez, 'Terminología jurídica', pp. 251, 263–5, who defines *iudicatum* as the fee paid to a judge; while it is clear that this did happen, it is also clear that most payments actually made *in iudicato* in these charters were made to court holders. Alfonso García Leal, 'Los condes Fruela Muñoz y Pedro Flaínez: la formación de un patrimonio señorial', *Anuario de Estudios Medievales*, 36/1 (2006), pp. 1–110, at pp. 32, 89; Martínez Sopena, 'La justicia en la época asturleonesa', p. 241, on the *iudicatum* and other payments. For words for judicial payments, see above, p. x.

110 On fines, see further below, pp. 41–3, 157, 198.

cases, property could be confiscated and bad men exiled, but there seems to be no evidence of a death penalty.[111] In practice, whatever the terms in which the penalty was evaluated, it was often paid in land. There are fewer records of compensation for the victims of such offences, although in one case the due penalty was payment of a horse worth 40 *solidi* to the injured party (compensation) and of another horse worth 40 *solidi* to the court holder (fine) – the latter, as so often, commuted to land.[112] Other examples support the likelihood that payment to victims was more common than recorded: a Galician case of assault, resolved in 952, hung on wounds assessed at a value of 10 cattle.[113] After assessment, the victim went to court and those who had committed the assault came to court to confirm that they would pay, on an appointed day. They duly came, and made a modified payment. The very fact that the victim went to court after his injury had been assessed indicates that he expected to receive something. We know about payments to court holders because they were wealthy aristocrats, lay and ecclesiastical, and they kept records; we rarely hear about compensation to victims because most do not appear to have kept records; so record-keeping habits mean that there is information about one kind of beneficiary, but not the other.

As a final penalty option, there is one case, of 994, that mentions penal slavery: a woman guilty of adultery, because she had slept with her father-in-law, should in accordance with the law have been reduced to the status of hereditary slave (*ancilla origenale*), but was permitted to make a gift of property instead, which went to the court holder.[114]

Good evidence of enforcement mechanisms comes from the use of sureties, personal guarantors, although both the activity of the *saio* and the role of the court holder indicate that they had a major part in enforcement too. *Saiones* were the people who got offenders to court in the first place, as in the Gordón case of ACO B.1.11, and they transferred property after the settlement of a case.[115] Court holders often presided over a hearing – they were a presence – and they received fines, as detailed above. Both were clearly critical to the working of the system. Sureties are perhaps less obvious, but nevertheless important: when the boundaries of properties on the slopes of the Cantabrian Mountains were agreed between the members of seven settlements and the monks of Pardomino in 944, the settlements provided seven sureties that they would stick to the agreement.[116] Sureties were the people who in practice saw that the terms of an agreement or of the resolution of a case were carried out. They might do this by paying up themselves if the loser defaulted, or else by forcing

111 See below, pp. 52–3, 183–6, for confiscations.

112 Liii578 (997); cf. Liii624 (1002), in which some vineyards went to Munio Fernández, the court holder, and others to the victim.

113 Sob103.

114 Liii561; see n. 90 above.

115 See further below, pp. 164–8, on both.

116 Li184.

a defaulting party either to pay up or to appear in court. They also performed other practical functions, like transmitting payments. When a man called Salomon was found guilty of theft in 931, in northern Galicia, and was required to pay 30 cattle, six sureties were named that he would not disappear before doing so, and if he did, the sureties were to pay the court 20 cattle.[117] When Astrario stood as surety for his sister and brother-in-law's debt to Celanova, he ended up handing over his hereditary property to the monastery.[118] When Velasco Hánniz and the abbot of Abellar were required to appear in court before the king in their disputed property case, their appearance was guaranteed by the surety, Fortes.[119] Although legal historians have tended to situate suretyship within the domain of private law, it is a mistake to see suretyship as purely private:[120] sureties may have had obligations to private individuals, but public endorsement of their obligations was extremely important to the functioning of the system.[121]

* * *

I shall now proceed to consider the texts recording judicial process, the differences between the kinds of text available, and the quality of their different perspectives as evidence of what happened in, before and after court sessions. In this diverse land, with its significant corpus of charters of the tenth century, how far does analysing the form and nature of these texts cast light on our understanding of judicial practice, and how far does it suggest regional difference?

117 Sob21. This is what the text says – it may not be an error, since penalties did get reduced; see below pp. 171–2, and Martínez Sopena, 'La justicia en la época asturleonesa', pp. 256–8.

118 Cel368 (p. 530).

119 Li256. The text appears to suggest he was surety for both, though in reality he may have been Velasco's surety only.

120 For a good discussion of the interplay between public and private roles, see Robin C. Stacey's discussion of Irish hostage-sureties in her *The Road to Judgment: From Custom to Court in Medieval Ireland and Wales* (Philadelphia, PA, 1994), pp. 82–111.

121 See Wendy Davies, 'On suretyship in tenth-century northern Iberia', in Julio Escalona Monge and Andrew Reynolds (eds), *Scale and Scale Change in the Early Middle Ages: Exploring Landscape, Local Society, and the World Beyond* (Turnhout, 2011), pp. 133–52.

Part I

The texts

2 The structure of dispute records

If we look at the charters that record disputes for which formal public action was pursued, we can see that those charters take many different forms. Some are long, and some short; some give considerable detail about procedure, while some simply record outcomes; some appear to quote the words of principal actors verbatim, but others use a very distant third-person narrative; some mention court proceedings in passing, and some focus fully upon them. Since the form of the record has a bearing on its value as evidence, the range of forms needs to be established and the attributes of each form described. The purpose of this chapter is to do that.

About a third of the records of disputes pursued in public explicitly refer to court proceedings. While it is clear that there must have been court proceedings behind events recorded in some other charters, they do not all give details; for example, many charters record the payments that were the outcome of court cases, but do not mention a court at all. Other charters detail several stages of a public dispute and its resolution without involving a court; this may mean that a solution was found without going through formal procedure, or it may mean that those who wrote or copied the record thought the formal procedure irrelevant and omitted it: many of these records are clearly incomplete, and a few are garbled; that court proceedings must have happened in some of these cases is indicated by reference to the actions of a legal officer, the *saio*, or by highly allusive writing that uses characteristic court outcome language (like 'we saw truth', *uidimus ueritatem*) without mentioning the court itself.[1] In order, then, to assess judicial practice and the public conduct of dispute resolution, we need to have more than records of judicial process in view. We need to look at those that only mention outcomes, those that detail protracted stages of a dispute, those that use court description language, and those that refer to legal officers as principal actors. In this analysis, I shall also include records of royal confiscations, since they are invariably the consequence of a protracted public dispute and seem to offer an alternative mode of resolution to that of the judicial court. And for the purposes of this study, I shall include records of the repayment of debts

1 For characteristic language, see below, ch. 5.

Table 2.1 Numbers of cases recorded

	No.	%
Accounts	59	20.42
Incidental	74	25.61
Fines	41	14.19
Confessions	15	5.19
Agreements	29	10.03
Oaths	5	1.73
Implied	10	3.46
Mixed	6	2.08
Confiscations	19	6.57
Debts	31	10.72
Totals	289	100

too, since this often appears to have been resolved in public and can reasonably be seen to have been a result of tension between two or more parties; debts may not often have been settled in judicial courts, but requiring repayment was a facet of the power politics at play at local level. As such, it must have been an element in the delivery of local justice.

Taking all this into consideration, I can identify 257 separate dispute texts, recording 289 separate cases, and I have divided the cases into 10 different categories.[2] Of course, some of the classification is arguable, some categories overlap, and inevitably a few texts are unclassifiable. But the taxonomy broadly works. The different forms, all of which occur as separate documents, are these: (1) Accounts of the progress and resolution of a dispute; (2) Incidental references to a dispute in the course of a record whose main purpose was to record something else; (3) Fines, fees and compensations following a court case;[3] (4) Confessions in court; (5) Agreements following a confession or other interaction; (6) Oaths taken in the course of a court case; (7) Implied disputes; (8) Mixed types; (9) Confiscations; and (10) Debts.[4]

2 Agustín Prieto Morera, 'El proceso en el reino de León a la luz de los diplomas', in *El reino de León en la alta edad media, II: Ordenamiento jurídico del reino* (León, 1992), pp. 381–518, is based on a more limited classification scheme, but is a paper full of useful observations, especially on procedure. I did not see the paper by Isabel Alfonso, 'El formato de la información judicial en la alta edad media peninsular', in Julio Escalona and Hélène Sirantoine (eds), *Chartes et cartulaires comme instruments de pouvoir. Espagne et Occident chrétien (VIIIe–XIIe siècles)* (Toulouse, 2013), pp. 191–218, until after I had developed my own scheme. Professor Alfonso's paper focuses on Sahagún dispute texts and on the reasons for making the records; her scheme of classification in this instance comprises Non-judicial transactions (including much that is in my Incidental category, but also Confiscations), Judicial transactions (transactions made for explicit judicial reasons, including some Debts), Confessions, Agreements and *Pleitos* (very close to my Accounts).

3 See above, p. x, for comment on the ambiguous terminology of judicial payments.

4 The calculations that follow refer to the total number of cases. If they were to refer to the number of records, the proportion of Accounts and Agreements would increase slightly, that of Debts would decrease slightly, and that of Fines would decrease by 4 per cent. This is because of the number of the latter in the Celanova inventories of the late tenth century, on which, see below, p. 42.

To begin with (1) Accounts: these are third-person, past-tense narratives of the course of a dispute, often quite long – much longer than a standard gift or sale charter – and often with detail of court proceedings, including reference to or citation of oaths, confessions and agreements.[5] As one of the largest groups in this analysis, they constitute a fifth of the corpus; since they tend to be detailed and there are many of them, they inevitably colour our view of what court procedure was like, and they have played an influential part in the historiography of Iberian dispute settlement.[6] They usually conclude with sanction and final protocol of date and witness or confirmer list, just like a standard charter of gift or sale (although cartulary copies may truncate the list); this is so in 92 per cent of cases, occurring in all regions considered; the exceptions can be explained by particularities of recording practice, for example by incomplete records in cartularies. Accounts also often include a confirmation of the outcome before the sanction, and the list of witnesses and confirmers usually includes a number (often an excessive number) of obviously high-status people. Many involve a king – 54 per cent of cases, although none of the dispute Accounts from Portugal or Castile does so; where there is no king, inclusion of someone called 'count' is common, particularly in the cases of Castile and Galicia. Many of these records begin with a standard formula: *orta fuit intentio* (or *contentio*), 'there arose a dispute', with which the date is sometimes associated rather than appearing at the end; this standard opening occurs from Portugal to Aragón, although not in San Millán records; it is – with nine variants – characteristic of 68 per cent of the records.[7]

Here is a typical, if short, example with a truncated confirmation list:

> In era 969 [931 AD] a dispute arose between the brothers of the monastery of San Julián, on the banks of the river Torío, in the outskirts of the city of León, and García son-in-law of Runfurco, on one side, and the inhabitants of Manzaneda and Garrafe on the other side. The brothers [of San Julián] had acquired those settlements by charter from a grant by the lord king Alfonso and Queen Jimena; confirmed subsequently by King García, and then by the charter of confirmation of King Ordoño and Queen Elvira. They said that the local men had made clearings within the properties (*uillas*) and within the boundaries specified in the charter so that they could obtain land from the brothers' portion. In order to resolve the dispute, both

5 The dispute recorded in Sam35 (944) occurs in the context of an account of the accumulation of the property of Samos and therefore does not follow the characteristic form of these Accounts. However, there is a lengthy narration of the depredations of a local bishop, consequent appeal to the king and restoration of property, ending with confirmation; I have therefore included it in this category as the best fit.

6 See above, pp. 18–20.

7 Variants, for example: *factum est altercatio*, AHN Clero Lugo 1325A–6 (922); *accidit contentio* in the middle of the text, SantA42 (961); *fuit contentio facta*, SJP14 (928); *abuit intenzio*, PMH DC 163 (991). For the formula, see further below, pp. 121–2; and Prieto Morera, 'El proceso en el reino de León', p. 390.

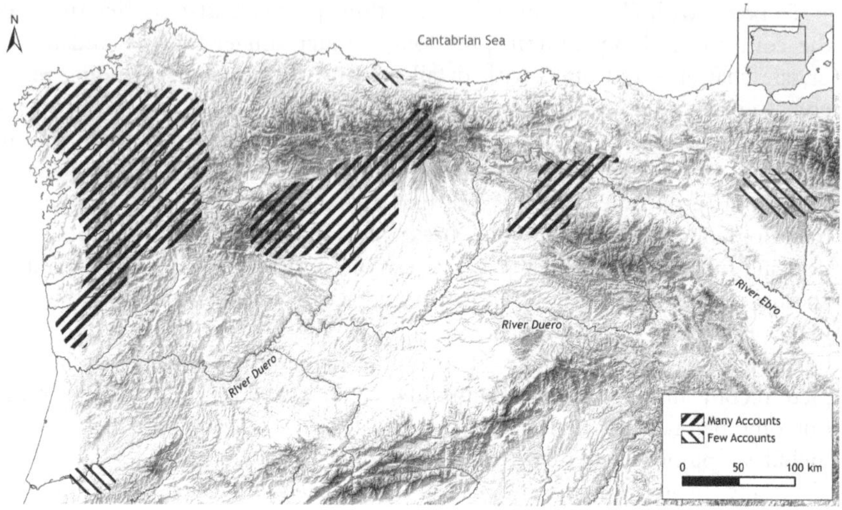

Figure 2.1 Distribution of Accounts

parties came before King Alfonso, son of the lord Ordoño, and at their suggestion he went to the properties together with the several magnates noted below in order to gather evidence. And they set the boundaries of Manzaneda where Runfurco had set them, that is from the river Avoceto . . . [detailed boundary]. We have perceived all this honestly in accordance with the charters and as the oldest men have related; and we decree that everything should remain for ever, without hindrance, so that no claim be allowed from outside. If anyone tries to take or claim anything from within those bounds without the consent of the brothers occupying that place, that person should pay twice or three times the value of those properties (*uillas*) to the monastery, as the Law of the Goths requires, in perpetuity.[8]

Noted on the 4th of the kalends of February, in the era cited above.

I King Alfonso confirm with my own hand that we have recognized the truth.

In the name of Christ, Bishop Cissila confirms; in the name of Christ, Bishop Oveco confirms.[9]

The charter survives on a single sheet, written in a Visigothic cursive hand, although most of the witness list has been cut off. There are two notes on the dorse, in a contemporary hand, saying 'Kartula de illos terminos' and 'Placitum de illos terminos' (charter, and agreement, concerning those boundaries).

8 *Lex godorum*, the Law of the Visigoths; see above, pp. 26–7.

9 Li89. See the Appendix to this chapter for Latin text of this and other translated examples.

Now, 75 per cent of these Accounts only survive in cartulary copies, and that high proportion may raise concerns about the credibility of the records; they are clearly retrospective accounts, and as such are likely to be framed from one point of view. However, some 25 per cent do survive as single documents on separate sheets (e.g. Figure 8.3); these include texts from Portugal, Galicia and the *meseta*, from 906 to the end of the century, so it is perfectly clear that records of this kind were indeed made in the tenth century, particularly given the standardization of the widely occurring opening. We usually do not know who the scribes were: even if a record has a scribal subscription, there is rarely enough information to identify individuals. However, there is a handful of instances in which a reasonable case for identity can be made. The priest Citayo who wrote up a case which was resolved in León in favour of the monastery of Abellar in 952 may well be the Citayo who joined Abellar three years later and may have been attached to the bishop's household at the time of the court hearing (the case was heard before the bishop of León).[10] The deacon and notary Felix who wrote up a case between abbots in León in 959 seems to be the Felix who recorded other transactions in and near León about that time and was clearly a cleric in León, whether or not explicitly attached to the bishop's household.[11] The notary Argimirus who recorded resolution of a case in favour of the bishop of Astorga in 878 was explicitly attached to the bishop.[12] And the priest Aloitus who constructed the long late tenth-century account of the dispute between the monastery of Sobrado (protected by Pedro bishop of Santiago) and the bishop of Lugo appears to have belonged to Pedro's household.[13] It is interesting that when we can hazard a guess at a scribe's identity, there is a strong episcopal context, but the number of cases is small and they are all cases in which a bishop had some kind of interest; it does not follow that all Accounts were drawn up in episcopal households. Overall, given their explicitly retrospective point of view and their focus on confirming outcomes, one could see these texts as records drawn up for the purpose of confirmation of an outcome by the winning party in a dispute, whether bishop, abbot, priest or powerful lay person.[14] This does not have to mean that they were untrue, but they are nevertheless partial, one-sided accounts; they are clearly not official court records nor notes taken in the course of court proceedings, although they could in principle draw upon records of oaths or confessions or other material if such existed.[15]

10 Li256, Lii288 (955); cf. Lii452 (977) and Lii494 (984).

11 Lii312; cf. S155 (957), S194 (961) and perhaps the interpolated Lii274 (954).

12 Ast5: 'Argimirus notarius qui assertor fuit de parte domini Indiscli episcopi manu sua scripsit.'

13 Sob109 (early 990s); cf. Sob49 (966–99), Cel5 (986), LaC102 (988), LaC110 (995).

14 On this point, see further below, pp. 93–4. Cf. discussion of Oviedo cathedral charter, ACO B.1.11, above and below, pp. 1–4, 51. Although it conforms in other respects to the form of these Accounts, I do not think the purpose of AHN Clero Lugo 1325A–9 (973, single sheet) was for confirmation; it lacks the usual long list of important confirmers (see fig. 6.2).

15 See further below, pp. 143–5, 147–8. Cf. Prieto Morera, 'El proceso en el reino de León', p. 387.

(2) Incidental references to disputes are just that, an incidental mention of a case in a text whose main purpose was to note something other than a dispute. They lie at the opposite end of the spectrum from the deliberate, retrospective Accounts. Two-thirds of them occur in gift charters, the remainder occurring mostly in records of sales or exchanges, with an occasional list or inventory too. Such references are brief and do not usually supply much detail of the dispute. For that reason, they have not featured so much in discussions of judicial procedure; however, since they are common and constitute a quarter of the total corpus, they offer some significant evidence of practice. The form of reference to the dispute is haphazard and does not conform to any standard template. Here is one example:

> In the name of God. I Cresciduru have agreed, in good will and of my own free will, to make a charter of donation for you Fruela Ansaloniz of the orchard which I have in the territory of Alvarenga, beneath Mount Ieronzo in the hamlet called Minudal. The orchard lies . . . [detail of boundaries]. I give you the eighth of that orchard, which was Aluito's, because of the dispute and the judgment I had before you, so that from today that portion of the orchard shall be transferred from my right into yours. You and your offspring shall have it in your power for ever. If anyone shall come to break this charter of donation then you shall have the power to take double the value from us, or as much as seems better to you.
>
> This charter of donation was made on the 18th of the kalends of March, era 975 [937 AD].
>
> I Cresciduru have confirmed this charter with my own hand.
>
> These are the witnesses: Rodorigu, Froigendo, Manulfu, Uiliulfu.
>
> The priest Sagado made the record.[16]

This is the second of two charters on a single sheet in favour of Fruela; the first is a gift of another part of an orchard and of a vineyard in the same territory, in 925, recorded by a different scribe.[17] The first looks like a straightforward gift, whereas we can see that the 937 gift arose because of a judgment made in court; we do not know why; and although we may speculate that the gift was in effect a fine paid to the court holder, the text does not say this.[18] Other examples of Incidental references to disputes make different kinds of point: a priest makes a gift to another priest because he had helped him when he was taken to court in chains; a couple makes a gift of property which they had (legitimately) acquired from a thief; another couple makes a gift of land which they had got from the man's father, who had acquired it from a man who had killed his serf; a priest makes a gift because the beneficiary of his gift had helped to clear him of a

16 PMH DC 43.

17 PMH DC 30. This is a completely separate text of twelve years earlier; it does not follow that it too was the outcome of a court case.

18 For court holders, see below, pp. 157–9.

charge of theft of horses; a woman sells orchards which her husband, who had committed homicide and appeared in court in León, had planted.[19] Sometimes the reference to a court case comes in a brief note about a past acquisition; sometimes, as in the example above, it is the immediate reason for making the transfer of property recorded. The explanatory comment is usually very brief, but it can be longer. Indeed, a few of the Incidental dispute records give quite considerable detail of court proceedings, although the purpose of these texts was still to record the transfer of property rights: a case of homicide, in which the killer had insufficient means to compensate the family and appealed to his lord to make up the difference; a case of property rights contested within a family, with a woman attacking her brother's gifts to his wife; a case of wounding denied, with the threat of an ordeal provoking confession and due payment.[20]

Examples of this kind of dispute record occur in most areas, but there are only two from Castile and none from Asturias. They occur throughout most of the tenth century, with a few ninth-century examples, but there are proportionately more from the 940s – 83 per cent of all examples. The proportion of lay beneficiaries is high (60 per cent); these lay beneficiaries were sometimes the victors in straightforward disputes over property between members of the laity, the dispute mentioned in passing when later transactions were recorded; but at least half of these lay men and women were also court holders, as were also at least half of the ecclesiastical beneficiaries, all of whom benefited from holding the court by receiving gifts or fines.[21]

I think it likely that many of these Incidental records were in reality records of fines paid to court holders – particularly where it is evident that the beneficiary was indeed a court holder, as in the example translated above. But not all were, and one cannot make such an assumption in all cases. There are, by contrast, some quite explicit (3) Fine (and compensation) records, and I have considered it important to be clear about the proportion of explicit Fines and keep them distinct. In what follows I use the single term Fine for all records of judicial payments, whether they detail a compensation, a penal fine or a court holder or other fee.[22]

Explicit Fines constitute nearly 15 per cent of the corpus; they also use gift format (see Figure 7.3). Here is a typical example of an explicit Fine record:

> In the name of God. Mondino and my wife Mirella and my daughter Bitillo to you Bishop Rosendo and the brothers of the monastery of Celanova.

19 S133 (951), S221 (964), Sam16 (989), Sob32 (941), Lii450 (977).

20 PMH DC 53 (943), Sam239 (985), OD31 (991).

21 For gifts, note especially LaC50 (947), in which the main actor had given gifts both to the bishop in whose court one case in which he had been involved had been heard and to the count in whose court another had been heard. (It is reasonable to differentiate gifts from fines – gifts were gifts, at least notionally freely given in recognition of some benefit, as the texts indicate; fines were explicitly required, and were increasingly noted from the late tenth century; see above, pp. 30–1.)

22 See above, p. x, for comment on terminology.

> We have agreed, of our own free will and without compulsion by anyone, to pay you our inheritance by the river Miño as a fine (*pariaremus*).[23] We give you the house which I had given my daughter as dowry (*casamentum*), in its enclosure with all appurtenances; we assign it to you before witnesses, and we are paying it because I gave my daughter in adultery to Brother Vidramiro. From this day on it shall be conveyed from our right into yours. If anyone should try to break it, he should pay double the value of the inheritance and you should have that in perpetuity.
>
> This charter recording a fine (*kartula pariationis*) was made on the 15th of the kalends of June, in era 990 [952 AD].
>
> We, Mondino and my wife Mirella and my daughter Bitilo [*sic*], confirm this charter with our own hands.
>
> These were present: Brother Donino, Pelagio, Lucido, Anditio, Vistroi.[24]

That Celanova was holding a court that dealt with lay offences is made explicit in several late tenth-century composite charters of acquisitions by its senior official, Cresconio. These composite charters are very lengthy documents which summarize records of a string of acquisitions, recording the main dispositive content, but without formal protocol; they include property acquired by gift, sale and exchange, in haphazard order, and also that acquired as fines. The latter include a gift from a man guilty of sleeping with (*perpetrabit adulterio*) his granddaughter, who complained before judges in the council of the monastery; payment of a fine from a man who disputed in court with another (apparently lay) man (it was paid *in iudicato*, the payment due to a court holder); and the property given by a man in lieu of the measures of wheat that *lex gotica* prescribed.[25] These composite inventories constitute an important corpus of information about publicly handled disputes – I have counted each Fine that is detailed in them as a separate event; this therefore inevitably skews the breakdown of beneficiaries in favour of the monastery of Celanova.

There are no examples from northern Galicia (although Sobrado Incidental dispute records often seem to record *de facto* Fines), Asturias, Cantabria, Castile and Navarre (see Figure 2.2). This is probably because most of the Fine records that we have arose from court activity; their survival depends on whether or not the archive of the court holder has been preserved. Although there are a few examples from the early tenth century, three-quarters come from the last thirty years or so of the century; this is significant because it does not reflect the overall distribution of charters and because it almost certainly does reflect the increasing tendency for major aristocrats to document court outcomes. That some formal court procedure was followed in these meetings is made absolutely

23 *Pariare* is the standard word in these texts for 'to pay a fine'; cf. classical Latin 'to make equal', 'to settle'.

24 Cel72; cf. PMH DC 58 (949), another case of a man paying a fine for his daughter's adultery with a monk, the fine this time going to a lay court holder.

25 That is, Visigothic law; Cel368 (975–1009), at pp. 530–31. See further above, pp. 26–7, 30, for the law and the *iudicatum*.

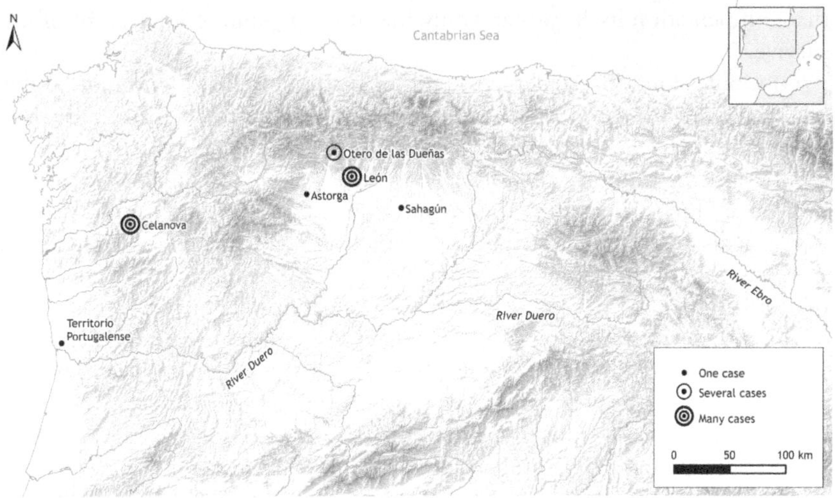

Figure 2.2 Distribution of Fine records

clear by cases such as that of the woman who committed adultery (*in adulterio*) with her godfather, whose Fine charter recounts that the *Librum* (the book of Visigothic law) had been consulted and it had been accordingly judged that she should become enslaved; however, after her confession it had been allowed that she make a gift of all her property, save that reserved for her children, to the layman who held the court.[26] These were not simply the arbitrary actions of powerful aristocrats leaning on peasants to make gifts; whatever their underlying intentions, some public procedure was followed. The beneficiaries of the Fines included the monastery of Celanova – at least 25 times – and seven different lay aristocratic court holders. It is perfectly clear that the court holder personally retained all or part of these payments because the properties handed over in such cases became family or monastic property; whether or not the court holder passed on a proportion to victims is unclear, although occasionally, as noted above, it was specified that one sum went to the court holder and another to the victim.[27] Most of these payments, defined by the dedicated vocabulary of *pariare*, *pariatio* and *iudicatum*, were made to the court holder (or to a judge), and there was also sometimes the *saionicum*, payment to the *saio*. However, in a handful of recorded examples, the payment following public resolution of a dispute clearly went to an injured party rather than to the court holder; for the purposes of analysis, we might prefer to think of such payments as compensation. Although they are much rarer in the record, this does not have to mean

26 Liii561 (994). Cf. Prieto Morera, 'El proceso en el reino de León', pp. 387–8.
27 For example, Liii578 (997).

that compensation itself was rare; only that it is uncommon for records of it to survive.[28]

(4) Confessions, (5) Agreements and (6) Oaths are records of a quite different kind from the three classes above. There are far fewer, and most are quite short (although elements of all can feature in the longer Accounts). To take Confessions first, often called *manifesta*.[29] There are 15 examples, just over 5 per cent of the total corpus. They come from all parts, except for Asturias and Navarre, although their distribution is quite different from that of charters as a whole – there are disproportionately many from Castile and Cantabria (8 of the total 15; see Figure 2.3); there are disproportionately few in the large collections; they run from 858 (there are in fact several ninth-century examples) to 995, and nearly all make explicit reference to court proceedings. They are interesting in that capturing the confession of guilt appears to have been the point of the record, rather than the conveyance of property, although many Confessions probably had property consequences in the long term. The form, and length, of these records varies, although many are in the first person and present tense; some give detail of the charges before recording the confession, and some give none of this; some give an indication of consequences, but others reserve that for a separate document. However much detail of the assembly may be recorded, it is clear that these documents relate to a rather late stage of the proceedings. Here is one kind of example:

> In the court of Flacenti, García Ordoñez and the rest of the council, I Flaino confess in response to the accusation of Elias, who speaks for Count Flaino Muñoz; I state that it is true, as I cannot deny, that in sin and at the devil's instigation, I Flaino had sex with a woman who is married to someone else and after that with her daughter. This confession is true and I have nothing to add.
>
> The confession was made on the 11th of the kalends of May, era 33 [i.e. era 1033, 995 AD].
>
> Flaino confirms this confession [with a sign].[30]

This document is preserved on a single sheet of parchment, together with the agreement made as a consequence.[31] Both are set out as separate documents on a thin strip of parchment, written in Visigothic cursive; there is no reason to think of them as anything other than original.

28 See above, pp. 30–1.

29 Prieto Morera, 'El proceso en el reino de León', pp. 395–7, argued that there was a distinct class of confession document called an *agnitio*, a record of acceptance of a judicial finding, especially used in civil cases, and argued that in the long term the *manifestum* evolved into the *agnitio*, at different rates in different regions. I am not persuaded by this argument; for use of the word *agnitio*, see below, pp. 127–8.

30 OD38.

31 OD39, of the next day. See below, pp. 48–9, for this record.

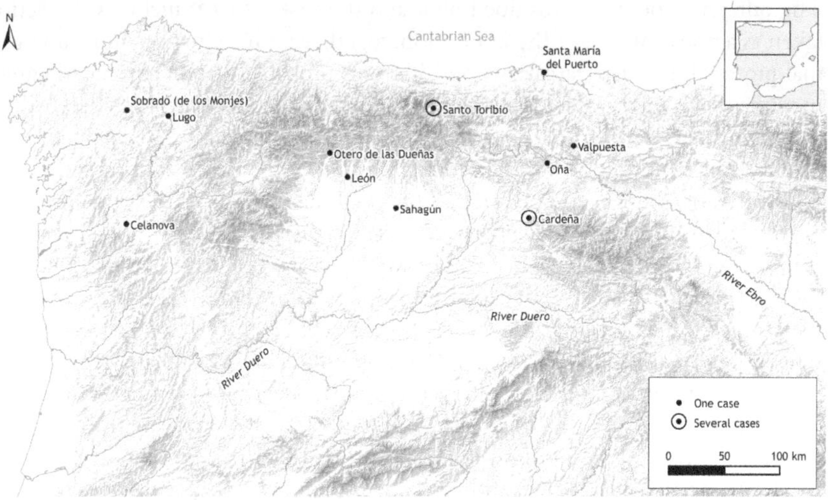

Figure 2.3 Distribution of Confessions

Here is a different kind of example:

> In the name of God. In the presence of our most glorious count Fernán González and many others, I the priest Gonzalo confess in response to the accusation of Abbot Lázaro, Fortes and all the community of the Holy Apostles Peter and Paul [of the monastery of Cardeña].
>
> I state that it is true, as I cannot deny, that I have possessed the church of San Justo, in Pesquera on the river Ebro, with all its appurtenances for three years; but I recognize and truly know that my uncle Alarico had it and gave it by charter to you.
>
> And today by the order of Bishop Basilio and of the count I consign it fully to you through the *saio* Tellu Offilo in perpetuity. This confession is true and I have nothing to add.
>
> And if I should have any other quarrel with you over that church, I myself or my parents or siblings or any of my successors, then you have over me the fact that I must pay the lord of the territory 300 *solidi*.
>
> This charter was made on the 15th of the kalends of March, era 979 [941 AD].
>
> I the priest Gonzalo make my sign on this charter of restoration that I have created. [Confirmed by] Munnio, Sanzone, Morelle, Albarus, Vincenti, Belasco, King Ramiro ruling in León, Count Fernán, Assur Fernandez.[32]

32 C35.

The difference between this document and the first is that it includes the action taken as a consequence of the confession, together with a sanction and some formal protocol. This is a cartulary copy; it seems probable that an associated agreement has been incorporated into the single text and that protocol has been added by the cartulary scribe, in accordance with standard procedure.[33] But the essence of the confession follows a similar format to that of the first example, despite the very different location and recording context. Indeed, some of the same formulas are used in both: *uerum est quod negare non ualeo, manifestum nicil abeo quod apponam*.[34] It looks as if there may have been a standard way of recording a Confession.

Another cartulary copy of a Confession, this time in the Celanova cartulary, may throw some light on the recording process.[35] Here we have a confirmation of an agreement following a court case, naming judges as well as both contesting parties, referring to the confession and to the subsequent assignment of a disputed property, fully witnessed. Appended to this confirmation are four separate documents: a Confession, a commitment by the representatives of both parties to appear in court, another commitment by the parties to appear in court with their statements before a different judge, and a final commitment to hand over the disputed property. All four of these documents have the *signa* of one or both parties but no witnesses. Very interestingly, the Confession includes the two formulas cited above, and indeed, in format it is extremely close to that of the confession by Flaino. So it looks as if a confession was recorded in a short document, in the course of or shortly after proceedings, as other key parts of the proceedings might be recorded in similarly short texts. Usually these do not survive, although the three commitments appended to the Oviedo single sheet ACO B.1.11 are very similar.[36] The confirmation that precedes the set of Celanova texts suggests that the case had involved formal proceedings, with judges and the active role of the legal officer, the *saio*.[37] Now, there is another copy of this charter later in the cartulary.[38] This is virtually identical to the initial confirmation, except for some corruption in spelling and a shorter witness list, but it does not have the four additional appended documents. It looks as if the confirmation was copied more than once, but the four additional documents were discarded. We should therefore consider whether court cases normally or

33 Since this happened in the count's court, it is extremely unlikely that the king of León was present; the reference to him probably derives from a dating clause, as the format of the reference would in any case suggest. That form is common, for example: 'Facta carta traditionis notum die XVIII kalendas decembris, era T.X.VIII, regnante rex Ranimiro in Legione et comite Garsea Fernandez in Castella', C180 (980). On such clauses, see Julio Escalona, 'In the name of a distant king: Representing royal authority in the county of Castile, ca. 900–1038', in *Early Medieval Europe*, 24 (2016).

34 For this formula, see further below, pp. 126–8.

35 Cel94 (987).

36 See above and below, pp. 1–4, 62.

37 It would be reasonable to classify the Celanova text as Mixed, like ACO B.1.11, but since the Confession section is clear, coherent and echoes other Confessions, and since the confirmation hangs on the fact of the confession, I have chosen to preserve this emphasis in my classification.

38 Cel150.

sometimes generated a few short documents, whether or not they were normally kept, and whether they might form a basis for Accounts or other texts constructed subsequently, as Roger Collins suggested in the 1980s.[39]

Getting a confession was clearly important, even if records of them were not often kept. This is amply demonstrated by an addition to a large royal donation charter to the monastery of Sahagún, on a single sheet: in the bottom lefthand corner there is a record of Confession of homicide and theft; both the royal charter and the Confession relate to places in Fuentes.[40] This record shares some of the wording of the Confessions above, although it does not have all the characteristic formulas. Given the interest in Fuentes, it looks as if the royal charter was an appropriate place to jot the Confession down – by implication, quickly; it may not have been intended as a permanent record in the archive, for it would have been near impossible to find if the donation charter was arranged with other royal gifts or in sequence or by geographical location.[41] But getting it down was important. A comparable process could well be the explanation for the apparently garbled cartulary copy of a sale record of 963.[42] Here a standard record of sale is interrupted by a first-person description of the vendor laying siege to a priest's house and burning it down, for which he went to court before the purchaser. This might have been a note of confession added in the margin of an existing sale document in the court holder's possession. In other words, although, as it now reads, it looks as if the attack happened first and the attacker/vendor then benefited enormously from the sale (for 100 *solidi*), in fact the attack followed the sale and we do not know the consequences of it. Altogether, then, records of confession look as if they were made soon after the confession was uttered and close in time to court proceedings – indeed,

39 See further below, pp. 143–4. Roger Collins, '"Sicut lex Gothorum continet": Law and charters in ninth- and tenth-century León and Catalonia', *English Historical Review*, 100 (1985), pp. 489–512, at pp. 501–2. See Roger Collins, 'Visigothic law and regional custom in disputes in early medieval Spain', in Wendy Davies and Paul Fouracre (eds), *The Settlement of Disputes in Early Medieval Europe* (Cambridge, 1986), pp. 85–104, at pp. 89–90, for his discussion of Cel94 and Cel150. His analysis of this text is arguable, but his main point that a single case might generate 'a plethora of documents' is very persuasive. (My main difficulty with his analysis is that I doubt that anyone other than the scribe 'signed' anything; I think the order in which the documents were produced was 3 4 2 5 1, not 3 4 1 2 5; I regard no. 1 as a retrospectively constructed agreement; and the mandator's suggested 'patronymic' (*Groupraviz*) must in fact be a corruption of *Et roborauim[us]*.)

40 S261, undated, but written on a record of 971. I am extremely grateful to Julio Escalona for sharing his views on this charter and pointing out the locations; he has argued, in a paper delivered in Madrid in 2014, that Sahagún was protecting interests in land and fishing rights in Fuentes, and that the royal charter was a very appropriate place to make the confession record.

41 The implication must be that the record, and perhaps the confession itself, was made in or near the Sahagún archive. The judges who heard the confession seem to have had access to a pack of documents; if the Placenti who wrote the record is the same as the Placentius of S237 (965), then it is likely he was a local priest in the valley of the Valderaduey (Ansur, purchaser in S237, seems to have used local priests to make many of his records), but of course he could have been a member of the Sahagún community. See further below, p. 85 n84, on this charter.

42 Lii360.

perhaps sometimes made in the course of court proceedings without troubling to record witnesses of the fact – some are not witnessed at all and four are only witnessed by major actors, like judges and *saio*.[43] The fact that there are a number of early examples, from the ninth century and that standard formulas were used suggests that this was a very long established practice.

(5) Agreements, of which there are 29 separate texts (10 per cent of the corpus), can be closely associated with Confessions, as in the Celanova and Cardeña examples above. Their distribution is similar to that of Confessions, although there is also one from Aragón,[44] and numbers from Castile and Cantabria are not exceptional; they run from 861 to 997. They too are written in the first person and present tense. If we take the Agreement associated with Flaino's Confession cited above as the first example of a Confession, it reads as follows:

> Elias, who is the spokesman for Count Flaino Muñoz, and Flaino, who speaks for himself through the *saio* Fortunio, by this our agreement we promise that we will present ourselves before García Ordoñez and Count Flacenti on Monday of the same era 33 [Easter Monday 995]. We will present ourselves and do as the law commands in respect of the confession which Flaino confirmed; and if anyone should falsify this agreement, he should pay 5 *solidi* and do as the law commands. We Elias and Flaino confirm this [with two signs].[45]

This is to the right of Flaino's Confession on the narrow strip of parchment and is clearly set out as a separate document (see Figure 2.4). A much earlier agreement from Lugo (of 861) reflects a similar situation. Here the priest Toresario had been in dispute with Bishop Gladila over control of a church. We have on a single parchment Toresario's Confession that until his mother's death due returns had gone to the bishop, but then he, Toresario, had diverted them, and also his Agreement to hand over the church, again set out as a separate document on the same parchment; there is also a third document on the parchment, an Agreement with the bishop made by another priest (see Figure 5.2).[46] It may be recalled that the copy of a Confession in the Cardeña cartulary was associated with an agreement immediately following within the

43 Not witnessed: OD38, S261, both on single sheets; witnessed by judges and *saio*: Flor74, T17, T30 (and also two unidentified), T66A (and also one unidentified). See further below, pp. 131–2, 211–13, on witnessing.

44 SJP31 (undated, tenth century).

45 OD39. For the date, see the editors' comments: since the preceding charter (OD38), on the same parchment, is dated 21 April 995, which was Easter Sunday, then this charter, dated Monday of the same era, is most reasonably understood as Monday 22 April 995.

46 Flor74 and Flor75; the third, Flor73, may well be the bishop's agreement with the priest who succeeded Toresario. The Confession was written first, and then the two Agreements, side-by-side in the space below. Amancio Isla Frez, *La sociedad gallega en la alta edad media* (Madrid, 1992), pp. 58–9, treats this charter as a forgery, although his comments on the Latin and on the formulas would not indicate forgery to me. In view of its similarity, rather, to other Confession records – coming from widely

Figure 2.4 A Confession and an Agreement of 995, AHDL, Otero 30A and B (OD38, OD39)

Source: Reproduced by permission of Archivo Histórico Diocesano de León

same charter:[47] where such cases constitute a single text, I have classified them together as Confession (or Agreement, depending on emphasis of the wording); where they were clearly conceived as separate documents, I have classified them separately.[48] Some stand-alone Agreements, however, have no associated confession; they may promise to make future payments or promise no future trouble; sometimes they split resources, like water, or concede that residents may have grazing rights. Most imply that there had been some dispute, although a few do not. Their forms vary: some have formal protocol, some do not; several are concluded before judges and counts; some have lengthy witness lists; some do neither. So while it is reasonable to suppose that recording a confession might quickly lead to the recording of a consequent agreement, as in the Flaino and Toresario cases, we do not have to assume that this was always so. It is conceivable that parties sometimes agreed a course of future action without a court case and without any open dispute, like the 974 agreement of Cendamiro and his brother to serve the bishop of Lugo from the church of Santa Columba.[49]

There are not many records that simply focus on (6) Oaths, but there are some – just five, less than 2 per cent of the corpus. These texts record oaths and not much else – there is little or no surrounding narrative – although they may include some explanatory prefatory material; they were oaths about evidence,

scattered parts, its correct use of standard Confession formulas (see below, pp. 126–8) and its association of Confession and Agreement, I think it unlikely that its content was fabricated. It does, however, appear to be a later copy of a ninth-century text; see further below, p. 85, on the hand.

47 See above, pp. 46–7.

48 As also T66A and T66B, where the cartulary copy has clearly run two or more separate documents together.

49 AHN Clero Lugo 1325A–11.

and they are known as *conditiones sacramentorum* ('terms of the oaths'). Take, for example, the sworn witness statements in a record of 911 from Valpuesta:

> ... We swear by God the Almighty Father, and by Jesus Christ his son, and by the Holy Spirit, who in the Trinity are the one true God; we swear by the relics of the holy Virgin Mary, mother of Christ; we swear by the relics of the Holy Saviour and his twelve Apostles and four holy Gospels; we swear by the relics of the priest San Millán, whose church is located in Gabinea, on whose altar we hold these oaths in our hands, while swearing. And so, as those aforesaid witnesses say, that is Ahostar, Simpronius, Paternus and Vigila, we were present and we have seen with our eyes and heard with our ears and we knew in truth that the priest Analso gave himself to the lord bishop Filimiro and the church of Santa María and the monastery of Valpuesta with all his rights, lands and vineyards, and everything in his power. And after that the bishop gave the priest Analso some of the land, where he built a house. And these things which we testify, we testify faithfully ...[50]

Many of the Accounts, and some other dispute texts, mention oaths in passing; indeed, it is often a focal point of a narrative that judges decided to give the oath to one party, with the names of those swearing then noted, together with an indication of the import of the oath, but no attempt to reproduce the words. The records that focus on the oath are different, and are interesting because – again, in first person and present tense – they appear to record the oath verbatim. They are long and invoke many holy people. They are very similar to each other, but vary slightly, particularly in the names of the holy persons invoked as well as in the particular content of the matter sworn. Although the group of texts is very small, it looks as if all examples conform to a standard pattern that was widely used; indeed, the summaries of some oaths which feature in other texts share some of the same characteristics. (The examples come from the *meseta*, Castile and Cantabria, with longer summaries from Galicia and Asturias.) Though tiny, this is an important group.[51]

There are two small groups of records that do not fit these categories: records in which disputes are (7) Implied but not detailed, and records of (8) Mixed type. There are 10 of the former and six of the latter and they constitute 3.5 per cent and 2 per cent respectively of dispute records. Disputes are Implied in, for example, a record assigning guarantors to the bishopric of Valpuesta that a man called Vermudo would not neglect his obligations and in a confirmation record of 945 which is described as a *scriptura agnitionis*, a record of acknowledgement,

50 V10; for the formulas, see further below, pp. 124–6.

51 The charter of Mixed type discussed above and below, pp. 1–4, 51, ACO B.1.11, also includes a verbatim oath, and the long and contorted account of Sob109 includes quite a long summary of an oath.

and details a complex previous history.[52] Some kind of dispute seems to lie behind such texts, but we have no detail. As with records of Incidental type, the main purpose of these Implied records was something other than recording a dispute or its outcome (mainly to record gifts or confirmations) – but in these cases the dispute reference is too abbreviated or too obscure to even count as Incidental. Numbers are so small the distribution and date range are unlikely to be significant, but it can be noted that examples fall across the tenth century and two if not three of them are Portuguese.[53]

Records of (8) Mixed type are just that – records which have elements of several types of record. Oviedo cathedral charter ACO B.1.11 is a good example.[54] This very large and very long dispute text, discussed in the Prologue to this book, lacks narrative detail, despite its very repetitive character; it has a long quotation of the oath taken by witnesses, a third-person note of an innocent going to the ordeal to test the evidence, six different witness lists and an appendix of three first-person commitments by the principal actors to appear in court, to accept the outcome and to accompany the *saio* for formal transfer of the disputed property.[55] Records like this do not fall into the regular record-making tradition, but clearly there was a court case, and a resolution, and someone with some knowledge of how such things were done wanted to make a record of it.[56] The other Mixed examples come from the Albelda, León and Celanova cartularies, and on two single sheets from León and Sahagún – a wide spread; again, all are from the late tenth century. The Celanova example is the long, rumbustious story of the doings of the monk Odoíno; this is largely story telling, but it includes a court case before the king and a final gift to the monastery.[57] The Albelda example is a record of a gift, to which are attached two statements, with witness lists, by the donor, denying the paternity of a child, together with reference to the fact that both he and the mother had undergone the ordeal of hot water in respect of this case.[58] The León cartulary example records a set of commitments to appear, to consign disputed property and to cause no further trouble and it also includes a verbatim oath. The León single

52 V43 (*c.* 968); cf. the same Vermudo as donor and confirmer in V38 (967) and V41 (968). S101 (945) – since the bishop confirms a royal grant, some episcopal interest is implied. For *agnitiones*, see n. 29 above, and below, pp. 127–8.

53 Ov3 (905), SMdelP4 (927), Cel509 (937), LaC71 (after 965), PMH DC 115 (976), PMH DC 167 (993); and perhaps Lor21 (974).

54 See above, pp. 1–4, for a longer description of the content of this charter.

55 OvC26; see also Wendy Davies, 'The language of justice in northern Iberia before AD 1000', in Andrew Reynolds, Jane Carroll and Barbara Yorke (eds), *Power and Place in Later Roman and Early Medieval Europe* (forthcoming).

56 Collins also discussed this text in '"Sicut lex Gothorum continet"', pp. 498–501. He rightly stressed its composite nature but his discussion does not touch on key points, such as the later addition of the high-status witnesses and the exceptional size of the parchment. See below, pp. 146–7, for further discussion.

57 Cel265 (982).

58 A27 (978) – a quite exceptional procedure.

sheet essentially records the progress of an appeal to the king for restoration of substantial episcopal property following a variety of disputes, and eventual royal confirmation of this.[59] And the Sahagún single sheet (which is an eleventh-century copy) records another royal restoration, this time to the monastery of Sahagún, with considerable back history of the property and an allusion to a court case, but no detail of it.[60] It is impossible to generalize about these records of Mixed type but, as in the case of the Oviedo charter, they can include quite significant detail of court proceedings.

Lastly, there are (9) Confiscations and (10) Debts – actions usually at one remove from the judicial court. Records that refer to confiscations suggest an alternative, largely extra-judicial, mode of public dispute resolution. Here is an example:

> King Ramiro to you Hermegildo, greetings. Our Glorious Serene Highness has approved that we give you all the inheritance of the homicides of Villa Matella, who killed our cousin Odoario Díaz. We give you arable, vineyards, orchards, mills and everything you can find in that villa, that you should have in perpetuity, you and your offspring having the power to do there whatever you wish. And whatever you want to take, do and judge there, let the power be given to you by us. We order that no-one should cause you any disturbance there.
>
> Noted on the 14th of the kalends of January, era 975 [937 AD].
>
> King Ramiro on this charter of donation made by us.
>
> Ordoño, the king's son, confirms.
>
> Sancho, the king's son, confirms.
>
> Confirmed by Ordoño, son of King Alfonso, Abbot Gonzalo, the priest Berulf, Osorius Monniz, Gundesindus Froilaz, Odoarius Gimaraz, Piloti iben Gibuldo, Olemundus iben Arosindo, Fortis Iustiz, Froila Gelmiriz, Veremudus Almoratiz, in the name of Christ Oveco by the grace of God bishop [and eight more names].[61]

These texts, which account for just under 7 per cent of dispute records, rarely give detail of the disputes, or the reasons for them, and for the most part record gifts of confiscated property (although there is one sale, one exchange and one confirmation text); they are in gift format. One might argue that reference to confiscation is purely incidental, but it is more than that. All but two of these Confiscations were made by kings.[62] One charter of 975 explicitly states that the king has power to take away property, and another, of 977, details

59 Li192 (946); Lii508 (985).

60 S276 (974).

61 Li123.

62 S322 (984), where the confiscation was by a count (from a lapsed priest), although there was an episcopal interest in the property. Lii479 (980), where the confiscation was by a bishop (from an adulterous monk).

the procedure: when a man broke down the doors of a church and killed the brother in charge, the king and his mother, the queen, sent the judge Gutino to confiscate the entire inheritance of the homicide, 'as was the custom'; the king and queen then gave away the property.[63] Mentioning confiscation is crucial to the record, for it supplies the justification for the king's power to dispose of the property, as it is also at the same time a statement of the royal power to command. This is specifically royal power in action, and reference to the king's *serenitas* (supreme position) is common in this kind of text. Most of the examples are from the *meseta*, where the king was most consistently present, although almost a third are from Galicia; there are no explicit cases from the north, Castile or regions farther east. There are examples from 867 to 998, and the beneficiaries were sometimes churches and monasteries, sometimes aristocrats.

Records of the payment of (10) Debts usually occur within unelaborated records of gifts of property, and are usually brief explanations of why the gift was made. They are of standard gift form (although many describe themselves as sales);[64] there is one exchange. Here is one example:

> In the name of God. I Lelle, and my wife Eilo, [greet] you Hermegildo and Paterna. There can be no doubt that we took a loan of grain from your community of Sobrado, wheat, barley and rye, and we did not have the wherewithal to return it to you. On account of that, we have agreed to make a charter for our share of the orchard planted by Geldemirus in the settlement called Gunderedi, that is, twenty apple trees and the land they stand on, so that from this day they shall be transferred from our ownership to yours. If anyone should be tempted to undo this, s/he shall pay you a fine of double the value of the trees, which you shall have in perpetuity.
>
> This charter of sale was made on the 11th of the kalends of January, era 990 [22 December 952]. Lelle and Gilo [place] our hands on this charter of sale [with signs], witnessed by Gresamarus, Spassandus, Munio.[65]

All such transactions are of relatively small scale, like this one, and the debts are most commonly wine or grain that was owed and could not be paid; hence, a gift of property was made in its place – and hence the implication of tension between the contracting parties. The beneficiaries were aristocrats and churches. These records constitute 11 per cent of the corpus of dispute texts, and more than three-quarters of them come from Galicia (with significant numbers in the Celanova inventories of the end of the century). The rest are from Asturias and the *meseta*, with none from Castile or parts farther east. They

63 Lii442; S287.

64 For gift and sale, and the difference between them, see Wendy Davies, 'When gift is sale: Reciprocities and commodities in tenth-century Christian Iberia', in Wendy Davies and Paul Fouracre (eds), *The Languages of Gift in the Early Middle Ages* (Cambridge, 2010), pp. 217–37.

65 Sob98. This is a cartulary copy; *signa* are indicated for the two donors, presumably a copy of signs made by the scribe of the original charter.

are a feature of the second half of the tenth century, and not of earlier records. Although in form they are not much different, they are a nice contrast to records of Confiscations. The latter deal with confiscation of landed property from aristocrats; these Debts deal with peasant problems and were the occasion for redistribution of property at a much lower social scale.

Concluding thoughts

Notwithstanding the occasional difficulties of classification and the debatable nature of some records, there are clearly several quite different types of record to consider when investigating the public settlement of disputes. There are some geographical differences in their distribution, most noticeably the smaller number of examples from Navarre and parts to the east – but that may be no more than a reflection of the overall number of charters that is preserved. Although there are plenty of surviving Castilian charters, there is a smaller range of types of dispute record than survives from regions to the west: there are no Fines or Confiscations or Debts; this must be partly a consequence of the recording and archiving tradition, for there are fewer peasant transactions in the record, and must be partly a consequence of the low survival of charters on single sheets: it may be that not everything was copied into the big cartularies that dominate. However, the absence of Confiscation records probably reflects the political reality of the limited appearance of kings in the region. Galicia, by contrast, supplies examples of all types of record. Its overwhelming proportion of Debt records cannot simply be attributed to a greater survival of texts of peasant transactions, for the corpus from the *meseta* has plenty of those. Rather, it is probably a reflection of proactive intervention in the peasant economy by very powerful monasteries like Celanova and Sobrado.

There are also some significant temporal differences in the incidence of types of record. The most obvious is that records of Oaths, Confessions and Agreements occur throughout the period surveyed and offer relatively many ninth-century examples, given the relatively low survival rate of ninth-century charters. Although their numbers are small, everything suggests that making records of this kind was a long-established practice, already old by the mid-ninth century. One could probably add to this the several records of formal commitments by principal actors to appear in court, to accept judgment, to hand over property, which are also first-person and standard in format, without witnesses.[66] They occur too rarely and too haphazardly (they are preserved in different contexts) to constitute a separate analytical category, but the consistency of form is suggestive. By contrast, the fact that records of Fines concentrate in the later tenth

66 For example, Cel94, Li191 (with witnesses), Li192 (with witnesses), OvC26; see further below, pp. 135–6, 147.

century, as do half of the Incidental records of disputes, may reflect changing practice in the handling of judicial cases on the ground, and not just changing scribal practice. Likewise, the concentration of Debt records in the later tenth century is almost certainly a reflection of the proactive monastic and clerical activity suggested above, rather than changing scribal practice.

As for structure, there are some fundamental differences between types. Firstly, there is a difference between the third-person, retrospective Accounts and the documents of several types written in the first person and present tense.[67] Secondly, within the first-person records there is a difference between those whose primary purpose was to record a conveyance of property, usually using standard gift or sale format (Incidental records of dispute, Fines, Confiscations and Debts), and those whose purpose was to record something else, in a range of different formats (Confessions, Oaths and Agreements). The latter tend to be short documents, may be scrappily recorded, and appear to have been made during or shortly after proceedings.[68] They seem less likely to have been kept in the longer term – they certainly survive in much smaller numbers – and were perhaps not intended to be kept; they often lack witnesses. Sometimes, however, such short documents seem to have formed the basis of a text that looks like a more standard charter, with full formal protocol – like the combined Confessions and Agreements noted above[69] – and sometimes the summaries of oaths and references to confessions that feature in the much longer retrospective Accounts look as if they could have used similar texts. If so, the short documents must have been kept for a period.

Dispute records survive in some very different formats, and there are some regional differences in distribution that are potentially significant. The processes which led to their construction are varied, and the outcomes of these processes have varying evidential value. But basic structure is only one aspect defining the form of dispute records. Physical form is another. We have already noted long and short documents, single sheets, annotations and cartularies. Chapter 3 will explore the range of material differences in the corpus and the potential significance of those differences for our understanding of the use of dispute records.

67 See further below, pp. 143–4.
68 See further below, pp. 147–8.
69 C35 and OD43; pp. 45–6 above.

Appendix: texts quoted in chapter 2

(1) Account

In era DCCCCLXVIIII[a] orta fuit contemtio inter parte de fratres de monasterio Sancti Iuliani, qui est fundatum super ripa de ribulo Torio, in suburbio ciuitatis Legionense, et pariter sub una uoce cum eis Garsea, genero de Rumfurco, contra omines abitantes in uilla Manzaneta et uillare quem uocitant Garrafi, quam fratres de supradicto monasterio per testamentos obtinebunt de concessione regum domnissimi Adefonsi principis et domne Scemene regine, seu et postea de regem domno Garsea et post eos simili testamento et confirmationis domni Ordonii principis et domne Giluire regine, quam pridem fecerant in sepedicto loco genitores et antecessores illorum, domnus Adefonsus et domne Scemena. Pro quibus dicebant omines qui infra ipsas uillas et terminos, quod in testamento resonat, ruptelas exerquerant quod de illorum erat termino et de sua presura illut obtinebunt. Dumque aberent pro hanc contemtio et disceptatione, uenerunt pariter in presentia principis domni Adefonsi, prolis domni Ordonii, et ad illorum sugessionem perrexit ill[e] ad ipsas uillas et plures magnati cum eo, subter annotati, pro [a]b[er]e testimonii, et posuerunt terminos de uilla Manzaneta per ubi eam Rumfurcus obtinuerant, id est: de ribu quod dicunt Auoceto, discurrente aqua per lumbano, de parte occidentis, usque in illa fracta super uillare Garrafi; et de parte orientys, per media fonte de tacos usque in Torio; et de parte superiore, discurrente aqua, per uia qui uadit per illa lumba usque in ualla Cabo et inde in termino de Aduocato. Hec omnia sepe memoratum, secundum in testamentos resonat et nos fideliter preuidimus et uetustiores narrauerunt, sic homnia cum summa integritate decernimus, absque huius inquietudinem, perenniter permanere, ut nihil exinde in parte extranea liceat uindicare, quod qui deinceps aliquid infra ipsos terminos sine consensum fratrum in ipso loco degentium, aliquid adpreendere uel uindicare temtauerit, pariet ipsas uillas in uoce monasterii duplatas uel triplatas, secundum lex continet godorum, omnia perenniter abiturum.

Notum die IIII° kalendas februarias, era quo supra.

Adefonsus princeps quod ueritatem cognouimus manu propria confirmamus.

Sub Christi nomine, Cissila episcopus confirmans. In Christi nomine, Ouecco episcopus confirmans.[70]

(2) Incidental reference

In dei nomine. Ego Cresciduru uobis Froila Ansaloniz placuit nobis adque conuenit per bona pacis et uoluntas et faceremus a uobis testum scriptura donacione in pumare que abemus in uilla que dicent Aluarenga subtus monte Ieronzo in uigo que dicent Minudal. Et iacet ipso pumare in alio uestro desueco de pumare de Tedon usque in larea calua. Damus uobis de ipso pumare integro que fuit de Aluito octaba integra pro intencione et iudicio que abui ante uos ita ut de odie die et tempore sit ipsa racione de ipso pumare cum suo terreno de nostro iure abraso et in uestro iure sit tradito uel confirmato. Abeatis uos et omnis posteritas uestra iuri quieto in temporibus seculorum. Ut siquis homo uenerit uel uenerimus contra hanc cartula donatione ad inrumpendum tunc abeas potestatem aprehendere de nos dublata uel quantum a uobis fuerit meliorata et uos perpetim abitura. Facta kartula donatione XVIII° kalendas martias. Era DCCCC LXXV. Ego Cresciduru in hanc cartula manu mea rouoraui. Id sunt testes. Rodorigu test. Froigendo test. Manulfu test. Uiliulfu test. Sagado presbitero notuit.[71]

(3) Fine

In Dei nomine. Ego Mondino et uxor mea Mirella et filia mea Bitillo, uobis domnus Rudesindo episcopo et fratribus monasterii Cellenoue. Placuit nobis propria nostra uoluntate nullius quoque gentis imperio nec suadentis articulo sed propria nobis accessit uoluntas ut pariaremus uobis hereditatem nostram propriam quam abemus integra iuxta fluuium Minei; damus atque paramus uobis ipsum kasa ab integrum quem ego Mondino ad ipsa filia mea dedi in casamento, sic quomodo iacet concluso in omnique giro cum omnibus suis per ubi uobis dilimittauimus et coram testibus adsignauimus et karacteres fitos, et pariamus uobis illo penis nostro facto quod filia nostra dedi ad adulterio ad fratrum Uidramiro. Ita ut de odie die uel tempore de iuri nostro sit abrasa et in iure uestro sit tradita atque confirmata. Et si aliquis homo ad irrumpendum uenerit uel uenerimus quomodo pariat uobis ipsas hereditates duplatas et uobis perpetim abituras.

Facta kartula pariationis XV kalendas iunii. In era D CCCC LXL.

Mondino et uxor mea Mirella et filia mea Bitilo in hanc kartulam manus nostras roboramus.

70 Li89 (29 January 931) = ACL1333.

71 PMH DC 43 (?14 February 937); 18th of the kalends of March is an impossible date; maximum number before the kalends is 16, which would give 14 February.

Qui presentes fuerunt: Fratri Donino ts. Pelagio ts. Lucido ts. Anditio ts. Uistroi ts.[72]

(4) Two Confessions

In iudicio Flacenti, Carcia Ordonizi uel cetero concilio, manifestum sum, ego Flaino, ad peticione Elias, qui asere uoce de comite Flaino Monizi, uerum est, cot necare non ualeo, quia peccato inpidiente et diauolo inmitente sic toliuit, ego Flaino, muliere aliena ad suo marito et fecit qum ea adulterio et post ec sic fecit qum sua filia, qum matre et filia. Et que manifesto uerum est factore et manifestu nicili abeo que opona.

Facto manifesto XI kalendas madias, era XXXIII. Flaino in hoc manifesto rouorabit.[73]

In nomine Domini.

In presentia gloriosissimi comitis nostri Fredinando Gundisalbiz uel aliorum multorum manifestus sum ego Gundissalbo presbiter a petitione Lazarus abba ita et Fortes et omnem collationem de Sanctorum Apostolorum Petri et Pauli.

Uerum est quod negare non ualeo, quia casa que est iuxta Ibero, in locum quem uocitant Piscaria, ecclesia que est sita Sanctorum Iusti et Pastoris et Sancti Saturnini, sic me cognosco in ueritate, quia odie tercio anno uel amplius ego illa possedi in meo iure cum omnes suos aditos et sua aiacentia, sic me cognosco et ueridice scio quia nostro tio domno Alaricus abuit illa uobis tradita et concessa per testamentum et scriptura que contra uos est.

Et odie per iussionem Basilio episcopo et mandatum de comite sic illa uobis consigno et persolbio per manus sayone Tellu Offilo, cum omni uoce et integritate in perpetim abiturum. Et in hanc manifestum nicil abeo quod apponam.

Et si, quod absit, aliqua querella uobis fecero pro ipsa casa, an ego seu parentibus meis uel germanis aut aliquis ex successoribus meis, tunc habeatis super me ut pariem a parte dominus terre CCC solidos in cautis.

Facta scriptura ista notum die XV kalendas marcias, era DCCCC.LXX. VIIII[a].

Ego autem Gundissalbo presbiter in hanc scedula restaurationis a me facta meum sygnum feci. Munnio rb. Sanzone rb. Morelle rb. Albarus rb. Uincenti rb. Belasco rb. Ranimirus rex princeps in Legione rb. Fredinandus comes rb. Assur Fernandez rb.[74]

72 Cel72 (18 May 952).

73 OD38 (21 April 995) = AHDL, Otero 30A.

74 C35 (15 February 941).

(5) Agreement

Elias, qui est mandatore de comite Flaino Monizi, et Flaino, qui responde sua uoce per saione Fortunio, per nostro placitum nobis cotpromitimus qualiter die II feria, uice ista era XXXIII, sic presentemus personas nostras ante Carcia Ordonizi, Flacenti comice, presentemus nostras personas et faciamus de illo manifesto que Flaino rouorabit que les mantare et qui mentire pacte solidos v et facia que les mantare. Elias, Flaino, rouorauimus.[75]

(6) Oath

Condiciones sacramentorum adque ex ordinacione Gondesalbo Tellizi. Iuraturi sumus nos prolati testes, id est, Ahostar et Simpronius et Paternu et Uigila . . . parte Tello abbati de Balle Conposita, testificantes contra parte Analso presbiter et Siberius presbiter, pro causa unde intentjo uertitvr inter eos. Proinde iurare debemus, sicuti et iuramus, inprimis per Deum, patrem omnipotentem, et Ihesu Christum, filium eius, Sanctumque Spiritum Paraclitum, que est in Trinitate unus et uerus Deus, iuramus per reliquias Sancte Marie Uirginis et Ienetricis Christi, iuramus et per reliquias Sancti Salbatoris et suos XII apostolos et sancta IIII euangelia, iuramus et per reliquias Sancti Emiliani presbiteri, cuius baselica scita est in Gabinea, super cuius altare as condiciones manibus nostris iurando tenemus. Quia, ut dicent sti iam supradicti testes, id est, Ahostar et Simpronius et Paternus et Uigila, presentes fuimus et hoculis nostris uidimus et aures audibimus et sapemus in ueritate quomodo sic se tradidit ste Analso presbiter ad domnu Filimirum episcopum et ad trium Sancte Marie uel ad zella de Balle Conposita cum omni facultate sua, uel terras et uineas uel omni quod in iuri suo abuit. Et post inde sic dedit ste episcopus sua terra de Regula et posuit stum Analso presbiterum et fecit ibi sta kasa cum sua conficta. Et hec que testificamus, recte fideliter testificamus, et in hanc iuramentum nullum fraudis inienium non interponimus. Quod testes testificauerunt iam supradicti, id est, Ahostar et Simpronius et Paternus et Uigila, quod determinauerunt pedibus suis. Et nos cognobimus, ego, Siberus, et Analso presbiter, quod uerum testificauerunt, pro ipsa tradictione que fecimus, sic tradimus nos cum omni facultate nostra ad domnum Filimirum episcopum uel ad regula Sancte Marie in Balle Conposita, in testimonio Dei et testamento eterno et iuramentum illius pretermittimus.

Ego, Analso, hic roboraui. Ego, Siberius hic roboraui.

Factum iudicius uel manifestum III idus magias, discurrente era DCCCC X^{L} UIIII. Regnante domno Garsea in Leione, et comite Gundesalbo Telluz, in Lantarone.[76]

75 OD39 ([22/4]/995) = AHDL, Otero 30B.
76 V10 (13 May 911).

(7) Implied

In Dei nomine. Ego, Uermudo, sic mito fidiatores Abayza et Mascecone contra Albaro abba si post odie die alica neglegentia fecero in ipsa casa de Ualle Coposita, aut con uicio aut in suprioli te fecero, que dimitam ipsas meas uacas in ipsa casa perpetuas. Et ego, Abayza, et ego, Mascacone, sic intramus fid[ia] tores super isto cauto de parte de isto Uermudo contra Albaro abba, et manus nostras roborabimus.

Ego, Uermudo, qui hanc fidiatura feci et relege[ndo] audibi, manu mea roborabi. Didacus [presbiter manu] mea roborabi. Nunnu Obeccozi manu mea ro[borabi]. Nunnu presbiter ts. Munnio frater ts. Feles ts.

Et ego, Uermudo, que factum, ego corona

[Fac]ta fidiatura XII kalendas I. . . [Regnante] rex Ranemiro, et comi[te] Fer[nando Gundesalbiz in] Castella.[77]

(8) Mixed

Petrus frater qui acsere, in sua uoce, et Uilifredus frater qui respondet, in uoce de Uictino, tibi saionni nostro Karoso per unc nostrum placitum tibi conpromitimus qualiter die quod est die IIII[a] feria, VIII[o] idus nouembris sic presentemus nostras personas in presentia Teodoredo Iustizi et Felix iudigum presentem ego Petrus mea persona et mea testimonia per quos firmetur super Uilifredo qui est uigarios de Uictino, quomodo segdente se Petrus in suo monasterio de Seuero de Seuero abba sic se leuauit Uictinus et inuitauit Petrum ad sua mensa et in alio die accesit ad illo uolumtas animo karo et spontania sua uolumtate et donauit ad Petrum terra uagua sua ratione et de sua muliere Fredildi et de Teodeuera uno consilio aderato et terra donada et assinada super placito et iuramentum quos fecissent ibidem monasterio ita et fecerunt et roborabit placito Uictinus in solidos C et monasterio facto et eglesia et kasas et corte clusa et ortum et pomare postum et aque metuta que ipso monasterio regat syc se leuauit Uictinus pro consilio de Uilifredo qui ipsa uoce autorigauit ad integritate et pro consilio de serore Gugina et per Teouera et de Fredildi bracio forcioso animo orrido et tullerunt ad frater Petrum ipso monasterio et ipsa ereditate unde placito rouorauerunt et tulliuit mici alia eglesia quem abeba de auios meos et uinia que donauit Seuero appa et serore Gogina ad Petrum et autoriauit Seuero appa ad Petrum in concilio de Gordone ante Teoderedo Iustiz et Felix iudigum in conuentum eglesie Sancte Marine. Si se leuauit Uilifredus et Uictinus et tullerunt mici ipsa uinia et ipso uino et ego Uilifredus qui sum uigarius de Uictino et de suas sorores mea persona pro ipsas testimonias accipere et qui minime fecerit pariet solidos V que Petro et Uilifredo in oc placito manus nostras (signo) fecimus. Ueruum tertium que testifigauerunt testimonias de parte Petrum contra Uilifredo qui est uigarius et mantutor de Uictino et de suas sorores id est Felix, Agila, Onorigus et alios plures numeros XXX[a]. Quia

77 V43 (*c.* 968); see editors' comments on the date (outside limits 966–75).

occulos uidimus et presente fuimus quando adduxo Uictinus fratrem Petrum ad sua mensa et sedente se Petro in suo monasterio su mano de Seuero appa si se leuauit Uictinus et accesit ad illum uolumtas animo karo et spontania sua uoluntate consilio aderato quum Teodeuera et Fredildi et rouorauit placito ad fratrem Petrum in solidos C de ipsa hereditate de Teodeuera et de Fredildi que donaberunt ad frater Petrum et donaberunt et assinaberunt ipsa ereditate que abebant in Paragiaio terra uagua que fecisset ibidem monasterio, ita et fecerunt, et monasterio facto eglesia et kasas et coorte clusa et ortum et pomare postum et aqua que ipse monasterio regat si se leuauit Uitinus per consilio de Uilifredo et de sorore Gugina et de Teodeuera et de Fredildi bracio fortioso et animo orrido et tulliuit ad Petrum ipsa ereditate et ipso monasterio et alia eglesia quam abebat de suos auios et uinia que donauit Seuero appa et sorore Gugina ad Petrum et autogauit illa Seuero appa in concilio de Gordone ante Teoderedo Iustiti et Felix iudigum et si se leuauit Uictinus et Uilifredus et tullerunt ipsa uinia et ipso uino ad Petrum et que testifigamus et iurare deuemus Felix Agila Onorigus confirmat. Conditiones sagramentorum adque ex ordinatione Teodoredo Iustizi Felix iudigum iuraturi sumus nos testes prolati qui sumus de parte de frater Petro testifigantes contra Uilifredo qui est uigarius de Uictino, id est Felix et Agila et Onorigo, iuramus inprimis ad Deum Patrem omnipotentem qui fecit celum et terra, mare et omnia que in ei sunt, iuramus pro XII profetas et pro XIIm apostolos et sancta IIIIor Euangelia, id est, Marcus, Mahteus, Lugas et Ioannes, iuramus pro reliquias Sancta Maria uirginis et genetrix Domini nostri Ihesu Christi, iuramus pro reliquias Sancte Marine uirginis in cuius loco as conditiones manus nostras tenemus sibe et pro diuina omniaque sunt sancta, quia occulis uidimus et presentes fuimus et bene nobis cognitus manet in ueritatem quanto aduxo Uictinus Petrum ad sua mensa et sedente se Petrum in suo monasterio sub mano de Seuero appa et si se leuauit Uictinus cuius uigarius est Uilifredus pro consilio de Teodeuera et de Fredildi et accesit ad illos uolumtas animo karo spontania sua uolumtate et donaberunt et assinnaberunt suas raciones quem abebunt in Paragiaio sic Uictino quomodo etiam et Teodeuera et Fredildi ad frater Petrum spontania sua uolumtate et rouoraberunt placitum ad fratrem Petrum de omnia sua ereditate quem abebant in Paragiaio ad integritate et roboraberunt placitum in solidos C et donaberunt et assinaberunt ipsa terra uagua quo fecissent monasterium ita et fecerunt et monasterio facto et eglesia et kasas et corte clusa et ortum et pomare postum et aqua mittuta qui ipsum monasterium inregat et ipso lauore facto sic se leuauit Uictinus pro consilio de Uilifredo qui ipsa uoce autorcauit ad integritate in concilio et pro consilio de sorore Gugina et de Teodeuera et de Fredildi et tulliuit ipsum monasterium ad Petrum et alia eglesia quam abebat Petrus de suos auios et uinia que donaberat Seuerus appa et serore Gugina ad Petrum et autorcauit illa Seuero abba ad Petrum in concilio de Gordone ante Teoderedo Iustizi et Felix iudigum in conuentum eglesie Sancte Marie et si se leuauit Uictinus et Uilifredus et tullerunt ipsa uinia et ipso uino ad frater Petrum et abent illo contra se et mentiuit ipsum placitum et abet et ereditate et placito contra se et qui iuramus recte et fideliter iuramus et in anc iuramento nunllo qui fraudis ingenio non interponimus et si mentimus et nomen Domini in falso tangimus comprendat nos iudicius Dei et pena kaldaria. Iuraberunt istas testimonias in eglesia Sancte Marie que exitata est ad porta Gordonens et pro eorum iuramentum ingresus est innocens ad pena kaldaria nomine Fredenandus qui in tercio die limpidus apparuit coram multorum testium qui II sunt conscripti uel signa facturi late conditiones, notum die XIImo kalendas dicembris era D CCCC LXL I[a]. Monnisso ubi fidelis fuit de amborum partibus et rogatus de frater Petrum manu mea roborabit. Assuri ubi fidelis fuit de amborum partibus et rogatus de frater Petrum manu mea. Furakasas ubi fidelis de amborum partibus rogatus de frater Uilifredo manum meam et nocentem sub custodia tenuit et in III° die limpidum presentabit mea. Teodoredus Iustizi quos iudicabi. Felix quos iudigaui. Gaudemiro. Fredenandus ubi innocens fuit et aserias conditiones iurauit et manum in kaldaria misit et ?? eiecit et in III° die in concilio limpidus apparuit manu mea. Karosus ubi saio fuit.

Qui preses fuerunt ad iuramentum id est Roderigus presbiter. Sunleani presbiteri. Fe? et Aurelius Senderigus Taurellus Tello Monninus ??? . . . on Karosus Pepinus Placinus. Ausanius pater et alios plures in conuentum eglesie Sancti Martini episcopi.

Qui preses fuerunt quando innocens ingressus est ad pena kaldaria id est Furakasas, abba Romanus confirmat. Ioannes confirmat. Uilifredus confirmat. Quintila confirmat. Tedisclus.

Qui ipsum nocente limpidum uiderunt id est Teoderedo Iustizi. Felix Rubio. Maximinus Nikeiti. Aurelius Ualerianus. Azmon Nunillani presbiter. Donnellus. Sabgildus. Seuero.

Petrus et Uilifredus tibi saionni nostro Karoso per unc nostrum placitum tibi compromitimus qualiter die quod erat die V[a] feria sic presentemus personas nostras ic in Gordone in presencia iudigum presentem ego Petrum mea persona et ipsa testimonia pro ad iuramentum et ego Uilifredus mea persona ipsas testimonias a iuramenture et qui minime fecerit parie solidos Vque Petrus et Uilifredus in placito manus nostras.

Petrus et Uilifredus tibi saionni nostro Kaoroso per unc placitum tibi compromitimus qualiter die quod sabbato sic presentemus personas nostras in presencia iudigum in Gordone presentem ego Uilifredus mea persona et meum pactum quantum lex mandat per sentencia et ego Petrus mea persona pro accipere ipsum pactum per manum saionis et qui unc placitum exserserit pariet solidos Vque et insuper compleat ipsu pactum. Petrus et Uilifredus in placitu manus nostras fecimus.

Petrus et Uilifredus tibi saionni nostro Karoso per unc nostrum placitum tibi compromitimus qualiter die quod quo die V[a] feria sic presentemus nostras personas ic in Ayrias et in Paragiaio presentem ego Uilifredus mea persona et assinnem ipsa uilla que in iudicio resonat per manum saionnis et ego Petrus mea persona pro ipsa uilla accepere et qui minime fecerit pariet solidos Vque Petrus et Uilifredus in placito manus nostras facimus.

Sub Christi nomine Gundesalbus aepiscopus sedis Legionensis confirmat. Gundesindus comes palatii confirmat. Uermudus Nunnizi comes palatii. Fortes Iustizi confirmat. Dextera uirtus [*recte* In Christi virtute?] Armentarius Dumiense sedis aepiscopus. Serenissimus princeps Hordonius. Altissimi manu protectus Gudesteus Ouetense sedis aepiscopus. Sanctius serenissimus princeps confirmat. Geluira prolis Ranemiri confirmat. Nebutianus presbiter.[78]

(9) Confiscation

Ranimirus rex tibi Hermegildus, salutem. Annuit namque serenitatis nostre glorie ut donaremus atque concederemus tibi, ad perauendum, omnem hereditatem de homicidanes de uilla Matella, qui occiderunt suprino nostro Odoario Didazi: terras, uineas, pomares, molinis uel quantum in ipsa uilla de eorum causa inuenire potueris, accessum uel concessum, omnia tibi donamus et concedimus perhenniter abitura, faciendi exinde quod tua institerit uolumptas, tu et omnis posteritas tua. Et quicquid exinde agere, facere uel iudicare uolueris, sit tibi a nobis concessa potestas. Neminem uero hordinamus nec permittimus quid tibi ibidem uel in modice aliquam faciat disturbationem.

Notum die XIIII kalendas ianuarii, era DCCCC LXX[a]V[a].

Ranimirus rex in hanc kartula donationis a nobis facta.

Ordonius, prolis regis, conf.

Sancius, prolis regis, conf.

[Ist column] Hordonius, prolis Adefonsi regis, conf. Gundisaluus abba conf. Berulfus presbiter conf. Osorius Monniz conf. Gundesindus Froilaz conf. Odoarius Gimaraz conf. Piloti, iben Gibuldo, conf. Olemundus, iben Arosindo, conf. Fortis Iustiz conf. Froila Gelmiriz conf. Veremudus Almoratiz conf. Sub Christi nomine, Queçco, Dei gratia episcopus.

[2nd column] Didacus archidiaconus conf. Berultus presbiter conf. Frede-nandus presbiter conf. Balderedus presbiter conf. Leouegildus confessor conf. Iohannes presbiter conf. Elias confessor conf. Dominicus confessor conf.[79]

(10) Debt

In Dei nomine. Ego Lelle et uxor mea nomine Eilo, uobis Hermegildo et Paterne. Non est enim dubium, set multis manet notum, eo quod leuauimus ceuaria inprestada de uestra casa de Superado, tricticum, ordeum et centenum, et non habuimus unde uobis reddere. Ob inde placuit nobis ut faceremus cartam de ratione que habemus in pumare quod plantauit Geldemirus in uilla uocabulo Gunderedi, et sunt mazanarias XX[i] cum suo terreno, ita ut de hodie

78 OvC26 (20 November 953) = ACO B.1.11.

79 Li123 (19 December 937).

die et tempore de nostro iure abrasas et uestro iuri et dominio sint traditas atque concessas. Si quis tamen contra hunc nostrum factum uenire temptauerit, pariat uobis ipsas mazanaria duplatas et uobis perpetim habituras.

Facta cartula uenditionis XI° kalendas iunuarii era DCCCCLX[La].

Lelle et Gilo in hac cartula uenditionis manus nostras, Gresamarus ts, Spassandus ts, Munio ts.[80]

80 Sob98 (22 December 952).

3 Material questions

A few hours in an archive looking at the single parchment sheets which survive from the ninth and tenth centuries are enough to reveal that there are some very considerable physical differences between charters, even between charters produced in the same year in the same place. This chapter is about those physical differences and the bearing they may have on the interpretation of the texts they record. Most of these points are very well known to palaeographers, whose work on early medieval texts during the past few decades has been of exceptional value and importance, but the materiality of the records still has to find a place in regular historical discourse.[1] My intention here is to bring this material into discussion not just of cultural context, but into that of social and political context too. Since it makes no sense to consider the physical attributes of dispute records in isolation from those of the total corpus of charters, I shall begin with a consideration of the physical characteristics of all kinds of charter of this period. For a few pages, then, we must leave the focus on dispute records and think about the whole corpus of pre-eleventh-century charters which survive on single sheets.

When we consider the appearance of a charter, we may be struck by its size, the extent to which utilization of the parchment surface is part of an overall plan, the layout of text and its decoration, if there is any, the style of handwriting employed and the quality of its execution, and the marks, if any, made by people other than the original writer. Other important details, such as preparation of

1 Very useful comment can be found in the prefatory material to recent editions, as well as in the editorial comment on individual charters, for example that by Emilio Sáez in *Colección documental del archivo de la catedral de León (775–1230), vol. 1 (775–952)*; José Antonio Fernández Flórez and Marta Herrero de la Fuente in *Colección documental del monasterio de Santa María de Otero de las Dueñas*, and Carlos Sáez and María del Val González de la Peña in *La Coruña. Fondo Antiguo (788–1065)*. Notable books and papers include: the list of royal scribes and other analyses of royal charters in Manuel Lucas Álvarez, *El reino de León en la alta edad media. VIII. La Documentación real astur-leonesa (718–1072)* (León, 1995), especially pp. 219–33; Carlos Sáez (ed.), *Libros y Documentos en la alta edad media. Los libros de derecho. Los archivos familiares. Actas del VI Congreso Internacional de Historia de la Cultura Escrita* (Madrid, 2002); José Antonio Fernández Flórez, 'Los documentos y sus *scriptores*', in *Monarquía y sociedad en el reino de León de Alfonso III a Alfonso VII* (2 vols, León, 2007), vol. 2, pp. 97–139; Jesús Alturo Perucho, Miquel Torras Cortina and Ainoa Castro Correa (eds), *La escritura visigótica en la Península Ibérica: nuevas aportaciones* (Barcelona, 2012).

Figure 3.1 ACL 890 (Li41), a royal gift of 917

Source: Reproduced by permission of the chapter of León cathedral.

the parchment, the abbreviations and contractions used in the text, the shape of chrismons and *signa* (personal marks), cutting and folding, and dorsal marks, may not be so immediately obvious, but nevertheless contribute to our appreciation of the text and the circumstances of its production.[2]

We can immediately notice a difference between what I shall call 'functional' and 'display' records: display records were clearly intended to be seen, perhaps to be publicly displayed, certainly to be shown to people; functional records, on the other hand, were not for show, but were purely for the purpose of having a record. Hence, display charters were relatively large (see Figure 3.1), whereas functional records could be very small (see Figure 3.2); display charters were often written in a practised, elegant hand, sometimes with flourishes, whereas the functional could be extremely straightforward in layout, occupying all the available space, and written with less concern for visual effect; display charters often had long columns of witnesses, with several or many elaborate *signa*, whereas the functional could have only a handful of witnesses and no *signa* at all. Typically, the records of large gifts to monasteries by kings, aristocrats and rich clerics were for display, like that of Ansur and his wife Ilduara's gift of an estate to the monastery of San Salvador of Pozuelo of 26 June 973; whereas records of sales of small plots from one peasant to another were functional, like the 980 sale

2 See Benoît-Michel Tock, *Scribes, souscripteurs et témoins dans les actes privés en France (VIIe–début du XIIe siècle)* (Turnhout, 2005), for an exemplary discussion of scribal marks and subscriptions. Chrismon: a sign invoking the name of Jesus Christ; for characteristic forms, see Carlos Sáez Sánchez, 'Crismones en la documentación particular de la catedral de León del periodo astur (864–910)', in Peter Rück (ed.), *Graphische Symbole in mittelalterlichen Urkunden* (Sigmaringen, 1996), pp. 439–42, and Susana Cabezas Fontanilla, 'De la *invocatio* en los documentos altomedievales (718–910)', in *VIII Jornadas científicas sobre documentación de la Hispania altomedieval (siglo VI–X)* (Madrid, 2009), pp. 43–78.

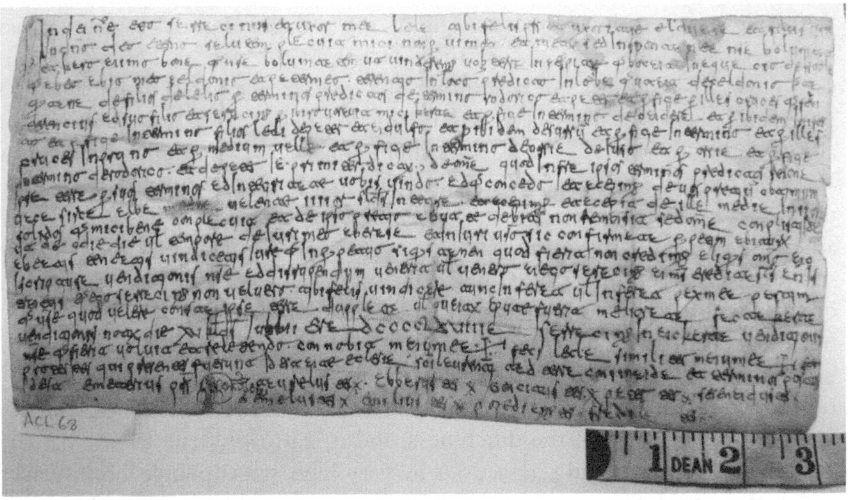

Figure 3.2 ACL 68 (Li88), sale of an arable plot in 930

Source: Reproduced by permission of the chapter of León cathedral.

by Cita and her son Álvaro to Auriolo of some arable which lay beside Auriolo's arable in cleared land, a plot which she and her husband had previously bought.[3]

Size

The size of the records varies considerably. Bishop Frunimio's 928 gift of two town houses and a garden in León, with plenty of material goods as well, to the church of Santa María and San Cipriano measures 620 × 410 mm (an area of 2,542 cm^2); King Ordoño and his wife Elvira's gift of Pardomino to two eremitic monks of 8 January 917 measures 620 × 345 mm (2,139 cm^2) (see Figure 3.1), and the priest Letimio's gift to the Galician monastery of Santa Marina de Paradela of 7 August 947 measures 425 × 625 mm (2,656 cm^2).[4] At

3 S269 (AHN Clero Sahagún 876–12); Ov22 (ASV 27), 1 January 980. Note my comments on use of the word 'peasant', essentially someone who laboured on the land, whether richer or poorer, tenant or small-scale proprietor; above, pp. ix–x.

4 Li76 (ACL 1330) on 12 January, Li41 (ACL 890), LaC50 (Archivo Parroquial de Santa María de Sar (Santiago de Compostela)). Cf. the chart of sizes of Sahagún charters published by Isabel Alfonso, 'El formato de la información judicial en la alta edad media peninsular', in Julio Escalona and Hélène Sirantoine (eds), *Chartes et cartulaires comme instruments de pouvoir. Espagne et Occident chrétien (VIIIe–XIIe siècles)* (Toulouse, 2013), pp. 191–218, at p. 212. See also the comments of Heinrich Fichtenau on the propaganda function of very large royal, imperial and papal charters of the central middle ages, 'Monarchische Propaganda in Urkunden', in *Beiträge zur Mediävistik* (3 vols, Stuttgart, 1977), vol. 2, pp. 18–36, at pp. 23–4; as also José Manuel Ruiz Asencio, 'Notas sobre la escritura y monogramas regios en la documentación real astur-leonesa', in José María Fernández Catón (co-ord.), *Monarquía y sociedad en el reino de León. De Alfonso III a Alfonso VII* (2 vols, León, 2007), vol. 1, pp. 265–312, at p. 271, on the large size, normally, of royal charters in the Astur-Leonese kingdom.

the other end of scale, the priest Fagildo's gift of half his goods to the deacon Savarigo, of 1 January 977, is less than a tenth of the size, at 200 × 107 mm (214 cm^2); a lay family's sale to a monk of a quarter of a patch of arable on 23 November 949 is even smaller, at 160 × 114 mm (182 cm^2); the sale of part of an orchard from one lay couple to another (31 May 948) is not much bigger, at 190 × 115 mm (219 cm^2), and the sale of an arable plot by another lay couple to a priest is a little bigger, at 270 × 130 mm (351 cm^2) (see Figure 3.2).[5] There are many sizes in between, and there is no perceptible change in the range of sizes across the century. While one might suppose that it would be the length of the text that determined the size of parchment chosen, that was clearly not the case: many have unused space, sometimes a considerable amount of unused space. If it was not the length of text that determined size, a correlation between the status of the actors and the size of the record looks like an attractive explanation of the differences, and it is broadly true to say that the very largest sheets record transactions by very high-status people, both secular and ecclesiastical. However, this is certainly not invariable: even royal transactions can be recorded on small *pergaminos*, like King Ramiro II's gift to Abbot Severo, noted on 8 July 932, on a sheet of 210 × 150 mm, or King Vermudo II's gift to his *fidelis* Fruela Vimáraz, noted on 10 March 989, on a sheet of 260 × 170 mm.[6] It is also perfectly clear that plenty of records of transactions involving aristocrats are of small size, as in the many cases of sales from peasants to aristocrats, such as the sales and gifts to Munio Flaínez.[7] This holds even where the record was made by the aristocrat's household scribe, like Munio's Fredmundo.[8]

If any patterns can be discerned in all this variation, they look like this: sales and exchanges between lay parties were usually recorded on relatively small sheets, like the sale from Beato to Menendo in Ujo, in the Cantabrian Mountains, at 130 × 120 mm.[9] This was the case even if an aristocrat was involved, and it was also usually the case for records of peasant sales to and exchanges with priests, monasteries and bishops: Baquina's 937 record of sale to the priest Vicente in the far north measured 105 × 186 mm; Andisilo's sale to the monastery of Abellar in 965 measured 150 × 92 mm, and the sale by Bellito and friends to Bishop Oveco in 943 measured 190 × 95/100 mm.[10] This is because transactions in which the principal actor was a peasant tended

5 Lii448 (ACL 131), Li207 (ACL 91) (though the hand is somewhat 'personal', it is described as very well executed by Concepción Mendo Carmona, 'La escritura de los documentos leoneses en el siglo X', *Signo*, 8 (2001), pp. 179–210, at p. 191), Li200 (ACL 89), Li88 (ACL 68).

6 OD2 (ACL Fondo R. Rodríguez 1, though a copy); OD30 (AHDL, Otero 24).

7 For example, OD6 (a gift), OD11, OD12 (AHDL, Otero 3, 9, 8), of 23 December 947, 31 October 961 and 1 November 961 respectively, at 195 × 190 mm, 210 × 110 mm and 230 × 155 mm.

8 OD6; see n. 7 above, and cf. Munio's wife's purchase of 13 October 962, recorded by the same scribe, on a small sheet, S205 (AHN Clero Sahagún 875–3).

9 Lii310 (ACL 104), 2 January 959.

10 Ov8 (ASV 5), 31 May 937; Lii383 (ACL 824), 2 January 965; Li160 (ACL 1338), 7 January 943.

to be recorded on small sheets;[11] the same is therefore true of peasant gifts to aristocrats, as in the Munio Flaínez case cited above. As for gifts to ecclesiastical bodies, not so many records of peasant gifts to monasteries survive on single sheets, although cartularies are full of them (which may suggest that if they were originally recorded on single sheets, no one bothered to keep and archive them), so we cannot generalize about them. But it is quite clear that other gifts to monasteries and to bishops tended to be recorded on larger sheets, like the very large sheets recording gifts to Pardomino and Santa Marina de Paradela noted above, or King Vermudo II's gift of land near Astorga to Bishop Savarigo of León, at 611 × 200 mm, or Count Fruela Vélaz's gift of a monastery to the church of Oviedo, at 530 × 285 mm.[12] They were by no means always as huge as these examples (in the order of 2,000 cm^2) but the sheets on which they were recorded were significantly larger (at 600–900 cm^2) than the typical 200–250 cm^2 of the peasant sale.[13] In particular, gifts which were confirmed by a king tended to be recorded on large sheets, like Bishop Vimara's gift of a church to the monk Alfonso, confirmed by King Ramiro II in 948, or the bishop of Segovia's gift of San Claudio to the bishop of León, confirmed by King Sancho, his sister Elvira and the future Ramiro III in 960, as indeed (except for the latter) the Oviedo dispute charter, ACO B.1.11, may have been.[14] As if to reinforce the point, many of the pseudo-originals constructed in later centuries were also particularly large, like the thirteenth-century purported record of Alfonso III's gifts to the episcopal churches of Oviedo and León, attributed to 906, at 3,857 cm^2.[15]

There are of course exceptions to these patterns. Firstly, it is important to say that some small sheets are small because they have been cut subsequent to the record being made, in the context of earlier or later archiving activity. In such cases, we cannot normally know the original size. Secondly, and consequently, a record of this sort must often have been one of a group of records recorded on a single sheet. A number of such composite sheets still survive, which allows us to see a recording practice that is different from the single sheet per record that is characteristic of many. These groups of records are of at least three kinds: the sheet with records of several transactions made on the same day; the sheet with records of a set of transactions in one location, sometimes constructed subsequent to the latest transaction; and the sheet to which transactions were added

11 By 'principal actor', I mean the person in whose name the charter was issued, normally donor or vendor rather than beneficiary or purchaser.

12 Liii548 (ACL 989), 29 July 991; OvC30 (ACO B.1.12), 14 March 976.

13 For example: LaC34 (AHDS 55–19), 10 December (932), 855 cm^2; Sam93 (AHN Clero Samos 1239–5), 17 February 951, 719 cm^2; S242 (AHN Clero Sahagún 875–16), 5 February 966, 894 cm^2; OD21 (AHDL, Otero 16), 18 July 976, 722 cm^2; Liii576 (ACL 827), 13 February 997, 596 cm^2.

14 Ov11 (ASV 6), 25 May 948, 1,212 cm^2; Lii333 (ACL 1340), 6 December (960), 1,160 cm^2. ACO B.1.11, 2,013 cm^2: see above, pp. 1–4, 51.

15 Li20 (ACL 348).

over a period of time – all of them witness to the archiving activity which was clearly in progress in the tenth century.[16] So, for example, the aristocrat Fruela Vimáraz clearly had a day, and presumably a meeting, for calling in debts on 6 June 995, on which several transactions in his favour were recorded on a long sheet, 120 × 335 mm; and the priest Gutier made purchases from different people on 28 February 994, recorded on a single sheet, 295 × 190 mm.[17] In such cases, a sheet of a size suitable for recording more than one transaction appears to have been chosen. On the other hand, the monastery of Sahagún made a number of purchases of small properties in Valdefresno. These included two on the same day, 1 January 965, for which a sheet of suitable size was chosen, 310 × 240 mm; two on different days in June of that year, which were recorded side by side on a thin strip of parchment, 430 × 100 mm; and four on different days in March and April of that year, recorded on a fairly large sheet, 330 × 290 mm. In the latter case, the latest transaction (2 April) is recorded first; this is followed by the second and first transactions (25 March, 15 March), and the last record is of the third transaction (also 25 March). This group of four records must have been retrospectively constructed for the purchaser, the monastery, in an act of deliberate record-keeping, subsequent to the actual transactions; the *signa* and the chrismons are the same for each record, the *signa* being simple crosses, with those of the vendors in irregular boxes (as is also true of the January and June transactions). Here parchments were chosen of suitable size for making composite records, so that this large and powerful monastery could control its archive.[18] The most extreme example of this process is that of the seven transactions of the priest Munio in and near Otero Vellosello recorded on a single large sheet (185 × 750 mm) in 978 and 979 (see Figure 3.3).[19] Here again the latest is recorded first (1 October 979), but the next five are then in sequence from 11 October 978 to 17 February 979; the seventh has no date. Here again the arrangement implies that the whole record was made retrospectively for Munio, but the clear sequence of numbers two to six suggests the copying of existing records. Differently again, the nunnery at Piasca, on the edge of the Liébana, bought small plots in and around Piasca, from a number of local people, recording them successively on 18 May 951, 5 July 951 and 10 April 952 on a single sheet; the monastery of Abellar bought plots in Villobera from different locals, recording them on 2 September and 23 November 939 on a single sheet; a man called Gundulfo made three purchases of plots in Negreiros in northern

16 See above, pp. 15–16.

17 OD40 and OD41 (AHDL, Otero 31); Liii563 and Liii564 (ACL 157).

18 S226 and S227 (AHN Clero Sahagún 875–10); S239 and S240 (ibid., 875–14); S236, S234, S233, S235 (ibid., 875–13) – the second record has one circular box and two rectangular boxes for the vendors. Miguel Calleja points out that we cannot always be sure that a date is that of performance of the transaction rather than that of making the record. However, the fact that records were constructed retrospectively remains clear in either event.

19 Lii471, Lii457, Lii458, Lii459, Lii465, Lii467, Lii472 (ACL 7255).

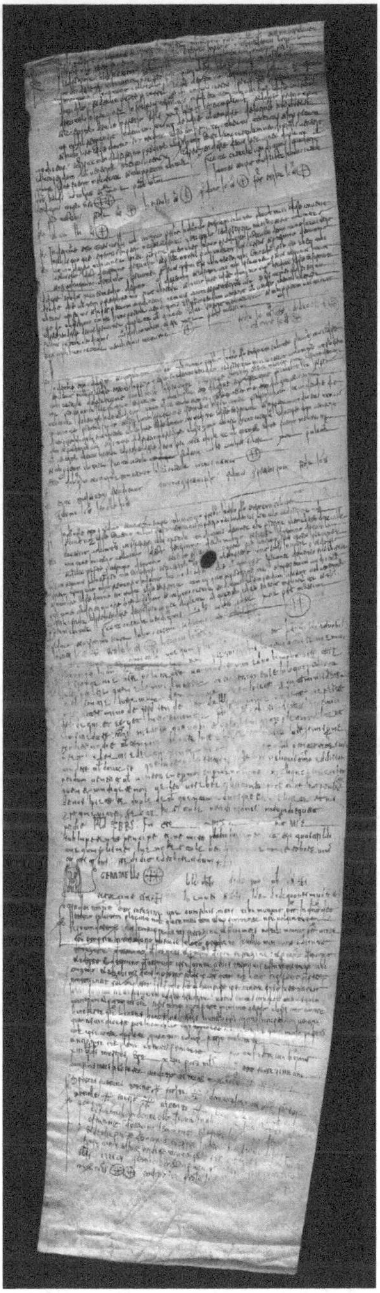

Figure 3.3 ACL 7255 (Lii471, Lii457 etc.), transactions involving the priest Munio in 978 and 979

Source: Reproduced by permission of the chapter of León cathedral.

Galicia on different occasions in 969–70, recording them on a single sheet.[20] Here, although the records must again have been made for the purchasers, the process was slightly different: a big enough sheet was selected and the first transaction recorded; when another transaction occurred, another record was added, and so on.

Some transactions involving peasants are recorded on larger than average sheets because a single charter records a complex of transactions, like the three sets of sales to Tano and his wife in La Braña on 18 December 942; here each of the three vendors received a separate price, which took more than the usual space to record, on a sheet 340 × 100/110 mm.[21] The exchange of arable plots in Marialba between peasant and priest on 19 February 943, contrary to normal practice, is recorded on a sheet that measures 330 × 165 mm.[22] Marialba lies in the land between the confluence of rivers to the south of León, and one of the plots was on the road to León itself; it is close to the city. Perhaps more resources were available in such locations, close to a centre of activity and culture, although Marialba (site of a late antique church) was a place which in itself attracted powerful interests – which might also explain the more generous provision of parchment.[23] It is also noticeable that records of peasant transactions near Oviedo tend to be made on slightly larger sheets than are those on the *meseta*: sales between lay parties in the tenth century are often recorded on sheets whose surface area is 300–400 cm^2.[24] Again, perhaps more resources were available in the hinterland of the former royal centre, and perhaps the priests who made the records came from a long-established pool of highly trained clerics associated with that centre.[25] Records of transactions of urban plots in León, and of the mills and mill waters of the rivers to the south of the city, are relatively large too, and the same explanation may well apply.[26]

One thing that emerges from this survey is that a careful choice of parchment was usually made by whoever procured it: the parchment was very large when royal *signa* and subscriptions had to be accommodated and sufficient space had to be left for all kinds of confirmer, but it was very small when the main need was to record simple transactions without wasting resources. Occasionally the choice seems to have been wrong: witness names had to be continued on the dorse, like those of the April 952 Piasca sale; and one gift and sale to the

20 S134, S135, S136 (AHN Clero Sahagún 874–1), 260 × 170 mm; Li132 and Li135 (ACL 818), 360 × 205/230 mm; LaC79, LaC78, LaC80 (AHDS 55–10), 205 × 290 mm.

21 Li158 (ACL 82).

22 Li161 (ACL 86).

23 Cf. the comments of Álvaro Carvajal Castro on royal interests there, 'La construcción de la monarquía asturleonesa en la meseta del Duero. Estudio de los procesos de integración territorial (s. IX–XI)' (Universidad de Salamanca, Tesis Doctoral, 2013), pp. 49, 579, 593, 600–603, 620.

24 For example, Ov5 (ASV 16), Ov6 (ASV 29), Ov7 (ASV 17, priest vendor), Ov14 (ASV 18), Ov25 (ASV 15), at 374, 395, 374, 296 and 393 cm^2 respectively (altogether dating between 917 and 994).

25 See further below, p. 105.

26 For example, Li97 (ACL 72), 8 March 933, sale *in suburbio* of León from Alderepto to Gemelo and his wife, 330 × 125 mm.

monastery of Abellar was clearly started on parchment that was far too small, because a substantial portion of the text continues on the dorse; the latter appears to have happened because the donor's daughter declared that she was herself fully empowered to alienate; one can almost see mother and daughter standing by the writer, and the daughter insisting that he should add that the land was part of her own inheritance from her father.[27]

So, it is not so much that all records of transactions involving aristocrats were large; rather, the records tended to be large if they recorded gifts to monasteries or bishops; if they recorded purchases from peasants, they were much more likely to be small. Charters recording any kind of transaction by peasants were highly likely to be small, although they could be larger if resources were available.

Layout

Just as the choice of large or small parchment was usually the outcome of some careful planning, so the layout of the text could also be part of the plan. Layouts ranged from the very deliberate arrangement for visual effect to a much more simple, optimal, use of the space available. The most elaborate of display documents were arranged stylishly and symmetrically, with text occupying the upper quarter to a half of the parchment surface and several columns of witnesses or confirmers below the text; as in other parts of Europe, the first line could occasionally be in much larger writing, like that of the record of Ansur's gift to the monastery of San Salvador of Pozuelo of 973.[28] An initial chrismon usually decorated the beginning of all types of text, and could be very large – 10 lines deep; in the case of a stylish display, a further chrismon characteristically formed a lefthand border for each column of witnesses, each of these witness chrismons having several 'bows', one bow for each witness name (see Figure 3.1).[29] The *signa* of witnesses and confirmers usually followed their names; they could be part of a planned decorative scheme, or alternatively purely functional. The writer's subscription and *signum* sometimes concluded one column, and at other times, especially in the more stylish cases, might be offset for emphasis; occasionally the scribal subscription was at right angles to the witness columns.[30] A high proportion of the most striking display documents had royal subscriptions, which were frequently either at the head of the

27 Li156 (ACL 819), 190 × 125 mm.

28 S269 (AHN Clero Sahagún 876–12); cf. S261 (AHN 876–8), possibly a copy – see above and below, pp. 47, 85, and AHN Clero Lugo 1082–3, a gift of 939, an eleventh-century copy.

29 The 'bow' is literally the abbreviation mark for Latin-*us*, such as terminates *Christus*, the chi-rho which lies behind the chrismon sign, Sáez Sánchez, 'Crismones'. On chrismons, see also Erika Eisenlohr, 'Von ligierten zu symbolischen Invokations- und Subskriptionszeichen in frühmittelalterlichen Urkunden', in Rück (ed.), *Graphische Symbole*, pp. 167–262.

30 For example, Ov25 (ASV 15), 17 July 994, a lay sale; Li168 (ACL 83), 28 April 943, a gift to the bishop of León; Liii560 (ACL 156), 11 January 994, a sale to the monastery of Santiago in León.

first column of subscribers or central to the witness space, although they do occur in other positions, like that of Ordoño II's *signum* at the bottom of the third column on a record of Bishop Frunimio's gift to the church of León;[31] wherever positioned, they tended to be larger than those of other subscribers, and their presence was part of the overall visual effect. Sometimes, later kings added an endorsement confirming the transaction, like the subsequent royal confirmations on the record of Ordoño II's gift to Pardomino (see Figure 3.1).[32] These must have been added in what was originally a blank space, which presumably explains the blank spaces still available on some display documents.

At the other end of the spectrum, as is particularly characteristic of small-scale sale records, the only element of visual planning appears to have been the initial chrismon (and it is rare for this not to have been present). Text was then written to fill all or most of the available space, and witnesses could follow on, in one or more horizontal lines, without even a new line start and – in the simplest cases – without *signa* or witness chrismons; the small record of a 930 sale of land on the River Esla from peasant to priest is a good example, with witness *signa*, but not chrismons: it is just a block of writing occupying the space, with a slightly enlarged date and now a rather faint initial chrismon, but otherwise no enhancements (see Figure 3.2).[33] Another good example is the record of a gift to the monastery of San Lorenzo de Carboeiro to clear a debt; again with an initial chrismon, it has no witness chrismons and only one very small, simple *signum* for the donor.[34]

Between these two extremes of very deliberate display and a block of writing, there are many variants, from stylish display documents without royal subscriptions to functional records with short witness columns, together with chrismons and basic *signa*; it is, in fact, relatively unusual for there to be no chrismons and no *signa* associated with subscriptions. Display documents could be decorated with elaborate opening initials, very prominent scribal or other subscriptions, and passages of larger writing. Parchments with more than one record are often the most functional of all, with no sense of display – like the three records of the priest Vincemalo's purchases at several dates in 943 or the two of the monastery of Abellar's purchases in 939.[35] It is often the case, though, that even the simplest designs have an enhanced feature that draws the eye: an elaborate initial letter 'I' for the opening *In nomine domini*; a scribal *signum* completed with a flourish or simply rather large; an enlarged dating clause.[36] While the document may not have been primarily intended

31 Li43 (ACL 1328), 26 June 917.

32 Li41 (ACL 890), 8 January 917; a mid-tenth-century copy, to which contemporary and later royal endorsements have been added, Ruiz Asencio, 'Notas sobre la escritura y monogramas regios', pp. 290–91.

33 Li88 (ACL 68).

34 LaC58 (AHUS 11), 956.

35 Li172/173/174 (ACL 87–8); Li132/135 (ACL 818).

36 For example: Ov9 (ASV 11), 11 March 946; Li207(ACL 91), 23 November 949; Lii398 (ACL 119–20), 23 October 966.

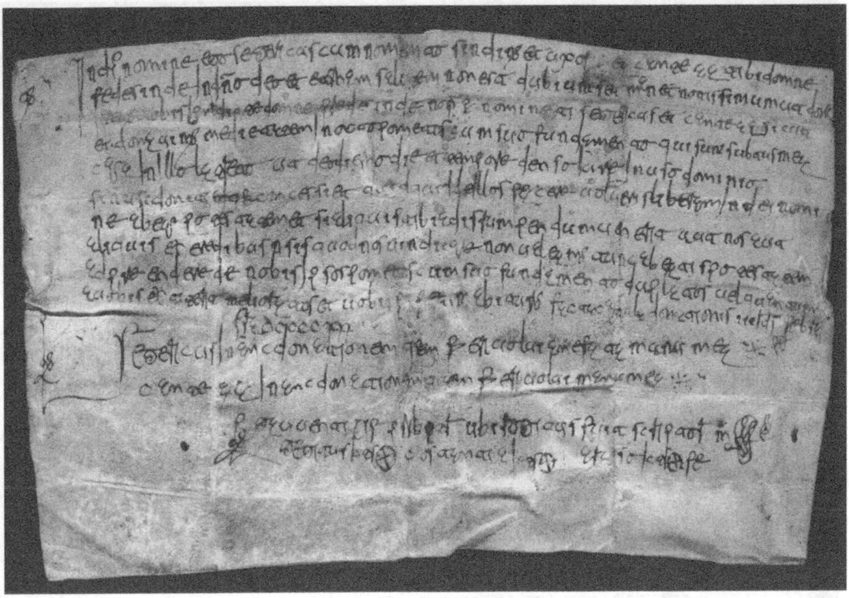

Figure 3.4 ACL 54 (Li11), lay gift to lay aristocrat of 897

Source: Reproduced by permission of the chapter of León cathedral.

for display, the writer included some element of decoration, however modest. Functional records, though simple and straightforward in plan, could be stylishly executed. Interestingly, records like this are often those in which the beneficiary was a lay aristocrat, like the charter recording a gift of apple trees to Doña Fredesinda in 897: it is on a small piece of parchment but enlarged letters begin the subscription of the donor (see Figure 3.4); or the strip that records a sale to Bonello and his wife in the far north in 962.[37] It looks as if the writers serving some aristocratic households took pride in their skills – even for modest transactions.

By contrast, a few documents were extremely untidy in plan, even if prepared in monasteries, and one or two have some puzzling spacing: a record of a sale of land in the Cantabrian Mountains to the aristocrat Flaino Muñoz, which includes an Incidental reference to a dispute, has spaces within words rather than between them; was this dictated to a writer who wrote by syllables rather than words?[38] The record of Odesenda's gift to the monastery of San Salvador de Matallana, prepared by Brother Bellito, can only be called extremely messy, with two very different hands recording the main text and with columns of witnesses pushed in above the rather large subscriptions and *signa* of scribe and clerics, the columns separated by untidy squiggles that bear

37 Li11 (ACL 54); Ov15 (ASV 22).
38 OD32 (AHDL, Otero 25), 15 July 992.

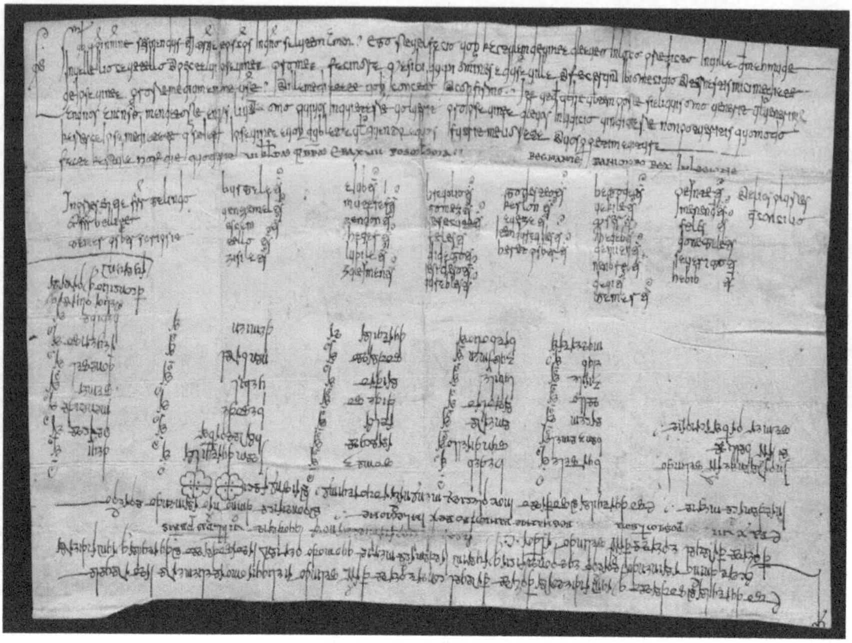

Figure 3.5 ACL 1341 (Lii463 and 464), a Fine paid to the bishop of León in 979 and a further document guaranteeing its payment

Source: Reproduced by permission of the chapter of León cathedral.

no resemblance to a chrismon; it is as if Brother Bellito began it, in a fine book hand, and after the first seven lines handed it over to a trainee with considerably less skill and with no sense of design.[39] A few were highly individual in design: the parchment recording two sales to Vermudo and Pascual in May 985 (two weeks apart) looks rather crude, but is clearly laid out for effect, with a very prominent near-central scribal *signum*, a very elaborate initial 'I' and a long chrismon running down the whole of the left side of the sheet; and the small sheet recording Revel's Fine paid to Bishop Sisnando, in respect of the homicide he had committed, as well as the separate commitment of his guarantors to see that the transaction would be completed, is striking because the second record is upside down on the same sheet and the quite long columns of witnesses for each record therefore meet in the middle, making a very arresting pattern (see Figure 3.5).[40]

A planned layout does not necessarily mean that all the words were written at one time. In fact, it looks as if text and chrismons were often written first, and witness names added later by the same or another writer or writers; this happens with all kinds of record, and indeed witness names might be continued

39 Liii531 (ACL 882), 989.

40 Lii501 and Lii502 (ACL 144); Lii463 and Lii464 (ACL 1341), 27 January 979.

on the dorse, as in the case of the April 952 Piasca sale.[41] Because of the pre-preparation of the text, space was quite often allowed for more names than were recorded. One Eslonza gift record even has individual words of confirmation and *signa* but no names on several lines.[42] The *signa* themselves were very often made by the writer who wrote the names, but they might be added later: sometimes space had clearly been left for important *signa* to be collected, and very occasionally these appear to have been autograph.[43] Later confirmations of King Ordoño II's gift to the monks of Pardomino in 917, from Ordoño III and Ordoño IV, are clearly added in different inks and hands (see Figure 3.1).[44] All this means that however careful the planning of the layout of a charter, in practice material could be added which upset the design, particularly if – as happened from time to time – extra columns of witnesses were fitted around the originally planned columns: an extreme example of this is the record of Isca and Filauria's gifts to Sahagún, which has witnesses added to the bottom of columns, at least one added column, and a further set of witnesses in a box; since many of these are located by reference to different settlements, sometimes together with an associated *saio*, it looks as if someone went round collecting the names of everyone who might be thought to have an interest in the transaction, after it had been completed.[45] The fact that additions were made is important because it means that the construction of some records was an ongoing process – a point easily demonstrated by the addition of witnesses in extra columns or in margins or corners or on the dorse, but also by the fact that other material could be added too.[46] An Agreement confirming that a deacon would keep his obligations was added on the dorse of a much earlier gift record;[47] a note of a gift to Piasca was added at right angles to a composite record of many separate gifts to the nunnery;[48] one of the sales to Sahagún of land in Valdefresno has marginal and interlinear additions;[49] and a whole charter

41 See above, p. 72, for Piasca 952. Very clear examples of witnesses added include: S5 (AHN 872–5), sale between lay parties in Piasca 7 May 904; Li73 (ACL 812), gift to the monastery of Abellar 22 April 927; Li165 (ACL 84), sale to a local priest 17 April 943; Ov13 (ASV 19), sale to a priest 10 July 949; Li213 (ACL 220), sale to Doña Paterna 5 March (950); Ov17 (ASV 24), sale to another priest 30 January 971.

42 E10 (AHN 957–13), 17 October 929.

43 On *signa*, see further below, pp. 79–82.

44 Li41 (ACL 890); see n. 32 above.

45 S164 (AHN Clero Sahagún 874–10), 9 April 959.

46 Cf. similar points about the ongoing process made in Julio Escalona, Isabel Velázquez Soriano and Paloma Juárez Benitez, 'Identification of the sole extant original charter issued by Fernán González, count of Castile (932–970)', *Journal of Medieval Iberian Studies*, 4 (2012), pp. 259–88.

47 Li10 (ACL 53), 19 September 895; the deacon's promise (Lii330) is on the dorse, dated 27 September 960, but confirmation of his gift is at the bottom of the *recto*.

48 It clearly belongs with S153, and seems to be an entry that was omitted initially (AHN Clero Sahagún 874–7), 13 February 957; it is in the same hand and ink as that record. It is published, however, as the last line of S154, which is the record of a simple sale to Piasca, in a different hand and ink, a much shorter record which was added to the parchment.

49 S233; see above, p. 70.

of confirmation of a gift by relatives of the original donors was woven around the witness columns of an original gift.[50] In any case, complete records might subsequently be recorded on the dorse of unrelated records: a sale of 913 on the dorse of an exchange of 909, an only partly legible charter on the dorse of a sale of 953, a gift of 987 on the dorse of a gift of 910, and a gift of 997 on the dorse of a gift of 990.[51] Gaps could be left in the text, to be filled in when information came to hand. Sometimes these survive as gaps, never filled in; sometimes they are completed in slightly larger or smaller writing, in different ink. Most obviously, gaps were left for the names of boundary points and of principal parties (like the gaps left for the names of Abita's children in the record of her sale to Abellar), or for prices, like the price gaps in two sales to the monastery of Piasca, or that in the local priest Vermudo's record of a sale to the monastery of San Cipriano del Condado, not far from León;[52] one can imagine the text of a sale being prepared in advance, then there was a negotiation about values, and finally the price was filled in.

Execution

The script of most charters was a Visigothic cursive, with the occasional use of Visigothic *redonda* and semi-cursive and very occasional Visigothic minuscule.[53] The hands ranged from very fine to rather crude; the most elegant tend to record gifts made by kings or other aristocratic donors to prominent monasteries, although the hands recording Abbot Abdie's 929 gifts to his sister and cousin have a 'calligraphic' quality (and a royal confirmation) and Aloyto Froylaniz's gifts to his wife in 965 (also with a royal confirmation) are 'very elegant';[54] those described by their editors as crude or coarse are overwhelmingly records of sales between peasants, although they include some sales to priests and some to monasteries.[55] There are charters with errors, blots and crossings out: the 953 sale of several plots by Sendino and his wife to Gontino and wife has

50 OD26, added to OD21 (AHDL, Otero 16r); the confirmation is dated 6 September 986, and the original transaction 18 July 976.

51 Li23 and Li31 (ACL 59), 27 April 909 and 29 January 913; Lii262 (ACL 99), 1 September 953; AHN Clero Lugo 1325A–4, 12 May 910 and 12 August 987; Liii534 and Liii575 (ACL 884), 1 March 990 and 1 January 997.

52 Boundaries: Liii587 (ACL 966), 30 July 999, for example; Abita's children: Li96 (ACL 815), 28 July 932. Prices: S134 and S135 (AHN Clero Sahagún 874–1), 18 May 951 and 5 July 951; Li221 (ACL 804), 29 May 950 – gap filled in subsequently.

53 There is some inconsistency in the terms used to describe scripts (e.g. *elongata* is used nowadays for some hands); I have followed the practice of the editions used for this book. The standard guide is Agustín Millares Carlo, *Tratado de paleografía española*, 3rd edn (3 vols, Madrid, 1983).

54 Li83 (ACL 67); LaC71 (ARG 495), surely intended to be passed on to a monastery.

55 For example, to priests: Ov8 (ASV 5), 31 May 937 and Li212 (ACL 95), 20 February 950; to monasteries: Li202 (ACL 806), 21 July 948 and Li227 (ACL 820), 23 August 950. In my opinion small-scale peasant transactions with monasteries were sometimes recorded by local priests; see further Wendy Davies, 'Local priests and the writing of charters in northern Iberia in the tenth century', in Escalona and Sirantoine (eds), *Chartes et cartulaires comme instruments de pouvoir*, pp. 29–43, at pp. 31–4.

Elias uxor cancelled before the first reference to Sendino and *Sendino* cancelled before Gontino in the price clause; the exchange between Rebelle and his wife Maosavara and Salvador and his wife has the *Mao* of Maosavara crossed out and rewritten, with *ut bynderemus* included in error before *tibe Salbatore* and encircled; the composite record of gifts to Piasca, of 957, has a mistake for Daui's wife, with Sendina crossed out and Quinegia written above it; the priest Vermudo's record of a sale to the monastery of San Cipriano del Condado has several erasures within absolutely standard formulas – an erasure within *de odie die uel tempore*, a redundant letter 't' in *in precio pro ipsa terra* and *si* squashed in subsequently in *Et si aliquis omo*.[56] The picture is in fact very mixed: while it is true to say that those with cruder hands and untidy emendations are much more likely to be records of peasant transactions, they do include records of peasant transactions with monasteries; equally, many records of peasant transactions, although simple in style and limited in visual effect, were written by skilful, practised hands.[57]

Some of the untidiest elements of visual display on a parchment could be the *signa* (personal marks) of witnesses or confirmers; although many were executed with confidence and some with a certain flair, some were executed unevenly and hesitantly. Understanding the use of *signa* is surprisingly complicated.[58] The *signa* of most witnesses were simple or very slightly elaborated crosses (elaborated with dots in the angles, for example), all made by the same writer (see Figures 3.4, 3.5 and 3.6). But some subscriptions were associated with signs of considerable elaboration, often with fanciful embellishments of swirls and squiggles (see Figures 3.1 and 3.6). The latter were sometimes all made by the same writer, but at other times they were clearly added to the document, in different inks, with different pens, at different orientations; some of these seem to be autograph *signa*. One might expect, as these look like personal identifiers, that different individuals would use different marks, but there are hundreds of cases of the use of the same *signum* by different people and a few cases of the use of different *signa* by one individual; personal identifier cannot normally have been the case in this culture. However, there are also circumstances where one individual consistently used the same *signum* (the scribe Amorino in upland Ujo, for example);[59] kings tended to use a *signum*

56 Lii262 (ACL 99); Lii388 (ACL 115), 17 April 965; S154 (see above, p. 77); Li221 (see above, p. 78).

57 I am grateful to David Ganz for pointing out the skill and speed of some of these local practitioners.

58 Although there is plenty of useful discussion: see Tock, *Scribes, souscripteurs et témoins*, especially pp. 145–90; Erika Eisenlohr, 'Monogramme und Invokationszeichnen in iberischen und fränkischen Urkunden', *Signo*, 1 (1994), pp. 35–50; see also Concepción Mendo Carmona, 'La suscripción altomedieval', *Signo*, 4 (1997), pp. 207–29, for a very helpful demonstration of the range of practice in Spanish charters. There is an extremely wide range of comment on the use of signs in charters in Rück (ed.), *Graphische Symbole*. Brigitte M. Bedos-Rezak, *When Ego was Imago: Signs of Identity in the Middle Ages* (Leiden, 2011), is much concerned with signs of identity, but focuses on seals of the eleventh and twelfth centuries.

59 Lii310 (ACL 104), 21 January 959; Lii357 (ACL 110), 15 December 962.

that was appropriate for their name (several kings called Ramiro used the same sign, those called Alfonso used another, and those called Ordoño another – the latter nicely demonstrated in Figure 3.1), and kings occasionally appear to have added the royal mark in the tenth century;[60] there is a long period in the tenth century when successive bishops of León consistently used the same *signum*;[61] and there is a tendency for judges, especially judges from in and around León, to use a distinctive judge's *signum*, six circles joined by diagonal lines, all within a frame;[62] monograms do also occur, although relatively infrequently, and they usually incorporate some letters from the principal actor's, scribe's, witness's or confirmer's name.[63] So there seems to be a rationale here, but not the kind of rationale one immediately expects. We could say this: it looks as if there was a large repertoire of established signs, a repertoire which must have been known to very many writers. Some kinds of sign were widely known to have been associated with certain kinds of people and were sometimes applied relatively consistently. Otherwise, writers chose from the repertoire as they saw fit. There must sometimes have been errors, and the copying of charters probably added to the levels of inconsistency, as well as purely capricious whim: what we see now was not necessarily what was intended. But where a charter occurs on a single sheet, especially in the case of large display documents, *signa* were sometimes added after the names were written; these must have been added by the named individuals themselves, or by their representatives, in which case one might suppose that they chose their own marks. Adding a mark therefore became part of the performance of completing a transaction, and to some extent such marks are indicators of ritual behaviour.[64] A high proportion of the elaborated and embellished *signa* is associated with clerics, who were presumably perfectly competent to make their own marks; even in local rural contexts, elaborate *signa* tend to be associated with the subscriptions of priests, while it is the case everywhere that the names of scribes are most often associated with relatively elaborate *signa*.[65] The *signum* of the priest Sendino, scribe for the

60 Ramiro II, ACL 83 (Li168, 943), ACL 890 (Li41, copy of later endorsement); Ramiro III, ACL 909 (Lii410, 968). Alfonso III, ACL 807 (Li18, 905), AHN 872–6 (S6, 904); Alfonso IV, ACL 813 (Li79, 928), ACL 1333 (Li89, 931). Ordoño II, III and IV, ACL 890 (Li41, 917 and two later endorsements); Ruiz Asencio, 'Notas sobre la escritura y monogramas regios', pp. 287–8, and see ibid., pp. 290–92, for Ordoño IV's autograph mark.

61 For example, Li41 (ACL 890), 917; E10 (AHN 957–13), 929; S98 (AHN 873–11), 945 (a copy); OvC26 (ACO B.1.11), 953.

62 For example, S145 (AHN 874–2), 955, and S33 (AHN 872–19), 925. AHN1235A–9, 973, has the symbol, but uses nine circles, as also Liii541 (ACL 2–2), 990; see Figure 6.1.

63 For example, *VER* in a monogram for King Vermudo, Lii508 (ACL 984; see n. 91 below); and *SAND* in the scribe Sendino's monogram, Liii562 (ACL 158), fig. 3.6. See the comments of Ruiz Asencio, 'Notas sobre la escritura y monogramas regios', with many clear examples illustrated, as at pp. 281, 286, 287.

64 See further below, pp. 247–9.

65 Cf. the comments of Michel Zimmermann, *Écrire et lire en Catalogne (IXe–XIIe siècle)* (2 vols, Madrid, 2003), vol. 1, pp. 140–47, on Catalan scribal *signa*.

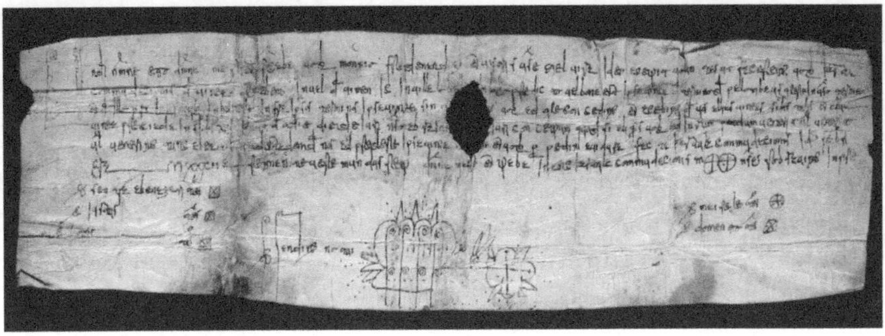

Figure 3.6 ACL 158 (Liii562), an exchange of a vineyard between lay parties in 994

Source: Reproduced by permission of the chapter of León cathedral.

aristocrat Munio Fernández, was particularly florid and visually dominates his record of an exchange of land in Valdevimbre between Munio and another lay party (see Figure 3.6).[66] The record of the sale of a small plot near Oviedo to the priest Vicente (for a pig) is witnessed by nine people, of whom four were priests and two were other clerics; while the vendor, confirmer and three lay witnesses all have *signa* in the form of a simple cross in a circle, all of the clerics but one and the priest scribe have elaborate *signa*.[67] As such, these elaborate signs become part of the decorative scheme; and while they clearly do not add authentication in the modern sense, and while – whatever their origins – except for the occasional royal mark, they cannot in practice have functioned as signs of validation in this period, they draw attention to the fact of a named individual's participation in a transaction.[68] The *signa* of principal actors, on the other hand – often simple crosses written by the main writer of the record – are different: they are conventionalized, in a conventionalized indication of that party's commitment.

66 Liii562 (ACL 158), 13 February 994; cf. very closely the cathedral cartulary, Tumbo de la catedral, f. 184v (Liii561), a cartulary copy of his record of a Fine paid to Munio on the same day, which appears to copy the physical characteristics of the exemplar. But even Sendino uses other *signa* too if Tumbo f. 195rv (Liii578, in which Munio is called count), a Fine of 15 September 997, also reproduces an exemplar (although it has some similar embellishments – extended triangles and lines of dots). For cartulary copies, see further below, pp. 83–4, 92–3.

67 Ov9 (ASV 11), 11 March 946. Cf. Mendo Carmona, 'La suscripción altomedieval', p. 222, on the possibility that priests, unlike others, were aware of a system behind graphical symbols.

68 For the value placed on the *signum* in Visigothic legislation, see Ángel Canellas López, *Diplomática hispano-visigoda* (Zaragoza, 1979), pp. 85–6. Much of the published discussion sets this material in the context of signs of validation (cf. Bedos-Rezak, *When Ego was Imago*, pp. 85, 87), and *signa* clearly did have validating functions in some early medieval material from other parts of western Europe; but for most of the Iberian corpus in this period functions were different, and I follow Tock, *Scribes, souscripteurs et témoins*, pp. 180–81, that in most cases the purpose of the *signum* was not to identify the person, but to draw attention to the subscription.

So what do *signa* tell us? Certainly writers liked to elaborate the display; they often liked to identify themselves, as did some other people, clerics especially; and they could assign identity to prominent people. But the consistent use of a personalized mark is very rare in this region.[69] Rather, *signa* are conventionalized signs of commitment, or more or less ostentatious 'graphic expressions of the confirmation expressed by the words [of subscription]', as María Isabel Ostolaza puts it.[70]

Copies

Overall, practice in constructing charters was extremely mixed, sometimes determined by the whims of individual scribal habit and the chances of circumstance: there was no single style of recording a gift or sale (despite the use of standard formulas). This variability raises a number of important questions. Leaving aside pseudo-originals, falsifications and obviously later copies, it is clear that some copies were made at or near the time of a transaction: where a single writer wrote an entire record (text, subscriptions and *signa*) in a particularly neat and regular fashion, without any of the irregularities that characterize most charters on single sheets, this looks like a contemporary copy rather than a primary record.[71] Leticia and Maia's gift to the monastery of San Salvador de Matallana is recorded in two versions: a straightforward simple charter and an elaborated text; it appears that the first version was abandoned in favour of the second, neatly copied by a single writer.[72] That being so, one might think that all charters completed by a single writer were in fact copies; and one might think that the *pergaminos* with errors, crossings out and blots were trial documents of which a fair copy has not survived. A record of a modest sale to the monastery of Valdevimbre has some trial letters below the main record, and a trial opening sentence of another record; since the scribe's name (Dominico) is in a different hand and ink, it looks as if in this case Dominico set a trainee to prepare the written record, at the end indicating his own responsibility (*Dominico notuit*) and adding the date, which the trainee seems

69 Contrast the northern Italian *signa* discussed by Reinhard Härtel, 'Zu Transformation und Bedeutungswandel graphischer Symbole in Unterfertigungen', in Rück (ed.), *Graphische Symbole*, pp. 121–41.

70 María Isabel Ostolaza, 'La validación en los documentos del occidente hispánico (s. X–XII). Del signum crucis al signum manus', in Rück (ed.), *Graphische Symbole*, pp. 453–62, at p. 459.

71 For example, Lii478 (ACL 1342), 8 August 980, a sale to Bishop Sisnando; Sam44 (AHN Clero Samos 1239–7), 29 August 975, a large Account recording restoration of a disputed church, classified as original by Ainoa Castro, *Colección diplomática altomedieval de Galicia I: Documentación editada en escritura visigótica (662–1234)* (A Coruña, 2011), no. 75.

72 The first version, Liii534 (ACL 884) was not only re-used for the record of another gift seven years later (Liii575), but it was folded so as to preserve this later record, allowing the first to become worn; the elaborated version of Leticia and Maia's gift (Liii535 (ACL 883)) is on a much larger parchment; both Liii534 and Liii535 have the same date, 1 March 990.

to have forgotten.[73] But cases where we can clearly see a trainee at work are very rare, and it is exceptionally rare to find evidence of preliminary drafts, like the Vorakten of the Sankt Gallen collection, where drafts of the essential detail of names of donor, property and witnesses in Alemannia were written on the dorse.[74] Although many charters have dorsal notes, these are usually identifiers of some kind – a note of the place transacted or the principal actors – and they are reflective of archival activity rather than document preparation. There is one case, however, in which a quite extensive dorsal note may indeed have been a draft: a sale of land on the River Porma to the monastery of Abellar in 961 has part of a record of a sale in the same location on the back, with a slightly different price (7 *arienzos* rather than 6), but this kind of draft is very unusual.[75] On the whole, then, while it is perfectly clear that contemporary copies were sometimes made, the surviving evidence does not support any suggestion that all charters written by a single writer were copies (the proportion of these is in any case far too high for that) nor that all those with errors were trial documents.

A final word on cartularies: cartulary copies of charter texts are clearly not originals and cannot be expected to have material characteristics that are pertinent to the issue of charter production, although of course the construction of cartularies is in itself an extremely important subject and has much to offer on the acquisition and management of property by the owner for whom a cartulary was constructed.[76] Eleventh- and twelfth-century cartulary copies of charters from the area covered in this book characteristically 'improved' the spelling and grammar of the originals they were copying but, where we can check against a single sheet, they usually did not make substantial changes to the content.[77] What is relevant in the present context is that some cartulary

73 Li227 (ACL 820), 23 August 950. There are also trial letters in the left-hand margin of ACL 122 (Lii416), of 2 January 972, quite a valuable house sale in León redacted and/or written by the priest Ceprigiane.

74 Karl Heidecker, 'Les actes privés de la période carolingienne dans les archives de Saint-Gall', *Annuaire de l'école pratique des hautes études, Section des sciences historiques et philologiques*, 139 (2008), pp. 372–7.

75 Lii345 (ACL 822); some of the writing on the dorse is illegible.

76 See, for example, Olivier Guyotjeannin, Laurent Morelle and Michel Parisse (eds), *Les cartulaires. Actes de la Table ronde* (Paris, 1993); David Peterson, 'Reescribiendo el pasado. El *Becerro Galicano* como reconstrucción de la historia institucional de San Millán de la Cogolla', *Hispania*, 69 (2009), pp. 653–82; David Peterson, 'El *Becerro Gótico* de San Millán. Reconstrucción de un cartulario perdido', *Studia Histórica. Historia Medieval*, 29 (2011), pp. 147–73; Leticia Agúndez San Miguel, 'Memoria, escritura y control social: la construcción de la memoria histórica en el monasterio de Sahagún (siglos X–XIII)' (Universidad de Cantabria, Tesis Doctoral, 2011); Elena E. Rodríguez Díaz and Antonio Claret García Martínez (eds), *La escritura de la memoria. Los cartularios* (Huelva, 2011); Wendy Davies, 'The composition of the Redon cartulary', *Francia*, 17 (1990), pp. 69–90.

77 Cf. the comments on this of José Antonio Fernández Flórez and Marta Herrero de la Fuente, 'Libertades de las copistas en la confección de cartularios: el caso del Becerro Gótico de Sahagún', in Emma Condello and Guiseppe de Gregorio (eds), *Scribi e colofoni. Le sottoscrizioni di copisti dalle origini all' avento della stampa* (Spoleto, 1995), pp. 301–19, and of María Josefa Sanz Fuentes, 'El lenguaje de los documentos falsos', in *Orígenes de las lenguas romances en el reino de León, siglos IX–XII* (2 vols, León, 2004), vol. 1, pp. 119–58.

compilers appear to have gone to considerable lengths to represent some of the physical attributes of the documents they copied. This applies particularly to witness lists, where occasionally the columns and more often the *signa* of the single sheet can be represented;[78] and in long or composite records, the paragraphing of the text can represent aspects of the single sheet(s). So, for example, the writers responsible for earlier folios of the León cathedral cartulary appear to take great care over this; the later folios do not.[79] This means that cartulary copies of charters can in some circumstances contribute to our understanding of the material attributes of the early versions of a record.

Records of disputes

Now, the range of physical characteristics of records of gift, sale and exchange is also characteristic of records of disputes. The distinction between functional and display records is particularly appropriate in this case, and dispute records occur on parchments of many different sizes: Fine records tend to lack elaboration and utilize only a small piece of parchment, like that paid by Segerico and friends to Munio Núñez in 940, measuring 140–90 mm maximum × 110 mm (see Figure 7.3); whereas the narrative Account of the dispute between Iñigo Garcés and the monastery of Cillanueva of Ardón, heard in the royal court, is extremely large at 560 × 340 mm and is laid out for show (see Figure 3.7).[80] If we consider the status of the actors in relation to the size of document, then the same principles apply as do to records of gift and sale. All of the largest dispute records detail events to the advantage of clerical beneficiaries; records of dispute which have some royal involvement are also large. All of the smallest records have principal actors who were peasants, although the beneficiaries might be bishops, priests, monasteries or aristocrats.

In fact, all retrospective narrative Accounts which survive on single sheets are large or very large, as are the few dispute records of Mixed type, and all Fines are recorded on middling or, more often, small sheets, as are records of Debts.[81] There is therefore a very clear size differentiation by type of record. Incidental records of dispute occur on sheets of all sizes, as might be expected, depending on the primary purpose of the record. Parchments with several records also tend to be large, for purely practical reasons: the mid-ninth century Lugo group of Toresario's Confession, his subsequent Agreement with Bishop

78 Cf. above, p. 81 and n66.

79 See further below, pp. 92–3. Cf. the comments of Marta Herrero de la Fuente, 'Cartularios leoneses. Del *Becerro Gótico de Sahagún* al *Tumbo Legionense* y al *Libro de las Estampas*', in Rodríguez Díaz and García Martínez (eds), *La escritura de la memoria*, pp. 111–52, especially pp. 138–41.

80 Li138 (ACL 76), 27 April 940; Lii410 (ACL 909), 4 October 968.

81 I have not been able to inspect a handful of dispute texts (especially Portuguese examples) on single sheets, but the number of these is so small it could not alter the tenor of these observations. For material characteristics of Portuguese charters, see António Joaquim Ribeiro Guerra, *Os diplomas privados em Portugal dos séculos IX a XII* (Lisbon, 2003).

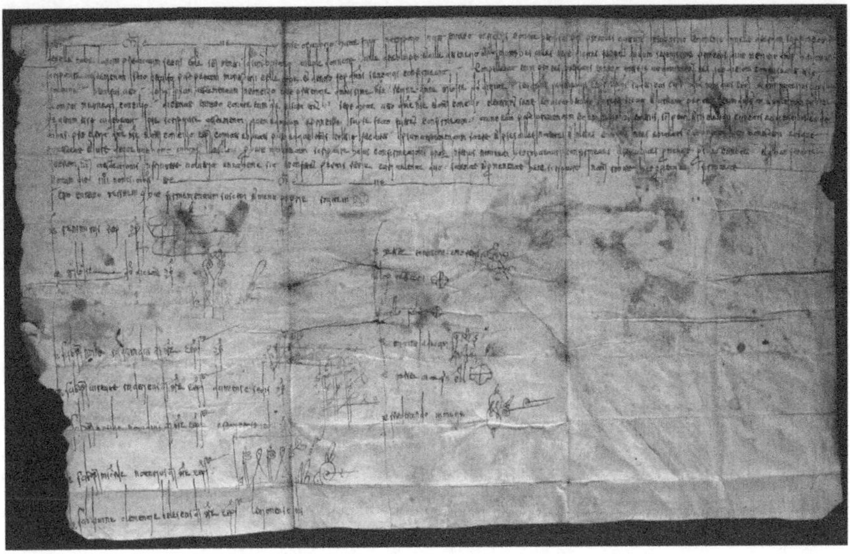

Figure 3.7 ACL 909 (Lii410), an Account of the court case between Iñigo Garcés and the monastery at Ardón in 968

Source: Reproduced by permission of the chapter of León cathedral.

Gladilano and Siseguto's Agreement with the same bishop are recorded on a long strip of 97 × 515 mm (see Figure 5.2).[82] Interestingly, with one exception, all other Agreements following the settlement of disputes are on small sheets, as is the other surviving Confession on a single sheet.[83] That means that the Accounts drawn up at some distance from court proceedings are recorded on large sheets, whereas the dispute texts that might be expected to have been recorded in or shortly after a judicial meeting are recorded on small sheets. The point is emphasized by the fact that the latter kinds of dispute record are sometimes added to a parchment whose principal function was to record something else. This is well demonstrated by the addition of the Confession to the large royal donation charter to Sahagún, discussed above.[84] Unfortunately no Oaths

82 Flor74, Flor75, Flor73 (ACLu 60 2), 5 June 861 for Toresario's Confession and Agreement; the year of Siseguto's Agreement, dated 15 May, is unreadable because of damage; it is usually assumed to belong to the same year. See above, pp. 48–9, on whether or not this sheet was a forgery; Ainoa Castro, in a personal comment, considers this to be an eleventh-century copy, as de Parga had also thought; I have to accept her palaeographical judgment, but it would seem that the writer went to great lengths to represent the ninth-century exemplar.

83 See below, p. 88, for the exception.

84 S261. See above, p. 47 n40, for Julio Escalona's argument that the royal charter is unusual, but is not only a credible record of *c.* 971 but that the sheet probably derives from that decade, with the Confession added shortly after, in a different hand. Assessment of the character of this record is complicated by the fact that the main royal grant on this parchment has been considered to be a copy (or even a forgery). See José Antonio Fernández Flórez, 'El fondo documental del monasterio de Sahagún y sus

survive on single sheets, but it may not be too fanciful to consider an analogy from late tenth-, eleventh- and twelfth-century England: there is widespread evidence of recording (vernacular) sworn witness statements in the margins and other blank spaces on the folios of liturgical and gospel books – that is, in odd spaces that were available rather than on new, separate sheets; it is particularly characteristic of manumissions and lists of witnesses and sureties, as well as oaths and agreements.[85]

As indicated above, Confessions sometimes survive in a physical association with consequent Agreements – as two separate documents on one parchment – and it seems likely that this was a common way to make the initial record.[86] Toresario's Agreement followed on the same day as his Confession, and Flaino's the day after, the latter written in the same hand; in each case, both documents are recorded on a single parchment.[87] In Toresario's case, his Confession to Bishop Gladilano comes first, across the long horizontal strip used to make this absolutely functional record; then the two Agreements (of Siseguto and Toresario) are recorded below the Confession, on the left and right respectively of the strip. Flaino's Confession before Flaino Muñoz is also recorded on a horizontal strip, with his consequent Agreement to the right of it (see Figure 2.4). However, Agreements were also written on the dorse of related or completely unrelated charters, where they usually occupy a tiny proportion of the space available – about an eighth in the case of Vital's Agreement with Piasca, some time after 989, and a quarter in that of Velito and Calendo's Agreement with the monastery of Santa Marina and in that of the deacon Arías's Agreement with San Martín de Noanca.[88] The Agreement of Crexes with the monk Romano (acting for the monastery of San Martín), recorded by the priest Arrano, is rather more untidy, beginning (at right angles) in the space below a sale record and continued on the dorse in a pattern which suggests the parchment was partly folded at the time of writing.[89] It is as if it were important to get a record

---

scriptores (siglos IX–X)', in Juan Ignacio Ruiz de la Peña Solar (ed.), *El monacato en los reinos de León y Castilla (Siglos VII–XIII), X Congreso de Estudios Medievales* (Ávila, 2007), pp. 125–46, at p. 140, who comments on the very unusual nature of the hand and on the fact that the scribe clearly was not used to preparing royal documents, but he does not comment on the addition of the Confession. Even if the main donation record were a copy, then it is likely that the Confession was also copied, for it looks as if it must have been added to the exemplar of the royal donation record; being a copy would therefore not invalidate this Confession record (and there would have been little point in forging it).

85 I am indebted to an enlightening paper by Julia Crick, Institute of Historical Research, London, 26 March 2014, for drawing my attention to this material. For examples, see David A.E. Pelteret, *Catalogue of English Post-Conquest Vernacular Documents* (Woodbridge, 1990), nos 78, 86 (agreements); Donald Scragg, *A Conspectus of Scribal Hands Writing English, 960–1100* (Cambridge, 2012), nos 781 (agreements), 862 (list of sureties, a tenth-century example).

86 See above, pp. 45–6.

87 Flor74 and Flor75 (ACLu 60 2), 5 June 861; OD38 and OD39 (AHDL, Otero 30), 21 and 22 April 995). See above, pp. 48–9.

88 S372 (AHN Clero Sahagún 875–16); OD43 (AHDL, Otero 16v), 1 June 997; Lii330 (ACL 53), 27 September 960, on the dorse of Li10 (895), for which see above, p. 77 and n47.

89 Liii597 (ACL 161), 24 April 1000, added to Liii593, 1 March 1000.

of such Agreements, as soon as possible, and it was therefore written, inelegantly, on the first parchment that came to hand. Differently, however, a record of one Agreement following intrusion into monastic property is written on the dorse of the original charter recording the donation of that property to the monastery twenty-one years earlier; here the record of the Agreement may have been made quickly and unceremoniously, but this time in a particularly appropriate place.[90]

The layout of dispute records for the most part fits the patterns and principles of the layout of gift and sale records. Nearly all retrospective Accounts are display documents, the text occupying a relatively small part of the available space (a quarter to a half), with witness and confirmer columns set out below that, accompanied by a number of elaborate *signa*. Several have royal *signa* in a prominent position, either central to the document (like that recording the determination of the boundaries of Manzaneda and Garrafe when challenged by the monastery of San Julián) or at the top of the first column (like that of the Iñigo Garcés case); the text of Mixed type, recording King Vermudo II's restoration of disputed property to Bishop Savarigo, has a central royal *signum* which appears to have been completed before the second chrismon and witness column, for they are laid out so as to respect that prominent position.[91] This was deliberate planning. Even the relatively simple layout of the Account of the royal restoration of confiscated property by the king to his loyal servant Menendo is stylishly set out.[92] The only exception to this practice of which I am aware is the Lugo Account of a property dispute between the layman Abregano and the priest Fafila; here the text occupies more than three-quarters of the parchment, with just two short witness columns below it; four of the six 'witnesses' are judges, one is a *saio* and the other the scribe (see Figure 6.1).[93] So there is no attempt here to display the presence of large numbers of witnesses of high status.

Just as Accounts are nearly always display records, so Agreements following Confessions or other kinds of settlements constitute basic, functional, unelaborated records if they are the main subject of a single sheet. They are all solid blocks of text, with witnesses (if any) set out in rows or in very short columns; although most have an initial chrismon, several have no witness chrismons; although the scribal *signum* is often quite prominent, some have no scribal subscription at all, however, and several either have no other *signa* or only simple

90 OD43, on the dorse of OD21 (AHDL, Otero 16r), 18 July 976.

91 Li89 (ACL 1333), 29 January 931 (see above, pp. 37–8, 56); Lii410 (ACL 909), 4 October 968; Lii508 (ACL 984), 16 November 985.

92 Liii559 (ACL 155), 30 September 993.

93 AHN Clero Lugo 1325A–9, 973. This parchment is cut off, but is cut below the witness chrismons, and there is space on the parchment for more names (see above, p. 39 n14). Possibly also Cañ41 (ACLu 11), an Account of a theft case between two laymen: it is laid out for display, with several columns of witnesses, but the text again occupies much more space than the witness columns (see fig. 8.2). This has also been cut off: there could have been more witnesses listed, but it is still unlikely that they would have occupied more space than the text.

crosses completed by the writer; the 955 Agreement of Pardomino monks with locals had two short columns of the locals added to the record – apparently an afterthought.[94] The only exception to this practice of recording Agreements in straightforward, unelaborated ways known to me is that of the Agreement between the layman Zezzon and Bishop Cixila over water rights in the River Torío, which is quite a large display document; even though the bottom has been cut off, there are still prominent witness columns with plenty of elaborate *signa*.[95] The size and style are not surprising given the interest of the bishop, but even so it is against the normal convention for the Agreements that survive. Confessions, of which few survive on single sheets, are similar in layout, although it should be noted that the layout of Toresario's Confession (unlike that of his Agreement) is deliberately stylish: although set out as a solid block of text, with witnesses in rows, the initial 'I' is elaborated, the date is in slightly larger writing, all the *signa* of witnesses are prominent and the subscription of the count (in whose court the case was heard) is marked out with a chrismon, unlike the others, and is almost central to the parchment. This suggests particular care in the construction of the record; it is unfortunate that we have so few originals to compare with it. Records of Fines and payments of Debts are for the most part functional, unelaborated documents, like the Fine paid to Munio Núñez by Segerico and companions, or the compensation for debt paid to the priest Braolio by Gogina and her children, although several have a touch of decoration in an elaborated initial 'I'.[96] Whoever the beneficiaries might have been, Debts and Fines belong with the style appropriate for peasant transactions – they usually involved the transfer of small plots of property, sometimes explicitly in lieu of chattels that could not be assembled.

The execution of dispute records is as varied as it is of other charters, although it is broadly true to say that the finest hands are found recording documents for display, especially those of Accounts, like the elegant hand of the Manzaneda and Garrafe Account, and the coarser hands record Debts and Fines. The same kinds of afterthought are evident in dispute records as in other records – corrections made to the text, a word omitted and subsequently added, extra witness columns squashed in, extra confirmers added, continuation on the dorse because a big enough parchment had not been selected.[97] Dorsal

94 Lii290 (ACL 101).

95 S33 (AHN Clero Sahagún 872–19), 8 July 925.

96 Li138 (ACL 76), 27 April 940; OD14 (AHDL, Otero 11), 25 February 964; both have the decorated 'I'. The Fine of OD37 (Otero 29) is a larger display document, as is the gift/sale of E24 (AHN Clero 958–7), which could arguably be regarded as a Debt (but not counted as such in this work); the negotiation of a reduction in penalty by *boni homines* in the former and the large number of witnesses (including three judges) in the latter appear to reflect unusually prominent occasions of settlement.

97 For example, the Incidental record OD29 (ACL Fondo R. Rodríguez 3) has corrections by a later hand, especially to the formulas; the Account of Liii559 (ACL 155) has a word added to the sanction; the Agreement of Lii290 (ACL 101), for which, see n. 94 above; the Incidental record of Lii378 (ACL 114), of 964, has two added confirmers, one of whom was the perpetrator of the original offence; the witness list of the Fine of OD34 (ACL Fondo R. Rodríguez 4) is on the dorse.

additions are not necessarily rushed and scrappy, and can be very neatly executed – they are often careful records, even though a new parchment had not been selected.[98] Many of the unelaborated records are nevertheless carefully executed, with prominent scribal *signa*, as it were declaring pride in the work, like the priest Domengo's subscription to his records for Fruela Vimáraz and Braolio's record of the Agreement following intrusion into Santa Marina's land; even the curious Confession added to the display record of King Ramiro's gift has a prominent scribal *signum*.[99]

Some records of disputes on single sheets appear to be copies, even if they were contemporary copies. The record of Velita's payment (apparently an enforced sale) to the monastery of Abellar in respect of her husband's homicide looks more like a training exercise than a record for someone to keep; it is extremely neat (described as a book-hand by Concepción Mendo Carmona), and there are some compass-drawn segmented wheels below the text, which look like decoration – perhaps doodles; the eight simple *signa*, added after the text was written, also look like decoration.[100] The Account of Rodrigo's dispute with the church of San Salvador (one of the Pardomino monastic community's churches) over control of a dependent, resolved in favour of the monastery, is recorded on an offcut of parchment of very irregular (and unusual) shape; Rodrigo had claimed that the man belonged to the *comissorio* (area of authority) of Ferreras and with the 'men of Ferreras' had taken his ox, but the king had ordered the monastery to present witnesses to swear on the monks' behalf; when they had done this, Rodrigo had given in, and the proceedings were recorded in the council (*concilium*) of Ferreras, not in the royal court.[101] The Account is framed as a backwards glance at what may or may not have been a full court case, presumably made for the benefit of the monastery. Physically, the record is written in a very tidy, even hand; it is not remotely for display: there is no sign of any *signa* by confirmers (as is usually the case with original Accounts), and the scribe's subscription is mixed up with those of the witnesses, rather than placed with some prominence; despite Rodrigo's status, this is not the kind of record usually associated with high-status individuals. It may simply be a copy made for reasons we cannot fathom. The large display record of King Vermudo II's restoration of property to Bishop Savarigo must also be a copy, although quite possibly a faithful and immediate copy of an original: it must be a copy because Bishop Pedro's *signum* at the end of the third witness column joins the chrismon for the scribe's signature, just as the *signum* of Salomon in the second column joins the chrismon for the third column.[102] Whereas chrismons were usually written before

98 But not the Agreement of Liii597, which its editor describes as 'very rustic'.

99 OD40 and OD41 (AHDL, Otero 31), OD43 (Otero 16v), S261 (AHN Clero Sahagún 876–8), on which see above, pp. 47, 85.

100 Lii450 (ACL 825), 7 May 977. Mendo Carmona, 'La escritura de los documentos leoneses en el siglo X', p. 188 and fig. 9.

101 Liii577 (ACL 887), 24 March 997.

102 Lii508 (ACL 984), 16 November 985.

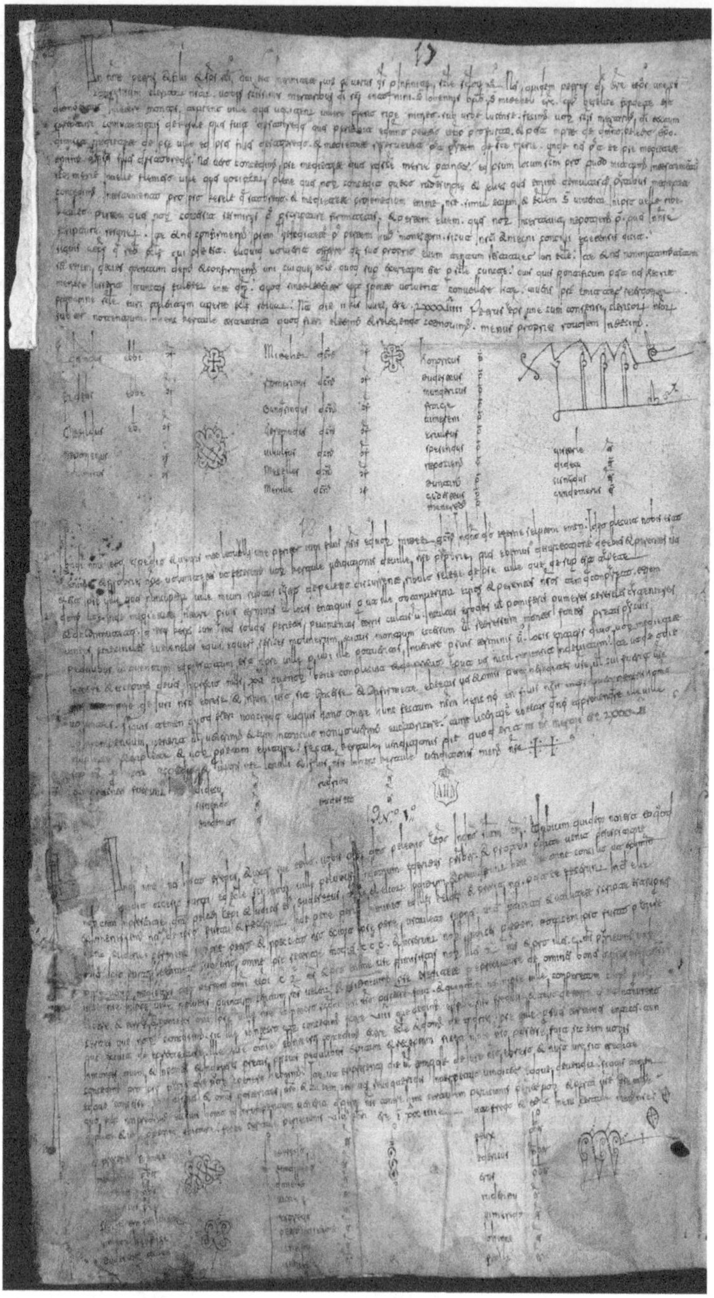

Figure 3.8 AHN 1325A–16 (Cañ65), the third text of a group of seven, an Account of a case of theft heard in the bishop of Santiago's court in 996

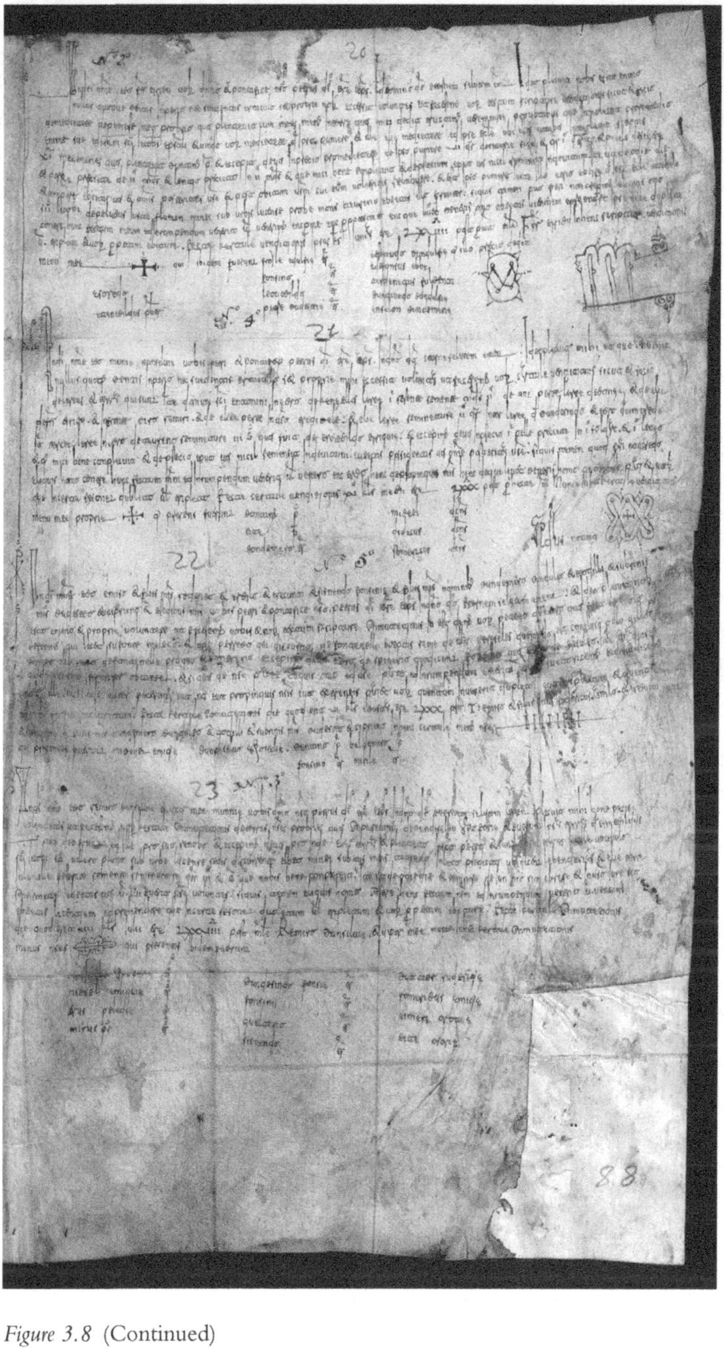

Figure 3.8 (Continued)

subscriptions and *signa*, here the scribe has not lifted the pen between *signa* and chrismons. A different kind of copy can be found in a set of seven charters in favour of the bishopric of Lugo; largely of the first half of the eleventh century, the group includes among the transactions an Account of 996 (see Figure 3.8).[103]

A number of important dispute records do not survive on single sheets, but are preserved in cartularies. That being the case, we have little chance of knowing what if any changes were made when they were copied, although we would expect changes to have been made to spelling and grammar. However, the layout of a cartulary item can in some circumstances indicate additions, like the additional payment appended to a Fine paid to Bishop Rosendo.[104] A few clues can also be offered by the cartularies which in some respects represent the layout and associated *signa* of witness lists. This is the case, for example, with the early folios of the Tumbo (cartulary) of León cathedral and with the first Sobrado cartulary. The single sheet of King Vermudo II's 985 gift to Bishop Savarigo has four columns of witnesses, whereas the cartulary version has only two columns and a selection, but not all, of the *signa*; this is a representation of the witness lists of the exemplar, but not a precise copy of it.[105] The León cathedral Tumbo is also particularly interesting in separating the text of some dispute records into separate sections: the Mixed record of the case against Mateo by the monastery of Santos Justo y Pastor and the Confession of Pedro and friends to the bishop of León – both cases prosecuted by the advocate Berulf – are copied as a series of distinct sections: in the Mateo case, the Oath is separated from Mateo's acknowledgment of guilt, which is separated from his first promise (to hand over the church), and the latter is separated from his second promise (to refrain from further provocation); in the Pedro case, Confession and subsequent commitment to hand over the disputed property are set out as two separate documents.[106] The Oath in the case over water rights brought by the monastery of Valdevimbre against Munio and his brothers, prosecuted by Velasco, is less straightforward but is set out as four separate texts, of which the second, third and fourth relate different aspects of the Oath (the testimony, the invocation of the holy and repetition of the testimony, with some verbal variation), preceded by the commitment of both parties to appear in court.[107] By contrast,

103 Though earliest in date, this is the third of the set; AHN Clero Lugo 1325A–16, published as Cañ65.

104 Cel393, 29 April 961.

105 Lii508 (ACL 984 and ACL Tumbo de la catedral ff. 14v–15v). Cf. the comments of Miguel Calleja Puerta, 'Cartularios y construcción de la memoria monástica en los reinos de León y Castilla durante el siglo XII', in Véronique Lamazou-Duplan and Eloísa Ramírez Vaquero (eds), *Les cartulaires médiévaux. Écrire et conserver la mémoire du pouvoir, le pouvoir de la mémoire* (Pau, 2013), pp. 187–97, at p. 197, on an intention to convey the same probatory value, such as it was, as had the exemplars.

106 Li192 (Tumbo ff. 39v–40v), 7 May 946; Li191 (Tumbo ff. 45v–46r), 17 April 946. See further below, p. 148. I am grateful to André Marques for pointing out that the same is true of the Livro Preto (Coimbra cartulary) copy of PMH DC 13.

107 Li34 (Tumbo ff. 205v–205bisv), 30 January 915; the editor notes that there are many errors in this record, since the scribe did not appear to understand the script of the original. It shares many of the characteristics of ACO B.1.11, however; see further below, pp. 146–7.

the cartulary Accounts of the 934 case of Abellar against Albura and friends and of the Iñigo Garcés case of 968, also prosecuted by Berulf, are simple slabs of text. Since we also have the Iñigo Garcés case on a single sheet, we can see that the cartulary copy (at folios 369v–370r) does not represent the appearance of its exemplar at all; it is as if the writer simply could not be bothered to do so.[108] In view of the deliberate sectioning of the texts of the three earlier folios, it seems reasonable to propose that they were copying separate documents, perhaps on a single sheet, just as we have seen that Confessions and Agreements were recorded as separate documents on single sheets.[109] The writer here seems to have been copying from existing documents of a type consistent with the single sheets that we have, and that gives us reason to think that those records reflect the visual appearance of their exemplars. However, clearly the practice of cartulary compilers was inconsistent, and one cannot always assume that cartulary copies reflect the physical attributes of originals.

Implications

Consideration of the materiality of charters has some important implications for our assessment of dispute texts. Firstly, it is clear that dispute records share the principal characteristics of other kinds of text recorded on parchment in the ninth and tenth centuries – that is of gifts, sales and exchanges of property. There was no special way of making a dispute record, and no hint that there was any special way of preparing the parchment or of writing on it; indeed, composite records of several transactions could include Fines and Debts among records of gifts and sales, as in the priest Munio's composite record of the late 970s.[110] The only hint of a distinctive feature is the fact that there was a greater tendency for Confessions and Agreements (and perhaps Oaths) to be recorded on odd corners or on the dorse of parchments whose primary purpose was to record something else, but even this was not invariable. There were, then, both functional and display records of disputes, with all the resourcing and archiving implications that that distinction has. In particular, retrospective, narrative Accounts of disputes are always display documents and are nearly always of large size and of deliberate layout for visual effect, with some decorative features and some eye-catching witness, confirmer and scribal *signa*. In this they resemble the display documents that principally record major gifts to bishops and monasteries by people of relatively high status. Looking at the physical characteristics therefore strongly reinforces my earlier suggestion that the principal purpose of drawing up such Accounts was to get confirmation of that outcome by one or more high-status individuals.[111] It is in any case clear that

108 Li99 (Tumbo ff. 387r–388v), 12 April 934, a text classified as 'reworked' by the editor; Lii410.

109 See above, pp. 84–6.

110 Lii457 etc.; see above, p. 70, and Figure 3.3 above.

111 See above, p. 39.

the Accounts were for keeping and displaying by the bishoprics and monasteries which were the beneficiaries.

At the other end of the scale, records of Confessions, Agreements, Fines and Debt repayments are functional. They tend to be on small pieces of parchment, laid out as a solid block of text; witnesses, if there were any, are often recorded in rows, although short witness columns do occur; these texts have little decoration and are only rarely laid out for visual effect, although scribal *signa*, if present, can be quite prominent. Of this group, Confessions and Agreements are more likely to be found in secondary contexts, as if recorded in a hurry on the nearest usable medium. It is not unthinkable that they were recorded during court proceedings, although they may well have been recorded shortly after; I certainly do not want to suggest anything like the stenographer of modern courts taking down every word as spoken, nor even the kind of 'court notary' that has been suggested.[112] What is important, however, is that these records were made much closer in time to the court meetings to which they relate than were the Accounts, and were primarily made to get a written record of what had just been conceded, rather than to display it. This means that such notes could lie behind parts of some of the retrospective Accounts; it does not follow that all were based on notes of proceedings, nor even most, and it does not stop them being one-sided, partial, accounts. But they were not necessarily at a total distance from the events.

⋆ ⋆ ⋆

The physical characteristics of dispute records are one aspect of the analysis essential to provide these records with context. Analysis of their words and language is another essential. Chapter 4 provides context for the language of dispute records by engaging first with the writing of all types of charter.

112 Compare Roger Collins, '"Sicut lex Gothorum continet": Law and charters in ninth- and tenth-century León and Catalonia', *English Historical Review*, 100 (1985), pp. 489–512, at p. 506. I consider the recording much more haphazard and less official than Collins suggested; see further above and below, pp. 54–5, 147–9.

4 Formulaic writing

Just as we needed to consider material aspects of the whole corpus of charters in order to identify the material characteristics of dispute records, so we also need to consider whether the writing of dispute records conforms to – or differs from – practice in framing other kinds of charter. Since the issues are complex, some time considering charter writing as a whole is essential before focusing on the language of dispute records. Areas of potentially distinctive local practice and indications of any norms of training would be especially significant.

Charter writing as a whole was characteristically formulaic, with standard formulas used to introduce the text (in what are known technically as invocation and address), describe the transfer of property and the rights that went with it (disposition), specify the sanction that applied in the case of default, introduce the list of witnesses and/or confirmers and the dating clause, and sometimes indicate the attestation of witnesses; charters of gift, in particular, might also have more or less elaborate preambles, again using standard formulas.[1] There were also non-formulaic elements, and these included the specifics of proper names, like the personal names of the principal actors and witnesses and the names of places transferred, and the specific detail of location, indicated by a short phrase or by longer or shorter boundary clauses; they might sometimes include some narration of the circumstances leading up to the transfer. The same formulas were used all over northern Iberia, and indeed are closely related to formulas used across western Europe in the early middle ages.[2] Some of them have a background of use in the Visigothic period, as demonstrated by their appearance on inscribed slates of the sixth and seventh centuries;[3] some of them were collected in formularies, providing models for use by those drafting

1 For a technical description, see the many diplomatic manuals, like the standard, Arthur Giry, *Manuel de Diplomatique*, 2nd edn (Paris, 1925); Harry Bresslau, *Handbuch der Urkundenlehre für Deutschland und Italien*, 2nd edn (2 vols, Leipzig, 1912–31). See also María Milagros Cárcel Ortí (ed.), *Vocabulaire international de la diplomatique* (València, 1994).

2 See the diplomatic manuals; and cf. Frankish formularies, as discussed by Alice Rio, *Legal Practice and the Written Word in the Early Middle Ages: Frankish Formulae, c. 500–1000* (Cambridge, 2009).

3 Isabel Velázquez Soriano, *Las pizarras visigodas (Entre el latín y su disgregación. La lengua hablada en Hispania, siglos VI–VIII)* (Salamanca, 2004), e.g. nos 8, 19, 40.

charters and other documents;[4] but in many cases their place and time of origin are lost.[5]

Here, for example, are some very common formulas:

Invocation – *In Dei nomine* ('In the name of God');

Address – *Ego NN uobis N in Domino salutem* ('I NN greet you N in the Lord');

Disposition – (a) *Placuit nobis atque conuenit, propria et spontanea nostra uoluntate, ut faceremus uobis kartula testamenti, pro remedio de parentum meorum* ('We have agreed, of our own free will, to make you a charter of donation, for the salvation of my parents'); (b) *Concedo ipsa terra qui est in locum predictum . . . ab integra* ('I give that land which is in such and such a place . . . completely'); (c) *ut abeatis illud firmiter de dato nostro, et quicquid exinde agere, facere uel iudicare uolueritis, sit concessa uobis potestas* ('so that you can have this gift securely from us and you are given the power to be able to do whatever you want to do thereafter');

Sanction – *Si quis contra hanc cartulam uenire temptauerit, tunc parte ipsius monasterii ipsa uilla dublata et uobis perhenniter habitura* ('If anyone should attempt to come against this charter, [we should pay] the monastery double [the value of] that property, and you will have it in perpetuity');

Dating clause – *Facta series testamenti* . . . ('The terms of this document were prepared [on] . . .');

Attestation – *NN manus nostras roboramus* [followed by *signa*] ('We NN have confirmed by our own hands [followed by marks]') or *N in hoc testamento quod fieri uolui et relegendo cognoui manu mea roboraui et signum feci* [*signum*] ('I N have confirmed with my own hand and made a mark [mark] in this document which I wanted to be made and which I have acknowledged by reading aloud').[6]

4 See 'Formulae Wisigothicae' in Juan Gil (ed.), *Miscellanea Wisigothica* (Seville, 1972), pp. 70–112, for a formulary, probably of Visigothic origin (whose formulas recur in ninth- and tenth-century charters), which is preserved in a sixteenth-century copy of a probable twelfth-century Oviedo manuscript; see Miguel Calleja Puerta, 'Ecos de las *Fórmulas visigóticas* en la documentación altomedieval asturleonesa', in *Les formulaires. Compilation et circulation des modèles d'actes dans l'Europe médiévale et moderne* (Paris, forthcoming). See Michel Zimmermann, 'Un formulaire du Xème siècle conservé à Ripoll', *Faventia*, 4/2 (1982), pp. 25–86, for a Catalan formulary. The fact that several formulas (including formulas for a loan, manumission and morning gift) are written in blank spaces in a ninth-century Iberian prayer book must mean that such formulas were available in some Iberian scriptoria and implies that they were used; see José Vives, 'El oracional mozárabe de Silos. British Museum, ms. Addit. 30852', *Analecta Sacra Tarraconensia*, 18 (1945), pp. 1–25, at p. 25. The prayer book itself is a Silos manuscript and is close in content to a prayer book of Tarragona origin. The three readable formulas reflect the three consecutive formulas on the same subjects in the Ripoll formulary (Zimmermann, 'Un formulaire', pp. 79–80), but the prayer book formulas are much simpler constructions; although they are clearly different from the Ripoll examples, it must be likely that they are of Catalan origin.

5 Cf. Jonathan Jarrett, 'Comparing the earliest documentary culture in Carolingian Catalonia', in Jonathan Jarrett and Allan Scott McKinley (eds), *Problems and Possibilities of Early Medieval Charters* (Turnhout, 2013), pp. 89–126, at pp. 100–101, who points to Frankish analogues, but also to differences so significant that the analogues cannot be the origin of the Iberian formulations.

6 Examples from Li203 (948), Lii292 (28 October 955), Lii293 (22 December 955), Sob17 (14 May 976).

Charters of sale use many of the same formulas, with the following regular variations:

Disposition – (b) *ut uenderemus uobis terra nostra* ('[we have agreed] to sell you our land'); (d) *acepit de uos . . . que mihi bene conplaqui, de precio aput uos nicil remansit in debito pro dare* ('I have received [this price] from you, which is agreeable to me; and there is nothing of the price remaining for you to pay');

Dating clause – *Facta scriptura uendiccionis* . . . ('This charter of sale was made [on] . . .');

Attestation – *NN in hanc kartula uendiccionis manus nostras [signa] fecimus* ('we NN made [marks] in this charter of sale with our own hands') or *N ic ts [signum]. N ic ts [signum]. N presbiter ic ts [signum]* ('N here [as] witness [mark]. N here [as] witness [mark]. The priest N here [as] witness [mark]').[7]

We find the same formulas used in northern Portugal, Galicia, Asturias, Cantabria, the *meseta*, Aragón and Catalonia. The key question is therefore: given that there were standard formulas, of widespread use, but with multiple variations, how can we explain the way that charters were framed, and how did they come to have the forms we see in the ninth and tenth centuries? One might suppose that using formularies, copying existing charters and memorizing the words of a master all played a part. Were there strong local or regional traditions that led to consistency of practice in certain areas? If so, one might deduce some element of local training and deliberate maintenance of the tradition; as a mechanism for sustaining shared experience, it would imply the involvement of a number of people, whether members of the group were from a single monastery or a monastic network or from a scatter of local clerics or religious households.

Cogentis/quoque gentis

The formulation of the Iberian corpus is remarkably homogeneous, but it is interesting (and potentially significant) that different scribes used the same formula in different ways. By way of demonstration, I shall begin with one formula which is extremely common: *placuit nobis atque conuenit nullius cogentis imperio nec suadentis articulo sed propria nobis accessit uoluntas ut uinderemus*, which literally means 'It is pleasing to us and it is agreed, without the command of anyone forcing [it] nor by the instruction of anyone persuading, but our own wish brought us to sell [to you]' – in other words, in normal language: 'we have agreed of our own free will, without anyone forcing or persuading us, to sell [to you]'.[8] This is exceptionally common, especially (but not exclusively) in sale texts, and it normally occurs in the first sentences of the disposition. I shall call

7 Examples from Lii294 (30 January 956), Lii299 (27 September 956), Lii305 (12 January 958).
8 S11 (910).

it Type 1. It has analogues in the Catalan Formulary of Ripoll and in Frankish formularies.[9] It also occurs in a second form (Type 2), which is even more common: *placuit nobis atque conuenit, nullius quoquegentis imperio neque suadentis articulo, set propria nobis accessit uoluntas, ut uenderemus;*[10] here 'no one forcing' has become 'no one' or 'no kin' (*quoque* is simply an intensifier, 'also'). There are other variants too, although they are not as common. Type 3 uses *egentis* or *quoque egentis*: *plaguit nobis adque conuenit nullius quod egentis inperiu(m) neque suadentis articulo set propria nobis accessit bone pacis uolu(m)tas* or in the form *placuit nobis atque conuenit nullis quoqueegentis imperio neque suadentis articulo set propria nobis accessit uolumptas ut uinderemus;*[11] here 'no one forcing' has become 'no needy person'. Type 4 is a variant on Type 3 and uses *coegentis*: *placuit nobis atque conuenit nullius coegentis imperio neque suadentis articulo set propria nobis accessit uoluntas ut uenderemus;*[12] now 'no needy person' has become 'no co-needy person', perhaps 'one of a group of'. Type 5 uses *congentis*: *placuit nobis adque conuenit nullisque congentis inperio neque suadentis articulo set probria nobis accescit uolumtas ut comutaremus*, where *congentis* might mean 'my own kin' or might not mean anything.[13]

I know of 40 apparent variants on *cogentis/quoque gentis*, although some of these are isolated cases and may well be errors rather than indicators of consistent variant practice.[14] Many of the others look different, but are simply orthographic variants of the five alternatives indicated above: *quogentis*, for example, is a reasonable way of spelling *cogentis*.[15] Grouping these variant spellings together, then, and leaving aside the isolated cases, there appear to be five distinctive practices (the five instanced above), each of which occurs in a range of spellings. These are: Type 1, *cogentis* (113 examples in this form), with variants *cogente, coientis, quogentis* (which occurs 45 times), *quoientis*, and perhaps *qoogentis* and *quolentis*; Type 2, *(quoque) gentis* (and *gentes*) (168 examples in this form, with a split between the words), with variants *ientis, quoquegentis* (which occurs 69 times, with no split), *coquegentis, coquigentes* and perhaps *quaquegentis* and *quegentis*; Type 3, *egentis* (19 examples in this form), with variants *eientis, eyentis,*

9 *Formulae Merowingici et Karolini Aevi*, ed. Karl Zeumer, MGH Legum Sectio V, Formulae (Hanover, 1882–86), pp. 10, 90, 186, 229 (Anjou 19, Marculf II 20, Sens 2 and Bignon 3 and 4), all sales (and see Rio, *Legal Practice*, for these formularies); Zimmermann, 'Un formulaire', p. 77. There are plenty of Catalan examples too (though using *ingenio* for *articulo*), for which see Michel Zimmermann, *Écrire et lire en Catalogne (IXe–XIIe siècle)* (2 vols, Madrid, 2003), vol. 1, pp. 253, 273; for an exhaustive search for Frankish parallels, see Jarrett, 'Comparing the earliest documentary culture', pp. 101–4. The Visigothic sale slates do not have the full formula; the closest is *auenit nouis bona uoluntate* of no. 41 (586–601), Velázquez, *Las pizarras visigodas*, pp. 234–9.

10 Li136 (940).

11 ACLu 60 19 (998); Li229 (950).

12 Li30 (912).

13 Li23 (909); cf. Li31 on the dorse.

14 *adgentis* (2); *adientis* (1); *cogitantis* (1); *cumegentis* (1); *degentis* (1); *entis* (1); *ingentis* (2); *uacentis* (1); *ynyentis* (1). See further below, pp. 103–104, on *adgentis/adientis*.

15 I owe this observation, with many thanks, to Roger Wright, who comments that *quogentis* could have represented [ko-]; it is not, as Jarrett, 'Comparing the earliest documentary culture', p. 101, suggests, a 'mistake'. Zimmermann, *Écrire et lire*, vol. 1, p. 278, also points out that there are variants, but does not develop the point; he adds the form *inioquegentis* (dated 902).

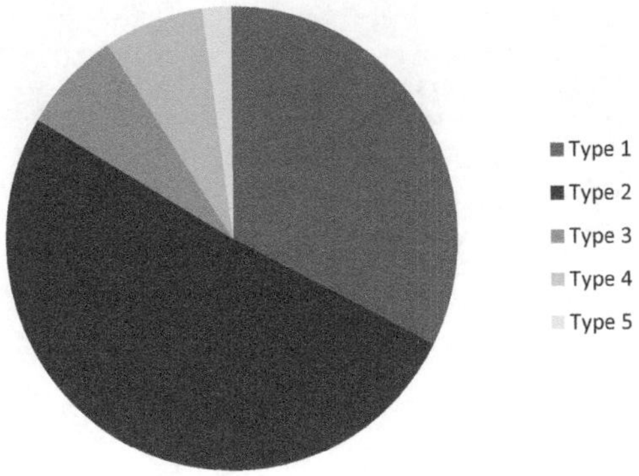

Figure 4.1 Proportions of Types 1–5 of the *cogentis* formula

quoqueegentis, *quoqueeientis*, *coqueegentis* and perhaps *quequoigentis*, *agentis* and *aientis*; Type 4, *coegentis* (10 examples in this form), with variants *quoegentis* (which occurs 23 times), *queegentis* and probably *coegtis*; and Type 5, *congentis* (7 examples in this form), with variants *congenti*, *conientis*, *cumgentis*.[16] As shown in Figure 4.1, of these, Type 1 accounts for 32 per cent of just over 500 cases, Type 2 for 50 per cent, Type 3 for 7 per cent, Type 4 for 7 per cent and Type 5 for 2 per cent.

Looking at the spatial distribution of these different practices, there seem to be some significant differences. Firstly, there is a broad picture. Remarkably, given the formula's widespread occurrence, two major collections, those of Samos and San Millán de la Cogolla, do not have this formula at all. Collections from Santo Toribio, Valpuesta, Cardeña, Albelda and Sahagún (that is, from the Liébana, Castile, the Rioja and the eastern *meseta*, in other words from the east of our region) all predominantly use the first (*cogentis*) form, Type 1, but so does the Sobrado collection in the north-west (see Figures 4.2 and 10.1). Collections from León, Astorga, Otero de las Dueñas, Celanova and northern Portugal all predominantly use the second (*quoque gentis*) form, Type 2 (that is, collections from south and south-west of the region). Collections from Oviedo in the north and from Lugo in the north-west are more mixed, but have more of Type 3 (*egentis*) than of Types 1 or 2.[17]

There are many possible lines of exploration of this distribution, but what is relevant for present purposes is this: in characterizing the distributions, I used the word 'predominantly'; in most cases, 'predominantly' means overwhelmingly, but not exclusively; where one Type is predominant, there are occurrences of other forms too in the region, but in small numbers. In the case of Celanova,

16 If no numbers of occurrences are cited, there are just one or two examples of each of these variants.

17 I have expressed these distinctions with reference to the location of current collections (single sheets and cartularies), for ease of reference. What is significant, of course, is place of original provenance, not ultimate collecting source, and I have tried to indicate the difference between original provenance and place of collection, where appropriate, in my comments.

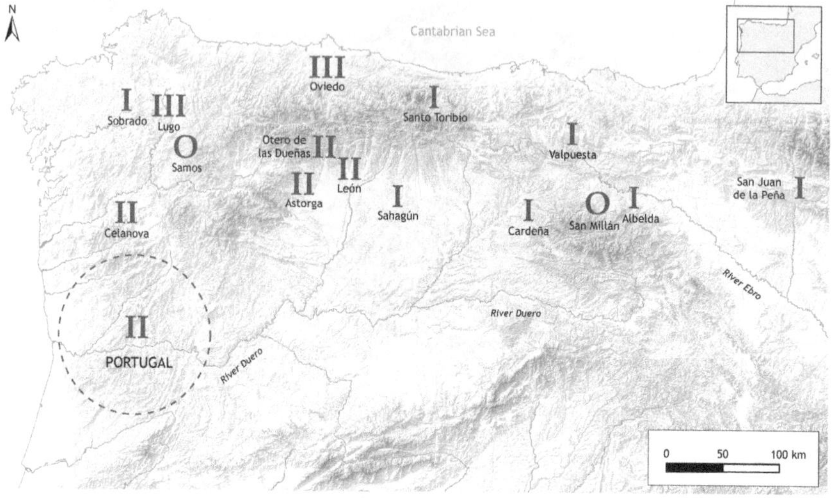

Figure 4.2 Predominance, by collection, of Types 1–3 of the *cogentis* formula

in southern Galicia, the predominance is by no means as stark as elsewhere, for 58 per cent of its uses of the formula are of Type 2 and 40 per cent are of Type 1.

The second kind of significant difference is this: there are differences in practice within distinct regions of ninth- and tenth-century northern Iberia, as well as the broad distinction between the practice of the east and that of the south and west; for example, that of León collections is different from that of Sahagún, only 40 km to the south-east.[18]

One can see some of the nuances in the distribution within some of these regions. Taking Galicia: this formula in the Sobrado collection is frequently and consistently of Type 1 (*cogentis*), with two exceptions.[19] Since all examples occur in a cartulary, one might think that they reflect the language of the cartulary compiler rather than that of the original redactors of the charters. However, the examples run from 827 to 950 and not beyond; in other words, they all derive from records made before the foundation of the monastery of Sobrado in 952. The many texts that record transactions which involved the monastery do not have any version of this formula at all. Use of the formula must therefore reflect the diplomatic of the region before the monastery was established (here, as in other areas, it is perfectly clear that records were being made long before the foundation of the great monasteries, which tended to absorb and archive records of earlier transactions concerning properties which the monastery

18 For much more detail on the spatial distribution of these formulas, and further comment, see Wendy Davies, 'Regions and micro-regions of scribal practice', in Stuart Brookes, Julio Escalona and Orri Vesteinsson (eds), *Polity and Neighbourhood in Early Medieval Europe* (Turnhout, forthcoming).

19 Sob15 and Sob27 *quoquegentis*. (I cannot see an obvious reason why these two charters should vary.)

acquired subsequently).[20] Use of the Type 1 formula appears to reflect some of the core properties of the founder of the monastery, Hermenegildo, and to reflect the local scribal practice of the well-defined region of the upper waters of the Tambre valley and neighbourhood.[21]

Celanova examples are again many; as noted above, about three-fifths of citations of the formula use Type 2 (*quoque gentis*) and two-fifths use Type 1 (*cogentis*). The choice of one form or the other does not seem to match any significant differences between transaction types nor in position of the charters in the cartulary. However, there is a difference in locations. Charters using the second form of the formula record transactions of property that lay within the hinterland of Celanova – Rabal, Bobadela, Amoroce – places which on the whole lay within 6 km of the monastery. Since some Type 2 records were made prior to its foundation, this looks like the local practice of the region, which had been picked up by the monastery and used in making its own records. By contrast, charters using Type 1 of the formula tend to occur farther north, relating to places like Quiroga, Bubal, the River Miño and the River Mao, just like charters of Sobrado and La Coruña (see Figure 4.3).

The León collections are the richest for the period and the richest for this exercise. The sources are several – the cathedral as well as a number of monasteries in the city and outside it; there are cartularies and also many charters on single sheets. It is very striking that Type 1 of the formula (*cogentis*) is exceptionally rare and Type 2 (*quoque gentis*) is extremely common (in a ratio of 1:19), and also that virtually every known variant occurs at some point in these collections. Type 2 is used in plenty of records of transactions between lay parties. Although assembled in León collections, the charters using this form come from a wide geographical area, occurring from León city, 40 km east to the River Cea, south beyond the confluence of Esla and Bernesga, and 100 km north into the Cantabrian Mountains as far as Ujo in Asturias (see Figure 4.4). By contrast, Type 3 (*egentis*) occurs almost entirely on single sheets, and almost entirely in or near León city, with nearly all the beneficiaries being clerics. It looks as if this practice belongs to a learned tradition and clerical culture. Type 4 (*coegentis*) occurs mostly in cartularies, mostly with ecclesiastical beneficiaries, frequently involving the monastery of Abellar, which lay on the River Torío, just to the north of León. This particular version seems to reflect Abellar practice.[22]

Although rare in these collections, Type 1 (*cogentis*) occurs almost entirely on single sheets, and nearly all beneficiaries of the properties conveyed are lay. The locations of these properties are very scattered, from Marialba on the River

20 In the case of Sobrado, much of this material appears to have come from a lay archive; see Adam J. Kosto, '*Sicut mos esse solet*: Documentary practices in Christian Iberia, *c*. 700–1000', in Warren C. Brown, Marios Costambeys, Matthew Innes and Adam J. Kosto (eds), *Documentary Culture and the Laity in the Early Middle Ages* (Cambridge, 2013), pp. 259–82, at pp. 269–73.

21 María del Carmen Pallares Méndez, *El monasterio de Sobrado: un ejemplo de protagonismo monástico en la Galicia medieval* (A Coruña, 1979), p. 31.

22 For Abellar's remarkable library, see Li75 (927); see María José Carbajo Serrano, *El monasterio de los santos Cosme y Damián de Abellar* (León, 1988), pp. 86–7, and ibid., p. 85 for the variety of formulas used.

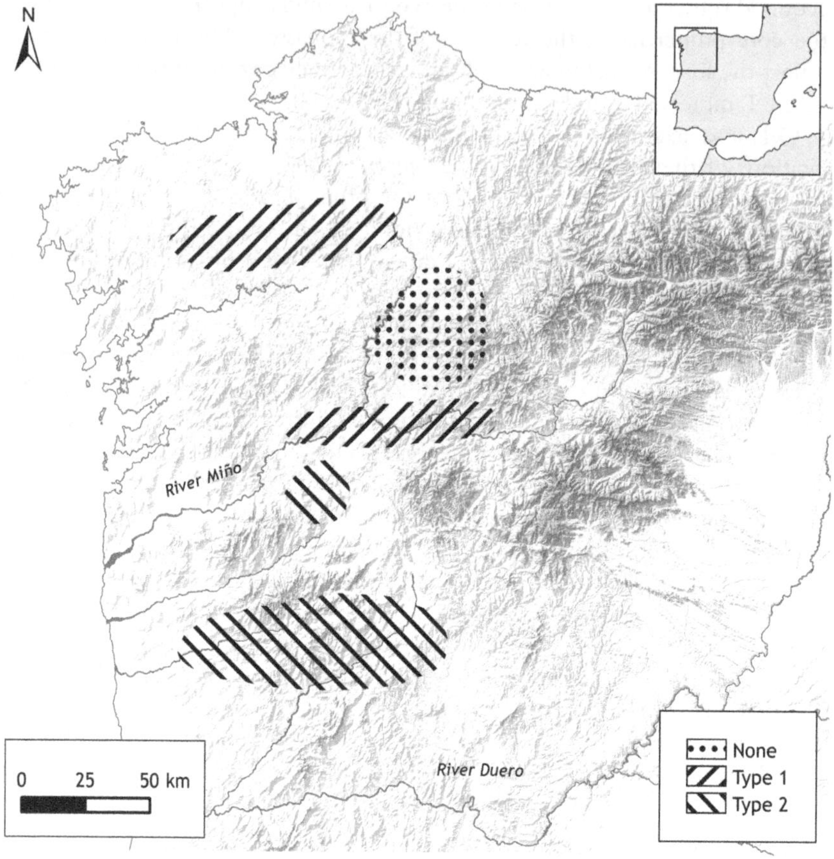

Figure 4.3 Distribution of Types 1 and 2 of the *cogentis* formula in Galicia

Bernesga south of León to the River Aller in the mountains in southern Asturias and to Viego, near the modern Embalse de Porma, also in the mountains. Their distribution overlaps that of the much more numerous Type 2 (*quoque gentis*), so clearly the areas of their usage were not exclusive (see Figure 4.4). But the single sheets and lay beneficiaries of Type 1 (*cogentis*) must reflect local practice, wherever it occurs: many were recorded at some distance from the centres of ecclesiastical administration, and they documented the ordinary business of lay people with each other, as must have happened for decades if not centuries before. Most of the miscellaneous others also occur on single sheets and to the advantage of lay beneficiaries, with the same geographical spread as that of Type 1. All of this seems to suggest that there were pockets of different practice, whether using the *cogentis* (Type 1) form or a more local variant like *adientis/agentis*, within the region of Type 2, *quoque gentis*, usage. That would therefore imply that Type 2 was by the tenth century a much more widespread common practice in the region, which had perhaps come to replace

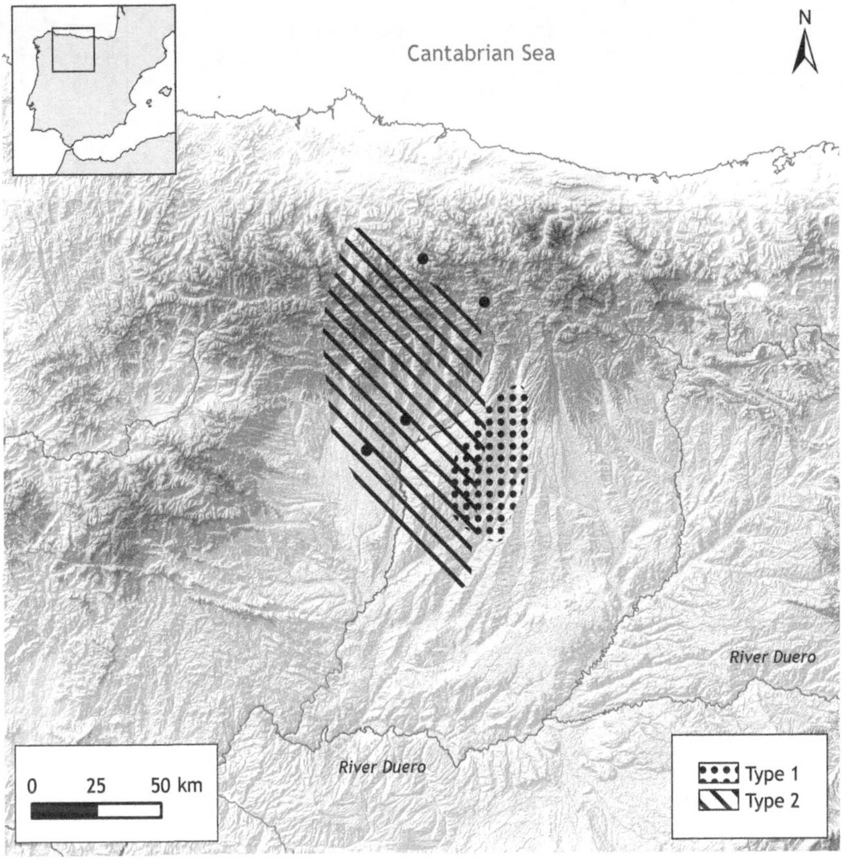

Figure 4.4 Distribution of Types 1 and 2 of the *cogentis* formula on the *meseta*

an original *cogentis* form (original because this is the form with the closest analogues beyond northern Iberia) and its more miscellaneous variants; *quoque gentis* clearly seems to have become the favoured practice of larger monasteries in the second half of the tenth century.

The local variants *adientis/adgentis/aientis/agentis* are found in both the León and Otero de las Dueñas collections, all charters being on single sheets with nearly all the beneficiaries being lay parties, although numbers of examples of these variants are small (a total of eight).[23] Although most of the beneficiaries are lay parties, three benefit monasteries. They occur in two quite separate regions: one in the zone of river confluences to the south of León (*agentis, aientis*); and the other in Valdoré and nearby places on the southern side of the Cantabrian Mountains (*adientis, adgentis, aientis*) (see Figure 4.5). Although the numbers are

23 Lii376 (964), Lii383 (965), Lii401 (967), Lii495 (984); Liii522 (988), OD8 (949), OD32 (992), OD33 (992).

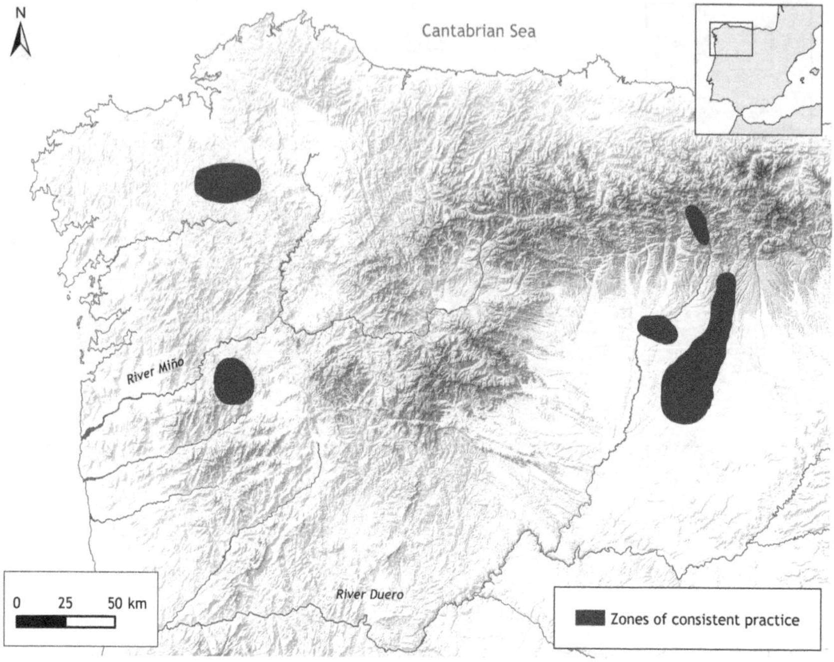

Figure 4.5 Micro-regions of variant practice in use of the *cogentis* formula

small, the single sheets and the high proportion of lay beneficiaries are significant: these look like the variant practice of two micro-regions, one a key area of continuing post-Roman use (not far from the church of Marialba, of fourth-century origin) and the other in the mountains.[24] They reinforce the suggestion that there were local pockets of consistent, sometimes variant, practice.

As for Sahagún: although relatively close to León, practice here overwhelmingly followed Type 1 (*cogentis*). A high proportion of the material is preserved in cartulary copies, but there is a significant number of single sheets and there are several lay beneficiaries; the examples of the latter presumably reflect local practice and not the standard approach of a monastic scriptorium. Nearly every variant from the *cogentis* form (including a few examples of Types 2 and 3) is in fact on a single sheet. Many of those on single sheets (Type 1 as well as others) are more limited to the north/south valleys close to Sahagún, especially the Cea valley and the plateau to the west of it. It looks as if the local practice of the Cea

24 Raquel Martínez Peñín, 'La secuencia altomedieval de la iglesia paleocristiana de Marialba de la Ribera (León)', *Estudios Humanísticos. Historia*, 6 (2007), pp. 47–64. Gisela Ripoll and Isabel Velázquez, 'Origen y desarrollo de las *parrochiae* en la *Hispania* de la antigüedad tardía', in Philippe Pergola and Palmira Maria Barbini (eds), *Alle origini della parrocchia rurale (IV–VIII sec.)* (Città del Vaticano, 1999), pp. 101–65, at pp. 123, 138–9 (with plan).

valley was mixed, but (like that of Rio Tambre) seems to have favoured Type 1 (*cogentis*); this type seems to have been picked up by the monastery's scribes and used all over its sphere of influence.

The examples that come from Oviedo and its neighbourhood are few, including both cathedral material, in cartularies and on single sheets, and material from the archive of the monastery of San Vicente, now in the monastery of San Pelayo, all single sheets. There are only two examples of the formula in the cathedral archive in this period,[25] but it occurs in some form in about three quarters of the San Vicente charters. About half use a short form of the formula, but the rest use the full formula, and they include examples of Types 1, 2 and 3 and one other variant. Scribes here seem to have been accessing at least three traditions, and I think something different may have been happening. The transactions are small-scale, for example plots with fruit trees (by the vendor's grandfather's house) sold to the priest Vicente for a hat, a goat, grain and cider in 949.[26] But there are many different scribes; and the places are all within a day's reach of Oviedo. Bearing in mind that until the early tenth century Oviedo was a royal centre, I suspect what was happening was that a pool of highly trained scribes was available there, and that transactors in its neighbourhood drew on that pool to get their records made. Hence we have local practice of a different kind: different traditions were available, and scribes chose from the traditions as their inclinations took them.

All of this shows us that there were different scribal traditions available, and that a variant, the Type 2 (*quoque gentis*) form, on an original Type 1 (*cogentis*) sale freedom formula, became a widespread standard by the mid-tenth century.[27] The number and nature of the variations on the word *cogentis* imply that it cannot have been understood at the point when the variations were coined, although some scribes continued to use it. It also shows that there are broad regions (in modern terms, two or three provinces) that show a preference for one tradition or another; but that different practices can be found within those regions, some of which – particularly when they are records which survive on single sheets, in favour of lay beneficiaries – appear to reflect local practice, apparently of much earlier origin; and that in a few cases there was a consistency of practice in a relatively small zone. These small zones include: the upper waters of the Tambre valley in northern Galicia (about 20 km long); the hinterland of Celanova in southern Galicia (about 12 km across); a zone on the southern slopes of the Cantabrian Mountains (about 14 km long); a zone across the confluence of the rivers Bernesga and Esla to the south of León (about 14 km

25 OvC32 (990), OvC33 (991).

26 Ov13.

27 But the variant must have developed well before that, since it occurs from the 870s, and perhaps from 845, in western Catalonia; Jarrett, 'Comparing the earliest documentary culture', p. 94; cf. Zimmermann, *Écrire et lire*, vol. 1, p. 278, who cites an example of 912. Given that *cogentis* occurs in the forms *coagentis* and *coagente* in the Frankish formularies of Sens and Bignon (see n. 9 above for references), loss of understanding of *cogentis* may well have occurred even earlier.

across); the Cea valley (60 km long) (see Figure 4.4). However, variation at micro-regional level was overall extremely inconsistent. Oviedo and its neighbourhood, by contrast, show scribes drawing on several traditions, so there were clearly some different approaches employed in the ninth and tenth centuries.

Other formulas

If we look at the treatment of other standard formulas, to see if the same zones had similarly consistent practice, then we immediately see how very distinctive the *cogentis* formula is. No other standard formula (and there are many) appears to have quite such striking patterns of use. Comparison is therefore extremely difficult. Variation there is in plenty, but in many formulas it can be so slight that it is impossible to attribute any significance to it. Variation also seems to operate in a different way. For example, a standard secular sanction (that is, a sanction that identifies a secular penalty) has a number of different elements – three or four distinct clauses, with a few amplifying phrases – which can feature in different combinations; the same is true of the standard price clause and to a lesser extent of the 'freedom' clauses of the disposition.[28] Sometimes there is an alternative version of one of the elements, although these alternatives rarely change the meaning of the formula; they are simply different ways of making the same point. What is astonishing is the widespread occurrence of the basic formulas, from central Portugal to northern Galicia, to the *meseta* and Castile, to Asturias and Cantabria, and less frequently to Navarre and sometimes Aragón. Given that there are early ninth-century examples of their use, they must represent a long-established tradition. The standard price clause occurs as *Pro quo accepimus de uos in pretium kauallum uaium, asinum et oues, que nobis bene conplacuit, et de ipso pretio apud uos nichil remansit in debitum*[29] ('For which we have received from you the price of a bay horse, a donkey and sheep, which is very acceptable to us, and none of that price remains owing by you'). There are two versions of the standard form of secular sanction, each of which occurs equally widely: *Si quis tamen, quod fieri non credo, contra hanc uendiccionis ad inrumpendum uenerit uel uenero, an quislibet homo de parte mea, que in iudicio uindicare non ualuero, tunc inferas uel infera, pars mea partique tue, ipsa terra duplata uel quantum ad uos fuerit meliorata* and *Si quis, tamen, que fierit minime credimus et contra han factum meum ad disrumpendum uenerit uel uenero, an fratribus, an filiis uel nepotibus meis, an de eredibus meis, an quelibet ommo, que ego uindigare non ualuero, quomodo pariet tibi ipsa terra duplata, quantum ad te fuerit meliora*[30] ('If anyone, or I myself, which

28 See above, pp. 96–7, for examples.

29 Li100 (934), a sale of land in Valdeduey to the monastery of Abellar.

30 Li125 (937), a sale to the monastery of Valdevimbre of a plot in the water meadows to the south of León; OD10 (951), a sale of land in the mountains near Noanca between lay parties. Elements of these formulas also occur in late eighth-, ninth- and early tenth-century Catalan charters; Jarrett, 'Comparing the earliest documentary culture', pp. 94–9; Zimmermann, *Écrire et lire*, pp. 369, 372, 382, 383.

I do not believe could happen, should come to break this sale/transaction, be it anyone on my side ['be it my brothers or children or grandchildren or my heirs or anyone on my side' in the second version], for which I could not provide a valid confirmation in court, then you should bring double the value of that land, or as much as seems better to you, from my part to yours ['then he/she should pay you double the value of the land' in the second version]'). Although the full forms occur often enough, it is equally common for this or that element to be omitted – for example, the fact that the very idea is incredible or the fact that the penalty could be adjusted to more than double the value of the land – and for the specification of 'anyone else' to be more or less detailed. Now, sometimes two or more charters on a single parchment, apparently written by the same scribe, will use different variants, like the two records of sales to the woman Leda (18 months apart), in the same hand, with very similar formulas but variations in the sanctions.[31] In other cases, however, two charters on a single sheet will follow the same practice: for example, two charters attributed to Durabilis, recording sales to the monastery of Abellar in Villobera nearly three months apart in 939, have minor variations, but essentially the same formulas and almost identical (deviant) spelling; and two charters recording sales to the priest Gutier on the same day in 994, probably both written by Diomaro, again have minor variations, but essentially the same formulas.[32] Frankly, it is not at all surprising that a scribe could use the same formulas on one day but introduce variations over the years, and it is certainly conceivable that some scribes could choose different formulas on the same day. Some variations therefore look as if they are simply the result of individual scribal choice, scribes clearly having a knowledge of much of the available repertoire. There are, however, pockets of what looks like the more distinctive practice of a local tradition here and there, in contrast to the varying practice of individual scribes: for example, the diplomatic of Valpuesta charters, while expressing very similar notions, is often formulated in a slightly different way;[33] moreover, omissions of one element of a standard formula sometimes look like a consistent local practice: for example, Cardeña charters often omit the 'acceptable to us' clause in the price formula, and Sobrado charters usually omit the 'confirm in court' clause from the sanction;[34] and a variant of the clause *que uindicare non ualuero* becomes common for sales in the Otero collection in the later tenth century: *que nos in concilio autorigare non ualuerimus* ('for which we could not provide a valid guarantee in

31 ACL 146 (Liii519) 17 April 987 and (Liii523) 30 October 988.

32 ACL 818 (Li132) 2 September 939 and (Li135) 23 November 939; I have argued elsewhere that Durabilis was local to Villobera rather than a member of the Abellar scriptorium; Wendy Davies, 'Local priests and the writing of charters in northern Iberia in the tenth century', in Julio Escalona and Hélène Sirantoine (eds), *Chartes et cartulaires comme instruments de pouvoir* (Toulouse, 2013), pp. 29–43, at p. 33. See also above, pp. 70–2. Gutier: ACL 157 (Liii563 and Liii564) 28 February 994.

33 For example, *Et accepimus pretjum de uos carnario, quod inter nos pacifice conuenit, quod uos dedistis et nos ad integrum accepissemus*, V24 (950).

34 On the significance of the 'confirm in court' phrase, see further below, pp. 119–20.

a public assembly').[35] Those writing for the priest Braolio in the Cantabrian Mountains in the late tenth century had a habit of writing *uoluero* for *ualuero* in the clause *que uindicare non ualuero*.[36] This still makes sense, but it may represent a misunderstanding of the formula by a small group of scribes.

So, while individual scribal choice seems to have played a part in some areas, sustaining a local tradition seems to have determined practice in others. There are two variations on the standard formulas of price clause and sanction which seem to indicate different regional habits. In the case of the price clause, a phrase indicating that the payment has been completed is sometimes added: *nichil remansit in debito, set omnia nobis bene conplestis* ('nothing remains owing and you have satisfactorily completed everything for us').[37] This is particularly characteristic of charters constructed in and around León, with a few examples from Sahagún and a corrupt form from Otero de las Dueñas.[38] There are also occasional examples of it in a passive form (*totum completum est*) from León and Otero, as also from Celanova and Samos in Galicia and from Oviedo cathedral in the north; however, the 'completing' phrase seems to be absent from most Galician collections (Lugo, Sobrado and La Coruña), from Castilian and Navarre collections (Cardeña, Valpuesta, Arlanza, San Millán and Albelda) and from the Liébana (Santo Toribio). The Otero corruption clearly did not become a sustained tradition.[39] This was basically *meseta* practice, and particularly that part of the *meseta* close to León; in other words, one could say that there is a loose (but imperfect) correlation with the *quoque gentis* distribution.

The second variation with regional significance occurs in the sanction, where the phrase listing those prohibited from interfering is expanded to include any substitute (what Zimmermann called a 'field of culpability'): *ad disrumpendum uenerit uel uenero an ego an subrinis uel quelibet subrogata persona* ('should come to disrupt [this transaction], be it I myself or cousins or any kind of substitute person').[40] This amplification is common on the *meseta*, including Castile, and

35 Cf. the Fines OD37 (994), OD40 (995). *Autorigare* appears more often in eleventh-century charters (cf. Liii866–870, all sales of 1030, all but no. 869 on the same single sheet). However, a version of the formula appears on a single sheet of 878 from northern Galicia (*in iuditio defenditare et obtorgare noluerimus*), LaC8; *autorifico* is clear in the text of C88, a confirmation charter of 955, and is differentiated from the more general *roboro* ('confirm'); and the Otero series starts in 963 (OD13). Luis García de Valdeavellano, 'Escodriñamiento y otorificación (contribución al estudio de la reivindicación mobiliaria en el derecho español medieval)', in *Centenario de la ley del notariado. Sección primera: estudios históricos* (2 vols, Madrid, 1965), vol. 2, pp. 125–335, at pp. 274–324, demonstrates unambiguously that the meaning of *autorigare* is to provide guarantees of the legitimate possession of a thing purchased.

36 Braolio as purchaser: OD13 (963), OD14 (964), OD15 (964), OD16 (964), OD19 (974); cf. OD17 (973) for the purchaser Fruela Muñoz, where *ualaero* has been overwritten to give *uoluero*.

37 Lii372 (964), sale between lay parties of a portion of property in Méizara.

38 OD11 (961), 'set omnia nobis adimplistis', sale between lay parties of land in *Tiulia* (probably Tolibia, Valdelugueros).

39 Cf. 'set omnia ad implestir', Ov5 (917), a sale between lay parties, but I have not seen any other examples.

40 S133 (951), a gift (with Incidental reference to a court case) from one priest to another of land on the River Porma. Cf. Zimmermann, *Écrire et lire*, vol. 1, pp. 380–82.

in the north; it occurs extremely rarely in Galicia, Navarre and Aragón.[41] On the *meseta* and in the Liébana, it also occurs in the alternative spellings *subrogita* and – much more rarely – *subroita, surogita, suroita.*[42] Orthographic variations of this particular kind might well reflect speech and perhaps imply that the word was commonly spoken in those areas. It is notable that charters on single sheets in the Sahagún collection use the latter (*subrogita*) forms, whereas charters from the cartulary use the more classical form; this suggests that the *subrogita* spelling (and other variants) was the norm in that area at the time of recording the transactions, whereas the spelling of cartulary copies was 'improved' as the copy was made. The point is reinforced by the extreme range of forms used in the single sheets of the Otero collection and by use of *subrogita* on single sheets in most other collections, although it is not invariable. There is also an interesting variant, using *subposita* or *supposita* or *suposita*: *inrumpendum uenerit uel uenero, an per me, an per qualibet subposita* ('should disrupt [this transaction), be it through me or through any kind of substitute').[43] The meaning is not significantly different, but the word is, although this variant can be found in charter sanctions in other parts of Europe, especially Italy;[44] the formulation *uel de aliqua supposita rogata*, duplicating the substitute point, looks like a corruption.[45] This variant is found on the *meseta* and also in Galicia, although it is in general rare, and particularly rare in Galicia; it does not occur in Castile. Overall, however, distribution of *conplestis* and *suposita* habits broadly mirrors that of *quoque gentis*.

These observations suggest that there was some consistent local practice in the application of long-standing traditions in framing charters. However, although these differences are interesting and suggest some broad regional distinctions in practice, they do not precisely mirror the *cogentis* distinctions. One cannot therefore suggest that there were discretely different approaches to the framing of charters in different regions.

Given that this enquiry is complicated by the fact of copying into cartularies and making changes in the process of so doing, do we find clearer patterns if we restrict the enquiry to single sheets, and especially to sales between lay

41 But it does feature in the Ripoll formulary; Zimmermann, 'Un formulaire', p. 78.

42 For example, S200 (962), a Grajal sale; E27 (957), a gift from Cañones; OD23 (978), a gift of properties near Oncina; OD40 (995), a gift from Posadilla, and on the same parchment *suprogita*, OD41 (995), another gift on the same day to the same lay beneficiary, recorded by the same scribe. Note also *surogidat* (Ov14 (950)), *subrogida* (OD44 (998)), *suroida* (S170 (959)), *subrogota* (PMH DC 114 (974)).

43 Li9 (894), a sale between lay parties of two houses on the River Torío.

44 See Fritz Boye, 'Über die Poenformeln in den Urkunden des früheren Mittelalters', *Archiv für Urkundenforschung*, 6 (1918), pp. 77–148, at pp. 95–100; I am grateful to Bernhard Zeller for this reference.

45 Li96 (932), a sale to the monastery of Abellar of land on the River Torío; cf. Li124 (937), also a sale to Abellar, this time of land on the River Esla; in the Fine record Liii590 (999), *subposita* and *subrogita* are both included in an additional sanction appended to the main text; *subrogita* does not appear to have been understood (*de Aloitu et de suas uxores subrogita et de aliquis homo*). Cf. the single-sheet Agreement Liii597 (1000), *si aliquis suposta . . . ac per aliqua suroita persona.*

parties – that is, for the most part to records of everyday local practice on sheets which may well have been originals? Records made in and around León in the first half of the tenth century commonly have these elements: *Placuit nobis atque conuenit nullius quoque gentis imperio nec suadentis articulo sed propria nobis accessit uoluntas ut uinderemus . . . accepimus de uos in pretium . . . que nobis bene conplacuit, et de ipso pretio apud uos nichil remansit, sed omni nobis bene conplistis . . . Ita ut ab odierno die uel tempore NN de meo iure sit abrasa et in tuo iure sit tradita, abeas [adeas, teneas, uindices ac defendas] tu et omnis posteritas tuas . . . Si quis contra hanc uendicc-ionis ad inrumpendum uenerit uel uenero, an ego uel quemlibet subrogata persona, que in iudicio uindicare non ualuero, quomodo pariet* [or other 'handing over' words] *tibi ipsa NN duplata uel quantum ad te fuerit meliorata.*[46] This looks like a package that constitutes regional practice; notably, it includes both the *conplestis* and the *subrogata* formulas (the latter also in the *supposita* form); it should also be noted that the variant spellings of *quoque gentis* are extreme in these cases (*quequoigentis, cumegentis, quegentis, qoogentis, coque uacentis*), once again strongly suggesting that the phrase cannot have been understood at the time these charters were framed, in the mid-tenth century.[47] There is a form which truncates the opening formula to *bono animo* [*et pacis uoluntate*] or [*et expontanea mea uolumtate*] without the *quoque gentis* phrase, particularly in the Cantabrian Mountains and farther north, although this too seems not to have been understood: *bone pacis uoluntas et animus conplaciendit, bono animo pacis et spontaneas nostras uoluntates, bono animo et propria nouis fuit uoluntas*; these charters often include (*in*) *debitum* in the price clause.[48] Such variation is not inevitable, however, and other mountain texts use the *quoque gentis* form. Notably, in the second half of the tenth century elements of the package continue, but occur less consistently together – it is as if communication was extending and traditions became more mixed.[49]

This suggests that elements of a standard way of recording sales between lay parties are particularly reflected in and around León and in the mountains in the ninth and earlier tenth century, but that that standard had broken down by the later tenth century; moreover, the standard was not used consistently even in the earlier period. Indeed, since there are variants within a single region even in the ninth-century corpus, it is impossible to identify distinctive and consistent regional practice. But there were certainly tendencies to include or prefer one element or another, by broad region. Indeed, the León 'package', without

46 For example, Li97 (933), Li162 (943) and Li205 (949) have all the elements, as do Ov14 (950), except for the *meliorata* clause, and C93 (958), except for the *conplestis* clause. As mentioned in n. 30 above, late eighth- and ninth-century Catalan charters also include several of these elements.

47 For example, Li13 (898), Li25 (910), Li205 (949), Lii361 (963). Zimmermann, *Écrire et lire*, vol. 1, p. 278, makes essentially the same point.

48 OD3 (936), OD7 (949), S136 (952) for the 'standard' truncations; Li60 (923), Li158 (942), and Piasca texts like S1 (857) for the variants – see the Lugo example in n. 11 above for the full form of words. Also reflected in Cañ30 (929), *placuit nobis bone pacis uoluntas*.

49 Cf. Calleja Puerta's comments on the mixing of elements of *Fórmulas visigóticas* in the tenth century in 'Ecos de las *Fórmulas visigóticas*'.

the *conplestis* and the *subrogata/supposita* formulas, and with a truncated form of the opening formula, occurs from Galicia across the *meseta*. Portuguese charters, for example, almost invariably use the truncated form of the opening formula: *plaguit mici bona pacis uolumtas ut uindere, plaguit nobis bone pacis uolumtas ut uindere, plaguit nobis per bone pacis uolumtas ut uenderemus*; and in the sanction they tend to use [*ad iudicio*] *deuindigare* for *in iudicio uindicare non ualuero*: *ad inrumpendum contra hanc kartula uenditionis que nos ad iudicio deuendicare non potuerimus que pariemus ad uobis* . . .[50] It is, then, use of the elements of formulas that can have local or regional significance – and it is the elements of formulas, rather than whole charters, that can suggest shared practice.

Trying to make sense of all the variations is as complex as trying to figure out the multiple variations in early medieval readings of the psalms and of chants – a particularly appropriate analogy given that formulas were used in chants.[51] Just as individual verses of psalms could circulate separately, and segments of the formulas of chants, it is presumably the case that individual charter formulas and even sections of charter formulas might have had separate circulation and transmission. Just as transmission of the elements of chant happened as a 'melodic vocabulary and a set of principles', in Rebecca Maloy's words, rather than as distinct individual melodies, perhaps we should be thinking of the transmission of charter formulas in the same way.[52] It was, perhaps, the vocabularies which were transmitted from generation to generation and from which the redactors chose in creating their texts – just as Martianus Capella has Lady Dialectic choosing an apposite phrase from a set of formulas inscribed on wax tablets.[53]

One would expect memory and aural training to have played a significant part in such transmission processes.[54] Clearly, the range of writing practice that can be seen in charters of the tenth century has other elements too: almost all the formulas of some charters were evidently copied from other charters and, since formularies existed, model documents were doubtless sometimes used too. Moreover, as argued above, it looks as if some individual scribes would pick and choose from a wide common palette, regardless of local tradition, preferring one or a group of formulas and changing their preferences from time to

50 PMH DC 41 (936), PMH DC 102 (971), PMH DC 155 (988); PMH DC 10 (883). Cf. José Mattoso, 'Sanctio (875–1100)', *Revista portuguesa de história*, 13 (1971), pp. 299–338, at p. 309.

51 See Rebecca Maloy, *Inside the Offertory: Aspects of Chronology and Transmission* (Oxford, 2010), especially ch. 2; see ibid., pp. 90–100, for formulas.

52 Ibid., pp. 87, 105, 135. Compare also the dissemination of glosses independently of the canon law texts on which they commented in early medieval western Europe; Abigail Firey, 'Canon law in the Carolingian era', in John C. Wei and Anders Winroth (eds), *Cambridge History of Medieval Canon Law* (Cambridge, forthcoming).

53 *Martianus Capella*, ed. James Willis (Leipzig, 1983), pp. 106–7 (= *De nuptiis Philologiae et Mercurii*, Liber IV de arte dialectica, § 328). I am very grateful to Irene van Renswoude for this reference.

54 Note the importance of memory in the transmission of chant: Emma Hornby and Rebecca Maloy comment that the textual variants on the text on which the chant *Deus laudabilis* is based 'attest to the role of memory in the transmission of Old Hispanic chant texts' in *Music and Meaning in Old Hispanic Lenten Chants: Psalmi, Threni and the Easter Vigil Canticles* (Woodbridge, 2013), p. 152.

time. Indeed, if one takes an example from the later tenth century of the records of seven transactions involving the priest Munio on a single sheet, it is clear that in a single neighbourhood, within a single year, involving the same group of people (the witnesses overlap), the formulas used could vary (see Figure 3.3).[55] The diplomatic is basically the same for all the records, but most miss out one or two elements, while the fifth and sixth (which are very close to the 'standard' León package) use *uoluntas* for the opening formulas rather than *quoque egentis* [*sic*], and the fifth adds *subroita* while the sixth adds *conplesti*.[56] There are also differences in orthography and in the way the locations are described. Recording in this locality fairly late in the tenth century was clearly not consistent; as already suggested by analysis of the *cogentis* formula, variation at micro-regional level could be very inconsistent.

So by the late tenth century, practice was very mixed. There was the shared experience of local tradition, of much earlier origin, still continuing in some parts, but clearly breaking down in the later tenth century; there was copying from written texts, whether existing charters or model documents; and there was individual scribal choice from a set of vocabularies, a palette of formulas.

Judgment language

There are some variants on formulas which make a rather different set of points about formulaic writing, but are particularly apposite when considering judicial process; these variations are sometimes reflected in the preambles and dispositions of charters, but occur more frequently in sanctions. These are the phrases that explicitly invoke the notion of judgment, particularly in the context of the Last Judgment. In the preambles and dispositions of charters, such phrases are associated with the reason for giving in the dispositive words of some texts: 'I give this so that you will support us at the day of the great judgment' (*ut ad diem magni iuditii subueniat nobis*); or 'when the Lord appears clearly to everyone to give judgment on the day of examination' (*in die examinis quando Dominus apparuerit cunctis manifeste ad faciendum iudicium*); or 'so that before the tribunal of our Lord Jesus Christ we will be worthy to find pardon for our sins' (*ut mereamur ante tribunal Domini nostri Ihesu Christi inuenire ueniam delictis nostris*).[57] Much more frequently, however, the Day of Judgment is invoked in sanctions, as a deterrent to interfering with a gift: if I or my relations or anyone else should revoke this gift, 'when he comes before the tribunal of the Lord . . .' (*dum uenerit ante tribunal Domini . . .*); or 'he will be condemned at the future judgment' (or 'on the day of the great judgment', or 'the day of examination of the wicked', or even 'the terrible' or 'terrifying judgment') (*in futuro iudicio . . . condemnatus*,

55 ACL 7255, records from 11 October 978 to 1 October 979; see above, pp. 70–1.

56 In the order of copying on to the sheet: Lii471 (1 October 979), Lii457 (11 October 978), Lii458 (11 October 978), Lii459 (11 October 978), Lii465 (31 January 979), Lii467 (17 February 979), and the note Lii472; five are sales, but the second and third are payments in settlement of disputes.

57 Cel246 (969); C82 (952); Liii570 (995).

in diem magni iuditii non resurgat, in diem examinationis reproborum, tempore terribili iudicii sui, in die illa tremenda iudicii).[58]

These formulations invoking the Last Judgment are particularly interesting in the present context because of the explicit references to judgment and its potentially adverse consequences. The references are widespread, but overall numbers of them are quite small, occurring in about 6 per cent of the total corpus of charters. They occur in cartulary copies and on single sheets, in charters from the early ninth century onwards, with relatively few in ninth-century contexts and relatively many (60 per cent) in the second half of the tenth century. This temporal distribution on the whole reflects the availability of charters, since far more charters survive from the tenth century, particularly from the middle of the century, although the weighting towards the end of the tenth century is disproportionate. Such formulas occur overwhelmingly in records of gifts to monasteries, although they also appear in a few records of sales to the monastery of Cardeña and very occasionally elsewhere.[59] They are not characteristic of records of transactions between lay persons, and do not appear to be an aspect of the long-established diplomatic tradition used for secular acts.[60] As such, one would not therefore expect to find the kinds of variation and corruption that characterize that tradition, as discussed above. The expressions are, however, more characteristic of some collections and regions than others, notably those of Cardeña, León (in records of the monastery of Abellar especially), Sahagún and Celanova, where they were clearly adopted at some periods as the normal diplomatic practice of the major monastery, although this does not mean that smaller monasteries did not sometimes use them as well: they feature in records of gifts to some of the smaller monasteries that feature in the León collections and in the Cardeña cartulary.[61] By contrast, although there is sometimes an occasional citation of such formulas, they are extremely rare in collections from Portugal, Samos, Sobrado, La Coruña, Otero, Oviedo, Albelda and San Millán, a list which includes some major monasteries with very active scriptoria (see Figure 4.6). There is also little correlation with collections which have significant numbers of dispute records: although both the León and Celanova collections certainly include many dispute records, so do those of Sobrado, Portugal and Otero, whereas those of Cardeña have relatively few; warnings of heavenly judgment clearly did not match an interest in keeping records of earthly cases. All of that being the case, it looks as if the

58 OD21 (976); Lii265 (954); Sam164 (989), A19 (950), S39 (930), Liii520 (987). Also reflected in the words of the oath in Gil (ed.), 'Formulae Wisigothicae', § 39; see further below, pp. 125–6.

59 See further below, pp. 116–17.

60 It is possible that the sale of C121 (965) was between lay parties, as it appears from the text, but the object of the sale was three parts of the church of San Martín, and it is likely that the purchaser, Gómez, was in fact a monk; a Gómez was a monk of San Martín in Villabáscones when it was given to Cardeña by its community, C108 (963), and he could well have remained in charge of that community, buying out the remaining interests of the lay locals in the monastery which they had originally founded (C45 (944–50)). Cf. also Brother Gómez of Cardeña, C190 (982).

61 For example, Li83 (929), Liii555 (993), Liii570 (995); C43 (944), C85 (954), C118 (964).

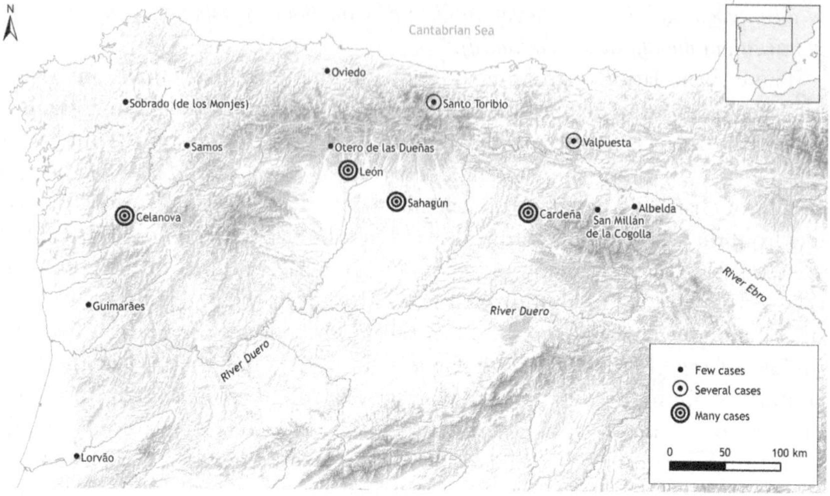

Figure 4.6 Distribution of charter collections which use Last Judgment language

differences in practice could result from the preferences of individual scribes and, especially, individual scriptoria rather than the simple fact of the strength of ecclesiastical interest.

Where these formulas occur in preamble or disposition, which – as noted above – is relatively rare, the charter almost invariably records a major gift, either from a high aristocrat or to a female community. The formula can be part of a long expression of piety: in a very long passage extolling the greatness and goodness of God and requesting mercy, in Fruela's charter of gift to his brother Bishop Rosendo of the site (and appurtenant properties) on which to build the monastery of Celanova, we find:

> Oh Lord you are a just judge. . . . When you appear, great and clearly visible, on high in sublime glory, at the day of reckoning, in order to give rewards to the just and evil to the wicked who deserve it, then may I be far from those evil ones and, as a man made clean, may I be worthy to mingle with the sheep to which from the beginning your father agreed to give the kingdom. . . . [I give everything to the Lord] as a result of which there will be a great reward for them [his parents] and for me at the eternal judgment 'since to each shall be returned in accordance with his/her own works'.[62]

62 *Domine tu es iustus iudex . . . Ut dum in examinis diem apparueris magnus et manifestus et in sublimi gloria excelsus reddere iustis premia, et malis que merentur mala, tum ego ab ipsis procul sim, et merear admisceri mundus ouibus quibus ab initio a patre tuo complacuit dare regnum . . .* [*Omnia dono Domino*] *qualiter illis et mihi magna occurrat mercis in eterno iudicio 'dum unicuique redditum fuerit secundum propria opera'*, Cel256 (12 September 936). I am grateful to Jinty Nelson for improving my translation of these passages. For sheep, see below, p. 118.

Not so lengthy, but still elaborately, the charter recording Vermudo Núñez's gift of a trading place in the market of Cea to the monastery of Sahagún prefaces its request for intercession with:

> I Vermudo, oppressed by the burden of sin, terrified by fear of the excessive punishments of hell, since I know that I must be judged for all my deserts at the last judgment; and therefore I collapse in the utmost despair, because I am alarmed with the witness of conscience; but what I am afraid to ask for through my own merits, I very often seek the support of the saints to grant because I know with certainty that the requests of the saints will have the strength to obtain for [this] sinner nothing of what his crimes deserve.[63]

Both donors inhabited royal circles, Fruela being first cousin of King Ramiro II of León and Vermudo a prominent aristocrat of the Cea valley;[64] Fruela's charter is attributed to the royal scribe Aloyto, although perhaps we might detect Rosendo's own drafting; Vermudo's was written by the Sahagún scribe Belido.[65] Less elaborately, but with the same sentiments, the record of the priest Sindamiro's gift of a substantial farm and stock, as well as vineyards, to the nunnery of Santiago in León has:

> I quake in the presence of the Lord Jesus Christ on the great day of judgment, like someone entirely stripped of good works, but yet with all the martyrs, virgins and confessors to rejoice for ever with the holy apostles, amen. . . . And as much as you shall find you have from me, you shall have and possess, so that, on the day of the great judgment, by your intercession I shall be worthy to be cleansed of my sins for as long as the Lord shall reign with his saints.[66]

It was written or redacted by the priest Iohannes, who may have been a member of the community, given that he wrote other charters for Santiago.[67]

Sindamiro's charter concludes with a sanction in the same vein: 'if anyone should try to break what I have arranged, firstly may the wrath of God descend on him and, living, may he lose the sight from his eyes [literally, 'lights from his brows'], and with Judas, the traitor of the Lord, may he bewail his punishments

63 *Ego Uermudo . . . mole peccatorum depressus, nimium gehenne penarum metu territus cum scio cunctis me pro meritis ultimi iudicii iudicandus et ideo me usque minime in desperacione deicio quia teste consciencia teste pauesco sed illut quod de propriis meritis impetrari pertimesco iubari sanctorum suffragia sepissime obto quia certissime sciens ualebunt impetrare postulaciones sanctorum quod peccatori ne quid promere flagiciorum*, S130 (31 January 951). Cf. the gift of Countess Justa, S355 (997).

64 Vermudo: S129 (950).

65 Cf. S34 (927–30), S51 (933).

66 *paueo presentia Domini Ihesu Christi et diem magnum iudici ut ad instar bonis operibus nudati et cum sanctis apostolis et omnes martires, uirgines et confessores exultare in secula, amen. . . . Et quantum inueneritis a parte mea . . . abeatis, possideatis, ut in die magni iudicci per uestra intercessione merear mundare a criminibus meis quantum regnare faciat Dominus cum sanctis*; Liii555 (3 January 993).

67 For example Liii586 (999), a sale conducted in the council of the monastery.

in eternal damnation', as well as specifying a fine of 500 *solidi* to the king.[68] As already indicated, reference, or allusion, to the Day of Judgment occurs much more frequently in sanctions than in dispositions or preambles, although it is still largely to be found in records of gifts to monasteries. The social range of the donors of charters using such sanctions, however, is much wider than that of donors of charters with dispositions using such notions. There are gifts made by kings and royal associates, by abbots and monks, by bishops, priests and deacons, by religious women, often using extreme expressions, like 'seeing [in error for 'living'? that is, 'in life'] may he lack both lamps in his brow, and after death may his [literally, 'their'] body not be buried with other Christians nor may his spirit join the society of the chosen, but on that day of terrible judgment, may his place be on the left side [that is the 'wrong' side] with those condemned and may he be then delivered over with the devil to punishments in eternal damnation',[69] by widows, and by wealthy and not so wealthy men and couples.[70] Of these, about three-quarters are lay donors, and in the order of three-quarters of those are clearly aristocrats, although it is notable that the associated donations include some quite small gifts. The judgment formulas are framed as straightforward warnings, particularly to the family of the donor, not to revoke the gift.

There are some limited exceptions to these patterns. More than half of the beneficiaries of gifts protected in this way are large, established monasteries or cathedrals, and nearly a third are less prominent monasteries. The exceptions remain religious: the beneficiaries named in such charters include an abbot, a few priests, a deacon, and one abbot gave his church to his sister and her deacon cousin.[71] The practice, therefore, is entirely ecclesiastical and is overwhelmingly monastic. The gifts which are the object of these charters are also overwhelmingly large gifts – whole estates, groups of estates, scatters of property in different locations, churches and their appurtenances – but about a fifth are clearly much smaller. These may be a field, a vineyard or a share of water rights, like Hermenegildo and his wife Zita's gift of a plot in Oteros to Santos Justo y Pastor in 959.[72] Records of small gifts associated with warning sanctions tend to occur in southern Galicia, in the *meseta* around León and in Castile, but not elsewhere. Since there are plenty of records of small gifts to monasteries that do not have sanctions warning of the Day of Judgment, it seems possible that their occurrence was specific to these particular donors – an intentionally strong warning directed towards an over-powerful or unreliable family, intended to

68 *si hunc meum factum aliquis homo inrumpere conauerit, inprimis ira Dei descendat super eum et ad frontibus suis uiuens careat luminibus et cum Iuda Domini traditore lugeat penas in eterna dampnatione.*

69 *ambobus a fronte uidens* [recte *uiuens?*] *suis kareat lucernis, post discessum uero eius cadauera sua non sepeliantur* [*sic*] *cum ceteris christianis nec spiritus societur cum electis, set in die illa tremendi iudicii cum reprobis pars illius sit ad sinistris, deinde cum diabolo in eterna dampnatione mancipetur penis.*

70 For example: Li79 (928), S155 (957); Li83 (929), Sam164 (989); S30 (922), S165 (959); Liii520 (987); C32 (939), Ov20 (978); Li177 (943), S123 (950); Liii536 (990?), S351 (996). For the latter, see Mathew 25:31–41; see below, p. 118.

71 Li83 (929), a single sheet.

72 Lii313.

shock when the charter was read out on a public occasion. Because they occur sporadically, this is the most obvious explanation. Although they are more characteristic of the second half of the tenth century, they do occur earlier. Records of other kinds of transaction (sales and a very occasional exchange) using such sanctions involve sales of small properties to the monastery of Cardeña or to other monasteries in that neighbourhood (there is a larger one to a priest in that area).[73] This practice is so clearly confined to that part of Castile that it presumably reflects a distinctive practice of the local region: some records of sales to monasteries were given religious sanctions evoking the Day of Judgment. Now, there are plenty of sales to monasteries, including Cardeña, which do not have this kind of formula; their sanctions usually utter a simple curse and state the secular penalty, or just do the latter; it seems possible, again – given the sporadic incidence of the judgment references – that the embellished sanctions were intentional and specific to those vendors.

Although the discussion so far has focused on formulas which specify the Last Judgment, it should be noted that the notion of a final judgment is implicit in many more formulas, particularly in those of sanctions. Fearing the sulphurous flames, condemned to the abyss of hell, constrained to share with Judas Iscariot the lower depths, all imply the consequences of judgment, although they do not refer to it explicitly, just as the requests for intercession imply the prospect of it.[74] So we find 'the wrath of God shall descend on him as it did on Dathan and Abiron, whom the earth swallowed up for their crime' (*descendat super illum iram Dei sicut descendit super Datam et Abiron, quos terra obsorbuit pro suo scelere*), protecting the gift of a church to the monastery of San Martín, Turieno; 'he shall join Judas, who betrayed the Lord, in the lower depths' (*cum Iuda, qui Dominum tradidit, participium habeat in infernum*), a warning attached to the gift to Cardeña of a modest share in a saltpan; 'he shall be excluded from the company of all the holy martyrs and be punished with the devil in perpetual hell' (*seclusus maneat a consorcio omnium sanctorum martirum set cum diabulo pena sit multatus in geenna perpetua*), of a royal gift of estates to Sahagún; 'in the sight of the Holy Spirit and of the martyrs of Christ he shall repeatedly be cursed, that is, damned to double ruin and damnation, so that like Dathan and Abiron he will forthwith be swallowed up at a stroke, still alive, and will bear the terrible penalties of everlasting torture with Judas, betrayor of the Lord' (*sit etiam in conspectu Sancti Spiritus et martirum Christi reppetita anathema maranata, id est, duplici perdictione damnatione damnatus et ut de hoc seculo sicut Datan et Auiron uibos continuo obsorueatur iatu* [recte *ictu*?] *et tartareas penas cum Iuda Domini proditore perenni perferat cruciatu in eterna damnatione*), of another royal gift; 'separated from divine company, he shall be rolled over and over with the deceitful one in the darkness of the abyss; and he shall have death without life, pain without end, torment without

73 C28 (936), C31 (939), C87 (955), C93 (958), C112 (963), C193 (984); C145 (969) to the priest Iñigo.

74 The record of Bishop Frunimio's gift to León cathedral does explicitly associate Judas with judgment, *et iudicium Iudes Scariotes summat*, Li6 (874).

release, and – punished with the most frightful ruin – he shall be lodged in one place with Judas, betrayer of the Lord, in the blackest, outermost darkness, for ever' (*separatus a diuino consorcio baratri caligine uoluatur cum dolo . . . et sit illi mors sine uita, pena sine termino, cruciatu fine* [recte *sine*?] *defectu et inmanissima strage multatus cum Iuda Domini proditore uno contubernietur in loco in tenebris exterioribus et caligosis longo per evo*), of the bishop of Santiago's gift to Celanova.[75] Without always going to the latter extremes, damnation alongside Judas was a common part of the sanction in charters of the big monasteries of Celanova, Cardeña and Sahagún, and of Portuguese Guimarães; it is again particularly characteristic of records of gifts to monasteries.[76]

This kind of writing is clearly characteristic of explicitly monastic diplomatic, employed as threat in the battle to secure gifts in perpetuity; to some extent, it was representative of monastic thinking. The note appended to a royal scribe's subscription to his record of a gift by King Sancho Garcés II Abarca of Navarre is explicit: 'I, Acisclo, have written this myself. Remember me if you find Christ merciful on the day of judgment' (*Acisclus . . . manu propria scripsi. Mementote michi si pium habeatis Christum in diem iudicii*).[77] The frequent occurrence of this kind of writing in forgeries reinforces the point, such as those in the series of fabricated records of royal gifts to Abellar.[78] All of this means that the notion of judgment was deeply embedded in the literate culture of the age. This is hardly surprising, as it was after all a recurrent theme of both Old Testament and New: 'O let the nations be glad and sing for joy: for thou shalt judge the people righteously' (Psalm 67:4); or 'False witnesses did rise up . . . Judge me, O Lord my God, according to thy righteousness' (Psalm 35:11, 24); or 'Thou, even thou, art to be feared: and who may stand in thy sight when once thou art angry? Thou didst cause judgment to be heard from heaven; the earth feared and was still. When God arose to judgment, to save all the meek of the earth' (Psalm 76:7–9); or 'But I say unto you, that every idle word that men shall speak, they shall give account thereof in the day of judgment' (Matthew 12:36); or 'When the son of man shall come in his glory . . . And before him shall be gathered all nations: and he shall separate them one from another, as a shepherd divideth his sheep from the goats. And he shall set the sheep on his right hand, but the goats on the left . . . Then shall he say unto them on the left hand, Depart from me, ye cursed, into everlasting fire, prepared for the Devil and his angels' (Matthew 25:31–41).[79] These were familiar concepts to those

75 T5 (828); C30 (937); S99 (945), a single sheet; S183 (960), also a single sheet; Cel461 (982). References to the traitor Judas and to the fate of Dathan and Abiron are also common in Catalan charters; see Zimmermann, *Écrire et lire*, pp. 389–402; both occur in Gil (ed.), 'Formulae Wisigothicae', e.g. nos 5, 7, 24, 39, 45, as does the Day of Judgment (cf. Zimmermann, 'Un formulaire', p. 79). Cf. Mattoso, 'Sanctio', pp. 314–21.

76 Cf. Mattoso's comprehensive analysis of elements of Portuguese sanctions in 'Sanctio'; see ibid., pp. 332–3 for the Celanova/Guimarães similarity.

77 A29 (985).

78 Li50 (920), Li54, Li55, Li56 (all 921). However, genuine ones have curses too.

79 Translations, and numbering, are of the Authorised version (for Vulgate numbers of psalms subtract 1; that is, Authorised Psalm 76 is Vulgate Psalm 75).

who followed the monastic day, or shorter rituals, and repeated the psalms as the liturgy required; and indeed, it is notable that many parts of western European liturgies pick up and repeat the judgment phrases from the psalms.[80] We know that such psalm-influenced liturgical practice is directly relevant in considering northern Iberia because of the evidence of the tenth-century Antiphonary of León: in that service book, Psalm 35 (cited above) is a source for the chant *Exsurge . . . et intende*, prominent in Passiontide services, and it is the basis for antiphons (such as *Iudica domine*) for Friday and Saturday of the fourth week;[81] and Psalm 109:7 ('When he shall be judged, let him be condemned') is a source for the *Deus laudabilis* chant for nones on Maundy Thursday.[82] Judgment language runs through and through this Antiphonary, and especially the repeated *Iudica me* of the Passiontide.[83] Indeed, one Otero charter, recording a gift to Santa Eulalia de Airas, specified support for the community of sisters *ad psalendum (et meditandum reculam monasterii et ofitia dibina)*.[84] There are, of course, analogues in ninth- to eleventh-century charters from France and other areas, as often discussed.[85] It is therefore not at all surprising to find judgment expressions borrowed into the language of northern Iberian charters. How far the ideas were communicated beyond the monastery is certainly arguable, but the ideas had the potential for impact on the culture of the judicial court, on the exercise of judicial practice and on the conduct of public meetings.

There is a further point to be made about sanction formulas: the sanction formulas that refer to confirmation in court have an important bearing on actual experience of judicial practice. It is particularly interesting that 'going to court' was a regular element of secular sanctions: *que in iudicio uindicare non ualuero*, referring to interference in a transfer of property that could not be justified in court;[86] it is more characteristic of La Coruña, Sobrado, León and Otero charters than of others (although there are versions of a comparable notion in Portuguese charters, in charters from the Liébana and in those of the Cardeña

80 Note Julia Barrow's recent book on the clergy in western Europe for the importance of regular psalm singing, *The Clergy in the Medieval World: Secular Clerics, Their Families and Careers in North-western Europe, c.800–c.1200* (Cambridge, 2015), e.g. pp. 43–4. For the influence of the psalms on the formulation of the wording of the liturgy itself, see Hornby and Maloy, *Music and Meaning, passim*, but especially pp. 155–243, for example, and Maloy, *Inside the Offertory*, pp. 50–57.

81 Antiphonary of León for Lent (ACL MS 8), fo. 138v, cf. ff. 141r, 144v (*Antifonario visigótico mozárabe de la catedral de León*, ed. Louis Brou and José Vives (Barcelona and Madrid, 1959), pp. 214–15, 221, 227); Hornby and Maloy, *Music and Meaning*, pp. 110, 165–7.

82 Antiphonary of León, fo. 163r (p. 265); Hornby and Maloy, *Music and Meaning*, pp. 57–8 (noting 'a long exegetical association with the Passion and Judas's betrayal of Jesus'), 310.

83 For example, Antiphonary of León, ff. 159v, 170v, 171v; 114r (*Antifonario visigótico mozárabe*, ed. Brou and Vives, pp. 259, 277, 280; 164).

84 OD29 (988).

85 See Lester K. Little, 'Anger in monastic curses', in Barbara H. Rosenwein (ed.), *Anger's Past: The Social Uses of an Emotion in the Middle Ages* (Ithaca, NY, 1998), pp. 9–35, at pp. 11–12; see also Wendy Davies, 'Anger and the Celtic saint', in Rosenwein (ed.), *Anger's Past*, pp. 191–202, at pp. 193–4. Lester K. Little, *Benedictine Maledictions: Liturgical Cursing in Romanesque France* (Ithaca, NY, 1993), especially pp. 52–85, draws attention on pp. 57–8 to *Liber Diurnus* as an influential model for sanctions.

86 See above, pp. 106–8.

collection[87]), and it underlines the fact that, at least in those areas, it was a common assumption that going to court – that is, to a public assembly – was the appropriate way to deal with property disputes; it was part of the customary culture. Accordingly, the language of the formula is occasionally reflected in a description of events: *secundum illam uindicamus per iudicio, in Legione, de Lub, ante comite domno Uelasco* (land near Ardón sold to the monastery of Santos Justo y Pastor which the vendors 'had [successfully] claimed from Lub in court in León, before Count Velasco').[88] The formula occurs in a high proportion of Otero charters, sometimes in the more explicit form *si allicus te in iudicio repedierit pro ipsa terra* ('if anyone should make a claim on you in court for that land'), which is especially interesting in view of the high proportion of dispute records in that collection and the fact that it was a lay collection.[89] Going to court was something to be expected of the lay community.

Looking overall at the treatment of formulas in charters, it is clear that although the same concepts were used across the whole of northern Iberia, the use of formulas varied by region and by micro-region. It is also clear that there were layers of older and more recent practice: there is something that looks like a long-established traditional practice for recording secular transactions, with packages of elements of formulas travelling together, while there were clearly new developments associated with the establishment of large monastic scriptoria; explicitly monastic concerns are reflected in the formulation of charters, especially in the recording of gifts to monasteries. It is particularly interesting that 'going to court' was a regular element of secular sanctions of earlier origin; it is also interesting that judgment (and condemnation) was a recurrent theme in records of gifts to monasteries. Both mean that we need to look at more than explicit records of dispute to understand the role of courts, judges and judgment in that society – a further reason why it was important to consider writing habits across the corpus of charters.

So how does this range of practice impact on the formulation of dispute records? How does the wider environment of charter writing influence – if at all – the writing of dispute texts? It looks as if there were some standard ways of formulating records of disputes, with widespread adherence. Does the writing of dispute texts show a set of processes similar to that of the writing of other charters?

87 Mattoso, 'Sanctio', p. 309; T67 (963): *insuper et pro temporali iudicia insistente pariat regi uel commite territorio eiusdem centum libras auri*; cf. T44, T60. C62 (949): *aut iudicium conpulsauerit*, cf. C164, C165. While the notion of authorizing legitimate possession – *au[c]torigare* – seems to have become common in sanction formulas in the second half of the tenth century (see n. 35 above), the core formula referring to confirmations in court (*in iudicio uindicare*) occurs from the ninth century onwards; according to Valdeavellano, 'Escodriñamiento y otorificación', pp. 244–7, 321, its origins lie in the provisions of Visigothic law, and ultimately in classical Roman law.

88 Li243 (952); cf., in similar terms, a gift to Abellar of land also won in a León court case, Li187 (944); cf. *auctorigato*, used of land to be legitimately sold, Liii560 (994).

89 OD3 (936).

5 The language of dispute records

Since there is a very strong narrative aspect to many dispute records, their language is for the most part specific to their context and content. Nevertheless, despite the free flow of these narratives and the detail of different circumstances, dispute texts are often marked by the occurrence of standard formulas, as other charters are. This is particularly true of Accounts, and can be true of the texts that record Oaths, Agreements, Confessions and Mixed types. Not surprisingly, the language of Incidental and Implied records of dispute, Fines, Confiscations and Debts tends to be influenced by the characteristic recording format of the transaction for which the record was primarily constructed, which was often straightforward gift format; in these cases, the language is dominated by the familiar formulas of gift and sale and its analysis needs to be viewed in the context of the preceding chapter. Inevitably, a significant proportion of the narratives of Accounts and of some other dispute records is not susceptible to formulaic analysis because of the free format; there are, however, the recurring formulas which pop up in diverse narratives and a few other formulas that seem to characterize particular types of dispute record. What, if anything, is the significance of the recurring formulas? Do they help us understand the process of construction of records of disputes?

Because these recurring formulas constitute a small proportion of extant texts, their incidence is not straightforward. But they have some characteristics that are obvious and immediately striking. Some are widespread, and some occur only in more limited regions. Some seem to come from a long tradition of describing court proceedings, and some seem to reflect recent developments. Some seem to belong with the brief records made shortly after proceedings, and others belong to the more distanced retrospective descriptions. Let me try and unpick this; and, since some categories, on careful examination, are quite clear, whereas others are more arguable, let me begin with the two clearest categories – the formulas which are particularly characteristic of narrative Accounts, and those which are particularly characteristic of Oaths and Confessions.

Accounts

I have already drawn attention, as others have done, to the occurrence of *orta fuit intentio/contentio* ('a dispute arose') as the characteristic opening of third-person, retrospective, narrative Accounts, an important large group of 59 texts.[1] This is an extremely common opening; it is virtually always in this format, with the words in this order; and it does not occur in other kinds of dispute record.[2] It is characteristic of records from nearly all parts of northern Iberia, from Portugal to Aragón, and is the introduction to over half of the Accounts. While it is not in itself a striking phrase, it introduces records from across the whole of the tenth century, from many different sources; it is, as it were, standard language to introduce the recounting of a past dispute. It occurs in records in cartulary copies and on single sheets, like the boundary dispute between the monastery of San Julián and locals of Manzaneda and Garrafe settled before King Alfonso IV in 931 or the Galician dispute of 975 between Fruela, son of King Alfonso IV, and the monastery of Samos over control of two churches.[3] Whereas it might be thought that this phrase was a characteristic addition by a cartulary copyist, it seems to have been just as characteristic of this kind of original record. It looks as if there was a shared language of description, and by using such a phrase, redactors were signalling that they were about to describe a past dispute.

Another apparently inconsequential but extremely common formula is *ordinare ut*, 'to order, arrange that': kings, counts and judges habitually gave instructions about what was to happen next in court proceedings, as Count Jimeno *ordinauit* two sets of Portuguese villagers to identify some reliable men to establish their disputed boundary and, more finally, judges in Présaras *ordinauerunt* Rezeuara and her children to restore some stolen sheep.[4] The formula is particularly associated with giving direction to provide witnesses or take an oath – that is, with critical stages in judicial proceedings. It is used in records from all areas and throughout the period under consideration; it is characteristic of Accounts, but also occurs in some Incidental records and some records of Oaths (unsurprisingly, given the common contexts). While this might seem to be so general a phrase as to carry no significance, it looks as if it was the phrase that came to mind when describing the giving of formal direction; in this, it serves to emphasize the formulaic framework, as also the authority of the president of the court.[5]

1 See above, p. 38; see also Agustín Prieto Morera, 'El proceso en el reino de León a la luz de los diplomas', in *El reino de León en la alta edad media, II: Ordenamiento jurídico del reino* (León, 1992), p. 390; Isabel Alfonso, 'El formato de la información judicial en la alta edad media peninsular', in Julio Escalona and Hélène Sirantoine (eds), *Chartes et cartulaires comme instruments de pouvoir. Espagne et Occident chrétien (VIIIe–XIIe siècles)* (Toulouse, 2013), p. 205. Cf., for the eleventh century, Andrés Gambra, *Alfonso VI. Cancillería, curia e imperio, I: Estudio* (León, 1997), p. 349, in the context of texts he describes as *placita* (but for *placita*, see below, pp. 234–5).

2 See above, p. 38 n7, for variants.

3 Li89 (ACL 1333), for which text, see above, p. 56; Sam44 (AHN Clero Samos 1239–7).

4 Lor36 (936), Sob23 (949).

5 On the significance of presidency, see Wendy Davies, 'Holding court: Judicial presidency in Brittany, Wales and northern Iberia in the early middle ages', in Fiona Edmonds and Paul Russell (eds), *Tome: Studies in Medieval Celtic History and Law in Honour of Thomas Charles-Edwards* (Woodbridge, 2011), pp. 145–54.

Other phrases which recur in Accounts are less regular, although those which evoke the notion of truth – *ueritas* – are common. Seeing truth, finding truth, receiving truth, having truth and being true are all phrases which feature in descriptions of judicial proceedings, particularly in stating the outcome of a case, although the associated verbs vary: *ueritatem uidimus, illorum ueritas est, sapemus in ueritate*; and *quod ueritas docet, deatis mici ueridatem.*[6] They occur most frequently in Accounts, but can be found in other kinds of dispute record – Agreements, Confessions, Incidental records; and although they occur on the *meseta* and in Castile, the phrases are preponderantly Galician. They feature from the early tenth century, but are more common in records from later in the century. Using this range of expressions about truth, therefore, looks as if it may have been a development – an increasingly standard way of evoking the resolution and of signalling which was the successful party. A similar usage is that which evokes the concept of 'foresight' literally, 'perception' effectively; words like *preuidere, preuisores* often described the process of judgment: everyone came together *ut preuidissent ueritatem* ('to establish the truth') in a case of disputed boundaries in northern Galicia; and Count Gonzalo came *ut preuideret ipsos terminos cum alios suos preuisores* in another Galician boundary dispute.[7] Particularly characteristic of Accounts, this too is a way of describing the outcome of proceedings and of reinforcing the statement of one party's success. Also later rather than earlier in usage, its citation is again predominantly Galician. Both *ueritas* and *preuidere* are used in records on single sheets as well as in cartularies, and therefore neither arises purely as a consequence of copying into a cartulary.

Phrases describing the activities, and often intervention, of *boni homines*, 'worthies' or 'elders', tend to occur in later texts too, particularly in the circumstance of negotiating a reduced penalty; again the precise form of reference to these men varies, although the verb *rogare* ('to ask, petition') is often associated with the term. These men could be significant actors in a case, and could change its course, and although reference to them was often formulaic, it could be more than a formulaic nicety;[8] they feature in Confessions, Agreements, Fines and Incidental records as well as Accounts. Phrases invoking the concept of the *iudicatum*, usually a penalty payable to the court holder, have a similar profile:[9] again relatively late in occurrence, not surprisingly these phrases are more characteristic of Fine records than of Accounts, although they do occasionally occur in the latter, as also in Agreements and Incidental records; they

6 Lor36 (936), Sob129 (942), V11 (919); S287 (977), OD27 (987), which are classified as Confiscation and Incidental respectively. For *agnosco/cognosco in ueritate*, which has a more specialized use, see below, pp. 127–8. Cf. Igor Filippov, 'Bible and the Roman law: The notions of law, custom and justice in the Vulgate', in *Lex et religio: XL incontro di studiosi dell'antichità cristiana (Roma, 10–12 maggio 2012)* (Rome, 2013), pp. 105–41, for some comments on the association of the notions of truth and justice in the Bible and in the works of Jerome.

7 Sob129 (942), LaC65 (pre-962); 'to determine those boundaries together with his other judges'.

8 But see below, pp. 169–76, for a more detailed discussion.

9 See above, pp. 10, 30.

are more common in southern Galicia and the *meseta* than elsewhere, especially in Celanova, León and Otero texts. Neither *boni homines* nor the *iudicatum* is characteristic of ninth- or early tenth-century texts.[10] Moreover, the concepts evoked by these words were not mere turns of phrase, for the concepts were descriptive of practice, and changing practice at that. Their increasing use in the later tenth century (as also their common use in the eleventh) reflects this changing world. Overall, usage of all four notions (*ueritas, preuidere, boni homines* and *iudicatum*) suggests some change in scribal practice in describing court cases during the tenth century, while that of the two latter terms may suggest some change in procedure as well.

Oaths and Confessions

The formulas used in Oaths and Confessions are of a different type. As already emphasized, these records tend to be framed in the first person and present tense. Although there are many references to the taking of oaths in Accounts and in other kinds of dispute record, in a handful of cases there survives what appears to be a verbatim oath, usually introduced by the technical term *conditiones sacramentorum*, literally meaning 'terms of the oaths'. All of these verbatim Oaths are extremely similar in structure and style, although they employ slightly different wording, as if the holy was invoked according to a standard format, with local variations, before proceeding to the detail of the evidence (five examples).[11] This consistency is particularly striking when we recall that the records were made several hundred kilometres apart – from the Cantabrian north coast to Old Castile to the southern side of the Cantabrian Mountains to the neighbourhood of León to the south-western edge of the *meseta* (see Figure 5.1). They all include swearing by God the almighty father, the twelve apostles, the four holy Gospels and the relics of a saint: most include the relics of the Virgin Mary, and one adds the relics of San Claudio, another those of San Emiliano, another those of St Peter, and another the holy altar of San Martín;[12] all but one add the twelve prophets, some add that God made heaven, earth, the sea and all that is in it, and the rest add Jesus Christ, the Holy Spirit and the Trinity.[13] They also all use the formula that they have seen with their eyes and heard with their ears and were present at the time when such and

10 For a couple of references to *boni homines* in the early tenth century, see below, p. 169 and n79. The earliest references to *iudicatum* in dispute texts are of 940 (Li138 and Cel456), and nearly three-quarters are post-975; if it had been a common term at an earlier period, one would expect it to have been used in Sob75 (858), but that is simply a *cartula pariationis*. As André Marques points out, *iudicatum* does occasionally occur in Portuguese sanctions at an early date, such as PMH DC 8 (875), where, if invoked, it would be payable to the *potestas* in control of the territory; however, I have some doubts about whether this sanction was original to the framing of this particular charter.

11 See above, p. 59, for a full example.

12 Li192 (946), V10 (911), Cast1 (927), SMdelP2 (927).

13 V10 does not have the prophets; including heaven, earth and sea: OvC26 (953), Cast1, cf. the Mixed text Li192; including Christ, the Holy Spirit and the Trinity: Li34 (915), V10, V11 (919), SMdelP2.

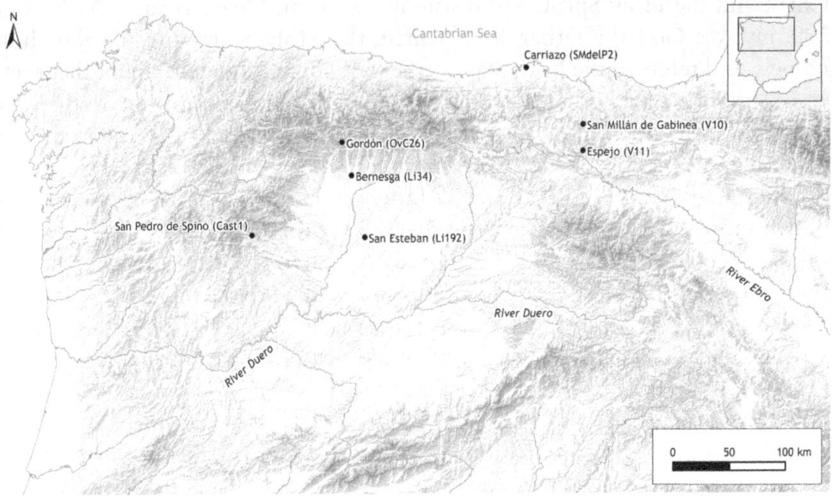

Figure 5.1 Records of Oaths

such happened: *iuramus quia occulis uidimus et aures audiuimus et de presente fuimus quando*.[14] One could imagine, during the performance of the court, the *saio* indicating to an attendant cleric to write down the words of evidence once the swearing of the oath was in sight. When the record was made, it rather looks as if it was standard practice to note the detail of the evidence, then the local version of the standard words of the oath, and then repeat the detailed evidence.[15] Whether this actually happened during the proceedings or was reconstructed for the record subsequently, the formulas are so distinctive and their use is so precise, despite the geographical distance between the locations of surviving examples, it must be likely that these verbatim oaths reflect ritual words uttered in court. It is, after all, clearly indicated in one charter that legal officers not only organized the oath-taking, but also organized the recording of oaths.[16]

Now, Oaths of this kind certainly occur in the extant Iberian formularies, as also on two of the Visigothic slates. The Ripoll formula invokes God the father, Jesus Christ, the Holy Spirit and the Trinity in the same terms as the charters; it also refers to the holy altar of a saint; and it has a similar version of being present, hearing and seeing.[17] The Visigothic formulas also invoke God the father, Jesus

14 Quoted from Li192; OvC26 and Li34 omit hearing with their ears.

15 This is essentially what happens in Li34, and it is repeated in the Mixed record Li192. The same practice is reflected in OvC26, with an additional partial statement of the evidence at the beginning of that text, and in Cast1, with a reduced initial statement of evidence.

16 Sob109 (early 990s): *scribserunt conditiones sacramentorum per manum saioni Fulgentio presbiter.*

17 Michel Zimmermann, 'Un formulaire du Xème siècle conservé à Ripoll', *Faventia*, 4/2 (1982), pp. 81–2.

Christ and the Holy Spirit.[18] And slate no. 39, from Diego Álvaro (Ávila), of *c.* 589, invokes God the father, Jesus Christ, the Holy Spirit and the four holy gospels, and refers to the holy altar of a saint.[19] There can be no doubt that there was a Visigothic background to this kind of oath, although it is interesting that the formularies and slates lack some of the standard detail of the charters – in particular, invocation of the twelve prophets, the twelve apostles, the relics of the Virgin Mary and of other saints. If there is any significance in the regional distribution, where the charter oaths diverge, the formularies (and slate) lie with the practice of Valpuesta and Santa María del Puerto (Old Castile northwards to the coast) rather than that of Gordón and Castañeda, farther west.[20] There is just a hint, then, of some regional divergence in formulation, while there is also a clear indication that some elements of the standard charter formulas used in the Oath had developed after Visigothic times.

Ritual utterance is also suggested by some recurrent formulas in Confessions.[21] Again, it is the repetition of identical words, in the first person and present tense, at widely distant geographical locations, that brings ritual performance to mind. The full formula of confession is *manifestus sum . . . uerum est quod negare non ualeo . . . in hanc manifestum nicil abeo quod apponam* ('I declare . . . it is true that I am not able to deny . . . [there follows the detail confessed] . . . in this confession I have nothing to add'). Of the 15 Confessions, all but three have all or part of the formula, and most of them have all of it.[22] These records occur both on single sheets and in cartulary copies. They range in date from 861 to 995, and they range in location from southern Galicia across parts of the *meseta* to the Liébana in the far north and Castile to the north-east. It is unthinkable that the same very precise words should have been used in such different locations across such a long period unless they represent a standard form of confession; given their occurrence on single sheets, several of which – given their physical form – may well be originals, the best explanation is that they represent the ritual words used in court, words which were recorded at court or shortly after its meeting. The slight variations in orthography and in

18 'Formulae Wisigothicae', ed. Juan Gil, in Juan Gil (ed.), *Miscellanea Wisigothica* (Seville, 1972), no. 39. For further discussion of the differences, see Miguel Calleja Puerta, 'Ecos de las *Fórmulas visigóticas* en la documentación altomedieval astur-leonesa', in *Les formulaires. Compilation et circulation des modèles d'actes dans l'Europe médiévale et moderne* (Paris, forthcoming).

19 Isabel Velázquez Soriano, *Las pizarras visigodas (Entre el latín y su disgregación. La lengua hablada en Hispania, siglos VI–VIII)* (Salamanca, 2004), pp. 210–19. Slate no. 92, also recording an oath, does not use these formulas; ibid., pp. 338–42. Cf. Roger Collins, '"Sicut lex Gothorum continet": Law and charters in ninth- and tenth-century León and Catalonia', *English Historical Review*, 100 (1985), p. 495.

20 The practice of Li34 and Li192, both relating to monasteries located to the south of León, is different from each other, suggesting more mixed practice in the region between Old Castile and the western edge of the *meseta*.

21 See above, p. 46.

22 S261 (post-971) and Sob75 (858) only have the beginning; see further below, p. 127 n25. Flor74 (861) and SMdelP1 (863) omit the last phrase, and T30 (922) only has the last phrase. Ar18 (965) does not have it; both Ar18 and Sob75 make much of the confession, without the formulas, but arguably one could classify them differently.

syntax make it perfectly clear that they are unlikely to have been copied from a written formulary, or from each other (for example *in iuditio nichil habemus quod oponamus* and *in iudicio nihil abemus quod eponamus*), and in a few cases the orthographic variation might suggest a reflection of speech: *nihil abeo que hoponam, . . . ad isto manifesto quia nichil abeo quid dicam* and *uerum est cot necare non ualeo . . . manifestu nicili abeo que opona.*[23]

The formulas of Confessions are in fact more complicated than this, but having identified the core constituents, we can perceive some complementary features. Four other formulas are common in records of confession: *in iuditio NN* ('in the court of NN'), *qui asseret in uoce* ('who was the spokesperson for'), *et que manifesto uerum esse fateor* ('and what I declare I admit to be true') and *cognoui in ueritate* ('I acknowledged the truth'), although the citation of the third is very variable and the last occurs in many other kinds of text as well as Confessions. Notably, the phrase *(scriptura) agnitionis*, '(record) of acknowledgement', which might easily be interpreted as 'record of confession', does not feature at all in any of these Confession texts; it occurs variously in other kinds of dispute text.[24] Most of the Confession texts begin with *In iuditio NN* (with the variant *in presentia (comitis)* in the Cardeña and Lugo records) and most have *qui asseret in uoce N*;[25] these two phrases appear to be part of the apparatus for introducing a confession, rather than words actually uttered in confession. But the first-person and present-tense formula, *que manifesto uerum esse fateor*, should belong with words uttered; its variant forms are: *manifestamus uerum esse faremur, que manifesto uerum est factore, hoc quod fecimus uera esse fatemus* and *quod ego manifesto uerum esse factum.*[26] While some of the variation here might be explained as simple slips of the pen, some of it suggests problems of comprehension; person and tense again suggest that it was part of a ritual utterance in public, although clearly it was an utterance of such ancient origin that some scribes had no idea what it meant.

The common formula *cognoui in ueritate* is another first-person phrase (in the past tense), but the pattern of its occurrence is different from those so far discussed:[27] it features in just over half of the Confession texts, but it does not feature in those texts which could be described as the raw confession – raw before it was packaged into a tidy cartulary or single-sheet version.[28] The two separate

23 Li191 (946), T30 (922); T66 (962), V33 (956), OD38 (995).

24 For example: Li128 (938), Li144 (941), S101 (945), Lii312 (959), Lii508 (985) (respectively Account, Account, Implied, Account, Mixed). Prieto Morera, 'El proceso en el reino de León a la luz de los diplomas', pp. 395–7, emphasized *agnitiones* as a class of document recording acceptance of a judicial finding; for comment on this, see below, p. 128 and n30.

25 *In presentia*: C35, C90, C151, Flor74; also S261; Ar18 has *in presentia (consilio)* in the course of the record; Sob75 does not have it, though, like Ar18, it has *ante iudicem*. Confessions lacking *qui asseret*: C35 (941), C151 (972), V33, SMdelP1, Sob75; S261 has *qui tinuit uoce de*.

26 Li191, OD38, T17 (885), T66.

27 It does also occur in present tense; see T30 (922), C35 (941), C90 (957), Ar18 (965), OD150 (1022).

28 Hence, it does not occur in OD38, V33, T17, T66, nor the confession appended to the main, 'tidy', text of Cel94. The Mixed text, Li192, does use *agnosco in ueritate* in a first-person commitment, which is a confirmation of an oath.

Confession texts of 987 included in the Celanova cartulary as Cel94 are particularly significant here:[29] in this case, the summary charter of a confession and its consequences has four attached documents, one of which is a document of Confession; whereas the Confession document does not have the formula, the summary charter does. It would appear that *cognoui* (or *cognosco*) *in ueritate* was a characteristic formula for referring to the fact that a confession had been made, but it was not one of the ritual formulas uttered in court by the person making a confession. Accordingly, it (and its variant *agnoui* or *agnosco*) features in some Agreements following confessions, as also in many other kinds of document that refer to confessions and their outcomes – Accounts, Incidental records of disputes, Fines and so on.[30]

So we might suggest this: the raw confession tended to be recorded in a standard format, beginning with a reference to the court (*In iuditio NN*), then making a reference to the spokesman for the accuser (*asseret in uoce N*), continuing with the ritual words of acknowledgement (*manifestus sum uerum est quod negare non ualeo*) and then the detail of what was confessed; the confession was then rounded off with the concluding ritual words (*que manifesto uerum esse fateor et in hanc manifestum nicil abeo quod apponam*). If a witness list was attached, which was not invariable, it might well name judges and officers but no one else, and the role of the judges might be indicated by the addition of the words *qui/quos/quod iudicaui* ('I have judged') after their names, as is the case in five of the Confession texts.[31] These raw Confessions must have been recorded near the time of the court meeting. As indicated above, Confessions sometimes survive in a physical association with consequent Agreements – as two separate documents on one parchment – and it seems likely that this was a common way to make the primary record (see Figure 5.2).[32] In a subsequent, secondary version, the two might be combined to make a single record, whose main function was to confirm the conveyance that was the outcome of proceedings (like the summary charter of Cel94, which precedes the four appended documents, which include separate Confession and Agreement).[33] Later, possibly much later, a third version might be drawn up, as an Account of the dispute, confession and subsequent agreement, sometimes for confirmation by

29 See above, pp. 46–7.

30 See n. 36 below. Prieto Morera, 'El proceso en el reino de León a la luz de los diplomas', pp. 396–7, argued that the formula with *agnosco* or *agnitio* unevenly and gradually from the early tenth century replaced that with *manifesto* or *manifestum*, especially in the west, as also that *agnitio* applied to property cases and *manifestum* to criminal, but I do not see this distinction in texts I have classified as Confessions. Note *manifestus sum* in the appended Confession text of the Galician property case of Cel94 (987), although the preceding summary charter does use *agnouimus*, clearly meaning 'acknowledge' here. For further comparison between the two, see further below, p. 131.

31 Flor74, T17, T30, T66, Li191; cf. the Mixed text Li192, which includes an element of confession.

32 See above, pp. 48–9; the classic cases are Flor74 and Flor75 (861) and OD38 and OD39 (995). Cf. OD150 and OD151 (1022), also a good example on a single sheet; the reported speech of OD150 is a near perfect expression of all the standard confession formulas.

33 See above, p. 46.

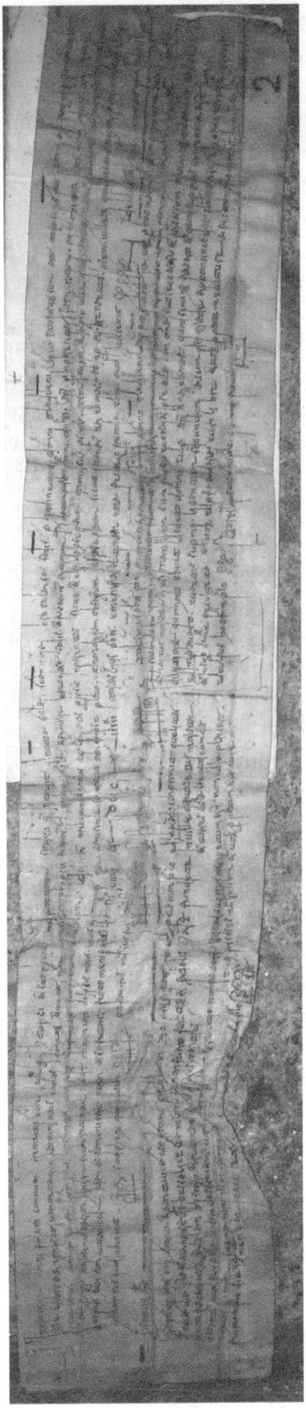

Figure 5.2 Toresario's Confession and Agreement and Siseguto's Agreement, ACLu 60 2 (Flor74, Flor75, Flor73)

Source: Reproduced by permission of the chapter of Lugo Cathedral; photo: Ainoa Castro.

powerful people; such Accounts could draw on the language of the summary Confession – especially *cognoui* or *cognosco in ueritate* – although they never appear to draw on the ritual words. We might then think of three stages of a recording process where confessions were concerned: the immediate words of the Confession, the subsequent summary charter, the later Account. There is no reason to suppose that all confessions stimulated the production of all three types, and there is plenty of reason to suppose that there was not much interest in keeping and copying the first, whereas passing references to confessions are widespread.

The Confession added to the parchment recording the royal gift S261 looks like a record of a raw confession, a primary record, although there is no associated agreement nor note of consequent action; it conforms to some extent to the standard pattern, but lacks nearly all the main ritual clauses of confession; however, its essential content and the language in which it is recorded is entirely credible as a first-stage record of a confession.[34]

Agreements

Turning to the formulaic character of Agreements, at first sight there are fewer indications of conventional practice, although there are some. This is partly because Agreements (of which there are 29) appear to have been recorded for several different kinds of reason – at the least, those recorded following a Confession arising from judicial proceedings, those that seem to have been recorded because of pressure from one party (powerful landlords pressing peasant cultivators to concede labour and/or rent, for example) and those that seem to represent deals done between equal parties.[35] There are also fewer indications of conventions of scribal practice because the records are of different types, and those types do not precisely match the different causation processes. One type is the associated Confession and Agreement: we have extremely good evidence that formal Confessions could be immediately associated with consequent Agreements to make recompense, as the priest Toresario agreed to restore the church of Villa Moreta to the bishop of Braga in 861 (see Figure 5.2) and Flaino agreed in 995 to pay five *solidi* for the adultery he had committed with a woman and her daughter; in each case, both documents are recorded on a single parchment.[36] Here the acts of recording the Agreement seem to have been very closely associated with making a record of the Confession – they were, if you like, 'immediate'. In other cases, we do not have a surviving Confession document, and in some cases there is no reason to suppose that there had been a confession or any judicial proceedings. Not surprisingly, then, we do not find the same formulas used over and over again, and it is much more difficult to detect the utterance of any ritual words.

34 S261 (post-971) (AHN Clero Sahagún 876–8). See above, pp. 47, 85.

35 See above, pp. 48–9.

36 Flor74 and Flor75, OD38 and OD39; see above, pp. 86–7 and Figs. 2.4, 5.2, for physical detail.

Nevertheless, there are some words and formulas that recur. There are those that recall the fact that a confession had been made, as Toresario confirmed his Confession (*manifestum roboraui*) and others acknowledged theirs (*cognouimus in ueritate*) in language recalling the act of confession.[37] A high proportion of all the Agreement texts (over three-quarters) use words that directly refer to an agreement: the word is most commonly *placitum*, but *pactum*, *conuenientia*, *compagina* and *atiba* are also used, the latter two implying a negotiated agreement, often explicitly through the intervention of *boni homines*.[38] One formula seems to reflect a standard way to record arriving at an agreement in a limited region on the southern side of the Cantabrian Mountains: *de iudicio deuenimus inde ad confragena*, *de iudizio et deuenimus ad atiba* and *deuenimus inde a lege . . . et copagina*.[39] Much more widespread is the fact that Agreements are often 'promised', a technical classical Latin legal term for two parties to abide by an agreement: *hoc meum placitum conpromito*, *placio facimus inter nos et uos et conpromittimus*, *nostrum placitum tibi compromittimus*, *per nostro placitum nobis cotpromitimus* ('I/we promise to abide by our agreement').[40] Note the dates and geographical range of these examples: they run from the mid-ninth century to the end of the tenth, and originate from central Portugal to the *meseta* to the Cantabrian Mountains to the north coast of Cantabria; this must reflect a standard way of recording a commitment, of some antiquity – indeed, perhaps even a standard way of declaring an agreement; the examples include the two Agreements on single sheets which are associated with Confessions.

There is another notable characteristic of many Agreements: short witness lists. The witness lists which conclude the vast majority of all charters begin with the name of the principal actor – that is, the donor or vendor (but not the beneficiary or purchaser), may continue with the names of some confirmers, and then conclude with a large or small list of witnesses of the transaction. The names which conclude a third of these Agreement texts are only those of both parties to the agreement – both parties, unlike the standard convention of charters of gift or sale. I cannot overemphasize the significance of the subscription of both parties, given that a single subscription of one principal actor is the normal convention. Interestingly, nearly all of these cases are also the texts which include the *placitum compromittere* formula.[41] This makes exceptionally good sense if the formula

37 S372 (post–989), OD43, for example.

38 For example, Lii477; see further below, pp. 172–3 for *boni homines* and negotiation.

39 OD4 (946) – this is the editors' (extremely convincing) reconstruction of a text which is very difficult to read, OD43 (997), Liii597 (1000). They are all variations on the meaning '[we came] from the court and arrived at an agreement'.

40 Flor75 (861), SMdelP3 (927), Lor35 (966–85), Cel94 (987), OD39 (995); cf. a reworked Account, Li99 (934), *placitum cauentes compromittimus*. For *compromitto*, see further below, pp. 135–6. For classical use, especially in the context of two parties agreeing to go to arbitration, see, for example, *The Digest of Justinian*, ed. Theodor Mommsen and Paul Krueger, with English translation by Alan Watson (4 vols, Philadelphia, PA, 1985), 44.4.4 *Si in arbitrum compromisserimus* ('If we have agreed to go to an arbitrator'), vol. 4, p. 632.

41 The exception is T62 (962), which has one additional name.

retained anything like its classical meaning: the Agreement was between two parties, who were each committed by the formal act of agreement; the text records their commitment; witnessing – unusually for charters – was irrelevant; the record was simply a record of the agreement, and is a primary record of that. There is, then, a group of nine Agreements which are primary records, unwitnessed, recording agreement between two parties, often following confession in court.[42]

Several of the remaining 20 Agreements have rather few witnesses, and a handful of these include both parties to the Agreement; the latter include three cases of negotiated agreement (negotiated with assistance); they all survive on single sheets.[43] The other Agreement texts are different: they do not have distinctive witness lists, for they conform to the standard model of the witness lists of donation charters.

There is a further point to make in respect of the three negotiated Agreements: all three of these records appear to be an attempt to represent what was actually agreed between the parties, in the words of the parties. This seems to be the case not so much because of their very unconventional orthography, but because in OD4 the short sentences read like speech: a story, a series of events, recounted, at times repetitively, by the party who initiated the case, without formulas; concluding with a final section in which the other party, also in the first person but now in the present tense, outlines the nature of their agreement. It is as if the two parties stood before the writer, who attempted to write down what they said, more or less as they said it. OD43 reads more like a scribe's attempt to summarize what had been said in court, although cast in the first person (*gongnobimus nos in ueritatem*), with patches of past-tense recounting, again concluding with first-person statements of commitment by both parties; the scribe here was Braolio, who was responsible for the records of several of Flaino Muñoz's court cases at this time.[44] This is the record which is written on the dorse of the original charter which recorded the donation of the land in dispute – as it were, making a record of the agreement in a very appropriate place.[45] Liii597, in which the priest Arrano records an agreement in the monastery of San Martín, to which the monastery was a party, again gives a voice to both parties, again recounts some of the events of the dispute that had passed, and again gives each party a voice in the commitment now made. This record was started in the space beneath another, unrelated, charter and continues on

42 Flor75, SMdelP3, Cel446 (959), T62, T66B, Lor35, OD39, Flor73 (?861), which was almost certainly a consequence of the Toresario case, Lii477 (980), which has the subscription of one party only plus two guarantors. T66B (962) is an incomplete record in its surviving form; see below, p. 136 n67, and below, Index of dispute texts. Note also in this category the Agreement appended to the Confession Cel94.

43 OD4 apparently (although it is very difficult to read), OD43, Liii597.

44 For Braolio, see Wendy Davies, 'Local priests and the writing of charters in northern Iberia in the tenth century', in Julio Escalona and Hélène Sirantoine (eds), *Chartes et cartulaires comme instruments de pouvoir. Espagne et Occident chrétien (VIIIe–XIIe siècles)* (Toulouse, 2013), pp. 35, 39.

45 See above, p. 87 and n90, for physical detail.

the dorse of the parchment. It is as if it had been important to get a record of the agreement as soon as possible, and it was therefore written, in a hurry, in a useful space on an unrelated parchment.[46] These three therefore also look like primary records.

Nearly all the primary records of Agreement discussed above explicitly followed judicial proceedings; they were directly and explicitly part of the arrangements for the resolution of the cases.[47] That such primary records were not normally kept is made clear by the record of Cel94, in which the constructed charter summarizing confession, agreement and subsequent action is followed by four brief documents individually detailing Confession, commitments to appear before the *saio* and consequent Agreement, which were clearly the primary documents. Repetition of the summary charter at Cel150 does not have the four attachments. A comparison between the formulas of the summary text and those of the primary documents is revealing: whereas the former (in first person) declares that the confession is confirmed and acknowledged (*agnouimus in ueritate*), it does not repeat the ritual words of confession of the latter; and although the disputed property is assigned to the monastery and an agreement made (again in first person) in the former, it does not repeat the *compromittimus* of the primary text. All the essentials of the proceedings are covered in the summary charter, but the ritual words of the primary texts are not repeated.

More than half of the Agreement texts lack the distinctive features of the primary records of agreement; two of these are third-person retrospective notes of an agreement, one is too fragmentary to allow full understanding of its nature, and the text of another is not available;[48] two others followed judicial proceedings and are probably subsequently constructed summaries of those cases.[49] The remaining 11 Agreement texts are of several types: Agreements concluded in public meetings before some kind of authority such as a count or judge, often to the advantage of a religious body; Agreements not to cause trouble to a monastery in the future; and Agreements which appear to have been made to the mutual advantage of both parties. The Agreements not to cause trouble look like another kind of primary record, prepared by a monastery for its own advantage: one, a commitment from a deacon to an abbot, is written on the dorse of another charter.[50] Agreements concluded in public meetings typically deal with cases of intrusion into monastic property, like the 21 peasants committed thereafter to make annual payments to the monks of Pardomino, a text

46 See further above, pp. 93–4.

47 Not explicitly Flor73 (?861), Lor35 (966–85) and Lii477 (980).

48 Endorsement to SantA28 (915), SJP31 (tenth century); S372 (post–989); there is also Ast25 (923), which defies classification because I have not been able to see the full text.

49 PMH DC 144 (985), Cel204 (pre–1005, p. 288) – both cases of aristocrats against peasants.

50 Lii330; the cartulary copies Lii400 and C103 (a guarantee document) could have been altered in copying, but look as if they derive from a text like Lii330. All three are witnessed, but by few witnesses.

probably inscribed with 21 simple *signa*, notionally locking each member of the group into the commitment.[51] They probably represent records made by the monasteries which were the beneficiaries of such concessions. On the other hand, Agreements made for mutual advantage without the pressure of a court case, like an Agreement with the bishop of Lugo to hold a church or another with the bishop of León to have shares in the water supply,[52] could in fact be primary records or could be subsequent constructions: the Lugo Agreement was folded while the ink was still wet.

The León charter 437, of 975, recording an Agreement of mutual advantage, must have been constructed subsequently and is instructive: two versions are preserved of an agreement between the monasteries of Sahagún and Abellar, in two different monastic cartularies, about access to water to power mills.[53] The versions are extremely close, but they vary in spelling and in grammar: the Abellar version does not respect classical endings as Sahagún does (hence *collegium* for *collegio*, *Ciprianus* for *Cipriano* and so on); it changes the word order slightly; it substitutes *quoque gentis* for *cogentis* in the 'free will' clause, nicely demonstrating the different practice of León and Sahagún orbits in respect of this formula;[54] substitutes *est* for *exit*, which makes rather less sense; varies some conjunctions; adds a phrase emphasizing that they share equal responsibility for constructing a weir; and slightly rearranges the witness list. These two texts, although obviously divergent, are in essence so close that they must depend on a single original text, presumably prepared by the deacon Erifonsus, whose *signum* concludes the record; it must have been prepared on behalf of Sahagún, whose abbot confirms, whereas Abellar's does not.[55] It is possible that the text was dictated, which seems the best explanation for this kind of variation. Here an agreement must have been negotiated, whether face-to-face or by letter, and then a definitive text drawn up by one party and dictated to writers for both; this text presents the agreement as a concession by Sahagún.[56] This is presumably indicative of the process which lies behind the creation of records for mutually advantageous agreements concluded between two parties; it is clearly quite different from the process of recording an Agreement consequent upon a Confession.

Whatever the type of Agreement recorded, it is clear that two levels of recording Agreements are preserved in the corpus: the primary record of Agreement, in which the commitment of both parties is recorded and then endorsed with the actual or notional signs of both; and the subsequently constructed charter,

51 Lii290 (955) – the beginning of a row of *signa* is clear, but a fold then obscures and there are 13 in columns below; Cel507 (985); probably also Sam247 (909).

52 AHN Clero Lugo 1325A–11 (974); S33 (925); both survive on single sheets. Also mutual advantage: Li94 (932), Lii437 (975), Cast5 (953).

53 The Sahagún version is S280.

54 See above, pp. 97–106, for *cogentis*.

55 The deacon Erifonsus was scribe for other Sahagún records.

56 Abellar was a good 40 km from Sahagún, but had property and representatives in the neighbourhood of the latter.

which records and summarizes the essential narrative and outcome and – invariably – the sanction that would apply if the terms were not kept. Although the Pardomino case cited an almost practicable penalty of 10 cattle per person in the event of default, some of the sanctions associated with other Agreements were excessively high – another demonstration of monastic sanction writing to its own advantage.[57] The subsequently constructed charters were clearly prepared in the knowledge of the terms of an agreement, whether before or some time after it was publicly declared; the primary records must have been prepared at or shortly after the moment of agreement. This could sometimes have been at a public meeting; if not, then shortly after the meeting.

Other conventions

As suggested above, there are occasional indications that another kind of written text was a standard part of court procedure: the first-person formal commitments by the principal actors in a court case to carry out the next stage of judicial procedure.[58] Like guarantor documents, these occur too rarely and too haphazardly to have been included as a distinct category of dispute texts in this book, not least because they clearly were not intended to be preserved:[59] they were part of an ongoing judicial process rather than any kind of reflection on the outcome. However, there are enough of them to permit some comment on their wording, which occurs both as discrete text and as an echo in a few narratives. I shall refer to these texts as formal commitments.

Five commitments, or sets of commitments, are preserved as discrete texts, and a further three are reflected in other texts. These are most obvious in the four texts appended to the Confession Cel94, and the three attached to the Mixed record from Oviedo, ACO B.1.11, but they also occur within the Mixed record Li192 and at the start of ACO B.1.11 and of the Agreement SMdelP3 and of the Oath Li34; they are incomplete in the Agreement T66B.[60] There is a standard format, in the first person and present tense. They begin *per hunc nostrum placitum tibi compromittimus qualiter die . . .* ('by this our agreement we promise you that on such and such a day . . .') and most frequently continue with *presentemus nostras personas in presentia iudicis N* ('we will present ourselves before Judge N').[61] They nearly always conclude with a sanction in the event of

57 See above, pp. 116–18, for monastic sanctions threatening doom and disaster.

58 See above, p. 54.

59 Guarantor documents are too rare to include as a distinct class, and they lack consistent, distinctive formulation. But they include V43 (for which, see above, p. 60, Lii464, attachment to T66B (for which, see n. 67 below); cf. the Agreements Lii477 (980), C103 (962).

60 See above, pp. 1–4, 62, 46, for ACO B.1.11 (= OvC26) and Cel94, and p. 92 for Li192. Collins, '"Sicut lex Gothorum continet"', pp. 499–501, has a different overall interpretation but makes similar points in respect of OvC26 and Cel94.

61 So, the beginning: OvC26 four times, Cel94 three times, Li192 twice, SMdelP3, Li34 in a slight variant, as also OD39; the continuation: OvC26 four times, Cel94 twice, Li34, SMdelP3, and also OD39. T66B has *tibi per hunc nostrum placitum qualiter die*, but lacks *compromittimus*.

failure to appear, and they are not usually witnessed by third parties.[62] Variants are the second attached commitment of ACO B.1.11, to abide by the decision reached,[63] and the several commitments to hand over disputed property, using the verb *assignare* or *consignare*.[64] Since the *saio* is sometimes explicitly the person addressed, it seems reasonable to suppose that these commitments were usually made to a *saio*, in the context of his handling the several procedural stages of a case. It is notable that they all use that classical legal term of commitment, *compromittere*. And since many are in the plural, representing the commitment of two adversaries, it seems likely that these were written formulas on which the adversaries, or their representatives, were invited to make a mark: both of the surviving single sheets have simple *signa*;[65] and if the texts had been records of words ritually spoken, one might have expected them to have been in the singular, and repeated for each individual. Interestingly, while the Visigothic formulas do include several instructions on court procedure, they do not include instructions for this particular aspect of it.[66]

The five examples come from the north coast of Cantabria, the hinterland of León on the *meseta*, the route from León to Oviedo across the Cantabrian Mountains and Verín in southern Galicia, and the incomplete example is from the Liébana. The language of commitment is also reflected at the beginning of one surviving Agreement from Valdoré, as discussed above, and at the end of a long Account of a dispute with the monastery of Guimarães in northern Portugal, where the third-person narrative is broken to record a first-person commitment to consign a disputed property.[67] The date range is 915–99. These places are hundreds of kilometres apart, and it is extraordinarily unlikely that there was any connection between the different recording sources (see Figure 5.3). That being the case, these few commitments must preserve a procedure that was widespread and of much earlier origin.

ACO B.1.11 is again important in highlighting another set of standard words found in dispute texts, those describing performance of the ordeal. Twelve charters make references of this kind, but the wording is not nearly as consistent as that which encapsulates formal commitments. There are three elements to the ordeal formulas: firstly, words indicating that an innocent man, a neutral party, entered the *pena caldaria*, the hot water ordeal, sometimes witnessed by *fideles*,

62 Sanction: OvC26 four times, Cel94 three times, Li192 three times, T66B once (identical to OvC26). The second and third of the texts in Li192 do have some witnesses.

63 OvC26.

64 OvC26 (*et assinnem ipsa uilla que in iudicio resonat per manum saionnis*), Li192, Cel94 twice, T66B; cf. reflections in PMH DC 183 and Li191. See below, p. 166 n63, for the language of consignment.

65 OvC26 (for each of the commitments), OD39; *signa* are also indicated in this position in the cartulary copies of Li34, Li192 (several times, for both parties and also for one party only), T66B, SMdelP3 (for one party only), and the texts appended to Cel94.

66 Gil (ed.), 'Formulae Wisigothicae', nos 40–43.

67 OD39 (see above, p. 59), PMH DC 183 (*tibi compromitto ut asignet tibi ipsa uilla . . . et tu asignes*). The incomplete T66B is followed by a separate guarantor document; the final document of the set in T66 records the handover of the property, but does not use the language of formal commitment other than *consignaui* and *consigno*.

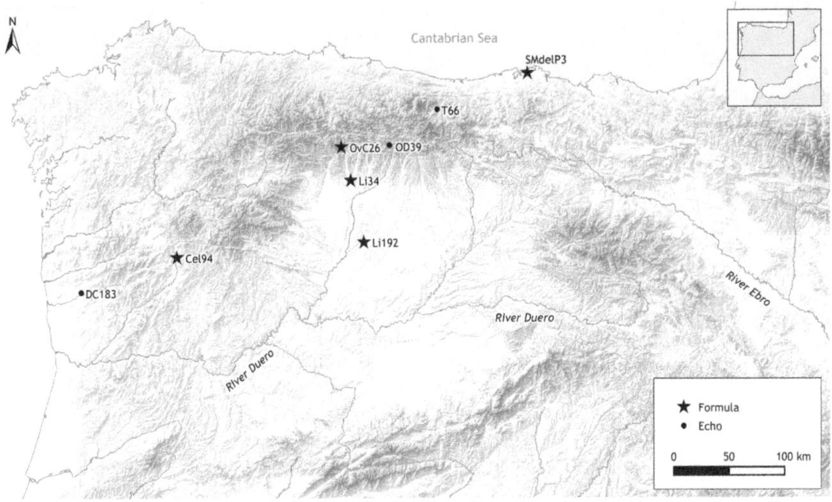

Figure 5.3 Formal commitments

trustworthy observers, like *ego innocens ad pena caldaria ingressus fui* ('I the innocent entered the ordeal').[68] Secondly, words indicating that the man (or very occasionally woman) put his hand into the hot water and pulled out (the hot stones), like *manum in kaldaria misit et* [?] *eiecit.*[69] Thirdly, words indicating that three days later, in a public assembly, the person's hand was revealed to be clean (and unharmed), like *in tercio uel in quarto die limpidus in concilio apparui.*[70] Two charters also cite statements associating the *fideles* with one or both parties.[71] Citation of these words is not consistent enough to suggest use of standard ritual words nor of a written formula in the ninth and tenth centuries: elements of some basic ideas appear to have been combined in different ways, rather like the way that elements of standard price clauses and sanctions were differently combined in sale and other charters.[72] They therefore seem to reflect elements of a standard mode of recording, rather than elements of performance, and this is even more loosely reflected in three further charters – one indicating that there was no need for an ordeal since sufficient oaths had been sworn, and the other two briefly suggesting that an ordeal had taken place.[73] Most of the references in any case feature in the course of Accounts, as part of a narrative about

68 Sob109; cf. *tornaui fideles et nocente de penna caldaria*, Cast1. See also OvC26, Cel252, SantA24 (with *fideles*), OD31 (with *fidelis*).

69 OvC26; cf. Sob109, OD31 and A27 (twice).

70 OvC26 three times (and also a list of witnesses of the revelation that it was clean), Sob109; cf. Cañ41; apparently reflected in PMH DC 160, *sacastis linpio de conzelio.*

71 OvC26, Sob109; *N ubi fidelis fuit de parte NN.*

72 See above, pp. 107–11.

73 SM27/BG391; AHN 1325A–9, Cañ65.

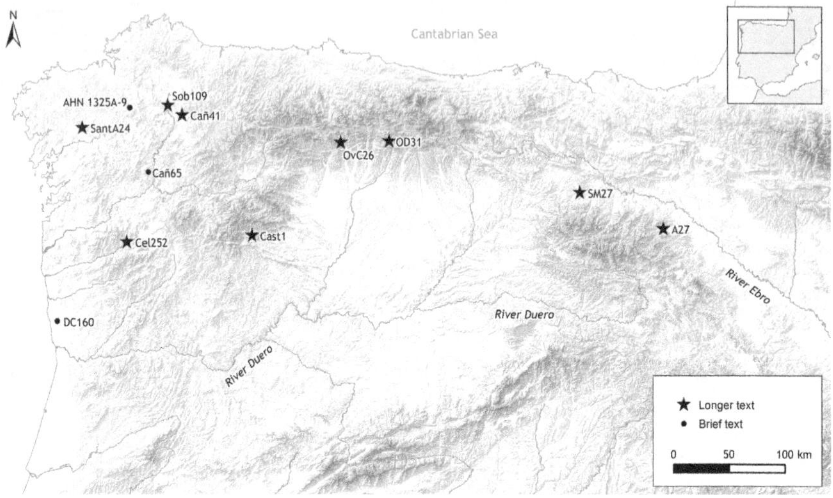

Figure 5.4 Charters referring to the ordeal

past procedure.[74] Overall, the texts suggest a retrospective view of a procedure, although the dates, which range across the tenth century from 912 to 1000, lie predominantly in the period from 973 onwards; the fact that one text of 991 is on a single sheet must mean that the practice was considered viable in the late tenth century.[75] The spatial distribution of the charters with such references is decidedly odd: with a weighting in Galicia (north and south, including northern Portugal), it extends to the western and northern edges of the *meseta* and then jumps eastwards to the Ebro valley and its tributary, the River Tirón (see Figure 5.4). The large region of the *meseta*, with its hundreds and hundreds of charters, is devoid of such references before 1000.[76]

The situation is complicated, and there is far too little material to be certain, but it looks as if we are dealing here with an old-established method of recording use of the ordeal, elements of which were put together in different ways by different scribes. These elements do slightly reflect a provision of Visigothic law dealing with the circumstances in which a judge might use the ordeal, and especially what should happen if a person emerged innocent from the hot water ordeal.[77] They reflect more strongly the words of an addition to

74 Not Accounts: OD31 and PMH DC 160 which are both Incidental, OvC26 and A27 which are both Mixed.

75 OD31; ACO B.1.11 (OvC26) is on a single sheet too, but must have been retrospectively constructed; see below, pp. 146–7.

76 Liii597 (1000) has *insuper caldaria*, but this looks like an error; later in the eleventh century, S542 (1050) and S575 (1055), both single sheets, clearly recount use of the ordeal.

77 *Leges Visigothorum*, ed. Karl Zeumer, MGH Leges nationum Germanicarum, sectio I.1 (Hanover, 1902), VI.1.8 (pp. 250–51).

this Visigothic corpus, which occurs in some later Spanish manuscripts: *manum mittere* is especially notable in this addition, but there is also an association of the procedure with innocence in the words *atque pueritia innocens, tota manu sana et totum corpus absque macula.*[78] The fact that the closer wording occurs in the addition to the corpus, rather than in the seventh- or eighth-century law, suggests that ideas about the ordeal, although apparently late Visigothic in origin, were being developed in the post-Visigothic period. Although it looks as if the practice of recourse to the ordeal was rare, the idea of it was certainly current in the later tenth century.

Texts primarily recording gift or sale

As noted above, Incidental and Implied records, Fines and Debts were primarily constructed to record gift or sale – that is, a transaction rather than a dispute – and therefore their formulas are essentially the formulas of gift, sale and exchange discussed in Chapter 4 (74, 10, 41 and 31 examples respectively).[79] Occasionally, none of the frequently used formulas found in those charters occur in this group of incidental records of dispute, but that is rare, and is usually a consequence of a record of non-standard form;[80] Confiscation records, on the other hand, nearly always lack these features, often because they reflect a distinctive, royal, diplomatic practice (19 examples).[81] Many of these incidental records use one or other version of the widely occurring *cogentis* formula, in accordance with the geographical distribution patterns outlined above, including the local *adgentis*-type variant in two of the Incidental records from the southern side of the Cantabrian Mountains.[82] The standard freedom clause, in one of its versions (the verbs vary widely), is almost invariable throughout: *ut de odie die et tempore sit ipsa [N] de iure nostro abrasa et in uestro iure sit tradita . . . abeatis firmiter de dato nostro, et quicquid exinde agere, facere uel iudicare uolueritis, sit concessa uobis potestas.* Given a tendency to frame Fines and Debts as sale records, the standard price clause features; its incidence reflects those of sale formula patterns, with the 'completing' clause (*set omni nobis bene conplestis*) added to León records, Incidental especially, but not elsewhere.[83] All, or most of, the standard sanction formula occurs extremely frequently in all of these types of record, and it is almost invariable in records of León, Otero and Portuguese collections and very common in those of Celanova: *Si quis tamen, quod fieri non credo, contra hanc uendiccionis ad inrumpendum uenerit uel uenero, an quislibet homo de parte mea, que in iudicio uindicare non ualuero, tunc inferas uel infera, pars mea partique*

78 Ibid., XII.3.18 (p. 463).

79 See above, pp. 40–1, 50–1, 41–4, 53–4.

80 For example, Cel144 and Sob46 (Incidental), S218 (Fine), V43 (Implied – a guarantor document), Cel411 (Debt).

81 See above, pp. 52–3.

82 See above, pp. 97–106; OD32 and OD33.

83 See above, pp. 108–9.

tue, ipsa terra duplata uel quantum ad uos fuerit meliorata, with the usual variant *ad iudicio deuendicare* in the Portuguese case. Like its occurrence in gift and sale records, the incidence of the full formula is less frequent in northern Galicia, and elements of the full sanction are more likely to have been omitted there. The additional *subrogata/supposita* clause features in Incidental records, Fines and Debts in records from the *meseta*, as also in one Celanova Fine and one Liébana Incidental, its distribution reflecting that of its occurrence in records of gift and sale.[84] The same is also true of the occurrence of *Iuda traditore* in some sanctions, reflecting warnings of the Last Judgment, sometimes with the variant *Iuda proditore*.[85] It is noticeable in Incidental texts recording gifts to monastic or episcopal beneficiaries.[86]

All of the above examples simply reinforce the fact that just over half of the references to disputes occur in the context of records whose primary function was to record a transaction. The element of dispute does not change the essential patterns of gift and sale formulas as they occur in these texts. However, two formulas which are characteristic of 'pure' dispute records occasionally feature in them: *agnoui/cognoui in ueritate* and *deuenimus ad iudicium*. The former occurs in mid- and late tenth century Incidental records and Fines from Galicia, especially, and the *meseta*.[87] The latter occurs in two of the same León records and one from Otero.[88] As discussed elsewhere in this chapter, these formulas appear to be characteristic of the way a scribe, at a second stage of recording, described the commitment of a principal actor.[89] It is similarly notable that the language used to record commitment to participate in due process is also occasionally reflected in these texts: *adsignaui* and *compromittimus* in Incidental records, as well as a note of a *uicarius pro consignare* in a Confiscation.[90]

Scribal considerations

As mentioned above, there remains one fairly common formula that occurs in a range of different kinds of text: *deuenimus inde ad/in iuditio/concilio*, 'we arrived from there at court/the meeting'. Although unremarkable and modest in meaning, the recurrence of this particular formulation in a number of different contexts is striking – in Accounts, Incidental records, Fines, Agreements and one Confession, across the period 922–1000, from Galicia to the *meseta*, on single sheets (in two-thirds of the cases) and in cartulary

84 Cel204 (p. 288); T41. Otherwise, for example on the *meseta*: C54, S133, Li148, E30, OD40.

85 See above, pp. 117–18.

86 For example: Ast84, C59, Lii432, LaC50, S221, Sam16, Sob43, AHN 1325A–5, Cañ69 (Incidental); Cel180 (Incidental and Fine); Lor21 (Implied).

87 Cel165, LaC61, Cañ49 (the latter two on single sheets); Cel197, Lii458 (single sheet), Liii556; also Cel509 in the third person (Implied).

88 Lii458, Liii556, OD37 (Fine).

89 See above, p. 131, and below, pp. 140–1.

90 LaC61, Cel527; Li253.

copies. It nearly always occurs in first person and past tense, nearly always continues *ante/in presentia N*, and is nearly always followed sooner or later by *cognouimus/agnouimus in ueritate*.[91] Basically, it belongs with the latter formula as a characteristic phrase in second-stage recording of the commitment by a principal actor to action following a dispute. Not normally the wording of a primary record (though occasionally so), it is characteristic of the way scribes who were constructing a record for preservation described the words of the principal actor. So the constructed summary of Cel94 includes the *deuenimus* formula (using *peruenimus*), but the appended primary records do not; the long composite record of acquisitions by Cresconio of Celanova has it in a summary of what must have been a record of a fine – *do . . . uobis propter actionem que nobis accidit de Gundisaluo . . . et deuenimus inde ante uos in iuditio et agnoui me in ueritate pro ipsa actione* ('I give [this] to you because of the dispute we had with Gonzalo . . . and we came before you in court and I honestly acknowledged [my part] in that dispute'); gift records have it when some detail is noted in passing of how the property to be transferred had been acquired; and, very appropriately, since they record consequences of proceedings, several Fines have it.[92] Its occurrence in Accounts is interesting, and reinforces the point: whereas in two records it occurs in the third person, as one might expect of these retrospective records, in another two it occurs in the first person.[93] Use of the first person in a Lugo record is striking because most of this record is cast in the third person – it is as if the retrospective Account drops into the first person as it encounters in some earlier record, or imagines, the first-person declaration. Overall, this looks as if it was a typical way for a scribe to formulate what an actor (usually a loser) would say when recounting what had happened. Choice of the word *superbia* to describe the act of rebellion reflects a similar process: it was the word that came to mind in certain particular circumstances.[94]

And what of the redactors of these records, whether they wrote them themselves or dictated them to others? The processes required in drawing up dispute records were different from those needed to construct a gift or sale record. In the latter cases, what was needed was the ability to learn and apply the appropriate formulas, whether memorized or copied from other written material, as well as to include the appropriate specific detail of person and place; in

91 Third person: Liii577 (997), S356 (998) (see further below, pp. 143–4; without *ante*: Liii577 (though *in presentia Ruderico* [*sic*] in the witness/confirmer list); without *cognouimus*: LaC50 (947) (the party was cleared), OD43 (997) (in which *deuenimus* occurs before this formula), Liii597 (1000), OD37 (994), AHN Clero Lugo 1325A–6 (922).

92 Cel197 (975–1011); LaC61 (958); Lii458 (978), Liii556 (993). See also n. 91 above, and pp. 112, 131.

93 Third person: see, n. 91 above; first person: AHN 1325A–6 (922), S295 (978).

94 For example, from a range of very different recording sources: SantA13 (886), Sob122 (960), Lii442 (975), Cel104 (994), Liii581 (998), TV15 (998).

most cases, the formulas occupied considerably more space than the particularities. At the highest level, scribes could elaborate the formulas with biblical quotations and expansive pieties, as is characteristic of the records of some royal and aristocratic gifts.[95] One might expect that the scriptoria of the great monasteries, and the scribes of royal and episcopal households, had such skill that they could turn their hands to the free narrative of a dispute text just as easily as they could fashion an elegant preamble. But what of the scribes in less elevated locations, and especially those who had dealings with people in local and regional courts? They must have had some capacity to write free text (and/or to listen to and transcribe what people said), and they must have had some knowledge, however it may have been acquired, of the conventional formulas for recording different aspects of judicial proceedings. Since many of those formulas (not all) were used both at the beginning and the end of the period under consideration, in a wide scatter of regions, they must have been of some antiquity; those that reflected classical legal technical language were clearly of very early origin, however they had been transmitted.[96] This implies a degree of specialized knowledge (just as knowledge of Visigothic law itself implies some specialized knowledge). Whereas the rural local priest could well act as notary for the recording of straightforward transactions, recording the outcome of a dispute is unlikely to have been a task for most local priests. Those who made records of what had happened at judicial proceedings must have been a rather special group – without going so far as to suppose they had the legal professionalism that was to develop in western Europe in the twelfth century and beyond. It must be likely that some were judges: although Brother Munnio *iudex* who redacted the record of a gift by King Vermudo in 990 clearly moved in royal court circles, plenty of judges operated at more local levels.[97] Some may have been *saiones*, and perhaps others were more than usually skilful clerics. We can put names to a few of them, but not many (fewer than a quarter of Oath, Confession and Agreement texts have named scribes), and even where we have a name, we rarely know anything about his social and political context. Both Braolio, who made records of the outcomes from Flaino Muñoz's courts, and Sendino, who did the same for Munio Fernández, in the late tenth century, appear to have been scribes attached to their aristocratic households – two scribes who clearly did a lot of court work (though both men used other scribes too).[98] Some of the named priests and deacons who also made judicial records may have been attached to larger or smaller monasteries – like the priest Arrano who recorded the Agreement in the monastery of San Martín, in or near León, while the deacon Erifonsus who recorded the Abellar/Sahagún

95 See above, pp. 112–16.

96 Of course, some of these characteristic terms are words that were also common in classical legal texts – *condicio, cognoscere, rogare, manifestum, sacramentum*, for example – but they are so common in classical literature that it is irrelevant to look for a specific channel of transmission; individual texts occasionally use classical expressions, like *rouorem inieci* ('validate') and *locupletes* ('trustworthy') of Sob109.

97 Liii541. See further below, pp. 160–4, for judges.

98 See Davies, 'Local priests and the writing of charters', pp. 37, 42.

Agreement seems to have belonged to the Sahagún scriptorium.[99] Some others were attached to episcopal households.[100] We can only guess about the rest.

Final word

I have argued that, although formulas do not occupy much space in dispute texts, nevertheless those that do occur are significant and can help us understand the process of construction of these texts. The formulas arise for different kinds of reason; hence, any attempt to summarize cannot be very tidy. However, it seems reasonable to suggest that there is an essential difference in kind between those formulas that characterize third-person and those that characterize first-person records, as well as some significant differences within each group.

The formulas characteristic of first-person dispute texts suggest that there were often two stages of recording Confessions and Agreements: firstly, a primary record that noted the raw details of a confession or an agreement, and secondly, a subsequently constructed charter which summarized the appropriate details of both, which might well have included a consequent conveyance and which always included a sanction in the case of default. It looks as if the primary records, which also include Oaths, could include quotation of ritual words uttered in court, like *iuramus quia occulis uidimus et aures audiuimus*, *manifestus sum uerum est quod negare non ualeo* and *nostrum placitum tibi compromittimus*, while the written formulas of formal commitment and perhaps guarantor documents also seem to have been primary records; such records were not normally intended to be preserved. Fortunately, by chance, some are. There were clearly conventional ways of constructing the subsequent charter and of characterizing the speech of the principal actor, like *deuenimus inde ad iudicio*. While it is conceivable that those who made the primary records actually did so in the course of judicial proceedings, this does not have to have been the case; it could easily have been done shortly after the meeting, the principal actor repeating necessary detail and the ritual words already well known to the redactor. In either case, the redactors must have been familiar with the conventions of judicial proceedings and must have had certain skills over and above those of the local priests who performed notarial functions for local communities.

The formulas that characterize third-person records include both signals that introduce a dispute text, like *orta fuit intentio*, and conventional phrases appropriate for the description of judicial proceedings, like *ordinare ut* and *preuidere*. Although most of the text was free narrative, these records were set within a formulaic framework of surprisingly wide use. They are representative of a third and different stage of charter construction, particularly associated with creation of narrative, retrospective Accounts. Most of these formulas are therefore notable in Accounts, but they can also be reflected in Incidental and Implied records of dispute and, especially, Fines. However, any of the formulas characteristic of

99 Liii597, Lii437.
100 See above, p. 39.

first-person records might also appear in these texts, as conscious or unconscious citation of pre-existing or imagined records. Both of the latter circumstances are conceivable, particularly in respect of Accounts: those who constructed Accounts sometimes may have had knowledge of or access to existing documents; but sometimes they may not have had access to any relevant written material at all.

Some of the characteristic formulas of third-person texts have more restricted use. Why *preuidere* should be characteristic of Galician texts rather than others is unclear, given its quite common occurrence in texts from other parts of western Europe of the early middle ages.[101] However, use of some conventional phrases, specifically those including the notions of *boni homines* and *iudicatum*, increases in frequency across the tenth century; this appears to reflect changing and developing judicial practice.

The formulas which appear to reflect the utterance of ritual words are particularly striking in their consistency and in their use across an extremely wide area. In this they differ from the characteristic formulas of gift and sale charters, with their multiple variations and pockets of local practice, and they differ from the formulas of charters making incidental references to disputes, which certainly do reflect those multiple variants.[102] Even the formulas used in secondary and tertiary records of dispute for the most part lack those patterns of multiple variation. Exceptions are the elements of Confession formulas that do not appear to have been understood or appear as variants; the elements of describing ordeal procedure, which appear to have been transmitted as elements rather than whole formulas; and use of *adgentis* for *cogentis* in a couple of the Otero Incidental records, linking their formulation to a pocket of distinctive local practice.[103] But there are relatively few exceptions of this kind. The consistency of many of the formulas used in dispute texts is important because it suggests a smaller pool of redactors and a shorter history of use, restricting the development of so many variations. Although some formulas clearly have a background in Visigothic material, there is less suggestion of the Late Antique than attaches to some of the gift and sale formulas. Moreover, there are some positive suggestions of development in recording practice after the Visigothic period (for example, in the formulas of Oaths) and of further changing practice in the course of the tenth century, especially in the second half of the century. In this latter respect, the framing of dispute records matches the framing of other charters, as communication extended, procedures began to change and large monasteries began to mould diplomatic practice in their own distinctive ways. Many records of disputes were clearly written by monastic beneficiaries, but some were not, and these records emerged – often imperfectly – from the process of

101 With much the same sense of 'to judge' in Italian texts and with the sense of 'to survey, estimate', especially in the contexts of land survey, in Frankish texts; see Jan Frederik Niermeyer, *Mediae Latinitatis Lexicon Minus* (2nd edn, Leiden, 1984), s.v. *praevidere*.

102 See above, pp. 97–106, 139–40.

103 OD32, OD33.

the courts. The difference between these two kinds of origin is of considerable importance in assessing their value as evidence of what happened in the course of judicial process. Just as important is the difference between, on the one hand, all the records primarily concerned with the proceedings and outcome of court process and, on the other, those records which include incidental references to disputes in charters whose main purpose was to record something else.

Coda

What, then, should we make of the large and puzzling single sheet ACO B.1.11?[1] It would appear that this was a retrospective attempt to create a charter covering the Gordón case and its outcome in order to record confirmation of that outcome (in favour of the monastery) by the king of León. Ordoño III's subscription is central to the layout of the charter, which suggests that such a confirmation is central to the rationale behind the record; if it happened, it could have been as early as 954, a year after the case. However, this could easily have been a retrospective record, and it is perfectly clear that most of the subscriptions of members of the León court were added to the charter (although several of these people could in fact have been present in the 950s). It must be likely that the record was produced before 981, the date of the subsequent endorsement, which is intrinsically credible and which lies below the witness subscriptions.[2] There is no strong reason to doubt that a court case did actually happen, given the quantity of circumstantial detail, although the record is probably highly selective and there is doubtless much that we do not know of proceedings. It is also possible that there was confirmation by Ordoño III; given that there were royal interests in the area, in the fort of Gordón, it was appropriate to seek royal confirmation. The charter appears to have been constructed from materials produced near the time of the court sessions, for it includes

1 See Figures 0.1 and 0.2 above and pp. 1–4, for a description, pp. 60–3 for the text, and also pp. 69, 124–5, 135–8.

2 For several of the León court group (Ordoño III, Bishop Gonzalo of León, Gundesindo and Fortis Iustiz), all of which except the last are recorded in the same hand, compare Lii280 (a royal confirmation of 12 November 954). The subscriptions of Bishop Gudesteo of Oviedo, Sancho, Elvira and the priest Nebutiano form the second column of witnesses, below Ordoño III (Sancho and Elvira also subsequently added to the November 954 event of Lii280). These are in different hands and ink and at different orientations from the first group, and must be subsequent additions; as also Bishop Armentario of Dumio, at the bottom of the first column, in yet another ink and at another orientation. The opening words of Armentario's subscription (which do seem to read *Dextera uirtus*) are clearly in error for *in/sub Christi uirtute*, often used by bishops. All of these must be additions after 954, and since the bishops Gudesteo and Armentario took office *c.* 992 and 985 respectively, they cannot have been added before the very late tenth century. The subscription of Armentario, which lies above the 981 endorsement, could have been inserted into a blank space.

four formal commitments, an Oath, an account of an ordeal and several lists of different witnesses of different parts of the process; the form of the Oath is testimony, then invocation of the holy, then repeat of the testimony, which appears to have been standard recording procedure for oaths.[3] The core of the story must have been copied from a written source because of the nature of the variations in this threefold repetition – these are the kind of variants that derive from copying or miscopying a written text, not from pure invention.[4] Since there are obvious errors in the repetition of some names, inconsistencies in the testimony and an additional initial statement of the testimony, this material emerges as partly garbled. This would suggest that what we have on the single sheet was constructed at some distance from the sessions, whether distant in time or place or both, although it makes sense to suppose that the core material originated in the monastery of Gordón. On balance, it looks as if the record was constructed some time between 954 and 981, although many of the high-status subscriptions must have been added subsequently, not before the very late tenth century in some cases. In my view, then, difficult as this text is, it is valuable both because it must derive from materials relating to a court case of the mid-tenth century and also because it provides an extreme example of the kind of subsequent elaboration those materials might receive in order to provide a confirmable Account.

* * *

Drawing together the multiple threads discussed in Part I, I would emphasize the points that follow. The language of regular charters of gift, sale and exchange between lay persons, and in particular the widespread use of a standard sanction referring to a claim made in court, shows that going to court was the natural place to pursue a disputed transaction; it was part of the customary culture. The language of many charters of gift, particularly those recording gifts to monastic beneficiaries, as well as that of much of the liturgy, shows that the idea of judgment was embedded in literate culture and that it was often associated with punishment.

Records of the settlement of disputes in a public forum survive haphazardly and imperfectly, but it is perfectly clear that judicial process was recorded in a number of different ways. Of those different ways, there is an essential difference between, firstly, retrospective narratives of judicial process recorded at some distance from the events they describe (Accounts); secondly, material directly deriving from the activity of the court (Oaths, Confessions, Agreements, some elements of Mixed records, and formal commitments); thirdly, a range of records in which judicial process is explicit but briefly mentioned, or implicit, because the main purpose of the record is to record a transaction of some kind (Incidental and Implied records and Fines); and fourthly, records

3 See above, pp. 124–6.

4 For detailed comparison, see the Appendix below.

deriving from some kind of dispute which was not necessarily handled in a judicial court (Debts and Confiscations).[5] Material in the second category – that deriving from the activity of a court – survives as a primary or a secondary record; in the first case, raw data that was not intended to be kept, and in the second, elements of that data reworked to become a coherent charter. Both of these might be subsequently used in constructing a narrative Account.

These retrospective Accounts tend to have been constructed as large display documents, like ACO B.1.11, deliberately laid out for effect with plenty of space for the subscriptions of important people – rather like records of major gifts to cathedrals and monasteries. Since a disproportionate number of these Accounts has one or more confirmations by kings, the principal purpose of drawing up such Accounts, which were essentially records of how a certain outcome (like the transfer of property) came about, appears to have been to secure confirmation of that outcome by one or more high-status individuals, regardless of whether or not those individuals had actually been personally involved in the proceedings.

By contrast, records deriving from court activity tended to be small and functional, and could be written on an odd corner or the dorse of an existing charter. This means that there was sometimes some kind of note-making during or shortly after judicial proceedings, on behalf of interested parties; it does not follow that it always happened, and the emphasis is very much on interested parties rather than on objective reporting – individuals making quick notes within a formulaic framework that must have been long established. Indeed, since their formulation is remarkably standard across a wide area (although occasionally there is a hint of a pocket of local practice), some of the words of these texts seem to represent ritual words uttered in court. Judicial practice itself appears to have been long established. While some of the formulas used in standard charters of gift and sale must ultimately have been of late Roman origin, given their occurrence in Italy and Catalonia,[6] some of the practice, and of the records describing it, including the origin of the Oaths, must be of Visigothic origin. Other formulas appear to be from more recent, post-Visigothic, times: while some of these look as if they were of eighth- or ninth-century origin, others reflect monastic strategies of the later tenth century and still others seem to reflect some real changes in judicial practice in the later tenth century.

The scribes who wrote the charters of the third and fourth categories, which are strongly influenced by the diplomatic habits of charters of gift, sale and exchange, came from as wide a range of contexts as did those who wrote those charters of gift and sale, from royal notaries and members of the scriptoria of great monasteries to more or less isolated local priests. The scribes who created the Accounts appear to have come predominantly from monastic scriptoria or

5 It is, however, clear that settlement of some debts was handled in a public meeting, as also that orders for confiscation often came from a meeting of great men and women attending the royal court.

6 See above, p. 98.

episcopal households; many of the identifiable scribes are from episcopal households.[7] Bishops may well have been especially concerned to create and keep records, but their apparent prominence is probably misleading: certainly, big monasteries (bearing in mind the monastic sanctions and warnings of doom), but also powerful aristocrats and other powerful clerics would have been just as concerned to have and to keep records. The single sheets that record the calling in of debts make the point: there was the aristocrat Fruela Vimáraz, who clearly called debtors before him on a given day and had records made,[8] and the priest Munio, who kept a sheet of his several transactions, including gifts in lieu of debts (see Figure 3.3).[9] Some of the charters in the Sobrado cartulary must have come from similar sheets.[10] Lay court holders, like Munio Fernández, Hermenegildo and the Flaínez family, seem to have been particularly concerned to do this, but there are some less prominent aristocrats, like the Fruela who seems to have presided in court in 963, who must also have done so.[11] As for those who made notes in or shortly after a court session, they must, as discussed above, have had some special skill, and it seems reasonable to suppose that some or many were judges with legal expertise.[12]

These different kinds of text have different kinds of evidential value, and their consideration is therefore an essential prologue to considering judicial practice in action. In what follows, on people, practice and social process, I shall pursue the potential significance of those differences.

7 See above, p. 39.

8 OD40 and OD41, on the single sheet AHDL Otero 31, of 6 June 995.

9 See above, p. 70.

10 For example, Sob98, Sob99, both of 22 December 952.

11 Lii360, a sale record, which must include a note of a separate court case, for which see above, p. 47. For lay archives, see Adam J. Kosto, '*Sicut mos esse solet*: Documentary practices in Christian Iberia, *c.* 700–1000', in Warren C. Brown, Marios Costambeys, Matthew Innes and Adam J. Kosto (eds), *Documentary Culture and the Laity in the Early Middle Ages* (Cambridge, 2013), pp. 259–82.

12 See above, pp. 140–3. Roger Collins, '"Sicut lex Gothorum continet": Law and charters in ninth- and tenth-century León and Catalonia', *English Historical Review*, 100 (1985), pp. 489–512, argued for a standard package of confession, oath and judge's account. Much of his argument depended upon Catalan material, and the argument may hold good for that area; the Leonese texts he used are far from typical, and he did not use some of the important texts from, for example, the Otero collection.

Appendix

Here is the core of the narration of ACO B.1.11, a core that is repeated three times. My purpose in this Appendix is to demonstrate the excessive variation in the telling of this story. The main text is that of the opening version of the story, B the first repetition and C the next repetition. See above, pp. 00 [ch. 2] for the complete text. Italics indicate words that do not occur in B; underlines indicate words that do not occur in C.

ego Petrus mea persona et mea testimonia per quos firmetur super Uilifredo qui est uigarios de Uictino, quomodo[13] segdente[14] se Petrus[15] in suo monasterio *de Seuero*[16] de Seuero abba sic[17] se leuauit Uictinus[18] *et inuitauit Petrum ad sua mensa et in alio die* accesit ad illo[19] uolumtas animo karo et spontania sua uolumtate[20] *et donauit ad Petrum terra uagua*[21] *sua ratione et de sua muliere Fredildi et de Teodeuera uno* consilio aderato *et terra donada et assinada super placito et iuramentum quos fecissent ibidem monasterio*[22] *ita et fecerunt* et roborabit[23] placito *Uictinus*[24] in solidos C[25] et monasterio facto *et* eglesia et kasas et corte[26] clusa et ortum et pomare postum

13 B: ad[d]uxo Uictinus [fratrem] Petrum ad sua mensa et; C, as B, less letters within [].
14 B and C: sedente.
15 B: Petro; C: Petrum.
16 B: su mano; C: sub mano.
17 B: appa si; C: appa et si.
18 C: cuius uigarius est Uilifredus pro consilio de Teodeuera et de Fredildi.
19 B: illum; C: illos.
20 B: uoluntate; C: et donaberunt et assinnaberunt suas raciones quem abebunt in Paragiaio sic Uictino quomodo etiam et Teodeuera et Fredildi ad frater Petrum spontania sua uolumtate et rouoraberunt placitum ad fratrem Petrum de omni sua ereditate quem abebant in Paragiaio ad integritate.
21 B: but see n. 20 above.
22 B: quum Teodeuera et Fredildi.
23 B: rouorauit; C: roboraberunt placitum.
24 B: ad fratrem Petrum.
25 B: de ipsa hereditate de Teodeuera et de Fredildi que donaberunt ad frater Petrum et donaberunt et assinaberunt ipsa ereditate que abebant in Paragiaio terra uagua que fecisset ibidem monasterio, ita et fecerunt; C: et donaberunt et assinaberunt ipsa terra uagua quo fecissent monasterium ita et fecerunt.
26 B: coorte.

et aque[27] *metuta*[28] que ipso[29] monasterio regat[30] syc[31] se leuauit Uictinus pro[32] consilio de Uilifredo *qui ipsa uoce autorigauit*[33] *ad integritate*[34] et *pro consilio* de serore[35] Gugina et per Teouera[36] et de Fredildi bracio forcioso[37] animo orrido et tullerunt[38] ad *frater* Petrum ipso monasterio[39] et ipsa ereditate[40] *unde placito rouorauerunt et tulliuit mici*[41]alia eglesia quem abeba[42] de auios meos[43] et uinia que donauit[44] Seuero[45] appa et serore Gogina[46] ad Petrum et autoriauit[47] Seuero appa[48] *ad Petrum* in concilio de Gordone ante Teoderedo Iustiz[49] et Felix iudigum *in conuentum eglesie Sancte Marine*.[50] [51]Si se leuauit Uilifredus et Uictinus[52] et tullerunt *mici* ipsa uinia et ipso uino[53]

27 B: aqua.
28 C: aqua mittuta.
29 B: ipse.
30 C: qui ipsum monasterium inregat et ipso lauore facto.
31 B: si; C: sic.
32 B: Uitinus per.
33 C: autorcauit.
34 C: in concilio.
35 B and C: sorore.
36 B and C: de Teodeuera.
37 B: fortioso et.
38 B and C: tulliuit.
39 C: ipsum monasterium; 'Petrum' and 'monasterium' reversed.
40 B: 'monasterio' and 'hereditate' reversed.
41 B: et.
42 B and C: quam abebat; C: + Petrus.
43 B and C: suos.
44 C: donaberat.
45 C: Seuerus.
46 B: sorore Gugina; C: Gugina.
47 B: autogauit illa; C: autorcauit illa.
48 C: abba.
49 B: Iustiti; C: Iustizi.
50 C: Marie.
51 B and C: the sentence runs on with 'et'.
52 B and C: Uilifredus and Uictinus are reversed.
53 B: + ad Petrum; C: ad frater Petrum.

Part II
Implications

6 Roles

As some of the formulas of the earliest sanctions in charters make clear, there was an expectation that people with a case to make should make it in court.[1] There was a functioning system of judicial courts across the whole of northern Iberia, with established procedures and dedicated officers, experts, written law and scales of penalty, throughout the period under consideration; it was clearly not new when our detailed evidence begins. Toresario's confession of failure to pay dues associated with the church of Villa Moreta in central Galicia was made in 861 before a count in a formal court; the record, which survives on a single sheet in the Lugo cathedral archive, uses formulas which are standard in confession records: already at this point there was certainly a standard way of handling and also of recording such cases.[2]

Just as close attention to the writing of the texts can differentiate between an immediate primary record, a secondary reconstruction and a tertiary, retrospective Account, so close attention to the content of these texts can highlight the principal actors in court proceedings. There are several kinds of consistent role played in court cases: those of presidents, judges, *saiones* (legal officers) and *boni homines* (literally 'worthies', people of good reputation), as well as providers of evidence, oath-takers and guarantors. I shall deal with their functions in turn, before considering their social status.

Presidents

We do not always know who presided at a court hearing, because the texts are often ambiguous and sometimes completely silent on the matter; the identity of the president is unambiguous in just over a third of the records which detail or imply court cases.[3] Although there are too many cases in which the identity of the president is unknown or unclear, there is nevertheless sufficient material to

1 See above, pp. 119–20.

2 ACLu 60 2 (Flor74); see above, pp. 44–8, 126–30, for confession formulas, and pp. 84–5, for the charter; if it is a copy, as seems likely, I would regard it as a careful copy of a ninth-century record.

3 See further Wendy Davies, 'Summary justice and seigneurial justice in northern Iberia on the eve of the millennium', *Haskins Society Journal*, 22 (2010 [2012]), pp. 43–58, at p. 48.

have some idea of the kind of person who presided and the range of functions he or she performed – we know of some women who did this, so it was not an exclusively male sphere.[4] It might be thought that phrases like *ante N* ('before N') and *in presentia N* ('in the presence of N') identify a president, but analysis of all occurrences of such phrases makes it perfectly clear that they do not: rather, they indicate important people present at a session; these might include the president, but did not necessarily do so.[5] When the content of a charter is sufficiently detailed for us to see him or her clearly, we can see that what the president did was take the chair (perhaps literally) and preside over the conduct of judicial proceedings: the implication of the sanction formula *ante tribunal* is that president (and judges) were expected to sit on a special seat or bench.[6] He or she might receive appeals and complaints, and might initiate proceedings as a consequence; or an investigation beyond court might be ordered, as King Alfonso IV ordered the boundaries of Manzaneda and Garrafe to be inspected when representatives of the locality and the complainant monks of San Julián appeared before him;[7] or people could be ordered to appear before the president or a delegate, as King Ordoño III ordered Velasco Hánniz and the abbot of Abellar to appear before him on one Sunday in August 952, or if he were to be delayed, before the bishop of León;[8] or someone else might be instructed to take action. In court, he or she might order oaths to be sworn or documents to be produced; he or she might order the restoration of disputed property, as Count Suario ordered his *saio* Braolio to consign a church to Munio Gutiérrez after a long case with the priest Cristofor.[9] Sometimes the president joined the judges in judging, and very occasionally the president explicitly made the final decision.[10] The fact that the president may or may not have taken part in the judging makes it quite clear that the function of presidency was separable from that of judging: whereas presidents tended to take initiating and concluding actions in the conduct of a case, on the whole it was the judges who were concerned with the detail and with what lay between start and finish.[11] Presidents did join in the judging on occasion, but for the most part they let others deal with the details of evidence. Some 21 individuals who presided over courts are

4 See further below, pp. 159, 183, 192–4.

5 For detailed analysis, see Wendy Davies, 'Holding court: Judicial presidency in Brittany, Wales and northern Iberia in the early middle Ages', in Fiona Edmonds and Paul Russell (eds), *Tome: Studies in Medieval Celtic History and Law in Honour of Thomas Charles-Edwards* (Woodbridge, 2011), pp. 145–54, at pp. 150–53.

6 See above, p. 112. Note *sedente* ('sitting') *in Toro*, of a judge, S356 (998); and of the bishop, as judge, *sedente domno episcopo cum clero in concilio*, Li256.

7 Li89 (931); see above, p. 56.

8 Li256.

9 Sob130 (992).

10 For example, Lor36 (936), Sob103 (952), Jaca (958), Sam126 (960). Final decision: SM50 (948) (= BG 531).

11 For the detailed argument on this point, see Davies, 'Summary justice', p. 54.

recorded as joining the judges in making judgment; these were all figures with political power – kings, counts and bishops.[12]

The president was also, on most occasions, the court holder. There are times when the court holder delegated the holding of a particular court session to someone else, as in the very clear case in which the king of León ordered a further session and provided that the bishop of León should preside if he himself could not attend; in such cases, the identities of court holder and president were separate. The court holder doubtless acquired political influence from the proceedings and some measure of control over the community served by the court, but he or she also got the fine, in effect payment for providing the court and seeing the proceedings to a conclusion – in other words, court holder fees.[13] In some cases, particularly those concerned with low-value offences, the court holder received the fine, but the record does not assign him or her any part in the proceedings; here presidency was implicitly delegated to someone such as a *saio* or a *iudex*.[14] Clearly, then, it could happen that someone other than the court holder presided over the court proceedings, and it may have been common for low-value cases.[15]

Those who held courts and presided were clearly figures of authority: kings, counts, bishops and sometimes other landowners. There are explicit indications that anyone with control of territory was entitled to receive fines (that is, the people described as *potestas* or *dominus terrae*), and therefore that anyone with such territorial control could in principle hold a court: one charter from Otero de las Dueñas provides for half the fine to be shared between the *potestas* ('local power') and the judge.[16] In practice, the best examples of fines going to territorial lords come from the large monastery of Celanova in southern Galicia, from which we have the inventories of multiple properties accumulated in the late tenth and very early eleventh centuries. These inventories include detail of how the properties had been acquired, and they make it perfectly clear that the monastery had received some lands in lieu of fines, as territorial lord, for hearing cases of adultery, theft and property disputes between lay persons.[17] This is very good evidence that court holding, deriving from control but not necessarily ownership of territory, comparable in some respects to the seigneurial

12 See further below, p. 188, on the circumstances in which presidents joined in the judging.

13 See above, p. x, for comment on my use of the term 'fine'; note that it does not carry any implication of a penalty paid to the state.

14 For example, Sob31 (951), OD31 (991), perhaps Sob75 (858); there are also cases in the jurisdiction of an identifiable but absent person which were heard before a judge, e.g. T62 (962).

15 For a longer discussion of the issues here, see Davies, 'Summary justice', pp. 53–5.

16 OD21 (976). A standard sanction formula from the Cardeña scriptorium indicates that the fine should go to the *dominus terrae* (literally 'lord of the land'), C22 (932), C35 (941), C54 (945), for example; and another Castilian charter provides for the fine to go to the *principes terrae* ('lords of the land'), Ar18 (965).

17 See above, pp. 42–3, for these texts. Inventories: Cel181 (1005), Cel192 (1001), Cel197 (975–1011), Cel203 (1007), Cel204 (1005), Cel205 (975–1011), Cel368 (975–1009).

lordship of northern Europe, did actually happen.[18] How much land was subject to territorial control of this kind is impossible to know, and we should not assume that all of it was so controlled: we need to bear in mind that many of the phrases suggesting the capacity of territorial lords to fine people occur in sanctions, where their function was essentially that of deterrent, rather than in descriptions of practice. We do not know whether all landowners had such powers, but it seems very unlikely that they did so, given the numbers of small-scale proprietors in some areas. Nor do we know how such territorial control was acquired.[19] However, there are certainly some clear cases of courts, which followed all the standard procedures, being held by secular landowners: Dona Dimitria, for example, in Portugal, appears to have presided over a case in which a dispute between two priests over control of a church was settled; and the layman Ablavel Godestéiz had acquired property, which he gave to a monastery in 988, from a layman guilty of abduction, by implication in his role as court holder.[20] So there were landowners who held courts by virtue of their powers of territorial control, but we do not know how such powers originated nor what qualified such landowners to be court holders.

Of the actual cases in which presidency of court proceedings is clear, 39 per cent of presidents were kings, 23 per cent were counts, 15 per cent were bishops and 23 per cent were other aristocrats (including in this latter figure the monastery of Celanova).[21] But we should remember that we often do not know who presided – many records are ambiguous – and that it is clear that court holders could and did delegate the function of presiding to others. In a number of records, it looks as if abbots presided; some were certainly present

18 On the difference between domanial lordship (landlord power over dependents), seigneurial lordship (landlord political power over dependents and freemen) and the more developed, 'concrete', *seigneurie* (characterized as *propiedad dominical, dominio señorial, señorío jurisdiccional*), see the important work of Carlos Estepa Díez, 'Formación y consolidación del feudalismo en Castilla y León', in *En torno al feudalismo hispánico. I congreso de estudios medievales* (Ávila, 1989), pp. 157–256, at pp. 161–3, further developed in Carlos Estepa Díez, 'En torno a propiedad dominical, dominio señorial, y señorío jurisdiccional', in Gregorio del Ser Quijano and Iñaki Martín Viso (eds), *Espacios de poder y formas sociales en la edad media: estudios dedicados a Ángel Barrios* (Salamanca, 2007), pp. 67–76; although the full applicability of these concepts relates to the central and later middle ages, the principle of the distinction between types of power is relevant for the tenth century. Beyond Spain, see the classic work of Georges Duby, *La société aux XIe et XIIe siècles dans la région mâconnaise* (Paris, 1953), especially pp. 173–90.

19 Compare discussion of delegation, above, pp. 24–5.

20 PMH DC 163 (991); OD29 (988).

21 The percentages are of the total number of records, not the total number of cases. The Celanova inventories include several cases per inventory (Cel368 has at least 16 if debt records are included); if I were to total the cases, rather than the records, the percentage of other aristocrats as presidents would increase. Since these inventories constitute a very particular set of records, counting by case would distort the picture; hence my decision (but the alternative approach would be completely viable). These percentages differ from those I published previously because I have added more material (e.g. that from Lugo) and because I have not included cases as 'comital' unless the individual is explicitly called 'count' in the record; see Davies, 'Summary justice', p. 48; on counts, see above, pp. 20–6.

at court cases and were members of panels that took decisions; however, all of the possible cases of abbot presidents are ambiguous, and I have therefore not included them in the figures.[22] Of course, it is entirely possible that some abbots did preside over judicial courts, just as Cresconio, officer of the powerful monastery of Celanova, did; but it is much more likely that they did this by virtue of their territorial lordship rather than because of their role as monastic leaders.

If we think about the structure and types of dispute record in which this information is recorded, there are some further points to note. Just over half of the records that make the identity of the president clear are Accounts – the long, narrative retrospective records of the course of disputes and their outcomes; a fifth are the more functional Fines, Oaths, Confessions and Agreements; and the rest (another fifth) are Incidental records of disputes.[23] When kings are cited as presidents, this nearly always occurs in Accounts: three-quarters of cases. Citation of kings is also regionally limited: it is much more characteristic of León and southern Galician records than of others. Nearly half (45 per cent) of the cases of presidency by bishops occur in Accounts, and the rest are split evenly between, on the one hand, Fines, Oaths and Confessions and, on the other, Incidental records. The explicit presidency of counts occurs in nearly all categories of dispute record, two-thirds in Accounts, a quarter in Fines, Confessions and Agreements, and the rest in Incidental records. In significant contrast, the presidency of aristocrats and other landowners is mentioned overwhelmingly in Fines, Confessions and in Incidental records (89 per cent of cases), although there are two references in Accounts.[24] Virtually all of the fines that appear to have been paid – as opposed to threats of the fine due in the case of contravention – were actually paid to counts and to other landowners; that being the case, the closer-to-court and incidental records, although relatively small in number, may well in fact offer a better reflection of practice; in practice, was it counts and landowners who did most of the holding of courts and taking of fines? Landowners clearly could preside over public meetings that were not judicial courts, as Domna Sancha seems to have done when the sale of water rights to the monastery of Villabáscones was confirmed.[25] Of course, this does not mean that kings and bishops did not do so – one would expect them to hold courts for all kinds of purpose, as well as dealing with judicial disputes – but it may well mean that proportions derived from raw citations of explicit presidency are misleading: in reality, there may have been fewer kings and bishops and rather more landowners presiding over judicial proceedings. It also suggests that the frequent citation in Accounts of kings as presidents, and

22 For example, T17 (885), T30 (922), C55 (945), C103 (962), T66 (962 – it is more likely than not that Abbot Opila presided at some of these sessions); cf. Liii577 (997), in which an abbot took an oath, but we do not know who presided.

23 Also 6 per cent Mixed (which have much of the Account about them).

24 If the individual items of the Celanova inventories were added to the total, that would increase the proportion of Fine and Incidental records even further.

25 C88 (955).

to a lesser extent bishops, was in effect a strategy to boost authority, particularly that of kings;[26] by contrast, the citation of counts and others, secular and ecclesiastic, in more functional records was largely incidental to the purpose of the record, and is more likely to reflect practice on the ground.

Judges

Judges are much more commonly, and unambiguously, mentioned than presidents, and it is clear that they had a significant role in determining the outcome of cases. It is important at the outset to differentiate between those who did the judging in court (*qui iudicabat, qui iudicauerit,* 'he who was judging, he who has judged') (see Figure 6.1), and those to whom the label *iudex* was attached, whether in court or outside it. The group doing the judging, the group of *iudices* in the plural, might include, or indeed be entirely composed of, individuals who carried the label *iudex*, but usually it also included others; to do the judging, you did not need to be a *iudex*, although you might be.[27] Being called a *iudex* was a sign of expertise – people carried the label with them, and it was applied to them when, for example, they witnessed uncontested sale transactions; in other words, the label *iudex* and the act of judging were separable.[28] A *iudex* (in the singular) was a person of special status and special skill; he must usually have been literate (given the cases in which a scribe is termed *iudex*), and he is likely to have known some law. A *iudex* could also preside over a hearing if the court holder so required.[29] Doing the judging, by contrast, was something in which other leading people could participate; hence the common references to *iudices*, in the plural, as the people doing the judging; in a case about control of freedmen in Galicia, an additional three people were

26 The judicial functions of kings are much discussed; see Gonzalo Martínez Díez, 'Las instituciones del reino astur a través de los diplomas (718–910)', *AHDE*, 35 (1965), pp. 59–167, at pp. 67–81; Alfonso Prieto Prieto, 'La potestad judicial de los reyes de León', in *El reino de León en la alta edad media, II: Ordenamiento jurídico del reino* (León, 1992), pp. 519–64. In the past, there has been some tendency to overemphasize the capacity of kings to delegate judicial power in the ninth and tenth centuries – see, for example, Luis García de Valdeavellano, *Curso de historia de las instituciones españolas. De los orígenes al final de la edad media* (Madrid, 1968), p. 503; José María Mínguez, 'Justicia y poder en el marco de la feudalización de la sociedad leonesa', in *La giustizia nell'alto medioevo* (2 vols, Spoleto, 1997), vol. 1, pp. 491–546, at pp. 502–6, 521–2; Juan José Sánchez Badiola, *El territorio de León en la edad media. Poblamiento, organización del espacio y estructura social (siglos IX–XIII)* (2 vols, León, 2004), vol. 1, pp. 454–5 – but for a nuanced recent appreciation, see Álvaro Carvajal Castro, 'La construcción de la monarquía asturleonesa en la meseta del Duero. Estudio de los procesos de integración territorial (s. IX–XI)' (Universidad de Salamanca, Tesis Doctoral, 2013), ch. 5.

27 For a longer consideration of these issues, see Wendy Davies, 'Judges and judging: Truth and justice in northern Iberia on the eve of the millennium', *Journal of Medieval History*, 36/3 (2010), pp. 193–203.

28 Sánchez Badiola makes a comparable point in *El territorio de León*, vol. 1, p. 460; compare the Lombard texts which refer to the duke or gastald as *iudex* and the functionaries carrying out judicial activities as the *iudices*, François Bougard, *La justice dans le royaume d'Italie de la fin du VIIIe siècle au début du XIe siècle* (Rome, 1995), p. 141.

29 See above, p. 157.

Figure 6.1 Subscriptions of four judges, *quos iudicauit*, a scribe and a *saio*, in a record of a property case near Lugo in 973, AHN 1325A–9

Source: Reproduced by permission of Archivo Histórico Nacional of Spain.

selected from the assembled court to join the judging panel and probe the witness evidence.[30] Those who did the judging could be royal companions, abbots and monks, bishops and priests and minor clerics, and secular persons of some standing, often aristocrats.[31]

Judging was usually done by panels of anything from one to 12, the larger numbers being more typical of Galicia, the smaller of the *meseta*. What they almost invariably did was decide what should happen next in the conduct of a case. So they might determine that a given number of persons should swear an oath or that a given number of witnesses should be produced, as happened in central Galicia in 959, when the panel ordered five witnesses to be provided by the accused;[32] they might also make investigations themselves, as did those who measured the water levels in a León dispute over water rights;[33] they reviewed evidence provided by others, as the panel reviewed the documents brought to court by the priest Ansemondo in a Galician case of 922;[34] and they could decide a final outcome, particularly in cases of disputed boundaries, in which the panel might well walk the disputed land itself and locate the relevant markers; also,

30 LaC95 (985).
31 See further below, pp. 205–11.
32 Cañ41.
33 Li128 (938).
34 AHN Clero Lugo 1325A–6.

importantly, they could set fines where required, as a panel ordered a woman and her five children to return the value of sheep which had been stolen.[35] Sometimes precisely the same kinds of action taken by a judging panel were performed by people who were neither called *iudex* nor noted as a panel of *iudices*: in a boundary case in northern Portugal, in which the count and a panel of three went to inspect the land and find the boundary markers, judgment words are not used of their actions and none of them is called a judge, even though the case began in the count's court, the outcome was witnessed and they resolved the case in the characteristic manner of the courts.[36] This is a useful warning that the language of the records is neither consistent nor stable: it allows us to see something of what happened, but by no means all; doubtless there were plenty of other cases resolved by standard court procedure which are not recorded as such.

People who were given the status of *iudex*, whatever kind of activity was being recorded, must have been experts and must in effect have been professionals (although they may well have derived significant income from personal properties rather than from fees alone). Most of them must have been learned in the law, like the two judges in the Lugo case of 922 who, knowing *lex gotica*, pronounced that the documents that were presented in court were valid.[37] We have a few indications of the local context of some judges: Flacino, *iudex*, appears as witness to straightforward transactions in the Noanca/Cofiñal area on the southern flanks of the Cantabrian Mountains and appears to have had landed property there; he does not appear in other areas.[38] The royal judge Abaiub ibn Tebite seems to have had property in the Cea valley, his son continuing the interest in that region; Abaiub's son, like the royal judge Gutino Zelim, witnessed a major grant of property in that area in 970.[39] Gutino, whose base seems to have been an estate on the River Torío (by León), was called upon by the king to handle a confiscation in the Cea valley area.[40] Since this valley was about 40 km from the city of León, the royal base, it suggests that skilled judges might have lived at home (or in a monastery) and were called upon to serve in court when required, either locally or wherever the king might be. Indeed, I think it is helpful to think of these skilled judges as an independent learned class, rather like Irish judges of the early middle ages.[41] It is also clear that they

35 Sob23 (949).

36 Lor36 (936); the words *in ueritate* may reflect a resolution deriving from a judgment (see above, pp. 123–4. See further below, p. 224, for this case.

37 AHN 1325A–6: *iudices qui lex gotica docent*.

38 *Iudex* and sometimes witness: S115 (949), S116 (949), S148 (955); witness only: S41 (930), S57 (936), S92 (943), S106 (947), S117 and S118 (949); *termino de Flacino*: S198 (962).

39 S255 (a later eleventh- or twelfth-century copy); cf. *castro de Abaiub*, Li197 (947) and Li221 (950), although we cannot be certain that this was the same Abaiub.

40 S287 (977); Liii708 (1012) relates the earlier history of his interest in the León property.

41 Thomas M. Charles-Edwards, 'Early Irish law', in Dáibhí Ó Cróinín (ed.), *A New History of Ireland, Volume I: Prehistoric and Early Ireland* (Oxford, 2005), pp. 331–70, at pp. 349–62; Fergus Kelly, *A Guide to Early Irish Law* (Dublin, 1988), pp. 51–7, 242–63, and see Kelly's map of late medieval legal families at ibid., p. 255.

were paid fees for court work, which was therefore certainly a source of some of their income.[42]

If we look at the types of charter which record the presence of judges, there are two important points to be made. Firstly, almost half (49 per cent) of the 96 charters that refer to judges do so in the context of witnessing gifts and sales; all such references are to people with the status of *iudex*, the skilled experts. The remainder refer to judges in dispute cases, of whom some have the status of *iudex* and many are the other people involved in judging panels. As might be expected, given their prominence in the corpus of dispute texts, nearly half of this remaining group of charters are Accounts: in these charters, judging was mentioned and judges were named in the course of describing the course of a formal case, often in detail. However, it is very striking that a fifth of references to people who judged occur in Confessions – a quite disproportionate number, given that only 5 per cent of surviving dispute records are Confessions. This suggests strongly that judges were normally present when a confession was made and that noting the name of judges present was important, although the record was short. Judges are named in small numbers of other types of dispute record, with relatively few in the large number of Fines and Incidental records; the paucity of references in Fines and Incidental records presumably reflects the fact that the main purpose of those records was to record transfers of property to the beneficiary, who was very often the president and/or court holder. How the transfer had come about was largely irrelevant to the record.

What kind of people were judges?[43] Some of these judges were royal judges, explicitly termed *iudex regis*, the king's judge. Three such – Abaiub, Abozekar and Bello – heard a property case in León in 958; four such – Gudesteo Díaz, Mito Arias, Pelayo Arvaldiz and Tructesindo Nantildiz – heard a property case in Galicia in 1000; and unnamed royal judges (*iudices de reie*) heard a case by the River Órbigo in 994.[44] Others were royal women or royal companions: not termed *iudex regis* explicitly, but often found in the king's presence, accompanying him on business; such were Leander and Maurello in and around León in the 930s and 940s, and Lope Jiménez, judging a church case in Pando (Castile) in 956 and witnessing royal gifts on the *meseta* in 945.[45] There were also five counts, a *saio* and a notary (who, as *iudex*, was scribe of a royal donation made in León) who were involved in judging and were regular or intermittent royal companions.[46]

42 OD21 (976), and see above, p. 157. For fees, see Gonzalo Martínez Díez, 'Terminología jurídica en la documentación del reino de León. Siglos IX–XI', in *Orígenes de las Lenguas Romances en el Reino de León, Siglos IX–XII* (2 vols, León, 2004), vol. 1, pp. 229–72, at p. 265.

43 I have noted 176 individuals termed *iudex* or explicitly involved in judging in ninth- and tenth-century texts.

44 S159, Cel252, OD37.

45 Li128 (938), Li99 (934); V33 (956), S98 and S99 (945 – these two charters probably elaborated in the later eleventh or twelfth century; José Antonio Fernández Flórez, 'Los documentos y sus *scriptores*', in *Monarquía y sociedad en el reino de León de Alfonso III a Alfonso VII* (2 vols, León, 2007), vol. 2, pp. 119–20).

46 Fofus *saio*, Sob129 (942); notary: OvC34 (992).

Some other judges were ecclesiastical office holders: at least 16 abbots, five monks, four bishops, 17 priests and three deacons.[47] Abbot Cisila was one of a panel of 10 which judged a property case in northern Galicia in 942; Brother Munnio, *iudex*, was the scribe who recorded a gift in Oncina in 990; Bishop Froarengo was the judge who set the fine for theft and adultery in 858; in 980, the priest Christofor witnessed a sale of houses in Dueñas as *iudex*; and the deacon Adaulfo was one of the four who determined boundaries in the Portuguese case of 936.[48]

Many of the remaining 51 per cent involved in judging appeared in this or that locality, without any stated royal or ecclesiastical associations, just as Flacino did. They include Alrameliz, in Grajal in the Tierra de Campos, in the 980s, with personal property there, and Eita Godestéiz in the late 970s outside León, in Quintanella to the east, his heirs selling from there in the next generation.[49] Always men and appearing in limited regions, these seem to have been local people of the required standing and skill. Beyond the clear indications that some were landed aristocrats, and that many were propertied, we cannot generalize about their socio-economic status.

Saiones

Saiones have a recorded background in the very early middle ages, and occurred both in Ostrogothic Italy and Visigothic Spain. In both cases, the word initially appears to have referred to the armed followers of a leader, but more importantly, by the sixth century in both regions *saiones* appeared as executive officers attached to courts, with powers of enforcement and arrest.[50] They re-emerged in ninth-century Iberian sources as named individuals in charter texts. References are relatively rare: they occur in about 2 per cent of the corpus of charters (60 charters). However, they are widespread, occurring in almost every collection, from northern Galicia and Portugal to the Rioja (they also occur in Catalonia).[51] Because numbers are so small, numbers per collection cannot

47 Juan José Larrea Conde, 'Construir iglesias, construir territorio: las dos fases altomedievales de San Román de Tobillas (Álava)', in Jorge López Quiroga, Artemio M. Martínez Tejera and Jorge Morín de Pablos (eds), *Monasteria et territoria. Elites, edilicia y territorio en el Mediterráneo medieval (siglos V–XI)* (Oxford, 2007), pp. 321–36, at pp. 330–31, points out that Vela, one of the three judges of SM27 (940) (= BG 391), was in fact the priest of Tobillas.

48 Sob129, Liii541, Sob75, Lii478, Lor36.

49 S329 (986), S316 (983), cf. *terminum Hali Rameliz*; Lii458 (978), S341 (989).

50 For example, Cassiodorus, *Variae*, 4.47, 7.42, 8.27; *Leges Visigothorum*, II.1.18, II.2.4, X.2.6. For Ostrogothic *saiones*, see Patrick Amory, *People and Identity in Ostrogothic Italy, 489–554* (Cambridge, 1997), pp. 93, 103–4, 471–2.

51 There do not appear to be any pre-1000 references in collections from San Juan de la Peña, Albelda, Leire, Eslonza and the San Vicente (Oviedo) collections, all of which are small. However, Jeffrey A. Bowman only counts 25 Catalan references in the tenth and eleventh centuries (relatively fewer, and their functions and occasions of appearance are more limited than in areas covered by this book) in *Shifting Landmarks: Property, Proof, and Dispute in Catalonia around the Year 1000* (Ithaca, NY, 2004), p. 109.

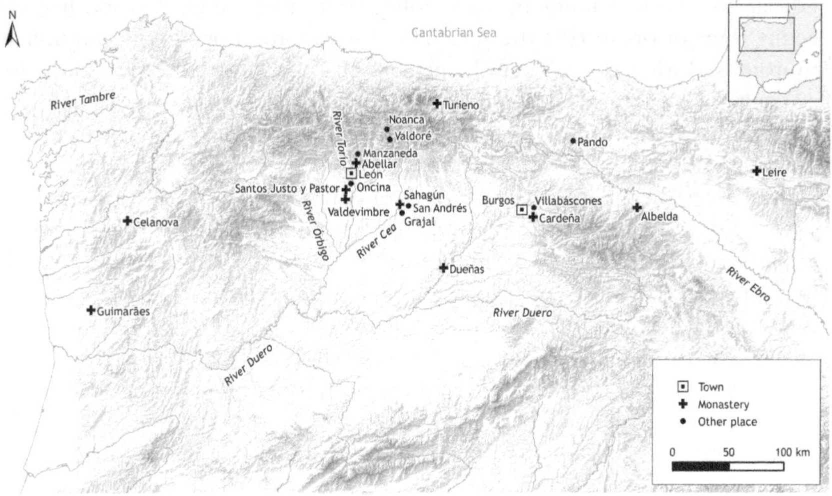

Figure 6.2 Locations noted in Chapter 6

be statistically significant, but it is worth commenting that there are relatively many in Otero collections (8 per cent of the pre-1000 charters), which reflects the relatively high proportion of charters in that collection dealing with judicial business (and perhaps their origins in lay archives); by region, there are disproportionately more references in Galician and Castilian charters than in those from the *meseta*. The first reference to a named *saio* appears to be in a (false) Santiago charter of 844, and references continue beyond 1000 into the eleventh and twelfth centuries.[52] Numbers increase from the 940s but, by decade, there are most from the 990s (nearly a quarter), which is significantly disproportionate to the number of charters which survive from that decade. The charters name 64 individual *saiones*, but six of them name more than one *saio* (four with two, one with three and one with four), all six charters occurring in different collections, all but one from the mid-tenth century;[53] five charters record action by unnamed *saiones*, and one clearly refers to a *saio* without labelling him.[54]

Despite the small numbers, the functions of the *saio* (or *sagio*) in ninth- and tenth-century Iberia are very clear and consistent. They were overwhelmingly

52 Flor50.

53 C46 (944), OD4 (946), V33 (956), S164 (959), T66 (962), Sob130 (992); perhaps also Cañ41, for which, see n. 54 below.

54 SMdelP1 (863), LaC61 (958), Cel165 (963), S295 (978), LaC95 (985); there is an incidental reference to an unnamed *saio* in Cañ41 (959), but the priest Serenianus also appears as *saio* later in this charter. No *saio* is named in Flor75, although the text refers to an individual who appears as *saio* in Flor74 (both 861).

judicial, for *saiones* cannot be seen doing estate management work, like collecting rents or organizing the agricultural workforce, nor fighting on military campaigns. Rather, the *saio* was the person who got parties to court, sometimes by securing a promise to appear on a given day, sometimes by accompanying them or perhaps even physically leading them;[55] he was often (probably always) present in court to hear accusations and agreements;[56] he could present oath-takers and organize the recording of oaths;[57] he could require parties to provide a given number of witnesses;[58] he transmitted judges' orders to a party to confirm this or that;[59] he administered confessions;[60] he was the person who physically led the innocent to the ordeal and presented the unwrapped hand three days later;[61] and following the resolution of property disputes, he was the person who conveyed the disputed property from one party to another[62] (the texts never say how this was done, but there must have been a transfer of some symbolic object or a ritual performance of some kind, perhaps involving walking the boundaries[63]); and we occasionally see him getting his fee, the *saionicum*, in one case explicitly a quarter of the court holder's fee.[64]

So the *saio* was an executive officer in court, a person who organized proceedings. But he was also an enforcer, with a pre- and post-court role. A couple of texts, in echoes of the armed *saiones* of the sixth century, suggest that he might have used force: one mid-ninth-century text has a furious *saio* removing

55 SM27 (940) (= BG 391), Sob129 (942), Sob31 (951), Sam44 (975), OD39 (995), for example; cf. Cel165.

56 V11 (919), OD4, Cañ41.

57 Sob109 (early 990s).

58 PMH DC 183 (999).

59 Sob130 (992).

60 Li34 (915).

61 Sob109, Cañ65 (996) (= AHN Clero Lugo 1325A–16; see Figure 3.8 above).

62 Li144 (941), Sob129, OvC26 (953), Cel94 (987).

63 See above, p. 136, for the formal language of consignment. Cf. the explicit procedures for legal entry into property in early Irish law, such as lighting a fire, or crossing a burial mound on the boundary; Kelly, *Guide to Early Irish Law*, pp. 186–9, 280. There are two Spanish charters which suggest the importance of marking the boundaries in these circumstances: Cast1 (927), after resolution, *adsignauit ipsa terra . . . per terminos antiquos et archas* (recalling the searches for *archas* of Galician charters such as Cel95 (950, 951)); Cel94 (987), fourth attached text, *quomodo adsignemus tibi ipsam uillam cum omnia sua per terminos suos et locis antiquis*. Cf. C27 (935), an apparently straightforward comital gift record in which citation of the bounds is followed by *consygnato per manu sayone Apre de Lara*, referring to the formal handover of the property (and perhaps, then, a hint of a previous dispute). *Leges Visigothorum* X.2.6 (p. 394) deals with the circumstances in which a judge instructs a *saio* to handle a claim on property and refers to the sealing of doors or gates of nearby property, on which there is no claim, with the seal (*anulo*) of judge or *saio*. OD73 (1007) appears to refer to Judge Cidi's sealed letter or instruction, *segelo*, and Sob109 refers to the seals (*sigillo*) of the abbot and priest who witnessed the innocent enter the hot water ordeal as well as the revelation of the clear hand three days later (for the procedure, see above, pp. 136–9. These fleeting references to sealing suggest some ritual action at entrances with real or symbolic seal.

64 OD4. Cf. SM23 (936) (= BG 390): *saionia*. Sánchez Badiola, *El territorio de León*, vol. 1, pp. 464–5, has a nice description of *saio* functions.

monks from a disputed property in advance of any judgment, and a mid-tenth-century text has two men entering a house together with *sagiones* and seizing three men with such force that one of them died, presumably in an attempt to get them to court.[65] They resemble, then, a kind of policeman.

References to *saiones* by type of text are comparable to the pattern of references to judges, and – like those – suggest that *saiones* were normally present at judicial proceedings, as we would in any case expect from their functions: there are disproportionately many references in Accounts (a third of all of these references), Confessions (a sixth of all of these) and Oaths, the latter presumably reflecting his essential role in the conduct of proceedings. Again, there are relatively few in the many Fines and Incidental records and in Agreements; there are none in Confiscations and Debts, although one might have expected this of an enforcer. Again, these low proportions must be because the primary function of those texts was to record the transfer of property rights, irrespective of the reasons for the transfer, but it is interesting that it does not seem to have been important to record the participation of the enforcing legal officer; in the case of Confiscations and Debts, it may well be that these were often treated as a matter of personal property and not as a subject for legal proceedings.

What kind of people were *saiones*? There were kings' *saiones*, counts' *saiones*, and one *saio* acted for a royal household officer (the *cubicularius*, literally 'bed chamber man', 'chamberlain'). Several are referred to by personal adjectives – 'our', 'my', your' – which in two cases appear to refer to the monasteries of Celanova and Turieno.[66] However, for three-quarters of citations there is no indication of to whom, if anyone, they were attached. There are three kinds of point to make about this. Firstly, it looks as if court holders (of all kinds – king, count, monastery, lay aristocrat) had *saiones*, the implication being that they chose them and got them to manage the business of their courts. Secondly, it looks as if rural communities could sometimes choose a *saio*, and hence 'our' *saio* is sometimes 'our local man'. This possibility arises for a number of reasons. Some of them are designated by territory: a gift of 959 to Sahagún was witnessed by three *saiones*, two from San Andrés and one from Villa Nova, single settlements to the south of Sahagún;[67] on one occasion cited in the Valpuesta cartulary, four of them witnessed a declaration about property – neither a major case nor a major occasion, apparently, so they must have been local, with

65 SMdelP1 (863); Cel165 (963). Cf. clauses in eleventh-century *fueros* requiring them not to use force; Fuero de León (1017) 2.45 and 47, Justiniano Rodríguez Fernández, *Los fueros del reino de León* (2 vols, León, 1981), vol. 2, p. 23.

66 For example, king's: Flor50 (844), Cel252 (1000); count's: C90 (957), Sob130 (992); of a *cubicularius*: Li192 (946); *nostro*: T66 (962), Cel94 (987); *meo*: PMH DC 183 (999).

67 S164; cf. Ar17 (964). Later in the same year, San Andrés had a local monastery dependent on Sahagún (see the gift of the property to Sahagún in October 959, S165); perhaps there was one *saio* for the monastery and another for the lay community.

small-scale responsibilities.[68] Further, where two *saiones* had an active role in a single case, which happened several times, one of them was the court holder's *saio*, be it of count, king or monastery; that being so, was the other the local *saio*?[69] And, to go to much later evidence, the *fuero* (local bye-law) of San Miguel de Escalada of 1173 provides that the monastery's *merino* (agent) should require each place (*uilla*) to name a *saio*, who should be chosen from middle-range people (neither *maiores* nor *minores*) and who had to serve for at least a year; while that of Villacelama of 1153 required that no one should be a *saio* against his will.[70] Thirdly, it is explicit that some *saiones* had other roles: two king's *saiones* were doorkeepers, *ostiarii*, and at least two other *saiones* were priests; they had other things to do.[71] It is also striking that hardly any named *saio* features more than once, although several court hearings might take place in one location within a decade, for example in León or at Valdoré.[72] It is also impossible to trace most of them outside their appearance as *saio* – they do not turn up on other occasions.[73] Neither is their presence recorded at most royal occasions, even if royal household officers are named; nor is their presence recorded at meetings of the royal court which took place in the same years or at the same locations as those of court hearings with a *saio*. And it is rare to find them witnessing ordinary transactions of gift and sale – as one would expect if they were permanent office holders; they particularly contrast in this with the *iudex*, the semi-professional judge, whose status was quite often noted in witness lists. All of these considerations suggest that being a *saio* was a function rather than an office; that playing the role was certainly short-term, and sometimes temporary. Hence, Alfonso V made the priest Sampiro, an important royal notary and major chronicler, *saio* for a high-profile case between the bishop of Astorga and the aristocrat Munio Fernández in 1008.[74] Kings could clearly require someone to take on the role for particular cases; one can imagine that local communities got together and chose, asked or persuaded one of their number to take it on for a period of a year or two. Indeed, it is possible that the formula *ubi* or *unde fui(t) saio*, used when *saiones* witnessed proceedings, is an implicit reference to the temporary nature of the position: 'I/he was *saio* on/at this occasion'.[75]

68 V33 (956).

69 For example, Sob130, OD4, C46, T66.

70 Rodríguez Fernández, *Los fueros*, 21.11 and 38.6, vol. 2, pp. 81, 125. Cf. the prohibition of entry by the king's *saio* in the interpolated immunity of Lii433 (974).

71 Li191 (946), Sam44 (975); T17 (885), Sob109 (early 990s).

72 There is a Mun(n)io in C46 (944) and in Ar17 (964), and a Paterno in V33 (956) and S164 (959), who might possibly be the same individuals. However Vermudo of the suspect C153 (972) and OvC24 (942), Gudesteo of AHN 1325A–6 (922) and Cel94 (987), and Pedro of V11 (919) and Cañ65 (996) can hardly represent the same individuals. The remaining 54 names are all different.

73 The priest Fulgentius, who is named as *saio* in Sob109, was probably the priest Fulgentius who recorded Sob130 (992) at about the same time.

74 Liii669.

75 For example, *ubi* T17, OD4, T66 (962); *unde* Flor74 (861), Sob129 (942), Li191, Sob109.

Boni homines

People referred to as *boni homines*, literally 'good men', sometimes took an active role in the court cases recorded by these charters. This was a term which was widely used in early medieval Europe to refer to trusted people who were called to give evidence or from whom judges were chosen – in other words, respected people (nearly always men) of good reputation. They feature in texts from Brittany, Italy and the Frankish Empire, as well as Spain and Portugal, and even once in translation in the ninth-century record of settlement of a dispute in west Wales (*degion*, literally 'good men').[76] Their presence and assistance at court cases was therefore part of a common heritage in western Europe: in discussing the late antique origins of the term, Nehlsen-von Stryk stressed their functions as suitable, qualified witnesses, *testes idonei*, and the extension of the term in the Frankish formularies to judging and arbitrating functions.[77]

There has been some notable discussion of *boni homines* by Spanish scholars, with some differences of opinion on their social status, and in recent years considerable emphasis on their role as mediators.[78] They do not feature clearly in Iberian charters before the 940s, although there are references to their role as evaluators in Visigothic law texts, and it may just be chance that there are no earlier charter references; four apparently earlier references all occur in dubious or false charters.[79] Use of the term is also quite rare, occurring in about 2 per

76 Karin Nehlsen-von Stryk, *Die Boni Homines des frühen Mittelalters unter besonderer Berücksichtigung der fränkischen Quellen* (Berlin, 1981); Dafydd Jenkins and Morfydd Owen, 'The Welsh marginalia in the Lichfield Gospels, Part 2,' *Cambridge Medieval Celtic Studies*, 7 (1984), pp. 91–120, at pp. 91, 101.

77 Nehlsen-von Stryk, *Die Boni Homines*, pp. 244–6, 346–8. A Breton charter of 892 is unusually precise about what constituted the suitability of a witness who was to provide evidence: good behaviour, good character, an unbribable nature, with a love and knowledge of justice, right and truth; *Cartulaire de l'Abbaye de Redon en Bretagne*, ed. Aurélien de Courson (Paris, 1863), no. 271.

78 María del Carmen Carlé, '*Boni homines* y hombres buenos', *Cuadernos de Historia de España*, 39/40 (1964), pp. 133–68, in a thoughtful survey, stressed their status as free proprietors and the fact that they had several functions. Pascual Martínez Sopena, 'La justicia en la época asturleonesa: entre el *Liber* y los mediadores sociales', in Ana Rodríguez (ed.), *El lugar del campesino. En torno a la obra de Reyna Pastor* (València, 2007), pp. 239–60, at pp. 245, 248–9, reviews earlier considerations, and stresses their role as mediators, pp. 248, 255–7; Mínguez, 'Justicia y poder', pp. 541–3, suggests that they were the wealthy peasant elite, the principal interface between local communities and lords; Fernando Luis Corral, 'Lugares de reunión, *boni homines* y presbíteros en Valdevimbre y Ardón en la alta edad media' (forthcoming), develops both of these approaches in the specific context of the zone south of León, stressing the mediating role, the wealthy peasant elite, and the interface between lords and communities (and I am very grateful for permission to see this in advance of publication). Josep M. Salrach, 'Prácticas judiciales, transformación social y acción política en Cataluña (siglos IX–XIII)', *Hispania*, 57/3 (1997), pp. 1,009–48, at p. 1,015, dealing with Catalonia, defines them as members of principal families of the locality where a hearing took place and members of the court holders' households; he emphasizes a function as interface between judicial power and those ruled.

79 AHN Clero Lugo 1325A–4 (910), PMH DC 17 (911), LaC14 (912), Leire 7 (938); Ainoa Castro, *Colección diplomática altomedieval de Galicia I: Documentación editada en escritura visigótica (662–1234)* (A Coruña, 2011), no. 23, treats AHN 1325A–4 as an original, although some of the text is surely doubtful as a

cent of the corpus of charters and 20 per cent of dispute records. References clearly increased in the later tenth century: two-fifths come from the 990s and four-fifths are noted from 960 onwards, and there are many more references in the eleventh century; it therefore looks as if reference to, and perhaps recourse to, *boni homines* was an increasing practice of the late tenth century and beyond.[80] It is also clear that some scribes in some regions either did not know the term or did not choose to use it: it is disproportionately common in Galician texts (nearly half of all cases), very rare in Asturian and Cantabrian texts, and rare in Castilian and Navarre texts; and although it is common enough on the *meseta*, it is rare in Sahagún material; in broad terms, its use lies with western rather than eastern diplomatic habits.[81] It is likely, however, as discussed below, that in some areas the functions of *boni homines* were performed without the term being used to describe those who performed them.[82]

In Iberian texts, the term *boni homines* is an expression used of people gathered together in public. The words are employed in three related but different ways, however. Firstly, they are used as a general term to refer to respectable people from whom oath-takers might be selected or before whom judicial proceedings were heard, like the confession made in 972 in the presence of Count García Fernández and the council of Burgos and *multorum bonorum ominum*, or the Galician property dispute of 995 in which King Vermudo II ordered one party to provide *suum iuratorem hominem bonum* to take the oath.[83] In this usage, the label seems to signify the presence of 'acceptable people', those of suitable standing; in some contexts, it appears to refer to great men, and in others to local worthies. On the *meseta* and in Galicia, this general usage is often expressed as *filii bonorum hominum*, the sons of law-worthy men, where the primary meaning seems to be 'other respectable people' rather than specific descendants; in northern Galicia in particular, it may also be reflected in *filii benenatorum*, 'sons of the well-born', which is used in much the same way, although the underlying concept is different and refers to status rather than respectability.[84]

Such references either specify no individual names at all, or do specify some names, concluding with a general 'and other *boni homines*'. Where *boni homines*

---

record of 910. *Leges Visigothorum*, at VI.1.5, IX.1.21 and X.1.17 (pp. 253, 365, 389), feature *boni homines* in contexts of evaluating the worth of slaves; suitable witnesses are noted at II.4.3 and II.5.16, and in the former case, their essential qualities are specified as being of free status, good reputation and wealthy.

80 Cf. above, pp. 123–4.

81 See above, pp. 99–106.

82 Pp. 172–3.

83 C151; Cel215.

84 For example, a gift on the *meseta* done in the presence of *filii multorum bonorum hominum* (Lii490 (983)), or *multi filii bene natorum* who confirmed a gift in north-west Galicia in 965 (LaC71). *Benenatorum* also occurs in OvC24 (942) and Ast128 (974), indicating that its use was not confined to Galicia. I do not support Sánchez-Albornoz's distinctive view that *filii benenatorum* was a tenth-century term for *infanzones*; Claudio Sánchez-Albornoz, *Estampas de la vida en León durante el siglo X* (Madrid, 1924), p. 74, n. 114.

are named, disputes were heard and truth established in their presence, sometimes explicitly in the presence of named judges 'and other *boni homines*'. All but one of these cases are Galician, and all but one are recorded in Accounts; clearly, this was a common Galician practice when drawing up retrospective Accounts.[85] The texts come from different parts of Galicia, from northern Portugal to the Verín area in southern Galicia to the Tambre valley and to La Coruña in the north-west – a good spread. Disputed boundaries were also fixed by named *boni homines* in the Verín area in the mid-tenth century, men who were sent from the count's and king's courts.[86] Oaths were sworn by *boni homines* in a dispute between Bishop Rosendo and the bishopric of Santiago over control of fisheries – the bishops named four and five respectively to take the oath.[87] While the naming of individual *boni homines* certainly adds a sense of precision to these records, it looks as if the main reason for using the label was to add an aura of respectability and authority to the proceedings, whether there were personal names or not.

In a second usage, *boni homines* might exercise the specific function of intercession in court (on which occasions they are never named). In such cases, they would speak on behalf of an accused person in order to get a penalty reduced, like those who spoke for people who had debts to the aristocrat Fruela Vimáraz – debts which were reduced in the mid-990s[88] – or those who got the penalty for incursions on to monastic land in Valdoré reduced in 997,[89] or in a more dramatic Portuguese case fifty years earlier, those who spoke for a convicted killer and persuaded the lord Ansur (probably the court holder) to make up the deficit in the due compensation to the dead man's family.[90] On another occasion, they petitioned a powerful aristocrat to permit an adherent to make a sale of some property.[91] This kind of *bonus homo* was clearly not a judge, since it was the judges or the court holders who were petitioned; they appear to have been other people who were present at court. Except for the Portuguese case of 943, all the examples of intercession come from the *meseta* and from the 990s, and there are many more in the eleventh century. This kind of reference is clearly in part simply a developing diplomatic habit, for the phrase *rogare cum bonis hominibus* is a standard way of describing the petition.[92] The fact that none is named is surprising, and might suggest that all this was just a turn of phrase; but it

85 The exception is the Mixed record, Lii508 (985), the format of which is an unusual *cum omnem togam palatii sui, filii bene natorum et pontificum multorum*.

86 Cel502 (940), Cel93 (950).

87 SantA42 (961).

88 OD37 (994), OD40 (995), OD41 (995).

89 OD43; cf. S358 (998).

90 PMH DC 53 (943).

91 Liii560 (994).

92 See Martínez Díez, 'Terminología jurídica en la documentación del reino de León', pp. 260, 261–3, and Martínez Sopena, 'La justicia en la época asturleonesa', pp. 241, 245, 248; also above, p. 123.

appears that debts and penalties did in practice get reduced, since the point of making and preserving these records was to document the transaction in property that was transferred in lieu of the specified fine or debt. A few texts appear to refer to the practice in a slightly different way: there are *rogatores* (petitioners) sent to the king by an imprisoned rebel and *fratres* sent to a duke to request the return of Odoíno's property.[93] Occasionally, there is a sense of performance about the process: Salvador prostrated himself, with the *boni homines*, in the king's court before coming to an agreement.[94] Since there was more than one way to refer to the act of intercession, it looks as if this was more than just a diplomatic habit and that the diplomatic reflects in reality a developing practice of intercession in the later tenth century.

A third, quite different, usage is this: in certain circumstances, it was *boni homines* who fixed a price for a transaction or who saw to the fair distribution of property. When half a property was sold in Portugal, the record of the sale provides that if the other half of the property were to be sold, the *boni homines* would fix a just price; and in another Portuguese case, a sick woman was taken to the *boni homines*, who led her to the monastery of Guimarães, where she gave instructions about what should happen to her property.[95] A note attached to the record of a León sale of 980 records that one party had come with *omines bonos* to request a further exchange with the other party.[96] Several charters name *boni homines* who witnessed or corroborated transactions of gift and sale: the witness list of another León sale charter begins *Homines bonos qui ibi preses fuerunt, hec sunt* ('The *boni homines* who were present there are:') and goes on to name four people, though the more usual format is to name some people and round off the list with 'other *boni homines*'.[97] All of these witness lists date from the mid-tenth century onwards, and most from the late 970s onwards; two-thirds of them relate to properties near León.[98] Clearly a practice of restricted use (but nevertheless from a number of different sources), some lists have no names at all, the label *boni homines* being no more than a way of indicating that there were witnesses without going to the trouble of recording the names.[99] One might think this the abbreviation of a cartulary copyist, but the format can be found on single sheets.[100] Why these few scribes chose to emphasize the suitability of

93 SantA57 (993), Cel265 (982). Martínez Sopena, 'La justicia en la época asturleonesa', p. 256, argues that *rogadores* were sometimes differentiated from *boni homines*.

94 Liii559 (993) – *prostrauit se Saluatorem ad rocum cum ommines bonos in ipso concelio de regem*, recorded in the church of San Salvador.

95 PMH DC 79 (960) – *pro pretium iustum quod omines bonos apreciaberunt*; PMH DC 81 (960), cf. Lor17 (957). For price-fixing, see also Catalonia: Josep María Salrach, *Justícia i poder a Catalunya abans de l'any mil* (Vic, 2013), p. 147.

96 Lii477.

97 Liii551 (992); OD23 (978), Lii445 (976), Liii516 (987), A8 (?941), Leire 13 (997), AHN 1325A–4v (987) – see above, p. 14 n28, for this charter.

98 A8 is the earliest; not León: A8, C88 (955), LaC71 (965 – *benenatorum*), AHN 1325A–4v from Lugo (*bene natorum*), Leire 13.

99 For example, Liii547 (991), Liii590 (999).

100 Liii547, OD23.

the witnesses is unclear – it was much more common simply to say 'and others' in such circumstances – but it is of course possible that there was some hidden background of uncertainty or dispute about the properties transacted.[101]

Given that there are clear examples of *boni homines* fixing prices, it may well be that some charters refer to precisely the same function of price-fixing without using the distinctive term, just as hundreds, if not thousands, of people witnessed transactions without being termed *boni homines*. One late tenth-century Galician Account records that, following proceedings in a case of theft, an estate valued at 100 *modii* was paid by the convicted thief, *et asignamus ipsa ereditate pro apreciatura de omines bonos*, in other words the *boni homines* are explicitly associated with the valuation (*apreciatura*) of the penalty in this court case.[102] When charters refer to a sale of property 'priced at' (*adpreciatum*) such and such a value, someone must have done the pricing. This kind of language is notable in charter collections which do not refer to *boni homines*, like those of Oviedo, Valpuesta and Santo Toribio, although it is not confined to them.[103] One Celanova record of a gift includes a note on a debt owed; the witness list begins *Qui presentes fuerunt et ipsa uilla apreciauerunt* ('Those who were present and valued this property'), and goes on to name 14 individuals. Were these 14 people men and women who might elsewhere have been described as *boni homines*?[104] Summaries of other Celanova sales refer to a *legitimo precio* ('a legitimate price').[105] Was it groups like the *boni homines* who conferred legitimacy? And were there far more people undertaking such roles than those described as *boni homines*? The implication of this set of material is that suitable people characteristically assisted in the conduct of property transactions, whether called *boni homines* or not; and, given the evaluation references of *Leges Visigothorum*, that the practice was of long standing.

Since the number of references to *boni homines* is small, one cannot be sure that differences in distribution reflect any realities; for what it is worth, hearing disputes was essentially Galician; interceding was essentially a feature of the *meseta*; being present at transactions and fixing the terms of transfer occurred in many parts, although prominent on the *meseta*. One might suggest that these references did not have any practical meaning at all and were

101 I cannot see anything distinctive about the scribes (many of whom are unnamed) nor the locations, although several charters are in favour of the monastery of Santos Justo y Pastor, just to the south of León. For the importance of Santos Justo y Pastor in this region, see Corral, 'Lugares de reunión'.

102 Cañ65 (996). *Modii*: a widely used standard measure of account; see Wendy Davies, 'Sale, price and valuation in Galicia and Castile-León in the tenth century', *Early Medieval Europe*, 11 (2002), pp. 149–74, at pp. 167–9.

103 Ov19 (978), V36 (960–1) – *pretium quantu ipsa ualuit* – for example; cf. T68 (963), *per mesura*.

104 Cel353 (999); the list includes two women. Cf. *Leges Visigothorum*, estimating the value of slaves, in n. 79 above, and Irmgard Fees, on *boni homines* as estimators of the value of land in northern Italy in the ninth to eleventh centuries in 'Tauschurkunden in Venedig und im Veneto', in Irmgard Fees and Philippe Depreux (eds), *Tauschgeschäft und Tauschurkunde vom 8. bis zum 12. Jahrhundert. L'acte d'échange, du VIIIe au XIIe siècle* (Köln, 2013), pp. 99–128, at p. 111.

105 Cel368 (p. 532), Cel180 (p. 254) (both late tenth century). Cf. 'just price': Cel180 (p. 255), Cel197 (p. 277); and 'they valued' (*apretiarunt*), Cel204 (p. 286).

simply a way of saying 'other people', as in part they clearly were. This is not just because numbers are small (after all, the number of references to *saiones* is comparable, but in that case their functions and appearance are so consistent and so specific there cannot be any doubt about the role), but because so many references to *boni homines* and analogous terms are extremely vague. On the other hand, reference to them cannot simply be dismissed as the odd practice of a few scribes or monasteries. They occur in texts referring to different regions and different locations within regions (Valdoré, Astorga, León, Santiago de Compostela, Santa María de Mezonzo, Verín and so on). They occur on single sheets (like the León sale witness list noted above[106]) as well as in cartulary copies; and the records were made by different kinds of named scribe, from scribes working for lay aristocratic households to local priests to smaller and larger monasteries (like those of San Salvador and of Santos Justo y Pastor to the south of León).[107] It was clearly a widespread habit. And although most references are framed in the context of a standard diplomatic, there are occasions when a scribe used the term in a non-standard note, like that attached to the Villaverde exchange of 980 or the Portuguese cases of price-fixing and distribution;[108] it is as if these were the words that increasingly came to mind in the late tenth century when describing useful and responsible collective action. But it was in the end a diplomatic habit, a way of writing – people performing exactly the same functions were sometimes called *boni homines* and sometimes not.

Not surprisingly, references to the involvement of *boni homines* in property transactions occur in regular records of gift, sale and exchange. References to their presence at court proceedings occur overwhelmingly in Accounts, whether to cases heard before them, boundaries fixed by them or oaths sworn by them, and whether they were named or not. By the late tenth century, this kind of reference was becoming part of the language of retrospectively recording disputes, especially in Galicia. References to the intercession of *boni homines*, however, are found in different kinds of record, although most intercessions took place in a court. Although there is one such reference in an Account, most occur in Incidental notes of disputes, Agreements, Debts and Fines – that is, to the closer-to-court records of the outcomes of proceedings, rather than in more distant descriptions.[109] Although the intercession formula also represents a diplomatic habit, it is a formula that was closer to the language of practice.

Because *boni homines* are not always named, and because so many references to them are vague, it is also difficult to be clear about their social status. Some

106 P. 172.

107 OD40 and OD41 (995); Liii516 (987); Lii445 (976); Liii559; Lii490 and Lii492 (983), Liii547 (991), Liii590 (999).

108 Lii477; Lor17; PMH DC 79 and 81.

109 There is also one in a Mixed record and one in a record of sale. See above, pp. 143, 147–8, for 'close to court'.

references were clearly to large gatherings of clerics, like those of the Lugo texts recording the corroborating presence of *benenatorum* when gifts were made.[110] Many other Galician references appear to refer to the great and good: they include bishops and counts, as well as abbots and priests and laymen with patronymics, and once *proceres palatii* ('prominent men of the palace'), and their contexts are aristocratic;[111] two of the royal judges of one record occur elsewhere as *boni homines*;[112] also, a Cardeña case involved an aristocratic court, and an Albelda case involved a royal court.[113] On the other hand, there is nothing about the names associated with corroborating or witnessing small-scale transactions of gift and sale that suggests aristocratic status, and it must be likely that these represent neighbours and members of a more local community.[114] Those who fixed a just price, or a legitimate price, must have been local and knowledgeable about the micro-topographical features that added or detracted from value. These were not necessarily the most menial of peasants, but they were presumably property holders of good local reputation – something closer to the 'local worthy' or 'elder' that one might expect – the people who came to local meetings.[115] The confirmation of Leire 13 is a royal confirmation, with many high-status witnesses, but there is a note which adds the presence of *filii bonorum patres de Saresacensi uallem testibus*, witnesses who were law-worthy people from the valley of Salazar (where the property was located).[116]

Overall, then, the texts reflect different kinds of use of the term and some differences in functions: an increasing habit of referring to participants in court proceedings, especially high-level proceedings in Galicia, as *boni homines* – this was essentially a diplomatic habit; an increasing habit of attributing the function of intercession to *boni homines* – this was a diplomatic habit too, but one that seems to reflect practice; and a substratum of more local references to the many people who assisted in the proper conduct of transactions. The import of the majority of references, and especially of participants in court proceedings, is that *boni homines* were much more likely to be aristocrats than peasant farmers; but for the ordinary business of day-to-day (or month-to-month) transactions, *boni homines* must have come from a lower social level.[117] Plenty of the people who performed these functions, and who had been performing the functions for some considerable time, were not called *boni homines*: what the tenth-century texts seem to show, then, was an increasing tendency to classify those who took on such roles as 'suitable' and 'qualified'. This suggests that there was a current of feeling by the year 1000 that sought to designate group presence and group

110 AHN 1325A–4r (910) and 4v (987).

111 Cel93 (950).

112 Gudesteo Díaz and Tructesindo Nantildiz of Cel252 (1000), in Sob130 (992) and PMH DC 163 (991). See further below, pp. 206–7.

113 C88 (955), A8 (?941).

114 For example, OD23 (978), Lii445 (976), Liii516 (987), Liii551 (992).

115 On meetings, see below, pp. 213–19.

116 On the role of local knowledge in court cases, see further below, pp. 211–13.

117 For further exploration of social status groups, see below, pp. 199–202, 228–9.

action by reputable people as legitimate; by so doing, in its turn it enhanced the legitimizing function of the actions.[118]

People passing through the courts

The preceding survey of the principal functionaries in court proceedings shows the relatively high status of most players. Kings, counts and bishops held courts, and so did some, perhaps even many, monasteries and lay aristocrats. Kings, bishops and counts might also act as judges, although any judging panel seems primarily to have been composed of abbots, priests and lay aristocrats on the one hand, and expert judges, with learning and specialized skill, on the other. These panels were not composed of people of the wealth and power of kings and counts, but they were nevertheless propertied and wealthy by comparison with the mass of the population, the abbots often controlling networks of dependent churches and attached properties, and the laity drawing income from a spread of scattered properties.[119] We might think of the professional judges – if they were not attached to the royal court, as some clearly were – coming from comfortable, propertied households of sufficient but not vast wealth. *Saiones*, as we have seen, came from mixed backgrounds. They were the proactive functionaries, even if they only served for a short term. They were primarily people who served others, high-level servants with practical skills, with a capacity to use force and with local knowledge; they might serve a king – as did Sampiro, a highly accomplished scribe and member of the royal household of León – or a count (as some judges also did), or a royal officer; they might hold the office of priest; they might even – particularly at the end of the tenth century – act for a local community. *Boni homines*, as we have just seen, were high aristocrats and high-status clerics who attended court proceedings, as they were also respectable people who went to local meetings and by their presence validated transactions – the latter apparently coming from lower social strata. A high proportion of the functionaries, then, were of high or middling high status.

Priests are particularly notable in performing a range of different roles in court; they came from a range of socio-economic strata; they could be attached to a monastery, could be as wealthy as the lay aristocrats, or could be more local, depending on properties of much more limited scale and spread.[120] Priests in court cases could come from royal or aristocratic households, from powerful monasteries or episcopal households, and from local churches; some were

118 Cf. 'the concept of the public hung directly on the participation of 'good men', *boni homines* and their innumerable variants'; Chris Wickham, 'Conclusion: Dispute processes and social structures', in Wendy Davies and Paul Fouracre (eds), *The Settlement of Disputes in Early Medieval Europe* (Cambridge, 1986), pp. 228–40, at p. 231. Mínguez, 'Justicia y poder', pp. 541–3, stressed that there were new developments in the late tenth century.

119 See further below, pp. 205–11.

120 See Wendy Davies, 'Local priests in northern Iberia', in Steffen Patzold and Carine van Rhijn (eds), *Men in the Middle: Local Priests in Early Medieval Europe* (Berlin, forthcoming).

high-level servants, and some came from propertied families of small scale and narrow horizons; we often cannot tell from the record of a court case what kind of priest was a participant. But priests acted as judges, as advocates for parties who did not speak for themselves, as *saiones*, as the companions of lay *saiones*, as members of investigating panels, as special witnesses of the ordeal or of oaths, as oath-takers in support of one party, as providers of notionally impartial evidence, as guarantors of outcomes and – at least once – as the innocent who went to the ordeal.[121] The priest Extrulphi was a member of the panel which heard a confession of intrusion into the land of the church of Villeña in 922; three priests were among the king's judges who heard a case in León between a woman and the monastery of Sahagún in 958; and another priest was a member of a judging panel in 978.[122] A priest was one of three sent by the king to fix the boundaries of Castroncán in 933, and the priest Viliulfo was Bishop Sisnando's representative when lands were divided between the bishops of Santiago and Coimbra in 906.[123] All of the latter were priests selected to serve on judging panels, but some priests were also expert judges, learned in the law: in 818 the priest judge Elarinus witnessed a gift, in 980 the priest judge Christofor witnessed a sale, and the priest judge Valiti confirmed a gift.[124] The priest Berulf acted as advocate on behalf of churches in several cases in the middle of the tenth century.[125] Priests also acted for lay parties in cases where there was no obvious ecclesiastical interest: the priest Ermegildo was guarantor for an agreement between two lay parties when the boundaries of a property were disputed in 946, and two priests joined four lay people in the Tambre valley in 931 to guarantee that a convicted thief would not default before paying the due fine – apparently a local issue and a theft of minor scale.[126] Two priests were members of the first investigating panel sent by the king to determine whether there was sufficient water to supply the mills both of the monastery of Valdevimbre and of the local community some time before 938.[127]

Such roles were taken by priests from Galicia to Aragón and from Asturias and Cantabria to the Duero, and from early to late in the tenth century; the first reference to a priest as *saio* comes from Cantabria in 885.[128] They clearly had skills which were very useful in court and status which was sufficient to make them suitable as supporters and functionaries, whether operating at royal or local level. Bishops and abbots were notable members of judging panels, abbots especially, and bishops were certainly court holders. We see less of them

121 For example, advocates: Li191, Li192, Lii410, Liii556, C129, Cel446, LaC95; *saio*: see n. 73 above; companions: C90; panel: Li128; special witnesses: Sob109, OvC26; oath: Li192, Lii410, SantA42, LaC95, TV135; evidence: SJP14 (928); guarantors: OD4, C103, V17; innocent: Sob109.

122 T30, S159, S295.

123 Sam46, PMH DC 13.

124 Sob43, Lii478, Lii479.

125 Li191 and Li192 (946), Lii410, for example. See Corral, 'Lugares de reunión'.

126 OD4, Sob21.

127 Li128.

128 T17.

as oath-takers and providers of evidence than we do of priests, although one abbot provided evidence for the layman Lovesindo in his case against the monastery of Guimarães, which in its turn had two abbots testifying on its side.[129] Unlike priests, they do not seem to have acted as guarantors. But both bishops and abbots were prominent protagonists in court cases, primarily disputing property rights. While many records of property disputes involving churches are Accounts, drawn up retrospectively for the purpose of confirming possession, it is perfectly clear that court cases of this kind had taken place; one could wonder whether the courts only existed to serve the interests of the church but for the fact that lay people clearly used the courts too.

Lay actors were less regular and much more varied in their appearances, and we know much less about them. Some great aristocrats held courts; while some of these were counts, and some acquired a comital title in later texts, some seem to have had no comital pretensions.[130] Such were the Portuguese lord Ansur, of 943, the sometime unfaithful *cubicularius*, Fortún Garcés, a couple of years later, the monastery of Celanova in the late tenth century; and there were other landowners who took judicial action of some kind, like imprisoning or taking fines.[131] The latter do not appear to have been great aristocrats, and were perhaps persons of lesser aristocratic status.[132] One text is particularly suggestive of this: when two dependent cowherds were wrongly accused of theft and their mistress's property was entered without her permission in order to apprehend them, the herdsmen were taken before 'another power', *alia potestate*, and held for fifteen days, although ultimately they were freed without any judgment being passed.[133] This is a small-scale issue, and seems to relate to the disputes of a lesser aristocracy. Lesser landowners, then, could be court holders too.

The people named as giving evidence or swearing oaths (or acting as guarantors) could be abbots, monks and priests, the latter especially, as indicated above.[134] But more lay people are named than clerics or monks.[135] We usually have no more than a single reference to a name, and we have no solid evidence of his or her social status or local position. However, while a few of these supporters in high-profile cases look aristocratic (Mumadonna at Guimarães, and

129 PMH DC 183 (999).

130 On the issue of counts, see above, pp. 20–26.

131 PMH DC 53, Li192 (cf. Lii482), Cel197 and Cel368; Lii378 (964), Lii474 (980), perhaps PMH DC 163 (991). See Davies, 'Summary justice', and Davies, 'Holding court', for court holders. Fortún Garcés had landed property in the Tierra de Campos and Lampreana; see Carvajal Castro, 'La construcción de la monarquía asturleonesa', p. 367.

132 See below, p. 200, for further discussion of this point.

133 Lii378.

134 Abbots: see above, p. 178; monks: LaC95 (985); priests: AHN 1325A–6 (922, where all five were priests), SMdelP2 (927), Li192 (946), for example.

135 That is, if the assumption that those without a clerical label were lay be correct. It seems reasonable to suppose this was the case if two of a group of six guarantors are labelled priests and the rest are not (Sob21) or one oath-taker is labelled priest and the other is not (Li192). However, see n. 47 above for the fact that priests were not always labelled as such.

many of those with patronymics), most are single names cited in very local contexts for very local issues concerning past owners and actions.[136] It must be likely that these people were local residents, as indeed that many of the priests were local priests: María and her son Rodrigo and Olidi and his wife Gota, both couples found guilty of providing false evidence in the case of a stolen pig, clearly had small-scale properties and clearly belonged to a group of peasant farmers.[137] Such people must therefore constitute an element of non-aristocratic participation in the business of the courts, and they seem to have been a frequent presence. Guarantors have somewhat similar profiles.[138] Of those named in the context of court cases (there were many more named for sale transactions), a few were priests, a few were clearly aristocrats, and the majority (three-quarters) are identified by a single name in a local context. The seven guarantors named in the case of the monastery of Pardomino against members of seven local settlements were explicitly to represent the settlements, presumably one for each; guarantors for small-scale debts in the Celanova orbit included a sister and brother-in-law of one debtor and the nephews of another; and the four who joined two priests to guarantee that a thief would not run away must have lived in the same neighbourhood as the thief and must therefore have belonged to the locality.[139] Again, lay people from different social strata were clearly frequent participants in this aspect of court business.[140]

Even clearer than these testifiers, oath-takers and guarantors is the fact that all kinds of lay person used the courts to pursue their own interests.[141] Lay aristocrats, like churchmen, had property disputes that passed through the court system. For example, in a case resolved before judges and *saio* in a church in Valdoré, one layman accused another of intruding into his land and moving the boundary markers.[142] There are even occasional cases in which members of

136 Aristocrats and patronymics: PMH DC 81, PMH DC 183, perhaps LaC95; local questions: Li34, for example.

137 Cel189, Cel190 (both *c.* 1000; the former is dated 1001 and the latter 1000, both on the same day, with reference to the same case; one of the dates must be erroneous). They are called *iudicatores*. Agustín Prieto Morera, 'El proceso en el reino de León a la luz de los diplomas', in *El reino de León en la alta edad media, II: Ordenamiento jurídico del reino* (León, 1992), p. 451, citing this case and Liii556 (*indigadores*), pointed out that the meaning was unclear, but that he was inclined to regard them as investigators; while I agree that the precise import is unclear, the content and context of these references suggests that the people were providers of evidence – in other words, people who responded to enquiries rather than people who made them.

138 See Wendy Davies, 'On suretyship in tenth-century northern Iberia', in Julio Escalona and Andrew Reynolds (eds), *Scale and Scale Change in the Early Middle Ages: Exploring Landscape, Local Society, and the World Beyond* (Turnhout, 2011), pp. 133–52, for longer discussion of the issues of suretyship.

139 Li184 (944); Cel368, Cel204 (late tenth century); Sob21 (931), see n. 126 above. For a clear aristocratic case: Cel215 (995).

140 Larrea, 'Construir iglesias', p. 331, suggested that guarantors came from pre-eminent families, operating at a supra-local scale; while that may well have been the case in the particular examples he considered, it would not apply to all cases.

141 See further below, pp. 190–5, for lay use of courts.

142 OD4 (946).

local communities, presumably peasants, disputed over the boundaries of their settlements and associated land and used judicial procedures to find a solution.[143] Courts also handled cases of theft, homicide, wounding, abduction, rape and adultery. There are many records of this, and the accused were for the most part peasants and local big men. The rural working population came to and through the courts as accused people, and that is the interaction we most often see; occasionally, they included servile dependents, like the cowherds wrongly accused of theft and the *servus* who ran away with a convicted thief, but most of those who appeared in court seem to have been free peasant proprietors, busy and active in their restricted local contexts.[144] There are also some rare cases in which local people took joint action, usually against an ecclesiastical landowner: the best example is the well-known case of the locals who took action, several times, against the monastery of Valdevimbre over water supply for their mills, notable because the locals won.[145] It was possible for the peasant community to use the courts, and to use them against more powerful landlords, but rare.

All of this means that records of court cases were not simply a creation of ecclesiastical interests, much as it might sometimes look like that. The number of records that come from lay archives, the proportion of Incidental records and Fines, the handling of purely lay matters by the courts, the use of courts by peasants to solve purely lay disputes over property, and the interaction of peasant individuals and communities with what was essentially an aristocratic and ecclesiastical mechanism makes this perfectly clear. While the business of the courts was largely a matter for semi-professionals, for people with ecclesiastical training and for aristocrats, others inhabited them too. Those others could play a part as witness, oath-taker, guarantor or litigant. They were mostly men, but women did feature as court holders, as litigants, as guarantors and as persons accused of theft or adultery; the action of aristocratic women in property disputes is not uncommon. Overall, the laity look to have played as much of a part in court business as churchmen. Moreover, what emerges from the inconsistent and irregular use of the term *boni homines* is the clear fact that there were people present at court proceedings who were not functionaries or litigants or providers of evidence: there were others who were simply there. Given the nature of the references, we cannot possibly know their numbers nor their social status, but it is important to remember that, even if silent, they were part of the proceedings.

143 Rare, though; see further, below pp. 221–6.

144 Lii378, Sob21. See further below, pp. 226–30.

145 Li128 (938). See below, p. 186, on the monastery's interest, nevertheless.

7 Power

The power that came with court holding could hardly be better demonstrated than the case of García Gómez presiding over a court hearing together with the Andalusian official *sāhib al-shurta* Ibn Abu-l-hawz 50 km north of the River Duero at Villalpando in 998.[1] García Gómez was a count, with a claim to be ruling (*imperantem*) from León in the early 990s, working with Muslim allies to pursue his interests at several points in the late tenth and early eleventh century.[2] The monastery of Sahagún had clearly appealed to García rather than to the king over the property that was the subject of this 998 case, as it did in another property case as well.[3] It makes sense to see Ibn Abu-l-hawz as an official – a super-*saio* – rather than as a judge, since one would expect judges to know northern Iberian judicial procedures and Visigothic law, and since the office he held is usually associated with security. The property dispute was pursued through a judicial court, and the would-be ruler and his political ally presided over that court – this was a political statement.

If we were to suppose that the judicial court in ninth- and tenth-century northern Iberia was an arena for displaying endemic alliances and enmities between individuals and families, as appears to have been the case in some parts of Europe, we would not get very far.[4] That is partly because there is too little detail in our documents about the background and connections of most of the players, and because personal alignments are often obscure (constructing cases would be possible, but they would depend on uncertain identifications and

1 S356. The *sāhib al-shurta* is a well-known office in Muslim areas, usually translated 'chief of police', but indicating something more like 'head of security'. I am very grateful to Ann Christys for assistance with this word. The initial reference to the pair is in a kind of *regnante* clause (for which, see above, p. 46 n33), which in itself implies ruling, underlining the political control of both; their base was located at Toro, on the River Duero.

2 Liii534, Liii535 (both 990).

3 See S444 (1036), which includes a retrospective account of this second property case.

4 Cf. Warren C. Brown, *Unjust Seizure: Conflict, Interest, and Authority in an Early Medieval Society* (Ithaca, NY, 2001), ch. 2 especially, but see also pp. 143–4, 156–7 (where the examples are Bavarian); Warren C. Brown, *Violence in Medieval Europe* (Harlow, 2011), pp. 77, 207–12 (in which most examples are English).

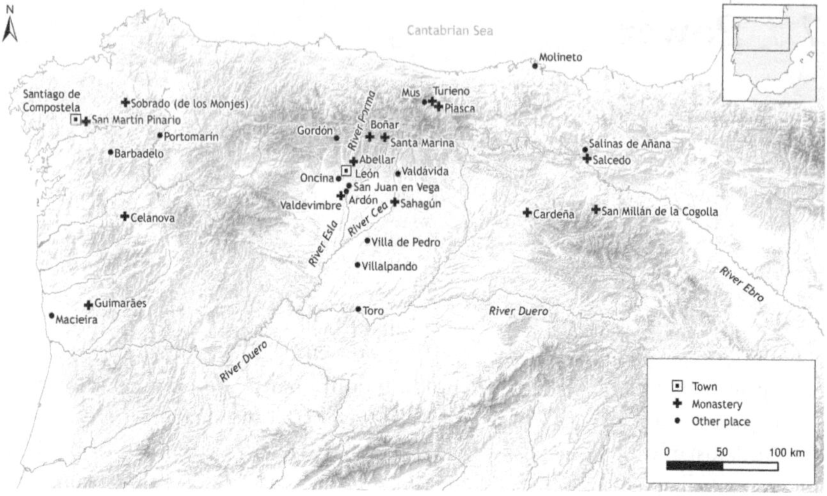

Figure 7.1 Locations noted in Chapter 7

much wishful thinking).[5] It is also because there is plenty of evidence to suggest that going to court was often about other things. Monasteries used courts a lot, to press institutional advantage, as Sahagún did in appealing to García Gómez; and lay people, even peasants, used courts to protect or enhance their material resources;[6] going to court here had more to do with materialities than personal vendettas. Expressions of enmity do surface in acts of physical violence – fighting, killing, besieging and setting fire to property – but we do not know whether these were isolated cases of momentary rage or symptoms of more deeply rooted and continuing hostilities: the fragmentary record of Lupi and his associates laying siege to a priest and his female companion at home, slaughtering some of the inmates, and then burning down the house, is tantalizing – but we simply do not know what this disturbance was about.[7] Some families appear to have been particularly disruptive, ranging round the countryside causing havoc, like Dom Patre and his gang of seven sons and cousins in Valdávida in

5 However, Vicente Ángel Álvarez Palenzuela, 'La nobleza del reino de León en la alta edad media', in *El reino de León en la alta edad media, VII, Estudios* (León, 1995), pp. 149–329, at p. 216, presents the Odoíno/Guntroda case in terms of competition between the Velázquez with Odoíno on one side and the Menéndez with Guntroda on the other. See Isabel Alfonso, 'Litigios por la tierra y "malfetrías" entre la nobleza medieval castellano-leonesa', *Hispania*, 57/3 (1997), pp. 917–55, for the role of land disputes in local politics in the much better-documented subsequent centuries.

6 For example, Lii474 (980).

7 For example, OD44 (998); Cel456 (940); Lii360 (963) – see above, p. 47, for the fragmentary record. The Icelandic burning of Njal, with his wife and family, comes to mind in the case of Lii360; *Njal's Saga*, trans. Magnus Magnusson and Hermann Pálsson (Harmondsworth, 1960), § 129, pp. 265–9.

the Cea valley, north of Sahagún, and Revel and his gang in the neighbourhood of the Villa Mahmudes, probably in the hinterland of León; these might suggest something more systemic, but these enmities tend not to be played out in court.[8] The most obvious displays of enmity are those expressed as rebellion against a king, action that was usually handled by summary confiscation rather than by any kind of judicial process. Although records of confiscations often situate the king in the presence of great men, they notably lack the language of judicial texts and any hint of the regular mechanisms of court procedure. To begin with open displays of enmity, then, how were confiscations managed?

Confiscations

The majority of recorded cases of homicide, though not all, were handled outside the court system.[9] This was predominantly the preserve of kings, who dealt with much reported homicide by confiscating the killer's property, and sometimes by exiling the killer. Dom Patre and his gang were exiled by King Ramiro II in 943, and their property was given to the high aristocrat Vermudo Núñez; the regent Elvira confiscated the property of the killers Valite and Jacinto on the banks of the River Esla near Castro Ardón in 969 and gave it to her uncle, the high aristocrat Aznar Puricélliz, and his wife; and King Vermudo II in effect confiscated the church of the homicidal priest Ero and gave it to the bishop of León.[10] Notice of these cases of homicide largely comes in straightforward records of gift, in which the point of the text was to record the assignment of the killer's property to someone else; the note of the killing is therefore largely incidental to the record. The procedure by which the king acted is consequently only dimly glimpsed, but it would appear that he was alerted to local reports and then took action, sometimes explicitly joined by his advisers. One could argue that, given that the record of levying the penalty is so brief, the action may in practice have been carried out with full court procedure, although it is notable that *saiones* do not normally appear to have been involved; certainly, the texts recording confiscations do not make a point of noting the involvement of a *saio*.[11] One charter is particularly useful in suggesting that the process involved summary royal action, and that this was normal. When the drunken and armed Rapinato went with others to a dependency of Sahagún (not named, but near Villa de Pedro), broke down the doors and killed a monk, King Ramiro III sent

8 S84 (943), Lii463 (979); cf. E25 (952), a gift to the monastery of Eslonza witnessed by Dom Patre, *gasaliane* of Abalza Adefonsi; see further below, pp. 183–4. Revel gave a vineyard *in uilla de Mahmude, in uallelio Cauetello*. This cannot be precisely located, but the Cavatello valley features in two suspect Abellar charters, of which one clearly cites the River Torío (Abellar itself lying north of León, on the river), while a person from Cavatello witnessed a charter of 1014 which clearly refers to the area north of León (between the rivers Torío and Bernesga); Li62 (914–24), Li99 (934), Liii732.

9 See below, pp. 198–200, for homicide cases that went through the courts.

10 S84, Lii411, Lii507 (985).

11 See above, pp. 164–8, for *saiones*.

his judge Gutino Zelim to investigate.[12] Gutino duly investigated, confiscated Rapinato's property in Villa de Pedro (in the Cea valley, south of Sahagún) on the king's behalf and gave it to the monastery of Sahagún. In detailing the confiscation, the charter adds that it was the custom (*consuetudo*) for kings to act in this way in cases of homicide. Confiscation for homicide therefore appears to have been viewed as a kind of royal prerogative, at least on the *meseta*.[13] As such, it was overtly political. However, some cases of homicide were handled in landowners' courts. We do not know what determined whether a killing should be handled directly by the king or by a court, but the indications are that, although proximity must have played a part, this was largely a matter of status: peasant killings went to the local courts, but those of and by aristocrats, and sometimes by middling men, went to the king – thereby emphasizing the political dimensions of the remedy.

Homicide was not the only occasion of confiscation. There is one case of confiscation for abduction, by order of king and bishop, although since the record indicates that the abductor confessed, there could have been a court case about this incident.[14] But there are many cases of confiscation by kings on account of rebellion and infidelity. The fact of rebellion at different points across the tenth century is noted by the chronicler Sampiro, like the rebellion of Count Fernán González of Castile and Diego Muñoz in 944, which led to the imprisonment of Fernán González in the fort of Gordón, by King Ramiro II.[15] King Vermudo II dealt with a series of rebellions in the late tenth century by making confiscations; he took property from Conancio, Salvador, Gonzalo Vermúdez, García Gómez, Ablavel Godestéiz, Gonzalo Menéndez and Suario Gundemáriz and gave it to faithful aristocratic followers, to high-status clerics and to monasteries; Conancio, whose property lay in Oncina, to the south-west of León, had spread rumours that the king was dead while he was away in Galicia; Gonzalo Menéndez had been joined in his rebel stronghold in Galicia by some of the king's servants – when the king asked him to send them back, or to send his son as a hostage, on pain of losing the key strategic property of Portomarín (as well as Recelle), Gonzalo replied that he could do whatever he liked with the place.[16] Rebellion and confiscation is particularly characteristic of this

12 S287 (977); for Gutino, see above, p. 162. (Gutino is not called 'judge' in this particular text.)

13 *ut consuetudo est secundum quod ueritas docet per canonica sententia aprehendit omnem hereditatem uel facultatem de ipso iam nominato homicida a parte dominica*; this literally says confiscation on the 'lord's' behalf, but the context makes it quite clear that it is the royal lord who was involved (as do other cases). The charter appears to invoke ecclesiastical, not secular, Visigothic law, but see Liii581 at n. 19 below; the latter also makes it clear that this view of royal power was not confined to the Sahagún scribe.

14 OD29 (988).

15 Justo Pérez de Urbel, *Sampiro. Su crónica y la monarquía leonesa en el siglo X* (Madrid, 1952), pp. 328–9, also pp. 338 and 341–2, and see his discussion at pp. 411–12, 426–7, 431–2. For Gordón, see also Julio Escalona, 'In the name of a distant king: Representing royal authority in the county of Castile, ca. 900–1038', *Early Medieval Europe*, 24 (2016), and see above, pp. 146–7, re ACO B.1.11.

16 Liii541 (990), Liii559 (993), Liii581 (998), OD90 (1012, a retrospective reference), SantA57 (993), Cel104 (994). Suario's rebellion involved an attack on royal castles in the Miño valley and led

later tenth-century period, but there is also a series of confiscations attributed to Alfonso III a century earlier, in which the confiscated property was channelled to the bishopric of Santiago.[17] One could question the efficacy of some royal action,[18] at any of these periods, but confiscated property undoubtedly ended up in monastic hands, whether through direct gifts to monasteries from the king or through gifts from lay *fideles* who had benefited from the confiscation. While confiscations look like cases of purely summary royal justice, there must have been an element of political consensus for confiscation to have been effective – one charter of 998, detailing the confiscation of Gonzalo Vermúdez's property in El Bierzo and its gift to Sampiro, cites holy law and Visigothic law on the proper treatment of rebellions and of opposition to the king;[19] clearly, there was a desire to proclaim a sense of legitimacy about this act, but it was a legitimacy that operated outside the regular courts. The rebels were aristocrats – sometimes, like Suario Gundemáriz, men who had moved in royal circles – and some of the late tenth-century rebel movements were clearly seriously disruptive, as the tales of servants and others who joined the movements suggest.[20] Royal action was inevitably about dealing with enemies, but it was also about the building and maintenance of alliances, built beyond the courts, not within them, and the beneficiaries were aristocrats, bishops and major monasteries.[21] Whether or not kings had always had the capacity to confiscate is arguable, and indeed unlikely, but the late tenth century, a time when they clearly did have such capacity, also emerges as a time of some conscious alliance-building –

---

to the gift of San Paio de Veiga to the monastery of Celanova; the same disturbance features in the more dubious Tumbo Viejo of Lugo, TV15 (998), in which it is claimed that Castro de Aguiar was subsequently given to the bishop of Lugo so that it could be destroyed and a church built, although the charter suggests that it was left to remain as a defence for the population.

17 SantA5 (867), SantA12 (885), SantA13 (886), SantA15 (895), SantA16 (895). Some of these charters have doubtful elements, but they are credible records of donation and are certainly consistent in suggesting the royal capacity to confiscate; in other words, there was a shared view that this was the kind of action that kings could legitimately carry out. Cf. Claudio Sánchez Albornoz, 'Rebeliones en Galicia', in *Estudios sobre Galicia en la temprana edad media* (A Coruña, 1981), pp. 159–82, who treats these charters as more than credible.

18 Cf. the case of Gonzalo Menéndez cited above, SantA57.

19 Liii581.

20 On joining rebels, see n. 16 above and Cel215 (995).

21 There is a very large bibliography on the construction of aristocratic families, their rebellions and their alliances. For a flavour of it, see Jose Manuel Ruiz Asencio, 'Rebeliones leonesas contra Vermudo II', *Archivos Leoneses*, 45–6 (1969), pp. 215–41, who deals with all the texts and with the chronology of rebellions against Vermudo II; Ermelindo Portela Silva and María del Carmen Pallares Méndez, 'Elementos para el análisis de la aristocracia altomedieval de Galicia: parentesco y patrimonio', *Studia Histórica, Historia Medieval*, 5 (1987), pp. 17–32; Álvarez Palenzuela, 'La nobleza del reino de León'; Margarita Torres-Sevilla Quiñones de León, *Linajes nobiliarios en León y Castilla (siglos IX–XIII)* (Valladolid, 1999); Amancio Isla Frez, *Realezas hispánicas del año mil* (A Coruña, 1999), pp. 59–71; Mariel Pérez, '*Rebelles, infideles, traditores*. Insumisión política y poder aristocrático en el reino de León', *Historia, instituciones, documentos*, 38 (2011), pp. 361–82, on the relationship between rebellion and the growth of autonomous aristocratic power.

certainly, in hindsight, a significant phase in the construction of royal, as also of aristocratic, power.[22]

Using the courts: monasteries, bishops and priests

If judicial courts were not the place for dealing with open enmities, to what extent were they an arena for the construction of political advantage; and if they were, who used them? In the case of the monastery of Valdevimbre's action against a group of local people from San Juan en Vega over water to power their mills, the monks twice claimed that the peasants were taking so much water there was not enough left for the monastery's mill; and the king twice sent judges to measure the water levels, declaring each time that there was enough water for everyone. The case is recorded because, although the peasants were successful in maintaining their access to water, the final declaration provides for them to give assistance to the monastery when its mill needed repair; despite their success, in the course of this case the peasants acquired an obligation.[23] There was a persistence in Valdevimbre's action here – the text says several times that the monks brought the case 'maliciously' – which in the end brought them some additional benefit, although they do not appear to have had a valid case. Persistence brought them an advantage, as it did to many monasteries.

There is an inevitable bias towards detailing the activities and successes of monasteries in the records that survive. While one might expect some exaggeration of the levels of success and some enhancement of outcomes (the Valdevimbre text is very unusual in indicating some limits), there cannot be any doubt that in the later ninth and especially in the tenth century, monasteries used the courts to gain advantages. These advantages were overwhelmingly proprietary. Monasteries went to court and initiated action against lay aristocrats and against groups of peasants, in roughly equal numbers, as also against lay individuals of uncertain status and now and then against other monasteries, priests or bishops; in the latter cases, apart from the occasional pursuit of errant monks or nuns, their actions were for similar reasons to those behind actions taken against lay persons – at this period, unlike later centuries, there is nothing especially distinctive about the suits pursued against ecclesiastical bodies.[24] So, for example, the monastery of San Martín Pinario in north-west Galicia, backed by the nearby bishopric of Santiago de Compostela, was involved in a court case against the aristocrat Dona Palla Díaz over the annual tribute due from the

22 For a thorough recent treatment of royal alliance-building, see Álvaro Carvajal Castro, 'La construcción de la monarquía asturleonesa en la meseta del Duero. Estudio de los procesos de integración territorial (s. IX–XI)' (Universidad de Salamanca, Tesis Doctoral, 2013), especially pp. 421–35, 457–8, 701–706; see also Álvarez Palenzuela, 'La nobleza del reino de León', pp. 179–239, and Pérez, '*Rebelles, infideles, traditores*', p. 382, who comments that the 'rhetoric of infidelity' masks the parallel development of aristocratic and royal power.

23 Li128 (938).

24 Against a monastery: SM50 (948) (= BG531), for which see below; a priest: C35 (941); a bishop: Sam126 (960).

freed men of Barbadelo; advocates made the case for each side, and the judges ordered witnesses to be produced for each; then three further judges ordered San Martín's witnesses to take the oath – which they did, and so the monastery won.[25] The monastery of Sahagún took Megito to court in 978 because he had entered their land at Fontasquesa, in the Upper Porma valley in the foothills of the Cantabrian Mountains, had cleared it and started ploughing; the case was heard before Count Fernando Vermúdez, Judge Pepi Braoliz and others, assisted by the *saio*; the man confessed, promised to keep off the land and paid the court fees.[26] The monastery of San Millán took action in 948 against the locals of Salinas, as well as against the monks of Salcedo and of Cardeña, over access to the saltpans of Salinas; the case was heard by Count Fernán González of Castile, and it was resolved that San Millán should have untrammelled access to the saltpans from dawn to dusk every Sunday.[27] This was perhaps not as much as the monastery wanted – the text speaks of every third day (*de tercio in tercio die*) – but it established the monastery's right of access and may well have resulted in an acquisition. By taking action, San Millán gained an advantage.

The actions taken by monasteries were primarily about the ownership of property, expressed as disputes over the control of small plots or large expanses of land, of churches, mills, water courses, saltpans and fisheries; this was sometimes expressed as dissent over the line of a boundary or as a response to intrusion across a boundary in order to plant and take a crop from monastic land, rather like Megito's case above; and it was sometimes expressed as insistence on a requirement to make a regular return from land or as insistence on the control of dependents. For example, when five families were held to have intruded on Celanova's land in Santa Eulalia in Lemos, they were taken to court, and the outcome was that they agreed that in future they would give the monastery a quarter of their grape and chestnut crop every year.[28] Other actions include cases over wounding, homicide and unpaid debts, although the number of these is very small (6 per cent) by comparison with the property cases (83 per cent).

All kinds of monastery, in all regions, behaved in this way, from the great monasteries like Celanova, Cardeña and Sahagún to those of lesser but significant size like Abellar on the outskirts of León and Turieno in the Liébana, to much smaller institutions like the female house at Piasca, or Santa Marina in the Upper Esla valley or the several monasteries involved in a Galician case about access to saltpans, of 956.[29] So many are these cases, it looks as if the courts were

25 LaC95 (985). I am very grateful to Juan Carlos Sánchez Pardo for identifying the location of Barbadelo; the placename is not in current use. See further José Miguel Andrade Cernadas, 'Villas regias y asambleas judiciales entre los siglos X y XI: el caso de Larín', *Revista Signum*, 12 (2011), pp. 18–35, for the location of the hearing at Larín.

26 S295.

27 SM50 (= BG 531). For a more detailed map of the locations, see the map associated with this charter in the online edition.

28 Cel446 (959).

29 S372 (989), OD43 (997), LaC59; one of the monasteries of the latter (Celanova) was not small at all, but the others included Camanzo, Salceda, Vilanova, Nogueira and San Lorenzo de Carboeiro, which – apart from San Lorenzo – are not prominent in the record in this period.

deliberately used as a tool by monks and clerics to extend their property base. The larger monasteries feature more often in dispute records, which may be a simple consequence of the preservation of a greater number of their records, or it may be an indicator of more pro-active strategies. Some powerful and well-documented monasteries do not feature so often – like Sobrado and Portuguese Guimarães – which may suggest that this was indeed a matter of strategy rather than survival of records: some monasteries were exceptionally pro-active. Although they might occasionally use the court of a landowner or of a royal official, on most recorded occasions monasteries went to a king's or a count's court, using the king's court in more than half of known cases in this period. Indeed, monastic strategy seems the best explanation for those records which suggest that court presidents joined the judges in judging:[30] at first glance, it looks as if it may have been the political interest of the court holder which led to his or her participation, but it happened overwhelmingly in cases in which monasteries, especially powerful monasteries, were the litigants – like the case of the monastery of Samos against Bishop Rosendo in 960, judged by King Sancho and others;[31] the court holders were overwhelmingly high-status people – kings or counts; and the cases are for the most part property disputes, and include relatively many disputes over the ownership of churches, sometimes at the level of a contest between bishop and monastery. Every one of these records is a retrospective Account. That being the case, reference to the participation of the court holder is more likely to be to do with the construction of the record than with any differences in the proceedings. The ecclesiastical authors of the texts wanted to associate the outcomes with the highest authority, and did so by presenting the court holder as one of the judges. In some of these disputes, the court holders, kings and counts, could have shown political interest by favouring these successful monasteries, but it certainly does not follow that they always did so.

This use of judicial courts by monasteries, then, was a dialogue with rulers and a bid for ruler support; using the court was a strategy invoking authority in several senses – the authority of the court, but also the authority of the highest conceivable kind of secular authority, secular not ecclesiastical;[32] and it was a statement that monasteries operated in the political sphere. Some of the great monasteries, like Sahagún and San Millán, went on to forge particularly strong associations with kings (of León and Pamplona respectively) in the eleventh century.[33]

30 See above, pp. 155–60, for presidency of courts.

31 Sam126.

32 We have very occasional evidence of church courts, but their business tended to be concerned with ecclesiastical discipline. See also n. 70 below for episcopal meetings.

33 Note the exemplary study of Sahagún's use of royal connections by Isabel Alfonso in Andrew Reynolds, Jane Carroll and Barbara Yorke (eds), *Power and Place in Later Roman and Early Medieval Europe* (forthcoming). For San Millán, see José Ángel García de Cortázar y Ruiz de Aguirre, *El dominio del monasterio de San Millán de la Cogolla (siglos X a XIII). Introducción a la historia rural de Castilla altomedieval* (Salamanca, 1969), especially pp. 137–92. By contrast, kings used monasteries too: see Carvajal Castro, 'La construcción de la monarquía asturleonesa en la meseta del Duero', pp. 503–20, for deliberate royal patronage of monasteries in the early tenth century.

Bishops sometimes backed the suits of monasteries, as the bishop of Santiago backed San Martín Pinario's case against the aristocrat Palla Díaz, but they also, of course, pursued their own cases through the courts, although – unsurprisingly, given relative numbers – there are not nearly so many records of these as there are of monastic cases (the ratio is 1:5).[34] Like those of monasteries, most of their recorded cases are about property, whether framed as an explicit argument about control of this or that piece of land or an argument about the line of a boundary.[35] Some cases were about ownership of churches, while that of the bishop of Braga against the priest Toresario was more explicitly about the income due from a church.[36] Bishops are most frequently recorded using the king's court, but they used count's courts at least twice too. Half of these proceedings are recorded in Accounts, one in a Fine and the rest in Confessions. In other words, the process involved in episcopal use of secular courts to protect or extend property rights is very similar to that of monasteries.[37]

While individual priests did not enter into court cases with the weight of monasteries or bishops, it is worth remembering how actively priests inhabited the court.[38] In addition to their practical functions, they were key providers of evidence. In 956, the priest Severo confessed on oath that the church of San Cipriano belonged to Valpuesta; in 961, two priests were named to swear on the tomb of Saint James on behalf of Bishop Rosendo in a disputed fisheries case; in 968, the priest Zuleiman took an oath on behalf of the monastery of Cillanueva; and one priest confessed, in the court of the count of Castile, that on a previous occasion he had sworn a false oath.[39] They also appeared as litigants in court cases, just as monasteries did. They were often in court as party to a property dispute, with both lay and ecclesiastical opponents. They conflicted with abbots over water rights and mills, as did the priest Abolmondar, who appeared in the count of Castile's court, along with neighbouring lay proprietors of mills, when the abbot of San Torcuato claimed there was insufficient water to power his own mill;[40] they were taken to court by bishops, by other priests and by laymen for failure to return income from their churches, as Toresario was;[41] they accused peasants and aristocrats alike of intruding onto their lands or taking their churches, just as the priest Fafila accused the

34 LaC95.

35 For example, Ast5 (878), Li191 (946), Jaca (958); boundaries: SJP14 (928), Cel93 (950).

36 T17 (885), OvC24 (942); Flor74 (861) – see above, pp. 48–9, 128–31, for the Toresario case; the text specifies Braga as the bishopric, even if in practice this was the bishop of Lugo, acting as successor to the see of Braga (the charter is preserved in the Lugo cathedral archive).

37 For the political influence of bishops in other fora, see Carlos de Ayala Martínez, *Sacerdocio y reino en la España altomedieval. Iglesia y poder en el Occidente peninsular, siglos VII–XII* (Madrid, 2008), especially cc. 6 and 7, although he readily admits (ibid., p. 214) that their role cannot always be deduced. Thirteen bishops attended a council in León in 950; ibid., p. 201.

38 See above, pp. 176–7, for priests as court functionaries.

39 V33, SantA42, Lii410, C151 (972).

40 C22 (932).

41 Flor74; see also V10 (919), Sob130 (992); cf. PMH DC 163 (991).

layman Abregano in a Galician court of 973 and five years later the priest Munio accused a peasant couple of occupying a vineyard he had bought on the *meseta*.[42] Priests were accused of, and confessed to, homicide, fornication and theft, as the priests Adulfo, Ero and Oderigo did; one priest appeared at a council (perhaps of Sahagún) in chains, where he was helped by the wealthy priest Melic, although we do not know precisely why this happened.[43] Priests were exceptionally active in court, as functionaries, as accused and as accusers. While to some extent they used the courts, like monasteries and bishops, to press for advantage, they are much more evident as members of the court and as its subjects; it is striking that the acquisitions of the powerful priests Vincemalo and Melic were overwhelmingly by purchase and partly through donations, not through property received as court-imposed penalties. Some of this activity was inevitably about local politics. We do not usually have sufficient information to unravel the personal relationships that animated these incidents but, again, the Valdevimbre case, in which the priest Gondemaro successfully led a group of local people against the monastery's claims, suggests that a local priest could identify with a local group.[44]

Using the courts: lay actors

Of course, there was no strict division between the ecclesiastical and the lay, and it may give a mistaken impression of divided spheres of operation to make one.[45] Lay families, like kings, patronized monasteries and used them to promote or extend their own interests, just as they did all over western Europe.[46] High aristocrats founded monasteries, as Ilduara and her family founded Celanova, and Hermenegildo and Paterna (whose son Sisnando became bishop of Santiago) founded Sobrado, in southern and northern Galicia respectively; or the Braoliz family, who founded Boñar, on the edge of the *meseta*; or the endowment of Bagaudano and Faquilona of San Martín Turieno in the Liébana.[47]

42 AHN 1325A–9, from Lugo, and Lii458 (978); cf. OD27 (987), AHN 1325A–6 (922).

43 PMH DC 53 (943), Lii507 (985), LaC102 (988); S133 (951).

44 See above, p. 186.

45 On interconnections, see, for example, Gregorio del Ser Quijano, 'Movilidad y promoción del grupo eclesiástico y su vinculación con la aristocracia. La diócesis de León en el período asturleonés', *Hispania*, 53/185 (1993), pp. 1053–67; Iñaki Martín Viso, 'Monasterios y redes sociales en el Bierzo altomedieval', *Hispania*, 71/237 (2011), pp. 9–38.

46 Mariel Pérez, 'El control de lo sagrado como instrumento de poder: los monasterios particulares de la aristocracia altomedieval leonesa', *Anuario de Estudios Medievales*, 42 (2012), pp. 799–822.

47 Sob1 (952); and see María del Carmen Pallares Méndez, *El monasterio de Sobrado: un ejemplo del protagonismo monástico en la Galicia medieval* (A Coruña, 1979); Cel256 (936) and Cel4 (938), and María del Carmen Pallares Méndez, *Ilduara, una aristócrata del siglo X* (A Coruña, 1998); for Boñar, E9 (929) and see Pérez, 'El control de lo sagrado como instrumento de poder'; for Turieno, see Abilio Barbero and Marcelo Vigil, *La formación del feudalismo en la Península Ibérica* (Barcelona, 1978), pp. 377–80, and Robert Portass, 'The contours and contexts of public power in the tenth-century Liébana', *Journal of Medieval History*, 38 (2012), pp. 389–407. Cf. the aristocratic founders listed in LaC59 (see n. 29 above).

High aristocrats held bishoprics, as did Sisnando, and Gutier and Ilduara's son Rosendo, and Vermudo Núñez's brother Oveco, bishop of León.[48] Widows endowed larger and smaller monasteries with substantial gifts of landed property, and it is certainly conceivable that family interests in that land were sustained beyond the widows' lifetimes, particularly since many of these lands had come to the woman from her own family; hence Mumadona's substantial gifts to Guimarães *c.* 950, Jimena's very substantial gifts to Sahagún of 985, Aragunta's less substantial gift to Celanova in 995, Velasquita's gift to Santa María of Osoño of land inherited from her grandmother, and Eldoara's gift to Santiago in León of property inherited from her mother.[49] There were also plenty of proprietary churches, owned by both clerical and lay families, and many owners benefited from the income from church properties. We can see family interest in Celanova and Sobrado across the tenth century; we can see the interest of the descendants of the founder of Santa Lucía de Montes supporting it against Osorio Gutiérrez in mid-century and that of the descendants of Mumadonna in Guimarães late in the century; however, on the whole, we do not know enough about the family connections of most abbots to know over how many generations aristocratic founders and endowers sustained their interests in the lands of the monasteries they had founded and endowed;[50] and the trend across the tenth century was certainly to alienate proprietary churches to the larger monasteries.[51] But there can be no doubt that there was an undertow of interconnection between many a lay family and monastery or church across the later ninth and tenth centuries. Despite all this, there is a difference between pursuing a judicial case as an ecclesiastical body and pursuing one as a lay individual, and for that

48 Ayala Martínez, *Sacerdocio y reino en la España*, p. 202.

49 PMH DC 76 (959), S328, Cel230, Cel492 (988), Lii425 (973). Widows also gave property which they had acquired with their husbands, for example S212 (963), Ov20 (978), Cel209 (997). Despite some good examples of morning gifts bestowed on wives by husbands, it is more difficult to demonstrate widows' gifts of land acquired from their husbands, although Sam239 (985), for which see below, p. 192, is probably one such case. For women's property rights, see my longer discussion in Wendy Davies, *Acts of Giving: Individual, Community, and Church in Tenth-century Christian Spain* (Oxford, 2007), pp. 164–79. For women's foundations and endowments, from both inherited and dower land, Karl Leyser, *Rule and Conflict in an Early Medieval Society: Ottonian Saxony* (London, 1979), pp. 49–73, remains fundamental.

50 Ast71 (952), PMH DC 183 (999); on the latter, see André Marques, 'Turning the bishop away but letting the king in: The *Livro de Mumadona* of Guimarães in the changing scenario of the 1070s', paper delivered at Leeds International Congress, July 2015, and see the forthcoming edition of *Livro de Mumadona*, ed. Luis Amaral. Pérez, 'El control de lo sagrado como instrumento de poder', pp. 816–17, argues that some families extended their interests by acquiring interests in an increasing number of monasteries across up to five generations.

51 For proprietary churches, see Susan Wood, *The Proprietary Church in the Medieval West* (Oxford, 2006); and for northern Iberia in particular, see Davies, *Acts of Giving*, ch. 2, and references there cited. María Isabel Loring García, 'Nobleza e iglesias propias en la Cantabria altomedieval', *Studia Histórica, Historia Medieval*, 5 (1987), pp. 89–123, makes the point that although many proprietary churches were given up by lay families, some great aristocrats retained interests in the monasteries that absorbed them through the eleventh and twelfth centuries.

reason, allowing always for the qualifications expressed above, I intend to treat ecclesiastical and lay actors separately.

Lay individuals used the courts in their lay capacity, despite the weight of monastic presence in dispute records and the monastic interest in their preservation. There are too many uncertainties about status to count the proportions of aristocrats or of peasants who did so, but it is perfectly clear that both kinds of person went to court, apparently voluntarily. Astotia took her brother Fruela Franquilaz to court, before Judge Diego Díaz in Samos, over the diversion of substantial family property to Fruela's wife.[52] Many litigants look as if they had in-between status – the local big men or middle-range people who seem to have had the resources, and the horses, to range around causing trouble, without the levels of wealth of the high aristocracy, people like Vermudo and Eldonça Petriz, who pursued a case against a priest over ownership of a church.[53] Again, more than half of recorded lay cases are property disputes, pursued against other lay people, and occasionally against monasteries, priests or bishops. At a very early date, some time before 818, Vittina and children displaced the children of Riquilani from what they claimed was their land; eventually, at the king's order, Count Aloito ejected Vittina from most of that land. Seseguto and Fernando argued over a vineyard in Mus in the Liébana in the 960s or shortly before that, an argument which ended up in court, with the involvement of two *saiones* and a (lay) surety also taking action against Seseguto. Sunilla and his wife Susana were involved in an action against Suario over an unpaid debt in southern Galicia late in the tenth century.[54] In an unusual case, a man called Lovesindo petitioned Count Mendo Gonçalves against the monastery of Guimarães over land in northern Portugal, and perhaps port rights, that his father had enjoyed; in the end, in 999, Lovesindo was in effect paid off with another farm and 28 *solidi*.[55] The aristocrat Rodrigo Álvarez was not so successful when he tried to claim control of a dependent (and therefore the income from that dependent) from the monastery of Pardomino, although he clearly tried.[56] In two cases on the eastern edge of Castile, the same laymen disputed with other laymen over land and over water power, invoking Visigothic law and taking oaths; and in another Castilian case, a group of six locals confessed before a judge that they

52 Sam239 (985), doubtless stimulated because the wife alienated property to Samos (which suggests that family interest was not sustained through the monastery in this case).

53 AHN Clero Lugo 1325A–6 (922).

54 Sob43, T66, Cel368 (p. 530).

55 PMH DC 183.

56 Liii577 (997). For this charter, see above, pp. 89, 141. The area, which was appurtenant to the castle of San Salvador, which controlled the basin of the River Curueño, was in the gift of the royal family, which had given control of it to the bishop of León in the 950s (Lii300). Rodrigo's control, which is suggested by *Ruderico Aluariz cum suos omines de Ferreras et preserunt ipso omine ut mitterent eum in comissorio de Ferrarias* (whether in his own right or that of someone else), was clearly in any case short-lived because the castle and its appurtenances were returned to the bishop of León by King Alfonso V in 999 (Liii588). See Carvajal Castro, 'La construcción de la monarquía asturleonesa en la meseta del Duero', pp. 574–5, 655–7, for detailed consideration of the role of the castle.

were using land that belonged to the count's daughter.[57] But lay people pursued each other in court for reasons other than property too: for theft, for fighting, for rape and for homicide; there was a man who stole a cow from each of three different people, and some brothers who stole horses; there was a man who laid siege to another's house, and there were men who fought and wounded others.[58] There are also occasional cases about paternity and servile status, although they are not prominent among the records that survive.[59]

Many of these cases make little impression in the corpus of charters because a high proportion of them (just under two-thirds) is recorded in Fines or Incidental records of dispute; there are indeed some Accounts, in which the course of the dispute gets some attention, and a few Confessions and Agreements, but most cases of lay people using the courts are noted because the winner made a grateful gift to someone who had assisted or because the loser had to pay a fine for the disruption caused; the ultimate transfer of property was the subject of the record, and the reason for making the record, not the dispute.[60] To take an example, in a straightforward charter of gift from Ausendo and his wife Zonza to Doña Trastalla of arable plots in the farm of Macieira, a charter which includes many standard dispositive formulas, we find the statement: 'damus uobis illos in oferzionem pro que nobis sacastis linpio de conzelio et sano pro parte de illo iudizio que noscum abuit Aderedo pro parte de illa ereditate que nobis Sendinus et Iulia uendiuit' ('we give them to you in recognition of the fact that you took us away from the council clear and clean, in the course of the court case we had with Aderedo about that property Sendinus and Iulia sold us').[61] Here, among the standard formulas of gift, we hear by chance that the beneficiary had saved the donors from a court case in which Aderedo was querying property they had purchased. We know nothing further about this case, and it is not clear whether Trastalla was the court holder or a patron who had intervened.[62] But the incidental nature of the reference makes it perfectly clear that local lay proprietors were using judicial process, and the likelihood must be – since the properties are of small scale – that they were peasant proprietors. The Cresconio inventories, from late tenth- and early eleventh-century Celanova, offer many comparable examples, recording, as they do, a great mixture of purchases, gifts and other modes of acquisition.[63] So, for example: 'ego Meola . . . in ripa deuesa mea ratione III[a] integra . . . do uobis [Cresconio] pro intentione que habeo cum Bellendo et do uobis illa in iudicato' ('I Meola give you Cresconio my one-third share of the enclosure [on

57 SM23 (= BG 390) (936), SM27 (= BG 391) (940), Ar18 (965).
58 T41 (932), Cel368 (p. 524); OD44 (998); Sob103 (952), probably Lii474 (980).
59 A27 (978), SantA24 (912).
60 For example, gift: C59 (947); fines: Cel456 (940), OD44 (998); cf. Lii473 (980).
61 PMH DC 160 (991), a charter on a single sheet.
62 Though the fact that they were *linpio*, clean, suggests they may have had to undergo the hot water ordeal; see above, p. 137, for this charter.
63 See above, pp. 42–3, 157, for these inventories.

the River Sorga] in respect of the dispute I have with Bellendo and I give it to you as court fees').[64] We do not know what the dispute was about nor what happened in court, just that there had been a dispute and that the monastery official Cresconio received the fine. Because these references are incidental, and brief, we do not know much about the players. The relatively few records of lay persons initiating action against monasteries or clerics are mostly recorded in Accounts, because in the end the monastery or cleric secured some kind of advantage which it was in their interest to record, as in the Valdevimbre case over water rights.[65] When Lovesindo petitioned the count in his case against the monastery of Guimarães, although the outcome was that he was successful in securing another farm, Guimarães nevertheless needed a record of its own case for keeping the farm which had been the subject of the original dispute.[66] Although most of these references to lay use of courts are incidental, they are important as a counterbalance to the monastic record; they show, without any shadow of doubt, that lay people used the courts to pursue or protect their interests, just as clerics and monasteries did.

It is worth noting that lay people seem to have used a wider range of courts than those characteristically used by monasteries. There are occasional hearings in the king's court, and several in those of counts, but purely lay cases were clearly heard in the courts of monastic officials (like the Celanova and Turieno cases cited above), and as many were heard in the courts of lay landowners.[67] At least one case was handled in an episcopal court, and several were heard before expert judges (who may have been king's or count's judges, but may perhaps – when there is no hint of royal or comital interest – have been independent judges who offered a service for a fee, given their special skill and expertise).[68] As suggested above, there may well have been many more landowner courts than those that are detailed in the record, for we get just a glimpse of lesser courts used by ordinary people.[69]

It is finally worth remembering that lay people (and clerics too) solved disputes and potential disputes without going to court – another fact that is not dominant in the record, for obvious reasons. There were written agreements and meetings involving representatives of both sides, sometimes assisted by *boni homines*; we often see meetings as a mechanism used by bishops in their conflicts with each other.[70] Disputes were resolved by making gifts and sales, by annulling documents, by paying fees and taking oaths; debts were cancelled because gifts of property were made in place of payments demanded. Halele and Zondai exchanged property and then made a written agreement that Halele would

64 Cel368 (p. 526).

65 See above, p. 186.

66 PMH DC 183; see above, p. 192.

67 See above, pp. 158–9, for relative proportions of records of landowner courts.

68 Bishop's court: Sob129 (942); before judges: SM23 (936) (= BG 390), Ar18 (965). See above, pp. 160–4, for judges.

69 See above, pp. 179–80.

70 Episcopal meetings: PMH DC 13 (906), SantA28 (915?), SantA42 (961).

not sell the property or exchange it with anyone else; the monastery of Abellar agreed to construct a fence after it had been given a route to access water, so that the donor's property would not be damaged by the coming and going; 'Brother' Ioanes extracted himself from the problems caused by failing to meet the terms of an earlier agreement by making a gift of land.[71] When Aderico and Sesina, the wicked cousins of Reparado and Trasvinda, abused the latter's bequest of their inheritance by ejecting them from their home and imprisoning them, Reparado and his wife revoked the gift and assigned the property instead to Bishop Rosendo.[72] And when Ydilo, one of the dependents of Celanova, claimed that a girl was the daughter of Arias, and not his own, Arias took an oath in public, with oath-helpers, to deny the fact.[73] Taking action in public to make an agreement or to settle a problem in some other way was evidently important to these communities. The public nature of the action is not always explicit, given the brief notice of these occasions, but it is evident from the contexts. A debt of 40 sesters of cider to the aristocrat Ilduara was cleared by a gift to her of orchards in 947; here the charter additionally notes in the witness list that the gift is to clear the debt – in other words, it was stressed before witnesses, in public.[74]

Getting to court

If we look at these issues the other way round – that is, rather than looking at those who used the courts to gain advantage or pursue their interests, we look instead at those who were the subjects of court procedure – does this provide a different slant on the power relationships of judicial process? Thinking about the kinds of people who passed through different kinds of court, we can note that virtually every kind of case was in fact heard in every kind of court; on the whole, courts were not differentiated by business. However, the extant records do not show kings dealing with adultery cases, nor indeed with petty theft of material goods – that is, with relatively low-value issues – and whereas property disputes were certainly heard in all kinds of court, there is far more evidence of them being heard in the courts of kings and counts. In other words, there is a tendency for the higher-level courts to be more concerned with property and with the lower courts to be more concerned with what we would nowadays call petty crime. There also seem to be some distinctions of status: while cases of homicide were handled both by kings and by landowners, essentially the killing of aristocrats went to the former and of peasants to the latter.[75]

71 Lii477 (980), Li94 (932), OD32 (992). See above, pp. 130–5, for the variety of surviving written agreements.

72 Cel228 (936).

73 Cel144 (n.d.): *et iurauit ipse Arias in concilio cum XIIm homines quia non erat sua filia*; certainly a public meeting (*in concilio*), but this could have been constituted as a court.

74 Cel229: *Offino a mea persona et de mea uxore Sauildi, in hanc kartulam quam fecimus pro ipsa sicera quod superius resonat manus mea.*

75 See above, pp. 183–4.

How, then, did people arrive in court, particularly if there was no explicit royal or comital order for action? While there are many hearings for which the first we know is that a person appeared before judges or before a court holder, with no indication of prior procedure, there are some charters which provide specific detail of the action which led to an appearance in court. We know that appeals were made to kings and counts by people with a grievance or by people who wanted to secure some advantage.[76] And we sometimes know what actions were taken as a result: the king might send assessors to inspect land or water; appeals to the king could sometimes result in a direct command from the king for aristocratic parties to appear before him; in the case of the layman Lovesindo who petitioned Count Mendo Gonçalves over property, a *saio* required both parties to appear before him with witnesses, and only after that did he send both parties on to the count's court for judges to assess the available written evidence and require oaths.[77] Here the count appears to have directed either his own *saio* or a local *saio* to take the initial action. There are many other cases in which it is clear that a *saio*'s instruction directly led to an appearance in court: when property was disputed between the son of a former king and the monastery of Samos, the *saio* took them both to appear before the current king; the thief Sentario, whose penalty had already been assessed, was taken before a judge by the *saio* to confirm he would pay the due penalty; when the ownership of property was apparently disputed between two sets of local people, the *saio* ordered them to court before judges.[78] It looks as if the *saio* sometimes physically took the accused to court, and at other times it is clear that he more formally delivered a notice to appear. The formal commitments to appear in court, which are occasionally preserved, make the same point: 'We Pedro and Vilifredo by this our agreement promise you *saio* Karoso that on Saturday we will present ourselves before the judges in Gordón'.[79]

The focal position of the *saio* is reinforced by the strong implication that there were pre-court procedures. The penalty for Sentario's theft was assessed before he was taken before the judge, and he confirmed before the judge that he had already confessed – presumably before the *saio*; the penalties for wounding Teverano and his wife, and for wounding Pater, were assessed before they pursued court cases to get payment of these penalties that were due; the level of compensation due from Adulfo for killing was known before he appeared before Ansur to deal with the deficit; and Lovesindo's complaint led to evidence being heard from both sides before the case was committed to the count's court.[80] It was the *saio*, in the latter case, who took the decision to move the case

76 For example, SJP13 (905–25 – this charter has suspect elements), Sam46 (933), Cel93 (950), Lii508 (985); Cel502 (540), and probably Li128 (938).

77 Li128, Sam46; SantA24 (912); PMH DC 183 (999).

78 Sam44 (975), cf. Li256 (952), Li192 (946), C90 (957); Sob31 (951); Sob129 (942).

79 ACO B.1.11: 'Petrus et Uilifredus tibi saionni nostro Kaoroso per unc placitum tibi compromitimus qualiter die quod sabbato sic presentemus personas nostras in presencia iudigum in Gordone'. See further above, pp. 135–6, for such commitments.

80 Sob31, Sob103 (952), OD31 (991), PMH DC 53 (943), PMH DC 183.

forward; and Pater's wounds were assessed at a value of 10 *solidi*, which was confirmed by the *saio* Frogia: 'in X solidos adprecitum et gum signale de sagionem Frogia'.[81] The unsuccessful litigant Rebello confessed that he had expelled the brothers of Santa María del Puerto and had occupied land in Molineto with the involvement of a 'hot-headed' *saio*, 'although there had been no judgment', the record comments; this is an implicit reference to the normal practice of a *saio* formally consigning property to the winning party after the resolution of a court case.[82] *Saiones* appear to have conducted assessment procedures of several kinds in advance of court cases, just as they had a post-court role in the formal performance of consigning property; their duties were not confined to the duration of a hearing.

However, there were other routes to court too. Some accused people seem to have been taken to court by their accusers, whether willingly or by force: it looks as if the priest Adulfo was taken before Ansur by the family of the man he had murdered; Bishop Endisclo made a claim before Count Gaton against a man caught ploughing his land, the man presumably being taken to the hearing by the bishop's agents; and, after his penalty had been assessed, Ermegildo was taken before Judge Braolio by the father of the man he had injured, because the assessed compensation had not been paid.[83] Physical capture or forceful distraint also feature: Tegino and a companion seized the cowherds Iohanes and Abdella, accusing them of theft, bound them for fifteen days and took them before an unnamed *potestas*; when Itilo accused Ranildi of theft, the record suggests that he held her in chains for eleven days; and, as noted above, two men together with *sagiones* entered another's house and seized three men so forcefully that one died – we do not know the whole story here, but this looks like a case of legitimate distraint (legitimate because the *sagiones* were advising) that went badly wrong.[84] Legitimate distraint – that is, taking action to force an adversary to acknowledge a dispute and come to court – is well known in some parts of early medieval Europe.[85] We also hear of the priest in chains and a monk in irons; clearly, physical constraint was an option.[86] Although action by a *saio* was evidently a very common method of getting someone to court, and perhaps the most common, it looks as if it was socially acceptable for other people to make a challenge and an arrest, and indeed to conduct the arrested person to court. Tegino's case is particularly interesting, although the procedure is only briefly mentioned: the record survives on a single sheet, and certainly looks like an original charter; it clearly states that he and his companion made their arrest *cum uoce de furto*, with a cry of theft. From an Anglo-Saxon background,

81 Perhaps confirmed not so much by his sign as by his seal; cf. above, p. 166 n63.

82 SMdelP1 (863); *per saionem caloratum*. For consigning, see above, p. 136.

83 PMH DC 53, Ast5 (878), OD31.

84 Lii378 (964), Cañ41 (959), Cel165 (963).

85 The early Irish law of distraint is particularly enlightening; see Daniel A. Binchy, 'Distraint in Irish law', *Celtica*, 10 (1973), pp. 22–71; Fergus Kelly, *A Guide to Early Irish Law* (Dublin, 1988), pp. 177–86.

86 S133 (951) – see above, p. 190, Sam156 (983).

one would immediately think of hue and cry, and of the early and later tenth-century legislation providing for the pursuit of thieves by local people (as also of citizen arrest in the more modern world).[87] It is also interesting that the charter specifies that they entered the property to make the arrest without the owner's permission and took the cowherds before another court holder, *alia potestate*, as if the more proper thing would have been to use the court of the herdsmen's landowner.

Why were people taken to court? It is evident that some landowners (including ecclesiastical landowners) held courts for dealing with offences by locals.[88] A good third of recorded offences were cases of theft – of food and animals especially, and occasionally of clothes; but there were rape, abduction, wounding and homicide, and quite frequent adultery cases too. Some purely civil, low-value, property disputes also seem to have resulted in a *iudicatum* paid to the court holder, as instanced above – here the fine must have been paid for court holder costs, in effect a fee for access to the court. More than three-quarters of the records of these cases are Fines or Incidental records; in the case of Fines, we see the outcomes but not the details of the offence, while the Incidental records may make no more than a passing reference to the judicial process. For example, the record of a straightforward exchange of property between lay parties in the Liébana includes the brief comment that one party, the powerful local couple Bagaudano and Faquilona, had originally acquired the vineyard which they now exchanged as a fine from a couple who had hidden a thief who had stolen three cows; Bagaudano and his wife presumably had held the court in which the charge of theft was heard and settled.[89] Despite the preponderance of Fines and Incidental records, there are a few Accounts, which give more detail, and a couple of Confessions. When there is detail of these small-scale, non-property cases, we can see that one or more expert judges (the expert *iudex*) were often present and that Visigothic law was invoked;[90] *saiones* managed the business, sureties were used to guarantee appearance in court or outcomes, and occasionally advocates spoke for accuser or accused;[91] fees and fines were paid to

87 For example, VI Æthelstan; cf. 'Ordinance of the Dunsaete'; texts in *Die Gesetze der Angelsachsen*, ed. Felix Liebermann (3 vols, Halle, 1898–1916), vol. 1, pp. 173–83, 374–9. See Patrick Wormald, *The Making of English Law: King Alfred to the Twelfth Century* (2 vols, Oxford, 1999; London, 2014), vol. 1, pp. 304–8, 381–2; vol. 2, pp. 161–91. (Volume 2 has been made available posthumously on the Early English Laws website as Patrick Wormald, *Papers Preparatory to the Making of English Law: King Alfred to the Twelfth Century, Volume II: From God's Law to Common Law*, ed. Stephen Baxter and John Hudson (London, 2014): http://www.earlyenglishlaws.ac.uk/reference/wormald/.) See Luis García de Valdeavellano, 'Escodriñamiento y otorificación (contribución al estudio de la reivindicación mobiliaria en el derecho español medieval)', in *Centenario de la ley del notariado. Sección primera: estudios históricos* (2 vols, Madrid, 1965), vol. 2, pp. 174–203, for *hurto* in the Spanish *fueros*.

88 See above, pp. 178–80, for further comment.

89 T41 (932) – *pariabit*; see further Portass, 'The contours and contexts of public power', for Bagaudano and Faquilona.

90 For example, Sob23 (949), OD31 (991), Liii556 (993); Liii561 (994).

91 For example, Sob31 (951); Sob21 (931); OD38 (995).

the court holder, compensation could be paid to the victim, and there seems to have been a system for arriving at an appropriate scale of penalty.[92] It therefore looks as if the same kind of judicial procedures were used for these cases as were used in civil property disputes. However, it is striking that there is very little of the evidential procedure that is common in property cases; we do not often find the accused (or the accuser) being asked to provide witnesses, nor either party being asked to take an oath.

Now, since most of the references to these cases are in Incidental records, procedure was irrelevant to the record; the lack of reference to evidence taking, therefore, may not mean that there was none, just that it is not recorded. However, the occasional indications of use of evidence in apparently low-level cases that we do have all occur in relation to litigants with some accumulation of property:[93] if they were peasants, they were wealthy peasants, and some of them look more like middle-range people. Taking evidence is certainly missing from some of the more detailed accounts in the Sobrado collection, from which it is clear that the assessment of penalties had happened before the accused got to court, as discussed above.[94] The point is clearly arguable, but it looks as if there were some differences in the procedure for dealing with these low-level offences. It looks as if some accusations arose as a matter of common knowledge and were handled by the *saio* (who could have heard evidence, of course), with the accused then taken before an expert judge, with no further evidence being required in court.[95]

Now, these are cases involving the peasant community (aristocratic homicide was handled in a different way, as we have seen).[96] As already indicated, the court

92 The court holder fee is evident in virtually all of these records; explicit compensation is rare, but see Liii578 (997), and above, pp. 30–1; scales of penalty: Sob21, Sob29, Sob31, Liii578, OD31.

93 These are OD31, in which no witnesses are called but the accused swore an oath in a case of wounding, his parents clearly having several properties in Valdoré; Cañ49 (975) (= AHN 1325A–12), in which a case about a priest and horse theft has witnesses and preparation for an oath, but the priest again had notable amounts of property; the theft case of Cañ41 (959), between two lay parties, which involved five witnesses, of whom two had to swear, but again there are notable amounts of property. The status of the two brothers of SM27 (940) (= BG 391) and SM23 (936) (= BG 390) is arguable, although they look like middle-range people or rich peasants; BG 391 is a case about control of a mill, and has witnesses and an oath; BG 390, of the same area, clearly looked for witnesses, though there were none, but has an oath; one of the judges of BG 391 came from an aristocratic family (on this, cf. Juan José Larrea Conde, 'Construir iglesias, construir territorio: las dos fases altomedievales de San Román de Tobillas (Álava)', in Jorge López Quiroga, Artemio M. Martínez Tejera and Jorge Morín de Pablos (eds), *Monasteria et territoria. Elites, edilicia y territorio en el Mediterráneo medieval (siglos V–XI)* (Oxford, 2007), pp. 330–31), but that is not necessarily a comment on the status of the parties.

94 For example, Sob21 (931), Sob23 (949), Sob31 (951). See above, pp. 196–7, for pre-court assessments.

95 Cf. the acute comments of Bruno Lemesle, *Conflits et justice au moyen âge. Normes, loi et résolution des conflits en Anjou aux XIe et XIIe siècles* (Paris, 2008), p. 150, dealing with eleventh-century Anjou, that whether or not there was a system of proof is irrelevant; what mattered was convincing a judge (in advance of the court hearing) that there was a case to be heard; and repeating it many times.

96 See above, pp. 184–6.

holders who dealt with offences committed by the majority of the population were very occasionally bishops, and sometimes explicitly counts, but they were overwhelmingly other landowners, lay and ecclesiastical.[97] Holding courts of this kind, dealing with the offences of agricultural workers, was something that landowners with powers of territorial control (*potestates*) did. This is not summary justice, for public procedures of ancient origin were used, although it looks as if standard procedures may have been adapted somewhat when these offences were committed by people of humbler status. Nor is there reason to think that these were simply courts for tenants; tenants and dependents were certainly involved – like the servants who stole – but free peasant proprietors, who gave away their property to meet fees and fines, were evidently involved too, and there are more surviving records of cases involving them than those involving dependents.[98] The acquisition of peasant properties as fines and court costs by these landowners could constitute a significant extension to their inherited properties, and is a major factor in the construction of the power of some aristocratic families (cf. Figure 7.3);[99] this means that holding court was to some extent a mechanism for controlling the (free) agricultural population. Local politics must inevitably have come into this, even if we cannot see the detail. But when witnesses from different settlements were added to records of transactions, one could read this as an attempt to establish local political consensus, as it were, noting the key players from neighbouring localities,[100] just as peasant conflict over property may sometimes have masked competition for local leadership.[101]

At least two factors appear to have influenced the kind of court before which the accused was taken: it was not the type of business, as such, but rather the status of the litigants and whether or not an appeal had been made to a court holder; there may have been other factors. If an appeal were made to a king or a count, the king or count dealt with the case, although the king might refer it on to a lay aristocrat (or occasionally to a bishop).[102] Otherwise, if the initiative came from a *saio* or from an aggrieved person, one can say broadly that if the accused were a peasant the case went to a landowner's court, and if the accused

97 Some were landowners who were not referred to as 'count' in the texts recording judicial proceedings, but who are labelled 'count' in later texts, or whose children were clearly counts – note especially Munio Fernández and Flaino Muñoz. See my longer discussion above, pp. 20–6.

98 For example, Sob75 (858), Sob21.

99 For this process, see, for example, Carlos Estepa Díez, 'Poder y propiedad feudales en el período astur: las mandaciones de los Flaínez en la montaña leonesa', in *Miscel·lània en homenatge al P. Agustí Altisent* (Tarragona, 1991), pp. 285–327; Alfonso García Leal, 'Los condes Fruela Muñoz y Pedro Flaínez: la formación de un patrimonio señorial', *Anuario de estudios medievales*, 36 (2006), pp. 1–110; Pascual Martínez Sopena, 'La aristocracia hispánica. Castilla y León (siglos X–XIII)', *Bulletin du centre d'études médiévales d'Auxerre*, Hors-série 2 (2008): http://cem.revues.org/10052; Davies, *Acts of Giving*, pp. 139–63.

100 For added witnesses, see above, pp. 75–8.

101 See further below, pp. 213–19, for local meetings and local leaders.

102 As in Sob43 (818), Cel95 (950), Cel252 (1000); Li256 (952).

Figure 7.2 'Isti sunt iudicati et damnati', Beato from ?Tabara, Pierpont Morgan Library Ms M 644 fo. 220r

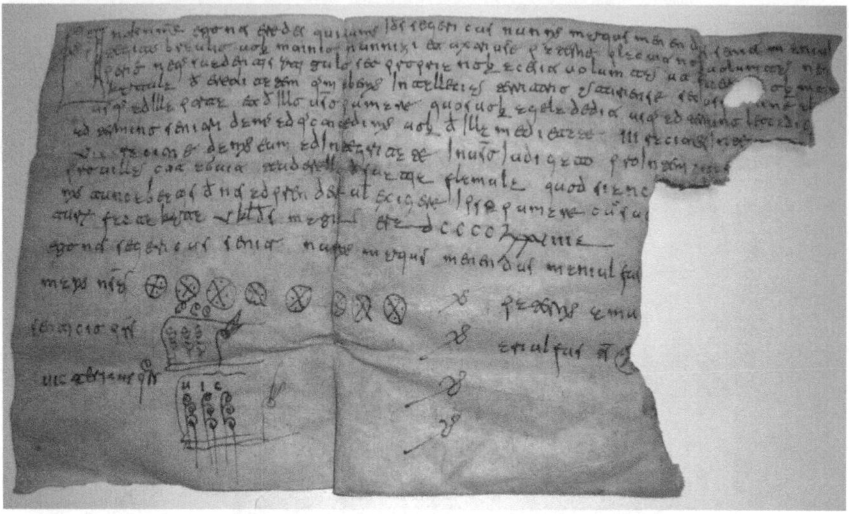

Figure 7.3 ACL 76 (Li138), a Fine of orchards paid to a lay court holder in Asturias, 940

Source: Reproduced by permission of the chapter of León cathedral.

were an aristocrat (and some middle-range people too) it went to a count's or a king's court.

★ ★ ★

So kings used disputes to manage aristocrats and patronize ecclesiastical institutions, and they used outright confiscation to manage – or try to manage – rebels in the complex interplay of building alliances. Courts were used as an instrument of control and as a means of securing advantage; courts obviously had political dimensions, although courts were certainly not the sole nor even the major arena for the pursuit of political interest. Courts were deliberately used as a tool by monks and clerics to extend their power; and the records of some purely lay court cases were made, though not always, by ecclesiastical bodies (rather than local priests) because churches developed an interest in the outcomes. Lay people, of higher and lower status, also used courts to protect their interests and gain advantage. But the fact that institutionalized procedures existed, and that they were used by all kinds of people, clerical and lay, means that courts had important social functions too. There were mechanisms for dealing with unprovoked theft, damage and harm, and in the end for the redress: when a neighbour stole a cow or a horse, the aggrieved owner went to court; when sons were wounded and daughters raped, parents went to court to get the compensation that had usually already been assessed; they do not appear to have relied on self-help mechanisms (although, of course, we do not know anything about unrecorded actions); they must have felt they were owed the compensation, and they must have chosen to go through the formal public procedure to get it. What looking from the subject's view therefore adds to the analysis is this sense that there were mechanisms for dealing with unprovoked attack and damage. One cannot read through the collection of reasons why lay people, especially lay people of lower status, went to court without supposing that they shared a sense of grievance.

The fact that landowners with territorial (and, as it were, seigneurial) power held courts does not make the system 'privatized': they used established public procedures and established legal officers,[103] they depended on a measure of local good will, and they were not in opposition to the work of the courts of kings or counts. They co-existed. And the fact that there were public procedures does not mean that they operated a state-organized, state-derived or state-controlled system. There was much more to the public court than the presence of the state: the system was 'public' because of the evocation of custom and of Visigothic law; because of the widespread use of the same standard procedures; because of its open and widely accessible character; because of the involvement of a range of people in decision-making and in the business of the courts; and because of the prominence of legal semi-professionals and of the dedicated legal officer the *saio*. So to try to characterize the system as either public or private simply does not work; the categories do not fit.[104]

There was therefore inevitably an element of the political about the use of courts. To hold a court was in itself a political power.[105] Kings, aristocrats, monasteries, bishops and probably some peasants used judicial process to gain personal or family advantage and to control other people; landowners, both ecclesiastical and lay, benefited directly from holding courts. But whatever other methods they may have used, people also used the court system to redress grievances; it is too easy to see those who passed through the courts simply as victims. Relationships were many-sided: some people played the system and benefited, but some people used the system to get what they felt was their due.

103 *Saiones* were involved in the procedures of the courts of several landowners, for example OD4, Cañ49 (unknown court holder, Suario Gundemáriz); Sam 239 and Cel368 (p. 528) (monasteries of Samos and Celanova); Sob129, Cañ65 (bishops); and by implication, that of Sandino Moñiz, Cel165.

104 The bibliography on public versus private is vast, but note the elegant comments of Matthew Innes, *State and Society in the Early Middle Ages: The Middle Rhine Valley, 400–1000* (Cambridge, 2000), pp. 254–9. See further below, pp. 251–2.

105 Cf. Jose María Mínguez, 'Pervivencia y transformaciones de la concepción y práctica del poder en el reino de León', *Studia Histórica. Historia Medieval*, 25 (2007), pp. 15–65.

8 Local responses

Court hearings took place in many different kinds of location. There were those associated with some particularly well documented court holders, like Valdoré and Sobrado: 'we came to court before Count Flaino Muñoz and his judges here in Valdoré' and 'in the presence of yourself and judge(s) here in Sobrado'.[1] There were also comital centres like Burgos and the royal centre of León and royal property like Larín in Galicia; and many sessions were held in a number of different churches.[2] In the Santa María de Mezonzo case of the 990s, a court moved from San Pedro in Présaras to San Julián of Nallar to an unlocated Santa Eulalia on the River Nallar and then to another San Julián.[3] Did the courts that were held in such places draw their participants from the immediate locality surrounding the place, or from a wider region? Clearly, if one hearing could move from church to church across 20–30 km, immediate locality was not the point. To what extent, then, was the immediate locality of a court functionally significant? And if it was significant, was this a locality of 5 km or 10 km or 50 km radius (see Figure 9.1)? In what follows, I shall use 'local' to refer to the neighbourhood of a main settlement – that is, to land within 2–3 km of the settlement;[4] for a locality comprising a group of such settlements, I shall use 'supra-local'.

1 OD43 (997): 'deuenimus indem ad iudizio antem gomite Fllaino Munizii uel suos iudizes ic in Orete'; Sob103 (952): 'in presentia uestra et iudicum hic in Superato' – *uestra* is Hermenegildo here.

2 On churches, cf. Fernando Luis Corral, 'Lugares de reunión, *boni homines* y presbíteros en Valdevimbre y Ardón en la alta edad media' (forthcoming); for Larín, see José Miguel Andrade Cernadas, 'Villas regias y asambleas judiciales entre los siglos X y XI: el caso de Larín', *Revista Signum*, 12 (2011), pp. 18–35, who points out that two judicial assemblies were held at the royal villa of Larín in the tenth century, both being high-status property cases. See also Julio Escalona and Iñaki Martín Viso, 'Los *palatia*, puntos de centralización de rentas en la meseta del Duero (siglos IX–XI)', in Alfonso Vigil-Escalera Guirado, Giovanna Bianchi and Juan Antonio Quirós (eds), *Horrea, Barns and Silos: Storage and Incomes in Early Medieval Europe* (Vitoria, 2013), pp. 103–26, at pp. 117–18, on an assembly held at a royal collection place in 1008, also a high-status property case.

3 Sob109.

4 Of course, settlement character varies between highly dispersed and heavily nucleated; many regions might have isolated farms or minor settlements within the neighbourhood of any 'main' settlement.

Collective judgment

Collective judgment was common in court cases; indeed, it was by far the most common mode of arriving at a judgment. From what pool of people were the members of the collective drawn? As already indicated, those who made a judgment might include court holder, clerics and expert judges, but they also included other, lay, people, many of whom look like aristocrats without any specialized legal skill.[5] Often we know no more of an individual who took part in judging than the appearance of his or her name on a single occasion. So there are inevitable uncertainties about the background, social contexts, status and relationships of many participants. But where there are reasonable indications, we can say this: of the 215 or so individuals involved as members of a group who judged or surveyed boundaries or before whom a case was heard, about half can be identified in some way: a quarter were clerics (including 19 abbots, 9 bishops and 13 priests), just over a fifth are identifiable laymen (that is, identifiable in the sense that they can be seen to appear in some other contexts), and 13 constitute a mixed group of royal women, kings, counts, an *alfierez* (officer) and a *saio*.[6] In what follows, I have not attempted to identify those for whom we only have a single name: there are far too many occurrences of single names to be sure of the identity of individuals. Where a name includes a patronymic, however, there is a greater chance of establishing identity, although even here we cannot always be certain: there can be more than one person with the same name and the same patronymic, like the two men called Gutier Osóriz who were active judges in the tenth century.[7] It turns out that we have more Galician evidence – there are more cases of group action and bigger groups – which means there is a Galician bias to the outcome.

As we have seen, some groups involved in judging were formed mostly or entirely of royal judges, like Abaiub, Maurello and Leander, who dealt with the San Juan en Vega dispute over water power in 938.[8] These were special cases. The men were in effect professional judges, with legal skills and expertise, close to the king of León and deputed by the king to deal with disputes he had been asked to resolve. Such cases tended to occur on the *meseta* in places within the

5 See above, pp. 160–4.

6 Numbers cited here are different from those cited in Chapter 6 above, for the latter are confined to people either explicitly involved in judging (using the verb *iudicare*) or termed *iudex* in some other context, such as witnessing transactions. In the count for this chapter, I have excluded the *iudex* who appears in other contexts, but have added all those involved in group decisions relating to dispute (e.g. those who walked boundaries or formed panels before whom cases were heard) even if judging words are not used in the text. A common format was that a case was heard *ante*, 'before', A, B, C, D or in the *iudicio*, 'court', of A, B, C, D; I have argued that this refers to the important people present whose authority enhanced the proceedings and the judgment; see above, p. 156. On the designation 'count', see above, pp. 20–6.

7 One cannot overstress the difficulty of making secure identifications; but where a name with patronymic appears more than once at about the same time and with the same associates, it seems reasonable to suggest that this name refers to a single individual.

8 Li128. For the case, see above, p. 186.

regular royal range, and they seem to arise from the interests of those who had relatively easy access to the king. But most judicial cases were not like this, and their panels included a mixture of lay aristocrats, clerics and some unknowns, and quite often a vague indication of 'many others', unnamed. So, for example, a property dispute in the Liébana between two laymen was heard in the court of Opila, abbot of Turieno, Vermudo Alfonsiz (son of Count Alfonso of the Liébana), Godino and Martino (*pueri regis*, perhaps king's attendants), in or before 962.[9] This is a composite document, combining four records from two related sessions; it is partly corrupted, but it is also clear that at least Opila and Godino were involved in the judgment that provoked the confession of one of the laymen, Seseguto. Farther west in Galicia, in 992, in the second phase of a dispute between Munio Gutiérrez and a priest over a church of Santa María in the territory of Présaras, eight named people ordered both parties to provide evidence to support their claims; and when witness evidence had been provided, the eight together with a further three named people as well as Suario Gundemáriz, who appears to have presided, ordered the church to be restored to Munio.[10] Suario Gundemáriz was a high aristocrat; as for the rest: in the first eight there was Gudesteo Díaz, who was a Galician expert judge, Vermudo Muñoz, who looks like a Galician aristocrat, an abbot, another cleric, and four unknowns;[11] they were joined by three further abbots for the final direction.

Of the lay people in the complete corpus of panel members, four overlapping categories of person are identifiable: expert judges, high aristocrats, aristocrats with a regional focus and royal companions. Incidental references to expert judges are much more common on the *meseta* than elsewhere (for example, as witnesses to uncontroversial sales), but they clearly existed in other parts too. Suario Gundemáriz presided over a case (involving the theft of a chestnut horse) together with 'his' (*suos*) judges, one of whom (Maurello Daildiz) was involved in judging another case sixteen years earlier; Elcino Quendulfiz and Ioacino Cartemiriz were two judges who knew *lex gotica*, Visigothic law, who perused the documents presented in a property dispute between a lay couple and a priest, heard before Bishop Nuño and Count Fruela Menéndez;[12] or there is Diego Díaz, the single judge who heard the property dispute between Fernanda and her sister-in-law.[13] Gudesteo Díaz, of the Présaras case above,

9 T66. For a recent assessment of Count Alfonso, and his limited power, see Portass, 'The contours and contexts of public power in the tenth-century Liébana', *Journal of Medieval History*, 38 (2012), pp. 389–407, at pp. 397–400.

10 Sob130; there is some corruption in transmission here: the names occur in several different versions, but the text is coherent. There is considerable doubt about which Munio Gutiérrez this might be – see María del Carmen Pallares Méndez, *Ilduara, una aristócrata del siglo X* (A Coruña, 1998), pp. 70–71, on the problem; cf. Margarita Torres Sevilla-Quiñones de León, *Linajes nobiliarios en León y Castilla (siglos IX–XIII)* (Valladolid, 1999), p. 327.

11 Vermudo witnessed a gift from the bishop of Santiago to the monastery of Celanova in 978 (Cel481).

12 Cañ49 (975) and Cañ41 (959), both Lugo texts; AHN 1325A–6 (922), another Lugo text. The count is otherwise unknown, but a Fruela Menéndez witnessed a confirmation by the Galician king Sancho Ordóñez to the bishopric of Santiago five years later; SantA50 (927).

13 Sam239 (985), for which see above, p. 192.

looks like an expert judge because we find him judging three cases in different parts of Galicia, in 992, 996 and 1000, recorded in three different collections, and in the second of these he is described as a judge attached to Bishop Pelayo of Santiago.[14] These experts often appear in groups with others of mixed backgrounds, as if it were normal for such groups to include at least one person with expertise in the law; the cases they judged include both property disputes (between lay parties and between lay and clerical parties) and offences like theft and assault. At other times, such experts appear alone or with the court holder – in the former case, presiding;[15] and in the latter, presumably providing necessary expertise for the court holder.

Secondly, high aristocrats.[16] Some prominent and well-documented high aristocrats are never listed as members of judging panels – men like Asur Fernández or Vermudo Núñez or the royal *armiger* Fruela Vimáraz or Fruela Vélaz – from which we have to presume that high aristocrats were not automatically assembled to judge cases.[17] But other high aristocrats were indeed listed. These were people who ranged widely across the kingdom, often found in the company of kings, from powerful families and with substantial landed property interests. Suario Gundemáriz, whom we have already encountered, married into the powerful Galician family of San Rosendo by marrying Gonzina, daughter of Rosendo's sister Adosinda; he is found holding a court in Galicia, acting as judge in Galicia and as witness of major occasions both in Galicia and on the *meseta*; some time before 994 he rebelled against the king.[18] Of similar profile, though different origins, a generation earlier, were Jimeno Díaz and Pelayo González, both married to sisters of San Rosendo. Jimeno was a court holder and was involved in judging a boundary case in northern Portugal; he was a major donor to the monasteries of Celanova and of Lorvão; and was a witness at many occasions in Galicia and sometimes on the *meseta*.[19] Pelayo was

14 Sob130, Cañ65 (see Figure 3.8 above), Cel252; see also Sob132 (1001), and cf. Torres Sevilla-Quiñones, *Linajes nobiliarios*, pp. 365, 371.

15 See below, p. 229, for cases with a single *iudex*.

16 There is an enormous literature on noble families. For a flavour of recent work, see, for example, José Mattoso, *A nobreza medieval portuguesa: a família e o poder*, 4th edn (Lisbon, 1994 [1st edn 1980]); Pascual Martínez Sopena, *La Tierra de Campos Occidental. Poblamiento, poder y comunidad del siglo X al XIII* (Valladolid, 1985), pp. 321–67; Ermelindo Portela Silva and María del Carmen Pallares Méndez, 'Elementos para el análisis de la aristocracia altomedieval de Galicia: parentesco y patrimonio', *Studia Histórica, Historia Medieval*, 5 (1987), pp. 17–32; Vicente Ángel Álvarez Palenzuela, 'La nobleza del reino de León en la alta edad media', in *El reino de León en la alta edad media, VII, Estudios* (León, 1995), pp. 149–329, especially pp. 179–231; Torres Sevilla-Quiñones, *Linajes nobiliarios*. For relationships between great aristocrats and tenth-century kings, Amancio Isla Frez, *Realezas hispánicas del año mil* (A Coruña, 1999), pp. 29–38, 59–65, is useful. See also above, pp. 185, 190–1.

17 Asur Fernández appears to be court holder in the case recorded at Oña 3 (944).

18 Sob130; Sob107 (968), Cel503 (985), Cel507 (985), Cel5 (986), S333 (986), Cel53 (988), for example; Cel104 (994), for confiscation for rebellion, and cf. the suspect TV15 (998), which records a further confiscation from him for the same rebellion. See above, pp. 183–6, for confiscations.

19 Lor36 (936); Lor33 (928), Lor34 (938), Cel7 (950); PMH DC 36 (931–50), Lor7 (933), Cel4 (938), Cel476 (941), Cel2 (942), S168 (959, though a suspect charter), for example. See Mattoso, *A nobreza medieval portuguesa*, pp. 139–40.

involved in judging in the León area and, with his sister Queen Aragonta, seems to have led the high-level panel sorting out rights to saltpans in Galicia ten years later, in 956 (and had founded one of the monasteries involved in the case); he was a frequent witness at major occasions in both Galicia and on the *meseta*.[20] Other high aristocrats with Galician connections and a wide field of operation include Gutier Osóriz, his son Osorio Gutiérrez and his son Gutier Osóriz (the younger), who were related to San Rosendo (Osorio was his second cousin); Rodrigo Gutiérrez, who it is argued was a brother of Osorio;[21] and Vermudo Magnidizi.[22] Tecton Luciti, involved in dealing with a theft case in 959, appears to be the man who accompanied Gutier Menéndez and Gutier Osóriz to witness royal gifts to the monastery of Abellar at much earlier dates, perhaps as a young adherent of one of the great aristocrats.[23]

Panels also included prominent aristocrats with an eastern base. The groups that acted with Count Fernán González of Castile appear to have included several aristocrats with Castilian interests, like the group which dealt with a water dispute in Castile in 932.[24] They included Fernando Díaz and the officer (*alfierez*) Gómez Díaz, who were probably sons of Diego Muñoz, and Nunu Fernández, perhaps son of Fernando Ansúrez, as well as an otherwise unknown Munio González and his son;[25] these belonged to prominent families of the region, and indeed of the kingdom.[26]

The groups that judged or surveyed or before whom cases were heard also included aristocrats with a narrower range of activity. Both Lope Jiménez and Fortunio Jiménez (who were perhaps brothers) were involved in judging a dispute over ownership of a church in Pando in Castile, and both also appeared

20 Li192 (946), LaC59 (956); Cel256 (936), Cel4 (938), Cel2 (942), S98 (945, charter elaborated in the late eleventh or twelfth century), Cel264 (949), S123 (?950), S129 (950), S132 (951), Cel54 (955), Lii295 (956), Cel356 (959), for example. See Mattoso, *A nobreza medieval portuguesa*, pp. 120–21.

21 Torres Sevilla-Quiñones, *Linajes nobiliarios*, pp. 300, 307.

22 For example: Gutier: SantA30 (917), Sam34 (932), Sam99; Osorio: S98, S99 (945, charter elaborated in the late eleventh or twelfth century), Lor1 (933), Cel2, S129 (later copy), S132 (later copy), Ast71 (952); Gutier the younger: S307 (980), Cel53, Cel5, Liii548 (991), Sam40 (993); Rodrigo: Cel2, Lor3 (943), S98, S99; Vermudo: Cel426 (951) – *maiordomus*, SantA45 (954), S212 (963), Sam32 (962), Sob107 (968). For Osorio, see Iñaki Martín, 'The memory of the "holy men" in Hispanic monasticism: The case of the Bierzo region', *Imago Temporis. Medium Aevum*, 6 (2012), pp. 165–90, at p. 184.

23 Cañ41; Li48 (919), Li86 (930); cf. SamS-2 (922).

24 C22.

25 If this was Gómez Díaz, son of Diego Muñoz, who died in 987, he must have been a young adherent of Fernán González in 932; see Álvarez Palenzuela, 'La nobleza del reino de León', pp. 200–203. About ten years earlier, Nunu Fernández, Fernando Ansúrez and Abolmondar Albus and his son Diego (possibly another name for Rodrigo Díaz; see Álvarez Palenzuela, 'La nobleza del reino de León', pp. 184–5), said to be ruling from Burgos, were captured by Ordoño II and imprisoned in León; Justo Pérez de Urbel, *Sampiro. Su crónica y la monarquía leonesa en el siglo X* (Madrid, 1952), ch. 19, p. 316. There is considerable uncertainty about the identity of these people; I am grateful to Julio Escalona for his views on the difficulties.

26 Note the appearance of Fernán González and Diego Muñoz and siblings (and Asur Fernández) as witnesses to Ramiro II's gift to the monastery of Dueñas; Dueñas 8 (936).

as witnesses of major grants on the *meseta*.[27] Munio Assuriz was involved in judging a case over mill rights in the River Tirón, near Siete Fenestras (Quintanilla de las Dueñas, Cerezo), at the eastern borders of Old Castile, just off the Ebro valley, and he also witnessed occasions in Castile, in the comital circle.[28] Galician aristocrats who were involved in panels of judges included Rodrigo's brother Suario Gutiérrez, Nepotianus Menéndez, Pelayo Tructesindiz, Tauron Mogaria and Oduario Tetoniz, the latter a donor to Celanova; they witnessed occasions in Galicia, but apparently not beyond.[29]

The last identifiable group consists of those often found in the company of kings, more consistently so than those great aristocrats with a clear regional base who made journeys to attend the king on special occasions. Some, or all, may have been royal servants. They include Domnon Vimarani, one of those who dealt with the wounding case on the River Cea in 946, Gutier Fernández, who judged the Castañeda case of 927, Sarracino Siliz and Piliolus or Piniolus Tructiniz, once described as a royal official, who judged a case about dependent status in northern Galicia in 985.[30]

This is not intended to be a comprehensive survey of those who were members of tribunals or assessment panels, but, rather, a representative snapshot; however, it should demonstrate very clearly that a significant proportion of the members of such panels was aristocratic, sometimes high aristocrats, and another significant proportion was clerical. Virtually every individual panel has some identifiable members, and this in turn makes it clear that usually a panel had mixed membership – some lay aristocrats, some clerics and some whose status is now unknown (a possible exception is the region of Castile, where gatherings seem to feature a disproportionate number of high-status lay aristocrats). We have no way of discovering the status of the 49 per cent of unknowns, but we might observe that they are likely to have been lay people (because clerics tend to have an indicator of status in all kinds of text – an abbot or a priest usually, though not invariably, tends to be called abbot or priest); and the unknowns do not appear to have been expert judges, since the latter tend to be

27 V33 (956). Lope: royal grants to Sahagún of S98 (945), S99 (945); Fortunio: S130 (951), Cel356 (959), an aristocratic gift to Sahagún and royal gift to Celanova. This was perhaps the same Fortunio Jiménez who led the initial panel considering the Jaca case, in Aragón, well to the east, some time before 958.

28 SM27 (= BG 391) (940); C42 (943), and just possibly C6 (913).

29 Suario and Nepotianus judging: Cel95 (950); Pelayo and Oduario judging: Cel94 (987); Tauron judging: Lor36 (936). Suario: Cel249 (941), Cel48 (941), Cel2 (942), Cel264 (949), Cel93 (950). Nepotianus: Cel7 (950). Pelayo: Cel275 (1005). Tauron: Lor1 (933), Lor34 (938). Oduario: Cel69 (1000).

30 Domnon (there were at least two individuals with this name): Li192 (946); Cel249 (941), Ramiro II's gift to Celanova, a Galician transaction, but perhaps not enacted in Galicia. Gutier: Cast1 (927); C20 (931). Sarracino: LaC95 (985); Cel5 (986), Cel53 (988), Liii581 (998), all royal gifts; SamS-1 (late tenth-century endorsement, royal confirmation). Pil[n]iolus: LaC95; Cel5, Liii548 (991), SantA57 (993), SamS–9 (995), Liii581, relating to a wide span of places, but with a royal interest in all the transactions.

identified as such. They were clearly people who did not consort with kings, since they do not appear as witnesses of royal transactions; conversely, and significantly, the majority of the people who did witness royal gifts do not feature in assessment panels. Nor do the 'unknowns' feature as witnesses of major non-royal transactions in east or west; in other words, they did not attend meetings that drew people from across a region. There does not appear to be any distinction between panels in respect of the type of case heard: many cases dealt with property disputes; these were heard by panels of expert judges, of mixed clerics and aristocrats, and of the latter with an expert judge or with one or more royal companions. There are therefore no clues about the unknowns to be gained from looking at types of case.

Now, the high aristocrats and royal companions cannot in many cases be supposed to have had local knowledge – surely essential for dealing with property cases, especially when boundaries had to be traced.[31] Kings sent their representatives considerable distances to deal with some of these cases: three envoys were sent to deal with bounds disputed between the remote (from the point of view of León) monastery of Samos and residents of nearby Castroncán. When the boundary dispute between residents of Sauto and of Leginoso came to Count Gutier's court, surveyors were chosen who were used to solving problems: it was the problem-solving skill not the local expertise that seems to have been valued (see Figure 8.2 below).[32] It must therefore be assumed that the requisite local knowledge lay with clerics – local abbots and priests – and with some of the unidentifiable members of panels. In fact, when the bounds of Santa María and Abedes (in southern Galicia) were disputed, Rodrigo and Suario Gutiérrez, to whom the dispute was presented, ordered all the *maiores natu* (elders) of Baroncelli (Verín) to walk the land; none of the 14 people then named is identifiable, although it includes three abbots and one other cleric (see Figure 8.2 below).[33] This group is highly unusual in that it does not include one or two identifiable aristocrats and in that its members are described as 'elders'; it is an exception. Bearing in mind all of the above considerations, it must be likely that the unidentifiable members of most panels were largely middle-range elites – that is, landowners with limited horizons but local knowledge – but one cannot rule out the possibility that sometimes they included some richer peasants.[34]

So while collective judgment was clearly extremely common, especially in property cases, the collection of people involved in any one case was usually

31 There are cases in eleventh-century England in which the great men who appeared on local panels can be shown to have had property in the area; I am very grateful to Chris Lewis for letting me see his work in progress on Great Tew. Social and political circumstances, as also the level of recoverable local detail, were so different in England from those of northern Iberia, I would not want to argue from this analogy; it offers a useful warning, however.

32 Sam46 (933); Cel502 (940): 'preelegerunt in ipso concilio preuisores qui antiqum solent comprobare'. See below, pp. 222–3, for this case.

33 Cel95 (950); see further below, pp. 221–2, on this case.

34 Identification by patronymic does not have to mean that individuals so identified were aristocrats; see above, pp. ix–x.

of very mixed origins and apparently of quite mixed status. We rarely know who all the members of any one panel were, but what we can say with total confidence is that they clearly were not normally drawn from any single local community;[35] many of the identifiable people came from far beyond the property in question or far beyond the place where an offence had been committed.

Local knowledge

If it was only rarely the case that panels of assessors came from a local community, as the 14 from Baroncelli may have done, what, if any, was the role of local knowledge in the settlement of disputes?[36] The records suggest that some cases were resolved on the production of written evidence, some were apparently resolved by the confession of one party, and some were resolved simply on the basis of statements made by the contending parties. Oaths and decisions were formally recorded;[37] *saiones* and judges required documents to be presented, and they were produced and studied in court;[38] documents were challenged, both successfully and unsuccessfully;[39] and documents were stolen and destroyed by parties who feared revelation of their contents.[40] However, living witnesses were also required or offered in several court cases, who one might expect to have been familiar with local detail. When the number of witnesses was very small, it is of course possible that they were simply friends of the litigant; but numbers could be larger, and sometimes the size of the reported group is extremely large. The most commonly cited number of witnesses is four or five per side, with the four witnesses provided by Bishop Rosendo in his dispute over fisheries with Bishop Sisnando of Santiago being 'too frightened to swear', thus giving the oath to Sisnando's five and the fisheries to Santiago.[41] One might suspect some Santiago manipulation of the text here, but it probably gives a hint of the pressures that often came to bear on witnesses. The bishop of Astorga was said to have produced fifty *testimonias* in a case of property disputed with a layman in 878; both Jimena and the church of Santa Eulalia produced 30 lay witnesses each in a Galician property dispute of 997; and the abbot of Celanova is said to have produced 356 against his opponent's 10 in a dispute over control of a

35 Cf. Juan José Larrea Conde, 'Construir iglesias, construir territorio: las dos fases altomedievales de San Román de Tobillas (Álava)', in Jorge López Quiroga, Artemio M. Martínez Tejera and Jorge Morín de Pablos (eds), *Monasteria et territoria. Elites, edilicia y territorio en el Mediterráneo medieval (siglos V–XI)* (Oxford, 2007), pp. 321–36, at pp. 330–31, who argued that judges were drawn from supra-local scale in the particular Castilian context he was considering.

36 Baroncelli appears to have been a name for a territory comprising several settlements, so perhaps supra-local; see below, p. 221.

37 Ast5 (878), Sob109 (early 990s).

38 C90 (957), Sam126 (960); AHN 1325A–6 (922), Li144 (941), PMH DC 163 (991); PMH DC 183 (999).

39 C55 (945); Lii410 (968). See below, pp. 242–3, for discussion of the role of written evidence.

40 Sob130 (992).

41 SantA42 (961). Comparable numbers: AHN 1325A–6 (922), Cañ41 (959), PMH DC 183.

church in 1000.[42] Perhaps more credibly, there were 12 and 10, respectively, in the dispute over control of dependents between the monastery of San Martín Pinario and the lady Doña Palla; while three were chosen to swear from an assembled 33 in the case about control of the monastery of Santa María of Gordón; and five older people (*senicas*) were chosen to swear from an assembled 37 in the Castañeda fisheries case.[43] We should probably assume some exaggeration of numbers, but there seems to be an underlying principle in this material that either the litigants turned up with one or two carefully selected witnesses committed to their support, or they arrived with a large band of people, from whom a handful was selected to take an oath. It makes sense to suppose that such bands were locals, who knew the land and its people and something of their history – hence the preference for older people, like the elders of Baroncelli and the *senicas* of Castañeda and perhaps the *bonos barones senes de illo bicinato* (the old worthies of the neighbourhood) of Jaca.[44] It is the same kind of principle as requiring the *auctores*, guarantors of legitimate possession, to testify in one of the disputed water power cases near León.[45] There are two further charters that are quite explicit that local knowledge was required: in the case of the disputed 'thirds' payable to the bishop by the abbot of Ocoizta (Acosta) in Álava, the 'elders of the land and people' testified in favour of the monastery; while in the northern Galician ecclesiastical dispute over control of the income of the church of Santa María de Mezonzo, representatives were at first sent to make local enquiries of 'the old men and wise elders' of the Tambre valley, and then two people from each of five sets of settlements were required to come to the session and swear that they had no knowledge (although in the end they did swear in support of the monastery of Sobrado – the record is inconsistent at this point); here, clearly what was required was supra-local input.[46] The expectation was that they certainly ought to have known about past obligations, although inquests like this are surprisingly rare among these records: it was much more common for oaths to be sworn on behalf of one party, as supporters.

42 Ast5, TV135, Cel252.

43 LaC95 (985), cf. Cañ49 (975); OvC26 (953); Cast1 (927).

44 Jaca. *Bonos barones* here must mean *boni homines*, worthies, people of good reputation (see above, pp. 169–76, rather than 'good barons'. Roger Collins, 'Visigothic law and regional custom in disputes in early medieval Spain', in Wendy Davies and Paul Fouracre (eds), *The Settlement of Disputes in Early Medieval Europe* (Cambridge, 1986), pp. 85–104, at p. 100, suggests that use of the term *barones* may have reflected Frankish influence, but it is a very unusual term in this corpus and does add to doubts about the tenth-century origin of this record; Collins also made the *bonos barones/boni homines* point (ibid., p. 99).

45 Li144 (941). See Luis García de Valdeavellano, 'Escodriñamiento y otorificación (contribución al estudio de la reivindicación mobiliaria en el derecho español medieval)', in *Centenario de la ley del notariado. Sección primera: estudios históricos* (2 vols, Madrid, 1965), vol. 2, pp. 125–335, at pp. 236–324, for the role of *auctores*, and ibid., p. 274 for this charter. However, see n. 104 below for the probable influence of *Leges Visigothorum* on the evocation of venerable knowledge.

46 SM98 = BG 221 (984): 'Et levaronse seniores terre et populi et testificaron que non habuerunt lege, nisi ad suos sanctos'; Sob109 (early 990s): 'homines senices et seniores sapientes'.

So there was a place for local and supra-local knowledge in cases concerning disputed property rights, and therefore some opportunity for local people to participate in judicial procedure. However, it is striking that local knowledge is adduced very rarely in these records, and equally striking that other methods of establishing truth were common (as also that some witnesses were of extremely high status); how far assembled witnesses provided any independent evidence is in any case arguable, given the emphasis of the texts on the small numbers who took the oath – in effect, many witnesses ultimately operated rather like oath-helpers.[47] It is also striking that a high proportion of charters that refer to witnesses (of any kind) are retrospective narrative Accounts and a high proportion are cartulary copies – about 66 per cent in each case. The frequency of Accounts is not surprising, given that these are the texts which give more detail of procedure.[48] Of the few charters that refer explicitly to local knowledge, only one (Jaca) is on a single sheet, and – single sheet or not – that is explicitly a retrospective record.[49] This raises the possibility that the citation of local knowledge was in fact a strategy employed by the redactors of dispute records to emphasize the totality of the successful party's victory. Even the one record of this group that is not an Account (Castañeda 1) was clearly drawn up in favour of the successful monastery. On balance, it looks as if in practice use of evidence from local residents did occur, but its occurrence was limited; that oral evidence was in fact taken is clear from the cases that note the delivery of false evidence: after all, two different couples in the Celanova orbit had to pay fines for giving false evidence in the case of a stolen pig.[50] But the idea, even more than the practice, of local input had a certain persuasive force: if adducing local knowledge was sometimes a strategic ploy, it was clearly expected to bring additional authority to final decisions; and local knowledge was cited from Galicia to Aragón, from all parts of the tenth century.

Local meetings and local leaders

Rural communities clearly had meetings at settlement level, from as early as we can see, although they were not necessarily large meetings; judging from the very brief witness lists attached to some charters, some had no more than a handful of participants. We cannot presume that they were inclusive, and we do not normally know the rationale behind who attended and who did not,

47 See above, pp. 28–9, and below, pp. 242–3, for this issue.

48 See above, p. 37, for the tendency for Accounts themselves to have long lists of witnesses.

49 Collins, 'Visigothic law and regional custom', p. 101, suggested that, because the terminology and the structure of this charter are unusual, it might reflect some local customary norms. It might, but since the charter is questionable as a tenth-century record and since we have very few charters from this region of this date, there is very little to compare. See further n. 45 above for the possible influence of knowledge of Visigothic law on such records. Charters on single sheets were not necessarily originals, of course.

50 Cel189 (*c.* 1000), Cel190 (*c.* 1000); see above, p. 179 n137, on the date of these charters.

but there is nevertheless some clear evidence of assembly.[51] The most obvious context for such meetings was for the public performance of transactions – this seems to have happened in all parts of northern Iberia throughout the period covered. That these transactions did indeed involve performance is strongly suggested by the material characteristics of some charters: the record of a gift from Aloyto Froylaniz to his wife in north-west Galicia in 965 has a number of (partly repetitive) added subscriptions, some with autograph *signa*.[52] It is as if the scribe went round the assembled group recording a complex ritual of confirmation.

That meetings took place in rural society is explicit in the use of the words *concilium* and *collatio* for gatherings, although – even without such words – the fact of meetings is obvious from the listing of witnesses. In some contexts, when associated with people of a named settlement, *concilium* clearly refers to an assembled group of people, a collectivity; *collatio* was used for the same purpose, and sometimes the two words were used interchangeably for the same group.[53] These words for assembly in effect refer to the decision-taking people of some places – that is, not so much to the residents of a place, but those who met and did things together, like 'the people of the council of San Juan en Vega' who took action against the monastery of Valdevimbre.[54] So in tenth-century texts there are expressions like *fecit collationem*, 'he called a meeting', in a Samos charter of 944, and *fecerunt concilio in illa terra*, 'they called a meeting on that land', in another northern Galician charter, recording distribution of rights in salt pans, of 956.[55] Of course, these words mean many other things too, but the fact that they could refer to meetings of lay people in rural localities is explicit in the listing of the names of those who participated in transactions at such meetings, in the listing of those witnessing such transactions, and in the nature and location

51 Compare Catalonia: Adam J. Kosto, 'Reasons for assembly in Catalonia and Aragón, 900–1200', in Paul S. Barnwell and Marco Mostert (eds), *Political Assemblies in the Earlier Middle Ages* (Turnhout, 2003), pp. 133–49.

52 LaC71, on a single sheet, apparently original. In a section to the right of the first column of witnesses we find 'In quorum presencia multorum benenatorum, abbatorum et confesorum ubi istas scripturas confirmauerunt, Sigeredus diaconus et Flamula Deo uota quod ad suo germano [uiderunt] rouorare quum omnes istos qui supranotati sunt, id sunt: Gundisalbus abba, Uisulfus abba, Ciprianus confessor [and 35 more names, including Gundisaluus abba]' (in the presence of many well-born [lay persons], abbots and confessors when they confirmed this writing, which the deacon Sigered and *Deo uota* Flamula confirmed to their brother with all those noted, that is Abbot Gonzalo, Abbot Uisulf, Ciprian . . .); and in a further section below that 'Coniunti in unum multi filii bene natorum et Flamulae Deo uota [space] uillas de Aloito Froylaniz ipsi preuisores id sunt: Lucidus [Teroni], Psalamiro Ariyulfiz, Petrus, Sigeredus' ([There were] gathered together many well-born and Flamula *Deo uota* . . . the villas of Aloyto Froylaniz; the surveyors were Lucidus, Psalamiro, Petrus, Sigered).

53 For example, in Liii577 (997). For full discussion of the usage of the terms *collatio* and *concilium*, see Wendy Davies, *Acts of Giving: Individual, Community, and Church in Tenth-century Christian Spain* (Oxford, 2007), pp. 201–7.

54 Li128, 'homines de collacione Sancti Ihoannis in Uega'; see above, pp. 186, 190.

55 Sam35, LaC59.

of the properties conveyed. Indeed, *concejo*, a borrowing from *concilium*, becomes the normal word for the rural local council in Spain in the central middle ages, and *collación* (from *collatio*) comes to refer to the association of parishioners. Several records emphasize performance 'in or before such and such a meeting': a lay couple gave another lay couple some land in Colinas (near Benavente on the *meseta*) in 960, witnessed by three named people and confirmed by seven named people 'and others from the council'; a woman gave her two daughters half a meadow in Orbaneja (in Castile), and sold them the other half, in 984, 'in the presence of the council of Villafria'; a sale of vines in Piniares to the monastery of Piasca (on the edge of the Liébana) was witnessed by nine named people and 'several others from the council', where we know that this group was not the council of the monastery because we have the (different) names of its 36 nuns.[56] Sometimes, not nearly so often, action was explicitly taken by the meeting: a gift of a field in Fontoria to the small monastery of San Juan was made in 932 by nine named people and 'all the council of Melgar', the council (*collacio*) here directly associated with the verb of giving in what was apparently a community gift.[57] The council (*concilium*) of Villabáscones made an agreement with the local abbot over water rights in 956, the charter citing 17 named men 'and all the council of Villabáscones' (and the meeting was mentioned three further times in this charter).[58] And the dispute between the aristocrat Rodrigo Álvarez and a monk of Pardomino in 997 over control of a dependant in Ferreras was heard at a meeting 'in the presence of the council of Ferreras'; Rodrigo confessed, and the outcome was then confirmed by 10 named people 'and many more of the council who were there'.[59] These examples come from Castile, the Liébana, the *meseta* and the southern slopes of the Cantabrian Mountains (see Figure 8.1).

As for the regularity and periodicity of meetings, if we look at all business transacted in public, and not just that of which the words *concilium* and *collatio* were used, it is clear that meetings happened in all months of the year and apparently on all days of the week. However, more meetings are recorded in the period November to April, particularly in April. Meetings seem to have occurred monthly or bi-monthly in winter and early spring, with a clustering around the Easter festival, but there are no data which suggest strictly regular meetings.

56 Lii331: *et aliorum de collacione* (grateful thanks to Álvaro Carvajal for this and many other identifications of properties on the *meseta*); C192: *in presentia de concilio de Uillafrida*; S136 (952): 'Felix hic ts, Octabius hic ts et alias plures de concilio, Iga ic ts, Carapellus ic ts, Fredenando Pepic, Asimondo ic ts', and nuns at S79 (941).

57 S44: *Ego Filauria* [+ 8 names] *et omni collacio de Melgare . . . damus . . . uno prato*.

58 C89: *uel omni concilio de Uilla Uascones*; the agreement was made with the monastery which the local community had originally established; see below, p. 219, and further charters C45, C87, C108.

59 Liii577: 'in presentia . . . concilio de Ferreras . . . et aliorum multorum de concilii qui ibidem fuerunt'. See above, pp. 89, 192.

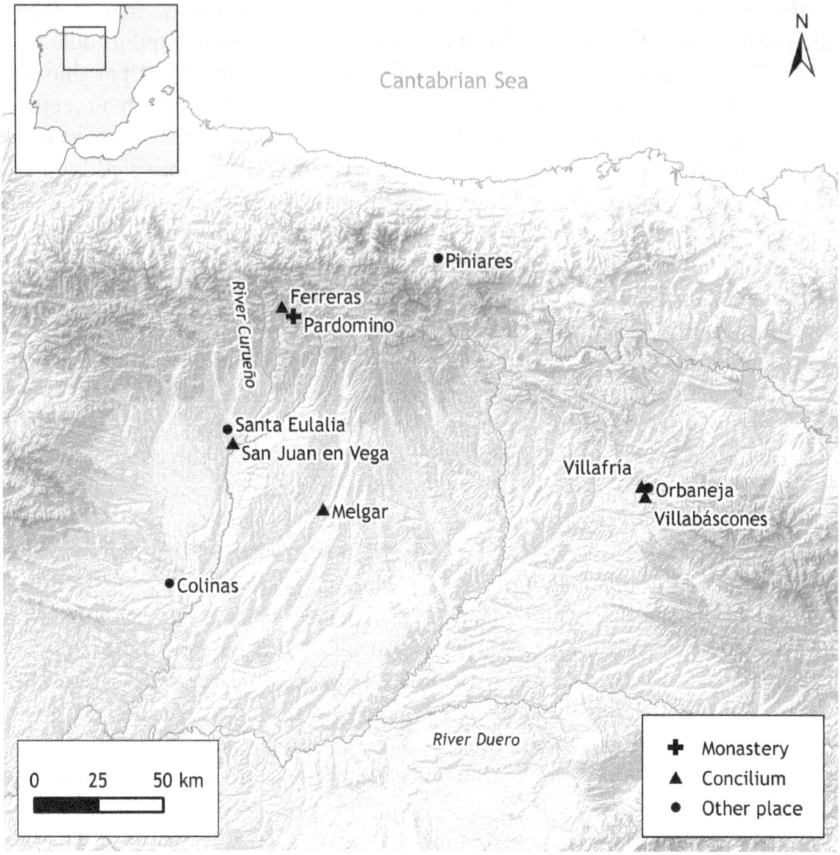

Figure 8.1 Locations of local meetings

The charters only rarely specify the precise location of a meeting, but there are references to meetings happening in or in front of churches, especially for the performance of transactions like sales between lay parties; for example, plots on the River Bernesga (near León) were sold by one couple to another in 953 in a church of Santa Eulalia.[60] Since local priests seem to have made records for local people, and perhaps kept them in a church box or cupboard, it is not at all surprising to find churches used as locations for transaction meetings. However, this does not rule out the use of other kinds of location: in areas of Europe where transaction places are normally cited in charters, as they were in eastern Breton charters in the ninth century, political centres and churches

60 Lii262.

were certainly used, but so were open spaces by buildings, fields, boundaries and other topographical features.[61]

Most of the *collationes* and *concilia* that are mentioned in charters were occasions – that is, meetings called for a particular purpose. References do not begin until 932, and most are of the 960s or later, but by the end of the tenth century occasions were clearly on the way to becoming institutions in some areas, although it took another two centuries to complete the process. The trend towards institutionalization is implied by the fact that the word *collatio* could be applied to territories by the end of the century – that is, the word could also mean the territory in respect of which the meeting acted.[62] This process was beginning to develop at the end of the tenth century. However, there were marked regional differences: in the tenth century, most of the evidence of the process comes from the relatively densely populated *meseta*, in the hinterland of the towns of León and Burgos and the market centre of Cea.[63] The institutionalization of meetings was not widespread across northern Iberia at this stage, although, as we have seen, people met for the performance of transactions in all parts. *Ad hoc* meetings were common and widespread; their transformation into something more regular and more formal happened unevenly, and took a long time in many areas.

Given that there were meetings at settlement level, were there leaders from the localities, and who were they? There is little suggestion in this material, at this period, that there were local office holders, operating at village or settlement level. The exceptions are the local priests, of which there appear to have been many, and who seem occasionally to have acted as community leaders; there was probably the occasional local *saio* too by the late tenth century.[64] However, some local groups did have representatives. Firstly, there are the representatives of family groups. For example, in central Galicia, when 17 people made gifts to San Xoán in 934, one or two were named as the representative of each of eight groups from Quiroga and Caldelas. The format of these references is 'N on behalf of myself and my brothers/cousins/wife'.[65]

61 See Wendy Davies, *Small Worlds: The Village Community in Early Medieval Brittany* (London, 1988), pp. 109–10, 137–8; see ibid., pp. 134–6, for examples of the standard recording formats. There is an occasional reference in Spanish charters to the performance of transactions on the boundaries of the land in question, e.g. Li88 (930), which happened to be in front of a church, and C20 (931).

62 For example, Liii547 (991): *terra nostra in Mataromarigo in collatione Sancte Llocadie.*

63 Also, however, Piniares, in the Liébana, S136 (952).

64 See Wendy Davies, 'Local priests in northern Iberia', in Steffen Patzold and Carine van Rhijn (eds), *Men in the Middle: Local Priests in Early Medieval Europe* (Berlin, forthcoming); see also Wendy Davies, 'Local priests and the writing of charters in northern Iberia in the tenth century', in Julio Escalona and Hélène Sirantoine (eds), *Chartes et cartulaires comme instruments de pouvoir. Espagne et Occident chrétien (VIIIe–XIIe siècles)* (Toulouse, 2013), pp. 29–43, at pp. 31–4. See above, pp. 167–8, for local *saiones*.

65 Cel224: 'Nos omnes qui sumus habitantes in Caldellas et Carioga . . . Dadinus confessor pro me et pro omnes meos germanos, Auderigu, Foffu, Lezenio, pro nostras mulieres . . .'. See below, pp. 219–20. Cf. the married couples in Cel95 (950, 951).

Other representatives of settlements give no indication of the rationale behind the representation: the seven *plebes* of the Pardomino hills had seven named representatives, who were formal guarantors of the agreement made with the monastery of Pardomino; as noted above, five sets of settlements in the Tambre valley in northern Galicia had to produce two representatives for each set to swear on oath that no one in their villages knew anything about past payment of rents; and in Aragón, some time in the tenth century, seven named people negotiated with an abbot in order to get land to replace their own worked-out land – and three or four people from each of seven locations witnessed.[66] In this last case, it looks as if the seven negotiators were representatives of seven named settlements, negotiation at supra-local level, and also that a few people also came from each settlement to witness the ensuing agreement.[67] There are other charters which record apparently straightforward gifts and sales, in which witnesses are grouped by named location; in such cases, it looks as if sometimes representatives came to witness the transactions of a neighbouring community, presumably transactions in which they were thought to have an interest. So, for example, a sale of several parcels of land in Ripa Rubia to Sahagún by the priest Arias in 946 was witnessed by people from seven different locations – seven of the witnesses from Ripa Rubia itself but the rest coming from nearby settlements.[68] Isca and Filauria's major gift to Sahagún of various possessions in Melgar (noted above) was also witnessed by people from at least six places, seven people coming from Melgar itself.[69] A sale to the monastery of San Vicente in Oviedo also has witnesses from seven different locations.[70] But other charters localize one or two places only;[71] and the majority of witness lists does not localize any at all. There are more examples of representation from settlements on the *meseta* than elsewhere, and they are perhaps a reflection of the more rapid crystallization of group identity in that area. We should remember that there are also charters in which many participating actors are named, but no one is picked out as a leader or representative of any kind. Such was the original Villabáscones gift to endow the local monastery, which was simply made by 24 named individuals, but there are plenty of other similar cases.[72]

Altogether, then, sometimes no one represented the local group, sometimes several people did, and sometimes it was just one or two. Of those single or

66 Li184 (944), Sob109 – see above, p. 212, SJP32.

67 'Et sunt testes Banzo Adogari et Galindo Garcianes et Mancio Lupi et Sancio Ennecones de Veniesse et Galindo Sancionis et Sancio Galindones et Belasco Fortuniones de Tolosana et Sorello et Moronta et Garcia Forti de Nabascosse et Annaia et Mancio Ennecones et Orobita et Asnari Banzones de Larosse et Asnari Galindones et Enneco Fortuniones et Sorello de Larota et Adogari Garcianes et Orioli Ennecones et Alariki Sanciones de Aranda et Galindo Manciones et Mancio Datones et Sorello de Capannas.'

68 Sii364.

69 S164 (959), in fact from several of the same places as Sii364; some of the names of the last column repeat those of the second. See further above, p. 77, and below, p. 230.

70 Ov19 (978), cf. E21 (946 – eight places).

71 OD9 (950), Li254 (952), Liii533 (990), for example.

72 For example, Cel224 (934) – 17, S142 (954) – 26, Lii290 (955) – 21.

pairs of representatives, several seem to have been heads of families and several were probably proprietors. The group which made a gift in Melgar to a local monastery in 932 seems to have been led by Filauria, since she is named first and we know from other charters that she was prominent; she seems to have been a wealthy peasant. But in most cases we have no idea who these individuals were. Representatives of local groups are likely to have been prominent local proprietors, although we cannot be sure of this; these were usually peasant proprietors, but middle-range landowners may well have acted in the same way from time to time.

Collective action

It is clear that some groups of local residents, whether they met in something called a council or not, took action together to make rent, boundary or water management agreements with landowners, or with other groups: hence, 'Nos omnes Galuarra, Galindo Soliz, Gazo, Laztago, Fortuni Appatiz, Ferro Sangiz, Galindo, Garcia . . .', listing the group of 24 locals who originally agreed to endow the church in Villabáscones.[73] The mode of reference in such cases is often an initial listing of individual participants, as here (there can be as many as 20 or 30), and thereafter 'we'. But throughout the corpus of charters, groups of people are overwhelmingly referred to by settlement name, whoever was making the record and whether or not the scribe was a member of the group or an external observer, as in 'the people of Place X': 'between the people of Villa de Sauto and the people of Leginoso'; 'we the people of the Fuentes settlements'; 'the people of Lemonioni'; and occasionally 'those living in Villa Santa María and Villa Abedes'.[74] Villa Báscones, literally the settlement of Báscones, is a different kind of group identifier, an unusual one, in its reference to a population group.[75]

The texts that appear to detail collective action form a difficult subset because most of them are clearly monastic records, in which it was in the interest of the monastery to present the locals as a coherent group. Whether or not we can really see group action is therefore an issue. Reports of collective action occasionally involved the pursuit of a legal case, but most did not. Some groups gave or sold property, jointly. We have seen above how nine named people and the Melgar meeting gave a field on the *meseta* to a minor monastery in 932.[76] Seventeen people ('all [of them] living in') Quiroga and Caldelas, in central Galicia, gave plots to the church of San Xoán in 934 – individual plots but

73 C45 (944–50).

74 Cel502 (940), *inter homines de uilla de Sauto et homines de Leginoso*; S289 (977), *nos homines de uillas de Fontes*; Sob129 (942), *homines de Lemonioni*, but also *neptos Lemeni*, implying a family relationship; Cel95 (950, 951), *habitantes in uilla Sancta Maria et uilla de Abdes*.

75 C45, *nos omnes, id est, de Uilla Uascones*. I am not aware of anything which suggests that these villagers were conscious of any connection between their settlement and any larger group.

76 See above, p. 218.

joint action.[77] Twenty-six named people, most of them married couples, sold their mills, water course and millstone in the River Cea, by Villaselán, to the monastery of Valdávida in 954 – joint action in respect of a shared resource.[78] It is not unreasonable to suppose that it was monasteries which made records in such cases, since they were beneficiaries, but there is no reason to suppose that they misrepresented the donating or selling groups. Such cases, then, are quite good examples of collective action by a group of local people. Somewhat similarly, the people (*homines*) of Fuentes were held to have agreed to pay regular rent to Sahagún in 977 – there is no original charter here, but the record of the agreement makes a point of identifying guarantors, in effect representatives of the residents, suggesting a credible transaction and continuing commitment; and a similar record suggests that all the inhabitants of Castellana were to pay rent to the bishop of León in 976.[79] In something of a contrast, the sale of the entire settlement of Villamol to Sahagún by 32 named individuals in 984 was accompanied by 24 separate payments, 5 *solidi* to Eugenia, 2½ to Stephano and Maluca, a vineyard to Diego, land and a cloak to Scape, and so on: although the residents may have decided as a group to make the transaction, the charter records that it was transacted as a multiplicity of separate sales.[80] This was more like a deal involving many parties than collective action. When the monastery of Pardomino negotiated with the residents of three places in its neighbourhood to pay annual rent, it clearly regarded the residents of each place as a distinct and separate group.[81] This agreement survives on a single sheet, and is probably an original. Twenty-one people are named, with a notional *signum* for most:[82] the negotiation was by settlement, but the individuals were held responsible. Local residents, then, sometimes clearly took collective action as a group; sometimes, even in similar circumstances, they clearly took individual action; and sometimes an ecclesiastical body required representatives of a group of local residents to be named and to take responsibility.

77 Cel224. 'Nos omnes qui sumus habitantes in Caldellas et Carioga. Id est Honorigo et frater meus Astruario, pro nos et pro omnes nostros germanos et heredes, Maurgato et suprinos meos, Dalinus et Busianus Crizila a persona de mea muliere Teodesenda, pro nos et pro omnes nostros germanos uel heredes . . .'.

78 S142.

79 S289 (the property had been given to Sahagún by the king), and see above, pp. 47, 85, for S261 and Fuentes; Lii443. Cf. Cel446, after a dispute.

80 S327. Cf., similarly, Lor32 (976).

81 'Nos omnes qui sumus habitantes in Campolongo et in Stabello siue et in Uayca', Lii290 (955). Each of the seven *plebes* of the Pardomino hills had its own representative (*uigarii*) in 944 (Li184): 'with all the inhabitants of Campolongo, Stabello, Ferreras, Utrero, Vegamián, Lodares, Noanca . . . we laymen who are representatives of the *plebes*' ('cum omnibus habitatoribus . . . de . . . Campolongo, Stabello, Ferraria, Uulterario, Meane, Lotares, Noantica . . . nos laici . . . qui sumus uigarii de parte plebium'). It is rare for a group to be termed *plebs*, literally 'the people'. See Reyna Pastor, *Resistencias y luchas campesinas en la época del crecimiento y consolidación de la formación feudal. Castilla y León, siglos X–XIII*, 2nd edn (Madrid, 1990 [1st edn 1980]), pp. 37–8, for this example.

82 See above, p. 88: some of the *signa* fall on a fold.

Control of water courses often led to open dispute, and could lead to collective legal action by a group.[83] The people of Villabáscones seem to have agreed water rights for the abbot of the church they themselves had founded within ten years of its foundation, without any court case.[84] But the priest Abolmondar, along with 22 named people from five settlements along the river from Quintanilla and Castañares to Burgos, was taken to court before Count Fernán González, by the abbot of San Torcuato, in 932; while the men of the council of San Juan en Vega won their case about water levels in the face of complaints by the abbot of Valdevimbre; and another group of locals, led by the priest Nemorelli, won another case (over the ownership of mills) against Valdevimbre in 941.[85] These legal disputes are recorded in monastic records because, whatever the outcome for local people, the monasteries nevertheless won some advantages through the case;[86] but some local groups and supra-local groups clearly took action in such circumstances to protect their own interests – interests which were critical to their survival. With sufficient provocation, collective legal action could, it appears, happen.

There are also records of disputes about boundaries which are recorded as disputes between local groups of residents (in addition to the boundary disputes which were explicitly between bishops or monasteries and local people).[87] A dispute is reported to have arisen between the inhabitants (*habitantes*) of Santa María and those of Abedes, Regaulfus and Saquetina, in the neighbourhood of modern Verín, southern Galicia, close to the modern Portuguese border, round about 950.[88] After an initial, apparently unresolved, dispute, the parties came before Counts Suario and Rodrigo Gutiérrez, who, as we have seen above, ordered the elders of nearby *urbs* Baroncelli (a hillfort, which in the early middle ages gave its name to a territory comprising several distinct settlements, and the forerunner of the surviving castle of Verín) to discover the truth (see Figure 8.2 below);[89] they walked the land, found markers, and eventually determined the bounds of Santa María (the modern parish of Verín). The finding was confirmed the following year. The dispute was not simply solved by the counts' assessors going out to survey the land: the assessors are described as local 'elders' (*maiores natu*); and it emerged that the successful protagonist was not in fact a group of local people who lived in Santa María, but the aristocrat, Countess Trudildi. In other words, it appears that the dispute was not between groups of

83 There are many charters specifying water rights – for example, C11 (921), Li66 (925); all potentially hint at a background of dispute. Cf. Pastor, *Resistencias y luchas campesinas*, pp. 97–8, for some of the cases mentioned here.

84 C89 (956); see above, pp. 215, 219.

85 C22; Li128 (938); Li144.

86 See above, p. 186.

87 See also Pastor, *Resistencias y luchas campesinas*, pp. 75–98.

88 Cel95 (950, 951). See María del Carmen Pallares and Ermelindo Portela, 'El lugar de los campesinos. De repobladores a repoblados', in Ana Rodríguez (ed.), *El lugar del campesino. En torno a la obra de Reyna Pastor* (València, 2007), pp. 61–87, at pp. 65–7.

89 See above, p. 212.

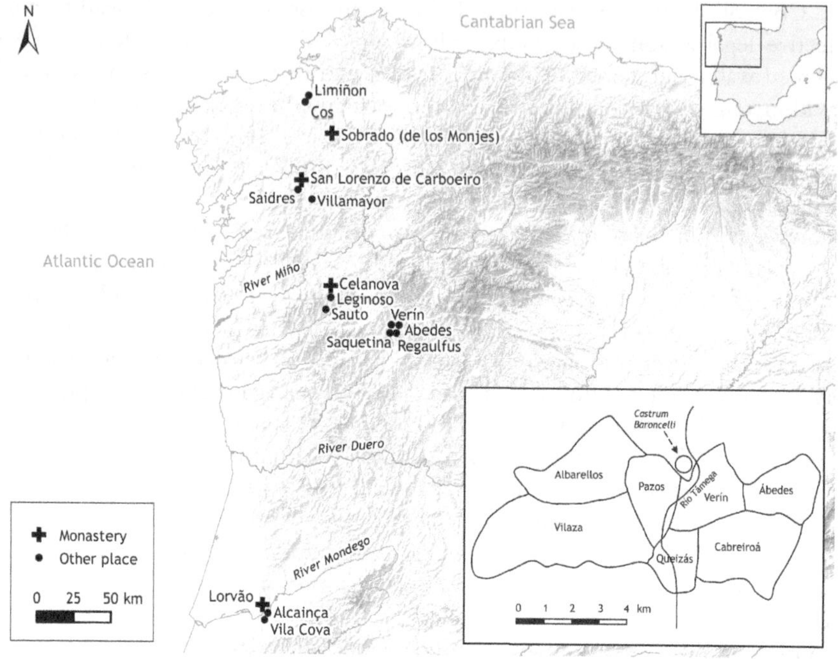

Figure 8.2 Boundary disputes in Galicia

Source: Inset after María del Carmen Pallares and Ermelindo Portela, 'El lugar de los campesinos. De repobladores a repoblados', in Ana Rodríguez (ed.), *El lugar del campesino. En torno a la obra de Reyna Pastor* (València, 2007), pp. 61–87.

locals at all, but between an aristocrat, who won, and groups of locals. Trudildi and her husband, it emerges, had acquired Santa María by exchange twenty years before the Santa María dispute.[90] It is also the case that this record is one of a set of records that run consecutively in the Celanova cartulary that deal with boundary disputes in the area of Verín.[91] In the earliest of these, Bishop Rosendo disputed with the inhabitants of surrounding settlements (Vilaza, Albarellos and Santa María) for Celanova's control of Pazos, which lies on the western boundary of Santa María; and in the latest, Abbot Manilán of Celanova disputed with more of them for Pazos. All of this, then, appears to be about aristocratic and monastic control of estates, and not at all about local groups and their local rivalries. There are, indeed, later charters showing Celanova's rights in the territory of Baroncelli.[92]

There are similar charters in this and other Galician collections. Slightly earlier, *c.* 940, comes the dispute between the people (*homines*) of Villa de Sauto

90 Cel460 (931).

91 Cel93 (950) and Cel94 (987), with Cel95, at ff. 37v–39v.

92 Cel117 (953), Cel152 (1000), Cel468 (1026), Cel148 (1031); cf. Cel35 (1032).

and those of Leginoso, partly bounded by a road to the River Limia.[93] These people went to Count Gutier Menéndez, who in a similar process chose assessors, who duly went to the area, walked the land and found the relevant markers. But despite the presentation of the dispute as one between two sets of local people, the monastery of Celanova certainly had an interest here, for a couple of generations later King Vermudo II confirmed service due from the men of Sauto to Celanova.[94] The essence of the dispute was whether or not Villa Parata was included with Sauto or with Leginoso, and the resolution was that it lay with Sauto. This suggests that the record of the dispute arose because Celanova wanted to document the fact that the disputed Villa Parata was included within the bounds of Sauto.

In a slightly different formulation, a Sobrado charter of 942 records a boundary dispute between two family groups, *neptos Lemeni* and *neptos Endulfi et Astruildi . . . habitantes in Codais* (descendants of Lemeni [in Limiñon] and descendants of Endulf and Astruild living in Cos).[95] Like Sauto/Leginoso, this was in effect a dispute about whether an intervening settlement (that of Paredes) attached to one or the other location. This dispute went to the court of Bishop Rosendo (of Celanova), where there were seven named people on the judging panel. Each party had a spokesperson, that for Cos being the deacon Salamiro, who was a monk of Rosendo's, while a Sisnando (son of Gondesindi) spoke for Limiñón. Rosendo and the panel, now with an additional three members, went to the disputed land and found the markers, thereby deciding that Paredes belonged to Limiñón. The *saio* Fofum was ordered to return Paredes, which he did in the presence of the Cos group; the Limiñón group then confirmed the bounds between Paredes and Cos. This was witnessed by 42 people, apparently including King Ramiro II and six bishops. Most of these 42 witnesses are unidentifiable, but they are clearly not the high aristocrats who appeared on other royal occasions, and if the king and bishops did confirm, it must have been subsequently. Limiñon was demonstrably an aristocratic estate in the late ninth century; by 952, Hermenegildo, founder of Sobrado, clearly had interests in orchards in Cos; and at some point in the later tenth century Sobrado clearly had interests in Paredes.[96] Though presented as a dispute between groups of local residents, all of these properties had been owned by aristocrats in the recent past, and most were subsequently claimed by Sobrado.[97] The places are about 30 km north-west of Sobrado.

93 Cel502. These places are difficult to locate, but Leginoso may well be Laioso, about 6 km due south of Celanova. Grateful thanks, as ever, are due to José Carlos Sánchez Pardo for his identification of and suggestions about Galician locations.

94 Cel5 (986).

95 Sob129.

96 Sob119 (887), a gift from Sisnando (perhaps an ancestor of Hermenegildo) to his wife; Sob1 (952), Hermenegildo's gift to Sobrado; Sob113 (n.d.), a reconstruction of land confirmed to Sobrado by Ordoño IV and Ramiro III.

97 Though individual elements are not specified, property in Nendos (the appropriate territory) was confirmed to Sobrado by Ramiro III in 968 and 978 (Sob107, Sob108).

There is a similar case from central Portugal, recorded in the cartulary of Lorvão, for which we know a little more of the history. Here the people (*homines*) of Alcainça and those of Vila Cova went to the high aristocrat Count Jimeno Díaz, who instructed them to take assessors to the disputed lands.[98] The three assessors and the count himself went to the locality; they found the stone which marked the boundary between Oliveiró and Vila Cova; after much further walking, they found the markers which separated Alcainça, Vila Cova and Louredo; and finally, crossing the River Mondego, they found the line dividing Vila Cova and Louredo. The record was made by one Adulfo, just possibly the deacon Adaulfo who was one of the assessors. The record is framed in language very similar to that of the other Galician cases, and the procedure was extremely similar. Again, local groups were apparently in dispute about boundaries; again, they appealed to a count, who walked the bounds with assessors, looking for markers. Now, another item in the Lorvão cartulary makes it quite clear why this record might have existed as a separate sheet and could have been copied into the cartulary. Two years later, in 938, Count Jimeno gave to the monastery of Lorvão a stretch of the River Mondego, including both banks and a landing place – a stretch that he had been given in recognition of the determination he had made between Vila Cova and Louredo, part of Alcainça.[99] The circumstantial evidence that the count received a piece of the land for his trouble is certainly credible, and indeed helps us understand how these procedures might have worked. A charter of 927 (recording purchase of some parcels on the banks of the River Mondego) makes it clear that that Lorvão already had interests in the area, which was only 5 km from the monastery itself.[100] The record of the count's grant to the monastery suggests that the record of local dispute is in this case credible, and therefore suggests that local groups could indeed have sometimes used this mechanism, although it must be likely that some of the disputed land went to the monastery shortly after settlement of the case. It also, very interestingly, makes the point that court holders might be given land that they did not particularly want as a fee.

There also survives a severely damaged original in which a Count Gonzalo was asked by the people (*omines*) of Saidres and those of Villamayor to settle a boundary dispute between them; the count took his surveyors, walked the bounds and settled the line of the boundary; the record was made by an otherwise unknown priest, Urban.[101] There does not appear to be any monastic interest in the property at the time of the dispute, but Saidres is very close to the monastery of San Lorenzo de Carboeiro, in north-west Galicia (about 2.5 km south of the monastery); the record was preserved in the archive of San Martín Pinario, which annexed San Lorenzo *c.* 1495; and Lucas Álvarez

98 Lor36 (936); see above, p. 207, for Jimeno Díaz.

99 Lor34: 'sicut illa prendidi pro mea determinatione quam determinaui inter Uilla Coua et uilla que dicunt Lauredo, que est de parte Alquinitia'.

100 Lor40.

101 LaC65 (some time before 962).

includes this charter in his San Lorenzo collection.[102] The monastery of San Lorenzo had been founded by Count Gonzalo Betote and his wife Teresa in 926, and there are twelfth- and thirteenth-century records detailing transactions of the monastery in Saidres.[103] Although there appears to have been no identifiable monastic interest in these lands at the time of the dispute, it seems possible that all or some of Saidres was included in Gonzalo's original foundation and that the 'dispute' recorded here was an attempt to clarify the bounds of Saidres by appeal to the donor. If so, then this would be a further case of action to preserve or extend monastic interest which was recorded as conflict between local groups. It remains possible, however, that we may again here have a case of two groups of local people in conflict, who went to a count to sort it out. Despite the monastic colouring of most of these texts, it looks as if such disputes between local groups could have happened. In other words, there really were a few groups of local residents who took collective action against each other in defence of what they believed to be their territorial rights. In doing this, they used a standard procedure of asking a count to send surveyors.

Overall assessment of these local boundary cases is not straightforward. The format and procedure is suspiciously similar in all cases – appeal to a court holder (usually a count), sending of surveyors, walking the land, finding markers. This procedure in fact harks back to the prescriptions and explicitly to the language of Visigothic law: in cases of disputed boundaries, people should be appointed go out and find the markers (*arcas*).[104] It is perfectly clear that prominent monasteries had an interest in the lands which are the subject of nearly all recorded boundary disputes, whether through an interest in immediately neighbouring lands or in the disputed lands themselves; and it is clear that most of the lands were in fact monastic or lay estates. Since all of these cases are recorded in retrospective Accounts, and since there were such strong monastic interests, it must be likely that they were framed by scribes aware of the wording of a long-established appropriate legal procedure; it must also be likely that

102 Manuel Lucas Álvarez, *El archivo del monasterio de San Martiño de Fóra o Pinario de Santiago de Compostela* (2 vols, A Coruña, 1999), vol. 1, p. 13; Manuel Lucas Álvarez, 'La colección diplomática del monasterio de San Lorenzo de Carboeiro', *Compostellanum*, 3 (1958), pp. 221–308, 547–638, at p. 253.

103 Lucas Álvarez, 'La colección diplomática del monasterio de San Lorenzo de Carboeiro', pp. 581; 241; 283, 616, 626. For Count Gonzalo, see Álvarez Palenzuela, 'La nobleza del reino de León', p. 186.

104 *Leges Visigothorum* X.3.1–5: keep landmarks; if boundaries are disputed, search for the landmarks (mounds of earth and 'arches'); people should be appointed to find the landmarks, especially the oldest residents. 'Quotienscumque de terminis fuerit orta contentio, signa, que antiquitus constituta sunt, oportet inquiri, id est aggeres terre sive arcas, quas propter fines fundorum antiquitus apparuerit fuisse coniectos adque constructas, lapides etiam, quos propter indicia terminorum notis evidentibus sculptos constiterit esse defixos', X.3.3 (p. 397); 'Cum autem proprietas fundi nullis certissimis signis aut limitibus probatur, quid debeat observari, eligat inspectio iudicantium, quos partium consensus elegerit; ita ut iudex, quos certiores agnoverit vel seniores, faciat eos sacramenta prebere, quod terminos sine ulla fraude monstraverint, et tamen nullus novum terminum sine consortis presentia aut sine inspectore constituat', X.3.5 (p. 399).

the presentation of a case as a dispute between two sets of local people was in effect code for a dispute between monastery and lay aristocrat or monastery and locals. It remains possible, however, given the fee paid to Jimeno Díaz and the fragmentary original relating to Saidres and Villamayor, that there really were some boundary disputes between residents of settlements, the 'peoples of Place X and Place Y'. Even allowing that this was possible, however, this material cannot be taken as good evidence of the existence of cohesive groups of local residents in these areas.

Local participation in judicial process

It has been suggested above that membership of panels that judged or surveyed might well include some middle-range local landowners, and even sometimes a rich peasant, but that the most common known element of such panels was the inclusion of high-status people from outside the locality concerned. Settlement of property issues was clearly not simply a matter for the local community. It has also been suggested that witnesses with local knowledge might be sought from local residents, particularly from those of age and experience, but that this was definitely not always the case, and indeed may have been rarely the case. Together, this suggests that local participation in the procedure of the courts was rather limited. On the other hand, the appearance of peasant offenders before a court, the courts of landowners called *potestates* especially, is well documented, and rural communities must thereby have been familiar with court procedure.[105]

This raises important questions about the status and independence of peasant communities in the face of judicial authorities. I argued in Chapter 7 that it is too easy to see peasants simply as victims of lordly self-interest – relationships were more complex, and peasants themselves did use the courts.[106] But were there in existence mechanisms for the protection of peasants and/or for their self regulation? Two patterns for the handling of peasant offences are visible: a hearing in a court, with all the apparatus of *saio*, judges, guarantors and advocates, sometimes involving an expert *iudex* and sometimes invoking Visigothic law; and alternatively a hearing before a single *iudex*, who appears to have been an expert, who either both presided and judged or judged in the presence of the court holder. What happened in these alternative arenas?

As discussed above, procedure in landowners' courts seems to have followed the standard pattern of that in kings' or counts' courts, but there is very little reference to the production of evidence.[107] Documents were produced in the

105 See above, pp. 198–202.

106 Pastor, *Resistencias y luchas campesinas*, is the classic treatment of peasant resistance to lords' oppression; see above, pp. 17–18, for the literature of developing lordly power.

107 See above, p. 199.

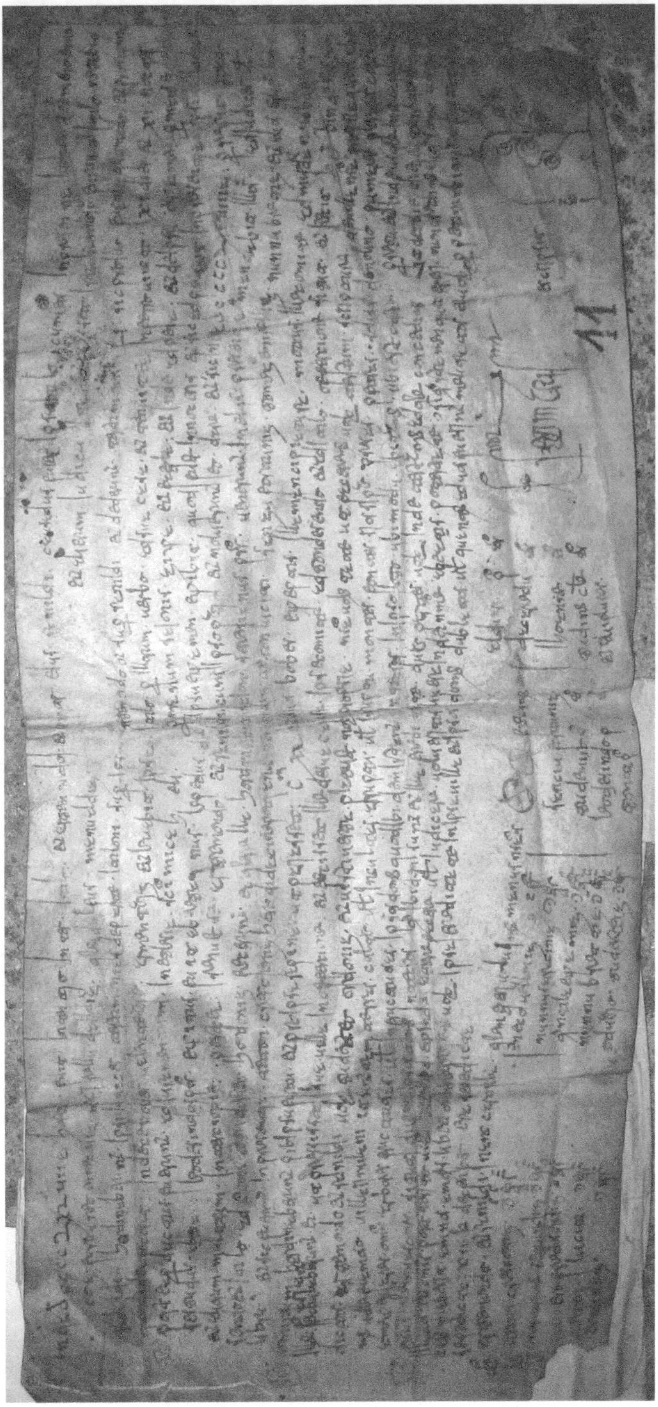

Figure 8.3 ACLu 60 11 (Cañ41), an Account of a theft case of 959 pursued between lay parties

Source: Reproduced by permission of the chapter of Lugo cathedral; photo: Ainoa Castro.

dispute between two priests over the church of Guilhabreu, heard in the court of Dona Dimitria, but that is the only time use of written evidence is recorded (and whether or not one should regard either priest as of peasant status is arguable).[108] I can only see one reference to the production of witnesses in any of the cases heard in landowners' courts, peasant or otherwise, although occasionally the accused or others were asked to take an oath, and occasionally the ordeal of hot water was used, or suggested, apparently to test the accused (rather than witnesses, as was more usual).[109] Panels of judges pronounced decisions – in cases of adultery, theft, disputed boundaries and disputed property ownership.[110] Confessions were often noted, in Galicia and on the *meseta*, both earlier and later in the tenth century.[111] Sentario committed theft at least twice, was due to make payments to two people of a cow and of goods to the value of 17 *modii*, and then was taken to court before a *iudex*; a couple wounded another couple, causing damage to the value of 10 oxen, and then they were taken before Hermenegildo and one or more judges in Sobrado.[112] The court was the place for public acknowledgement of the fault and of the consequent obligation to make recompense; and it was the place for fixing the day of payment. Any taking of evidence that happened must have been handled by the *saio* before the court met.

Now, in some of the cases of peasant offence – recorded in a number of different sources – the texts are explicit that the guilty person was taken before a *iudex*, a single *iudex*, at such and such a court. There are nine unambiguous cases in which a person appeared before a single *iudex*, in these circumstances surely the expert *iudex*. The court holder was sometimes present, but if a pronouncement was made, it was the judge who pronounced. The cases include theft, adultery, homicide and wounding, but there are also some property cases, and they run from 858 to 993. Most of them are associated with a court held at a place regularly associated with court hearings – Valdoré, Sobrado, León, Cerezo.

What happened in court before a single *iudex*? As already indicated, establishment of guilt and assessment of penalties appears to have taken place in advance of the court sessions. In nearly all of the cases of appearance before a single judge, what the accused party did was formally confess and agree to carry out the penalty – and sometimes deals were done, as in the homicide case heard in León.[113] These court occasions were, again, very public acknowledgements of guilt and commitment, whatever may have gone on beforehand and behind the scenes; the formal court session was about publication of what had happened.

108 PMH DC 163 (991). I do, however, regard the partly dependent priest Sagulfu as of peasant status.

109 Cañ49 (975); OD31 (991), Cañ65 (996).

110 Sob23 (949), Cel368 (p. 530, late tenth century), Sob129 (942), PMH DC 163. There is no indication of the procedure followed in landowners' courts in cases of theft (OD34), rape (OD33), property dispute (OD27, Li138, for which, see Figure 7.3 above) and unknown dispute/offence (PMH DC 43).

111 Sob54 (930), Sob21 (931), Cañ49, OD31, Liii561 (994), OD38 (995).

112 Sob31 (951); Sob103 (952). See n. 1 above.

113 Lii450 (977).

It was acknowledged that the deed had been done, and it was expected that the perpetrators would make the prescribed recompense or make a land grant in lieu of the assessed penalty payment if they did not have the means to meet the latter. There was inevitably an element of performance in this.

We might expect that the values at stake and the status of the accused would have determined whether offences were handled by a single, as it were professional, *iudex* or by a panel of non-expert judges.[114] The records are neither precise enough nor detailed enough to be certain, although a high proportion of the accused in single *iudex* cases (seven of nine) were demonstrably peasants, and values in some of these cases were clearly relatively low (for example, theft of one or two sheep), although the cases include wounding to the value of several cattle – clearly higher, but nothing like the value of the whole estates that might be transferred in aristocratic cases. On balance, then, it looks as if the single *iudex* dealt with peasant cases. Neither the court hearing with full apparatus of *saio*, judges and so on nor the hearing before a single *iudex* suggest much in the way of protective mechanisms for local populations, although it is clear that peasant groups could (if rarely) win court cases, even against very powerful landowners.[115] On the surface, then, it may look as if many peasants who committed offences were at the mercy of a single judge, but to some extent the very existence of a standard system, operated by dedicated legal officers, was a kind of protective shield – more so than the possibility of appeals to the king, which seem to have been rare, although it is perfectly clear that kings could send their companions some considerable distance to deal with larger property disputes.[116] So there was not much in the way of protection. What one would expect, by analogy with other parts of Europe, would be some self-regulating mechanisms at local scale, sufficient to deal with small-scale boundary disputes and social disturbance. In early medieval eastern Brittany, for example, formal courts and informal meetings, on a regular basis, are very well evidenced at village level; these courts dealt with petty theft and assault, as well as a mass of property cases; sureties to guarantee outcomes for the most part came from the home village, and witnesses came from the home village or a neighbouring village; judges were not professional, and tended to be drawn from a small group of immediately neighbouring villages – people of solid reputation.[117] There is none of this in the Iberian corpus. This does not have to mean that no such mechanisms existed. It could be that their activity simply did not hit the recorded horizon, although the Iberian charters that deal with local transactions are very similar in character to the Breton; and the whole corpus has plenty of localizable material

114 See further above, pp. 200–2, for the status point.

115 For example, Li128; see above, pp. 186, 190; cf. Li144 (941).

116 See above, p. 209.

117 See Davies, *Small Worlds*, pp. 146–60; and in more detail, Wendy Davies, 'Disputes, their conduct and their settlement in the village communities of eastern Brittany in the ninth century', *History and Anthropology*, 1 (1985), pp. 289–312, and Wendy Davies, 'People and places in dispute in ninth-century Brittany', in Davies and Fouracre (eds), *Settlement of Disputes*, pp. 65–84.

and plenty of circumstantial detail of petty cases – so much that one would expect a hint of a village-level court here and there if such had existed. It is in fact clear that local meetings happened in many parts – as discussed above – and there is indeed one case which appears to have been handled at the level of a single community meeting, but only one, and it involved an aristocrat and a monastery.[118] There were leaders, and there must have been followers at local level, but these leaders do not appear to have dealt with judicial business. If that was the case, it must mean that peasant offenders and minor landowners had to travel some distance to have their cases heard; they could not expect them to be handled by the community of local residents. *Saiones* must have travelled about from settlement to settlement, gathering people up, encouraging, forcing, leading them to attend the nearest court. Any estimate of how far peasants might have had to travel is limited by the fact that the location of meetings is relatively rarely stated. However, it may be relevant that people were drawn to testify from settlements within 6 km of Sobrado in the Santa María de Mezonzo case, and Santa María was itself 12 km from Sobrado. When groups of settlements acted together – eight in the Lóuzara valley in central Galicia, seven in the Pardomino hills on the edge of the *meseta*, five near Burgos in Castile, seven in Aragón – that clearly involved an element of travel.[119] We do not know how such supra-local groupings arose, but they may suggest a scale at which the holding of assemblies for judicial proceedings became viable, zones of the order of 15–25 km diameter.[120] There are also the occasions, as noted above, when witnesses to transactions came from several settlements, like that of Isca and Filauria's gift to Sahagún in 959, from within a zone of about 15 km diameter.[121] These are not huge areas (though significantly larger than the Breton average of 6–7 km across[122]), and one would in any case expect regional variation.[123] But this might offer a notion that a peasant might have to travel up to 20 km to get to a court (four or five hours' walk) – sometimes much less, and

118 See above, p. 215, for the case of Rodrigo, handled in the *concilium/collatio* of Ferreras, one of the Pardomino *plebes*.

119 Sam247 (909), Li184 (944), C22 (932), SJP32 (no precise date, but tenth century).

120 Travel to Burgos in the Castilian case was up to 11 km; the seven *plebes* which gave guarantees to Pardomino appear to have been within 10 km of the monastery (but two are unidentified). The area from which the Aragón group came was not enormous – about 6 km in diameter, centring on Pardina de Cillas; I am grateful to David Peterson for assistance with this. See further Juan José Larrea, 'La documentación de San Martín de Cillas. Un Ensayo de crítica de las fuentes altomedievales', *Revista de Historia Jerónimo Zurita*, 61–2 (1990), pp. 7–44.

121 S164. See above, pp. 77, 218, for this charter. The transaction appears to have been performed in Sahagún, but groups of witnesses, by location, were added to the initial listing, as if in an attempt to include those settlements that might be thought to have had an interest (whether or not they were actually present at the event).

122 See Davies, *Small Worlds*, p. 65.

123 All of the pre-1000 cases heard at Valdoré appear to relate to people who came from within its territory; for reconstruction of the territory, and map, see Álvaro Carvajal Castro, 'Sociedad y territorio en el norte de León: Valdoré, los Flaínez y el entorno del Alto Esla (siglos IX–XI)', *Studia Histórica. Historia Medieval*, 31 (2013), pp. 105–31. If this suggested reconstruction of the territory of Valdoré is correct, that zone was more like the Breton norm, much smaller, at 5–6 km across.

doubtless sometimes even more.[124] Formal courts at village/single settlement level do not appear to have existed.

★★★

It is perfectly clear that rural communities had meetings, and in some parts could have representatives. Institutionalization of meetings (and of communities) certainly happened in the long run, but it was late in the first millennium before this started, and it was regionally restricted. The main development came in the eleventh, twelfth and thirteenth centuries. The fact that the normal mode of reference to the community was by place rather than by group identifier – 'the people of Place X' – might suggest a relatively weak sense of community identity; and the fact that 'family' is the significant opposition to 'foreigners', a particular characteristic of the sanctions of many charters, might suggest that family identity was stronger than group,[125] although some charters are quite explicit that the group of residents that met or negotiated included more than one family. If one asks what qualified a person to be a representative, two things are prominent: family leadership and proprietorship; but there may obviously have been other factors as well, which we cannot see: we might expect standing, knowledge, experience, an inclination for action or for bullying, a capacity for persuasion. Representatives sometimes seem to have included lawyers (judges) among their number – evident in the cases where a *iudex* came from a neighbouring community to witness a gift or sale – maybe by virtue of their proprietary interests rather than their special skills.

Any sense of local community dynamics is elusive in this material. Meetings, representatives and collective action all make it clear that local residents could act as a group, even if community identity and community cohesion were relatively weak and were to develop much further in the central middle ages. The very fact that people met for the performance of transactions – in all parts at all periods – is critically important to this assessment. But if there were local self-regulating mechanisms, they are invisible. It is highly unlikely that judicial business was handled at the level of individual settlements, which makes these communities different from those of some other parts of Europe, and it looks as if even petty offences were often handled at a sub-regional (that is, supra-local) level. Counts, most *saiones* and wealthy landowners were beyond local society, but they must have been in view, on the horizon. That being the case, it is not surprising that local people played a relatively small part in judicial process and that local knowledge had a smaller role than one might have expected. Collective judgment there certainly was, but the collective that made the judgment was far from being the representative of 'local community'; rather, it was a collection of people from different places, some from a considerable distance. And for many offences at peasant level, collective judgment does not seem to have featured at all.

124 Most of the Sobrado theft cases relate to settlements within 6 km of Sobrado; see Sob54 (930), Sob21 (931), Sob23 (949).

125 'Si quis aliquis homo hanc kartula ad inrumpendum uenerit, an nos, utrum filii nostri, uel extranei aut propinqui' ('If anyone, one of us or our children, outsiders or relations, should come to break this charter'). See above, pp. 96, 116–20, for sanctions.

9 A view on Northern Iberia in the European context

There has been a good deal of discussion of conflict resolution and dispute settlement in early medieval Europe during the past generation, although national historiographies have much longer traditions of studying the history of law and its application and there is an even longer-established trans-national study of Roman law, a field which remains extremely lively.[1] Recent discussion has been occupied with social conflict in many kinds of arena, but sometimes, as in this book, it has focused on the handling of disputes within a judicial process, often strongly influenced by the legal anthropology of a generation ago, with its focus on law residing 'in the minds and practices of people in a society'.[2] Some of the most influential analyses of process have focused on the eleventh century;[3] and

1 Most influentially, Heinrich Brunner, *Deutsche Rechtsgeschichte*, 1st edn (2 vols, Leipzig, 1887–92); for England, see Frederick Pollock and Frederic William Maitland, *The History of English Law before the Time of Edward I* (2 vols, Cambridge, 1895). For Roman law, see, for example: Friedrich Carl von Savigny, *Geschichte des römischen Rechts im Mittelalter* (6 vols, Heidelberg, 1815–31), drawing on several centuries of existing scholarship; Fritz Schulz, *Principles of Roman Law* (Oxford, 1936); Caroline Humfress, 'Laws' empire: Roman universalism and legal practice', in Paul J. du Plessis (ed.), *New Frontiers: Law and Society in the Roman World* (Edinburgh, 2013), pp. 73–101.

2 See, for example, Susan Reynolds, *Kingdoms and Communities in Western Europe, 900–1300* (Oxford, 1984); Wendy Davies and Paul Fouracre (eds), *The Settlement of Disputes in Early Medieval Europe* (Cambridge, 1986); *La giustizia nell'alto medioevo (secoli IX–XI)* (2 vols, Spoleto, 1997); Warren C. Brown and Piotr Górecki, 'What conflict means: The making of medieval conflict studies in the United States, 1970–2000', in Warren C. Brown and Piotr Górecki (eds), *Conflict in Medieval Europe: Changing Perspectives on Society and Culture* (Aldershot, 2003), pp. 1–35, and Warren C. Brown and Piotr Górecki, 'Where conflict leads: On the present and future of medieval conflict studies in the United States', in Brown and Górecki (eds), *Conflict in Medieval Europe*, pp. 265–85; Nicole Castan et al. (eds), *La justice en l'an mil* (Paris, 2003). On legal anthropology, see: Sally Falk Moore, *Law as Process: An Anthropological Approach* (London, 1978), e.g. p. 244; Simon Roberts, *Order and Dispute: An Introduction to Legal Anthropology* (Harmondsworth, 1979); John Comaroff and Simon Roberts, *Rules and Processes: The Cultural Logic of Dispute in an African Context* (London, 1981).

3 Stephen D. White, '*Pactum . . . legem vincit et amor judicium*: The settlement of disputes by compromise in eleventh-century western France', *American Journal of Legal History*, 22 (1978), pp. 281–308; Stephen D. White, 'From peace to power: The study of disputes in medieval France', in Esther Cohen and Mayke B. de Jong (eds), *Medieval Transformations: Texts, Power, and Gifts in Context* (Leiden, 2001), pp. 203–18; Stephen D. White, 'Tenth-century courts at Mâcon and the perils of structuralist history: Re-reading Burgundian judicial institutions', in Brown and Górecki (eds), *Conflict in Medieval Europe*, pp. 37–68

while there have been excellent regional studies, there has also been some tendency to generalize about western Europe as a whole.[4] When this happens, it has the effect of making everywhere appear the same. There clearly was plenty of common practice shared across wide areas of western Europe before 1000, but there were some significant differences too. It is the purpose of this chapter to make some observations on northern Iberia in the western European context – what practice was shared and what diverged, and how far does northern Iberia fit the paradigms of the dominant historical interpretations?

Without wishing to suggest that all of northern Iberian practice was the same, for there were clearly some regional differences within Iberia, it is nevertheless the case that plenty of elements of judicial practice of northern Spain and Portugal in the ninth and tenth centuries were shared with those of other parts of western Europe in the early middle ages. The fact that there were standard procedures, and that they were followed, is normal everywhere. So is the fact that cases often took some time to complete and hearings were spread across several sessions of the court: cases in southern Italy could well take two or three years to reach a conclusion.[5] Having a court president was normal too, whether a single or a shared responsibility, as was flexibility in whether or not the president joined in the judging. Judgment was most often collective, and the primary role of the judges was to determine what should happen next in the course of a case, although they might make judgments too; whether or not they were likely to do so was one factor that varied across Europe.[6] Variation was also characteristic of the preference for this or that mode of proof: while the use of written evidence, the oral evidence of witnesses and the judicial oath all played a part in virtually every system, sometimes writing, sometimes witnessing and sometimes the oath was dominant. Putting down pledges was procedurally important in some parts and, although it has attracted less discussion, apart from that about Celtic areas, I suspect that use of sureties as an enforcement and/or guarantee mechanism was also widespread.[7]

(all reprinted in Stephen D. White, *Feuding and Peace-making in Eleventh century France* (Aldershot, 2005)). Patrick J. Geary, 'Vivre en conflit dans une France sans état: typologie des mécanismes de règlement des conflits (1050–1200)', *Annales ESC*, 41 (1986), pp. 1,107–33; Bruno Lemesle, *Conflits et justice au moyen âge. Normes, loi et résolution des conflits en Anjou aux XIe et XIIe siècles* (Paris, 2008).

4 For a generalizing approach, see Raoul Charles van Caenegem, 'La preuve dans le droit du moyen âge occidental. Rapport de synthèse', in *La preuve. Deuxième partie: moyen âge et temps modernes* (Brussels, 1965), pp. 691–753, at pp. 692–708: 'Le droit que nous étudions ici n'est pas celui d'une nation, mais d'une civilisation, celle du moyen âge occidental' (p. 692).

5 Huguette Taviani-Carozzi, *La principauté lombarde de Salerne. IXe–XIe siècle. Pouvoir et société en Italie lombarde méridionale* (2 vols, Rome, 1991), vol. 1, p. 607 (also citing a five-year case).

6 Compare Karl Heidecker, 'Communication by written texts in court cases: Some charter evidence (*ca.*800–*ca.*1100)', in Marco Mostert (ed.), *New Approaches to Medieval Communication* (Turnhout, 1999), pp. 101–26, at pp. 111–12, on Rankweil in Austria, with Chris Wickham, 'Land disputes and their social framework in Lombard-Carolingian Italy, 700–900', in *Land and Power: Studies in Italian and European Social History, 400–1200* (London, 1994), pp. 229–56, at p. 234, on Italy.

7 Wickham, 'Land disputes and their social framework', p. 233, but note change in the use of pledges in southern Italy in the later tenth century, Paolo Delogu, 'La giustizia nell'Italia meridionale

Available evidence

But there are outright differences too. While there is a kind of comparability about the numbers of surviving records of court cases per region, with more per square kilometre in Italy and fewer in Iberia,[8] there are major differences in the nature of those records. There does not appear to have been anything of the formal, lay, notarial tradition of Italy in northern Iberia, nor of the reflection of that tradition in the more formal recording practice of public scribes in Burgundy or the use of standard templates in other parts of the Carolingian Empire.[9] Although some standard formulas certainly recur in reporting court cases, suggesting the widespread sharing of a common recording tradition, there is nothing to suggest use of a standard template, nothing to suggest any element of official recording at court and nothing to suggest the existence of a professional notariate, lay or clerical, in northern Iberia.[10] Creating the record was a different process, and the form of the records of Iberian court cases was, thereby, much less standardized than those of many other parts of western Europe.

Since the formal *placitum* (the record of a court case) did not exist in northern Iberia, we cannot compare like with like. However, there is a certain comparability between the Accounts of northern Iberia and the records of so-called fictitious disputes from Francia, in that in both cases records were retrospectively constructed in order to secure high-level confirmation;[11] and the narrative element of Accounts is echoed in texts from many parts of Europe.[12] Recent commentators on judicial procedure beyond Iberia sometimes note that there are references to court cases in records other than *placita*, but it is

---

longobarda', in *La giustizia nell'alto medioevo (secoli IX–XI)* (2 vols, Spoleto, 1997), vol. 1, pp. 257–308, at pp. 301–302, as also replacement by the oath of pledges in compensation for homicide, in ninth-century Francia, Régine Le Jan, 'Justice royale et pratiques sociales dans le royaume franc au IXe siècle', in *La giustizia nell'alto medioevo*, vol. 1, pp. 47–85, at p. 67. Stefan Esders and Søren Kaschke, '*Ut sub fideiussoribus ad nostrum palatium veniat.* Gestellungsbürgschaft und Letztentscheidung des Hofgerichtes unter Ludwig dem Frommen' (forthcoming), notes the increased use of *fideiussores* under Louis the Pious. For Celtic areas, see Thomas M. Charles-Edwards, Morfydd E. Owen and Dafydd B. Walters (eds), *Lawyers and Laymen: Studies in the History of Law Presented to Professor Dafydd Jenkins on His Seventy-fifth Birthday, Gŵyl Ddewi 1986* (Cardiff, 1986), pp. 15–233.

8 Heidecker, 'Communication by written texts', p. 101, cites 550 cases for the Carolingian Empire north of the Alps before 1000 and over 500 for the kingdom of Italy during 774–1050, as against my count of 257 for all types of dispute record from northern Iberia (excluding Catalonia) before 1000.

9 François Bougard, *La justice dans le royaume d'Italie de la fin du VIIIe siècle au début du XIe siècle* (Rome, 1995), pp. 66–70; Heidecker, 'Communication by written texts', pp. 114–17; Warren C. Brown, *Unjust Seizure: Conflict, Interest, and Authority in an Early Medieval Society* (Ithaca, NY, 2001), pp. 108–20.

10 For formulas, see above, chapters 4 and 5.

11 Paul Fouracre, '"Placita" and the settlement of disputes in later Merovingian Francia', in Davies and Fouracre (eds), *Settlement of Disputes*, pp. 23–43, at p. 26.

12 Cf. the comments of Robert Jacob, 'Conclusions. Logiques et langages du procès autour de l'an mil', in Castan et al. (eds), *La justice en l'an mil*, pp. 149–67, at pp. 149–50; as also, in eleventh-century contexts, Lemesle, *Conflits et justice*, p. 88, on the *récits* produced by the victorious party following a court case.

difficult to acquire a sense of the totality and range of such records;[13] Patrick Wormald's listing of all of the 178 recorded late Anglo-Saxon cases is probably the closest set of *comparanda* available.[14] But comparison is inevitably uneven. In the case of this book, the large number of Incidental references to court cases – almost a third of the corpus – makes a significant difference to our understanding of process and of the social context of process. It is these Incidental records which make clear that lay people frequently used the courts and which allow us to see a fair degree of peasant activity, whereas most Accounts and the formal *placita* from beyond the Pyrenees largely focus on the activities of aristocrats and monasteries.[15] The Incidental records and the Fines are also our principal source of information on criminal cases, for which there is limited evidence in regions from beyond Iberia, but a significant corpus within Iberia, as also in England.[16] That makes the Iberian criminal corpus particularly important as a contribution to understanding judicial process in Europe, at least until the work of collecting comparable incidental references has been undertaken for other regions.[17]

The availability of written texts of legal collections is also pertinent. There has been an enormous amount of work on manuscript collections of legal texts in early medieval Europe in the past generation. Quite apart from increasing our knowledge of the circulation and dissemination of written law, this work has made it very clear that in many parts of Europe people were studying written law, not only making new collections of it but making summaries and selecting excerpts.[18] There were cadres of people concerned to capture and distil what was deemed relevant for practical use in the early middle ages.

13 Cf. Wickham, 'Land disputes and their social framework', p. 229, who cites 150 formal texts for the period 700–900 in north-central Italy, plus 15 'informal' (i.e. judicial texts not written using the *placitum* template).

14 Patrick Wormald, 'A handlist of Anglo-Saxon law-suits', *Anglo-Saxon England*, 17 (1988), pp. 247–81, counting to the late eleventh century, with a couple of cases added subsequently, bringing the total to 180 (Patrick Wormald, 'Giving God and king their due: Conflict and its regulation in the early English state', in *La giustizia nell'alto medioevo*, vol. 1, pp. 549–83, at pp. 551, 568). Tom Lambert, 'Theft, homicide and crime in late Anglo-Saxon law', *Past and Present*, 214 (2012), pp. 3–43, at pp. 33–9, notes the incidental nature of many Anglo-Saxon references to theft and homicide.

15 A few records of purely lay cases also survive in England (12 of 180 late Anglo-Saxon cases); Wormald, 'Giving God and king their due', p. 568. Josep María Salrach, *Justícia i poder a Catalunya abans de l'any mil* (Vic, 2013), pp. 84–94, notes the appearance of peasants in Catalan records, but principally as the subject of more powerful adversaries' attention.

16 See above, pp. 40–1, 199. For England, see Wormald, 'Giving God and king their due', pp. 558–62, also citing the small numbers of Ottonian and Carolingian cases.

17 For the problem of criminal records in Italy, see Bougard, *La justice*, pp. 235–9. The five criminal cases in the ninth-century Breton corpus do not have any detail of the procedure used to establish guilt; Wendy Davies, 'Disputes, their conduct and their settlement in the village communities of eastern Brittany in the ninth century', *History and Anthropology*, 1 (1985), pp. 289–312, at p. 296. Wickham, 'Land disputes and their social framework', p. 247, notes transfers of land resulting from fines, but the number of such records in Italy is small (personal comment).

18 For example, Rosamond McKitterick, *The Carolingians and the Written Word* (Cambridge, 1989), pp. 40–60; Bougard, *La justice*, pp. 30–36; Detlef Liebs, *Römische Jurisprudenz in Gallien (2. bis 8.*

Legal norms clearly existed in northern Iberia. Ninth- and tenth-century records of judicial process make reference to an existing body of law, secular and ecclesiastical, in the laws of the Visigoths, both the *Forum Iudicum* and the corpus of canon law.[19] Late tenth-century interest in this Visigothic material is obvious, for much was copied, surviving in manuscripts like the great codices of Albelda and San Millán de la Cogolla; the Albelda Codex dates from 974–76, and the San Millán Codex, much of which is a copy of the former, dates from a generation later.[20] While there was certainly plenty of copying of whole law texts in the late tenth century, I am not aware of much copying in northern Iberia outside Catalonia before this nor of any collections of excerpts made before 1000.[21] For example, of the 20 full or partial manuscripts of the Breviary of Alaric (otherwise known as *Lex Romana Visigothorum*), 17 sets of abbreviations and two sets of excerpts, only one manuscript is Spanish.[22] If there were no summarizing or excerpting activity in Spain or Portugal, this would suggest that the written corpus of law was not being studied and used in the way that Roman and Germanic law codes were studied elsewhere in the early middle ages. In Catalonia, by contrast, one important copier of law texts of the early eleventh century was himself a judge, and his law text is quite heavily glossed.[23] It looks from this glossing as if legal text was being prepared for practical use,

Jahrhundert) (Berlin, 2002), especially pp. 97–267; Wolfgang Kaiser, *Die Epitome Iuliani: Beiträge zum römischen Recht im frühen Mittelalter und zum byzantinischen Rechtsunterricht* (Frankfurt, 2004), *passim*, but see pp. 11–21 for an overview of early medieval manuscripts of, excerpts from and glosses on Epitome Iuliani (a version of the Novels of Justinian); Charles M. Radding and Antonio Ciaralli, *The Corpus Iuris Civilis in the Middle Ages: Manuscripts and Transmission from the Sixth Century to the Juristic Revival* (Leiden, 2006), pp. 35–65 (although somewhat dismissive of the early medieval period, this book offers a useful summary of the available manuscript evidence); Patrick Wormald, *The Making of English Law: King Alfred to the Twelfth Century* (2 vols, Oxford, 1999), vol. 1, pp. 30–35, 54–6, on Lupus of Ferrières; Magali Coumert, 'Isidorus Hispalensis and the Lex Salica', Leeds International Congress, July 2013, and further work forthcoming. Cf., on the citation of the Theodosian Code by a range of early medieval authors, Dafydd Walters, 'From Benedict to Gratian: The Code in medieval ecclesiastical authors', in Jill Harries and Ian Wood (eds), *The Theodosian Code: Studies in the Imperial Law of Late Antiquity* (London, 1993), pp. 200–216.

19 See above, pp. 26–7.

20 Codex Albeldense: El Escorial MS d.I.2, written by Vigila; Codex Emilianense: El Escorial MS d.I.1, written by Velasco and Sisebut. Earlier manuscripts of *Forum Iudicum* are Catalan or southern French; see above, pp. 11–12.

21 See Manuel C. Díaz y Díaz, 'La Lex Visigothorum y sus manuscritos. Un Ensayo de reinterpretación', *Anuario de historia del derecho español*, 46 (1976), pp. 163–224, for manuscripts of *Lex Visigothorum/Forum Iudicum*; see further above, p. 27, on the disjuncture in transmission of the texts. The very fact that the León palimpsest (a sixth-century copy of most of *Lex Romana Visigothorum*, a version of the first five books of the Theodosian Code) was overwritten in the tenth century with a Latin translation of Eusebius emphasizes the break in transmission; León, Biblioteca Catedral 15.

22 Liebs, *Römische Jurisprudenz*, pp. 109–10.

23 See Josep M. Salrach, 'Prácticas judiciales, transformación social y acción política en Cataluña (siglos IX–XIII)', *Hispania*, 57/3 (1997), pp. 1,009–48, at p. 1,020, and *Justícia i poder*, pp. 37–8. Judge Bonushomo of Barcelona wrote the surviving MS, of 1011: 'In nomine Domini incipit Liber iudicum

and in any case we have dispute texts that the same judge recorded.[24] Glosses on legal texts survive from many parts of Europe, and indeed there are Frankish glosses on the Breviary of Alaric.[25] But this kind of evidence of attention to text is lacking from most of northern Iberia, just as legal manuscripts are lacking until the late tenth century. All the more surprising, then, that written law was cited in records of judicial process in northern Spain well before that and it is found in other charters too (for example, in charters recording gifts from husband to wife, which reflect the provisions of Visigothic law on this particular kind of endowment).[26] These provisions were evoked relatively frequently, sometimes with explicit reference to the appropriate text.[27] While *Lex Alamannorum* is sometimes reflected in the charters of Saint-Gall, and *Lex Baiuuariorum* and *Lex Ripuaria* in Carolingian charters, these are reflections rather than explicit citations, which are rare, as also are citations of *Lex Salica*,[28] and law texts are not cited in English charters at all.[29] Although these differences in approach to legal manuscripts and to citation must partly be explained by the loss of manuscripts from Spain and Portugal, there do seem to have been real differences in legal culture between northern Iberia and much of the rest of western Europe.

---

popularis . . . scriptum uidelicet Barcilona ciuitate per institutione Bonushomo laeuita qui et iudice . . .V. idus iulii nauiter fuit anno scilicet. XVI. Roberto rege regnante in Frantia'; see Jesús Alturo, Joan Bellès, Josep M. Font i Rius, Yolanda García and Anscari M. Mundó, *Liber iudicum popularis. Ordenat pel jutge Bonsom de Barcelona* (Barcelona, 2003), p. 104; for glosses, see ibid., pp. 256–70, 705–85.

24 Salrach, *Justícia i poder*, pp. 187–8; cf. Alturo et al., *Liber iudicum popularis*, pp. 262, 267 – 'a veritable vulgarization of the principal text'.

25 See Liebs, *Römische Jurisprudenz*, pp. 209–20; cf. Kaiser, *Die Epitome Iuliani*, pp. 13–14, for glossing Epitome Iuliani. Cf. also the practice of early Irish lawyers: the volume of Irish legal glossing is enormous, and although the activity stretches into the late middle ages and early modern period, it began in the ninth century. For a complete edition of glosses, see *Corpus Iuris Hibernici, ad fidem codicum manuscriptorum recognovit*, ed. Daniel A. Binchy (6 vols, Dublin, 1978). For an accessible introduction to early Irish law, see Fergus Kelly, *A Guide to Early Irish Law* (Dublin, 1988).

26 For example, Sob119 (887), Cel577 (926), reflecting *Forum Iudicum* III.1.5.

27 See above, p. 26.

28 Cf. *Urkundenbuch der Abtei Sanct Gallen*, ed. Hermann Wartmann (6 vols, Zurich, 1863–1955), vol. 2, no. 408, a gift of 849–50; *Die Urkunden Pippins, Karlmanns und Karls des Grossen*, ed. Engelbert Mühlbacher et al. (Hanover, 1906), nos 13 (760), 84 (774); see Carl I. Hammer, 'Land sales in eighth- and ninth-century Bavaria: Legal, economic and social aspects', *Early Medieval Europe*, 6 (1997), pp. 47–76; cf., on *Lex Romana Curiensis*, Peter Erhart and Julia Kleindinst, *Urkundenlandschaft Rätien* (Vienna, 2004), pp. 44–5, 50; cf., on Lombard law, Radding and Ciaralli, *The Corpus Iuris Civilis*, pp. 45–6. See also Matthew Innes, 'Charlemagne, justice and written law', in Alice Rio (ed.), *Law, Custom, and Justice in Late Antiquity and the Early Middle Ages* (London, 2011), pp. 155–203, at p. 172; cf. Alice Rio, *Legal Practice and the Written Word in the Early Middle Ages: Frankish Formulae, c. 500–1000* (Cambridge, 2009), pp. 198–211 – her discussion focuses on formularies, but the same principles apply. For prescriptions within law texts on charter writing, see Harry Bresslau, *Handbuch der Urkundenlehre für Deutschland und Italien*, 2nd edn (2 vols, Leipzig, 1912–31), vol. 1, pp. 635–53.

29 Wormald, 'Giving God and king their due', p. 571; nor in those from the Loire in the eleventh century; Lemesle, *Conflits et justice*, pp. 83–4.

Procedure

While it is not impossible that some courts had a regular schedule of meetings, I am unable to detect this in the ninth- and tenth-century Iberian evidence. By contrast, regular meetings of the *mallus* were a particular feature of the Carolingian world, and from the tenth century so were regular meetings of the hundred and shire courts in England, in both cases because of direction from the ruler (two or three times a year in the former case, and respectively 12 times and twice a year in the latter).[30] Iberia seems to have been different. As for the locations of meetings: in most parts of Europe, meetings could be held in several kinds of place, inside and outside, in the open air, on disputed land, in a building, in a palace, in a church, and many courts were held in towns, in places as far apart as England and Italy.[31] While meetings in or in front of churches were quite common in Spain, meetings in the *atria* (porches) of churches were repeatedly prohibited in Francia, which may suggest they were common there too.[32] There is also a marked difference in officers serving the court, given the regular occurrence of the dedicated legal officer, the *saio*, throughout northern Iberia;[33] while most of the *saio*'s functions will have been performed in some way elsewhere, it is more usual to find officers with a range of different responsibilities, military and financial as well as judicial, beyond Iberia.[34]

The use of judges with legal expertise is characteristic of Iberian practice, as it is of Italian or Irish, and in all three cases there is reason to suppose this was a matter of family expertise, transmitted across generations;[35] expertise must also have been characteristic of Francia – *scabini* had experience – although perhaps not so much legal expertise. While the emphasis, everywhere, is on collective judgment, there were clearly cases in northern Iberia in which a single judge both presided and determined the outcome.[36] Despite the burden of much recent comment, it is equally clear that single judges did handle cases elsewhere,

30 François Louis Ganshof, 'Charlemagne et l'administration de la justice dans la monarchie franque', in Helmut Beumann (ed.), *Persönlichkeit und Geschichte* = vol. 1 of Wolfgang Braunfels (ed.), *Karl der Grosse: Lebenswerk und Nachleben* (5 vols, Düsseldorf, 1965), pp. 394–419, at p. 401; Bougard, *La justice*, pp. 205–209; Sally Harvey, *Domesday: Book of Judgment* (Oxford, 2014), p. 84.

31 Wormald, 'Giving God and king their due', p. 570; Bougard, *La justice*, pp. 209–12.

32 See above, pp. 216–17; on Francia, see, for example, *Capitularia Regum Francorum*, vol. 1, ed. Alfred Boretius (Hanover, 1883), pp. 174 (§ 21), 182 (§ 8), 284 (§ 14), of 813 and 818/819; *Capitularia Regum Francorum*, vol. 2, ed. Alfred Boretius and Victor Krause (Hanover, 1897), p. 269 (§ 7), of 853.

33 See above, pp. 164–8.

34 Bougard, *La justice*, pp. 158–70, 185–90; for a nice picture of the activities of a somewhat special Carolingian *missus* (Archbishop Arn of Salzburg), see Brown, *Unjust Seizure*, pp. 102–23.

35 See above, p. 162; Bougard, *La justice*, pp. 141–52, 281–4; Delogu, 'La giustizia nell'Italia meridionale longobarda', pp. 283, 287; Taviani-Carozzi, *La principauté lombarde de Salerne*, vol. 2, p. 773, stresses that family interest cannot be demonstrated before the eleventh century, but implies that it happened. Compare Kelly's map of Irish legal families, cited above, p. 162 n41. Cf. Salrach, *Justícia i poder*, pp. 40–43, 156, who argues for continuity of tradition in Catalonia.

36 See above, p. 229.

in Catalonia and southern Italy for example, and I am not sure that Iberian practice is distinctive here.[37]

Collective judgment was nevertheless a common feature of all areas, and in this northern Iberia was no different.[38] But who were the people who constituted the collective? Was this everyone present, or a particular group, like the panel of judges? It is a feature of some European records to associate the whole court, judges and others, with the final judgment and resolution of a case.[39] Where records explicitly make a point about the participation of the whole court, that may well be a reasonable conclusion, although we probably need to differentiate the scribe's desire to indicate political consensus from the practicalities of the process as it took place. However, many records of court cases (and these include the Iberian) do not make this point. If 'collective' has to refer to the judgment of the whole court, rather than to the judgment of a specified group, then Iberia, and many other places, were different. In a variation on the 'whole court' model, some historians propose that all witnesses, by virtue of their presence, in effect participated in the judgment. While at a very general level one might quite reasonably argue that the presence of anyone at a judgment meant that he or she bought into the system, this is not the same as making the judgment. Many records are in any case vague about witnesses – some appear to record meticulously all who were present; others indicate the names of a few; some listed witnesses do not appear to have been present at the transactions with which they are associated; some lists omit some of those present.[40] Precise recorded detail of what exactly happened at the moment(s) of judgment, and of who was involved, is often lacking, but it is useful to ask about numbers and about where those involved came from. Numbers present at court are difficult to assess, given the witness problem, but where specified they range from 10 to 20 to well over 100, in Iberia and beyond. Chris Wickham has argued that the size of assemblies changed in due course – large assemblies stopped being associated with judgment after the year 1080.[41] As for dedicated judging panels, on the other hand: numbers have in fact been counted in many

37 See Salrach, *Justícia i poder*, p. 21; Taviani-Carozzi, *La principauté lombarde de Salerne*, vol. 1, pp. 572–6; Delogu, 'La giustizia nell'Italia meridionale longobarda', pp. 265–7. Cf. also Monique Bourin, 'Les *boni homines* de l'an mil', in Castan et al. (eds), *La justice en l'an mil*, pp. 53–65, at p. 60, of southern France.

38 See above, pp. 205–11.

39 Bougard, *La justice*, p. 141.

40 See above, pp. 77, 172. Cf. Bernhard Zeller, 'Writing charters as a public activity: The example of the Carolingian charters of St Gall', in Marco Mostert and Paul Barnwell (eds), *Medieval Legal Process: Physical, Spoken and Written Performance in the Middle Ages* (Turnhout, 2011), pp. 27–37, at p. 29.

41 Chris Wickham, 'Public court practice: The eighth and twelfth centuries compared', in Stefan Esders (ed.), *Rechtsverständnis und Konfliktbewältigung. Gerichtliche und aussergerichtliche Strategien im Mittelalter* (Köln, 2007), pp. 17–30, contrasts large but unspecified numbers at eighth- to tenth-century assemblies, with eight at an important case of 1188, noting rarely less than 10 in late eleventh-century northern Italy; cf. Timothy Reuter, Chris Wickham and Thomas N. Bisson, 'Debate: The "feudal revolution"', *Past and Present*, 155 (1997), pp. 177–225, at pp. 203–5 (Wickham).

areas, including northern Iberia, and they usually range between two and 12, although they could be larger.[42]

Now, it seems to me that the collective judgment issue is not simply one of size, but also of composition: in Iberia, the collective that made the judgment was rarely drawn just from local residents, and was more usually a larger or smaller panel of very mixed provenance, some members travelling a considerable distance to participate.[43] By contrast, there is an underlying assumption in much western European literature that such panels, and indeed assemblies, must have been drawn from local communities, although there is relatively little work on who precisely joined panels and where they came from.[44] This 'local community' is rarely precisely conceived: was it the community of local residents? If so, were they the residents of the settlement in which the court was held, or the residents or representatives of some wider regional community? And if the latter, was this a region of – say – 10 km diameter, or 30, or 80 or 150 km (see Figure 9.1)? The differences between the smallest and the largest scale would imply a significant difference in the social standing of the participants.[45] In ninth-century Brittany, the panels which judged in village courts characteristically came from three or four surrounding villages (that is, from within a zone of no more than 20 km diameter), and from the wealthier levels of the peasantry.[46] Even in these very low-level courts, collective judgment was made by people from beyond the immediate home locality, although certainly not from far away. On the whole, the detailed work on this has not been done for most areas, although there is some work on panels which provided sworn evidence – clearly a different issue, but a useful comparator in the present context. For late eleventh-century England, there is a very large body of evidence about numbers and provenance of jurors, recorded in the vernacular

42 See Bougard, *La justice*, pp. 143–4, on numbers of *scabini*: from a college for each *ville*, usually seven, occasionally fewer, rarely more than 12, exceptionally 21; see Lemesle, *Conflits et justice*, pp. 63–5, on numbers present at hearings. Salrach, *Justícia i poder*, comments frequently on numbers of judges, and sometimes others present at a hearing, for example pp. 75, 77, 89, 93, 103 (3, 6, 9 – unusually high, 4, 5 judges, respectively). See above, pp. 160–4, 205–11.

43 See above, pp. 209–11.

44 The Breton evidence is particularly good at clearly differentiating judges from witnesses and at giving us a sense of where people came from; see Davies, 'Disputes, their conduct and their settlement in the village communities of East Brittany in the ninth century', and Wendy Davies, 'People and places in dispute in ninth-century Brittany', in Davies and Fouracre (eds), *Settlement of Disputes*, pp. 65–84. On 'local', see above, p. 204. On the notion of 'community', see the discussion of Fernanda Pirie and Judith Scheele, 'Justice, community, and law', in Fernanda Pirie and Judith Scheele (eds), *Legalism: Community and Justice* (Oxford, 2014), pp. 1–24, and their reminder that 'community' is 'a particular way of imagining the social', ibid., p. 24.

45 But see Julio Escalona and Andrew Reynolds (eds), *Scale and Scale Change in the Early Middle Ages: Exploring Landscape, Local Society, and the World Beyond* (Turnhout, 2011); Julio Escalona, in particular, has been consistent in addressing issues of supra-local scale in northern Spain; see his 'Scale change on the border: The county of Castile in the tenth century', in Escalona and Reynolds (eds), *Scale and Scale Change*, pp. 153–83.

46 Davies, 'People and places in dispute in ninth-century Brittany', pp. 78–82.

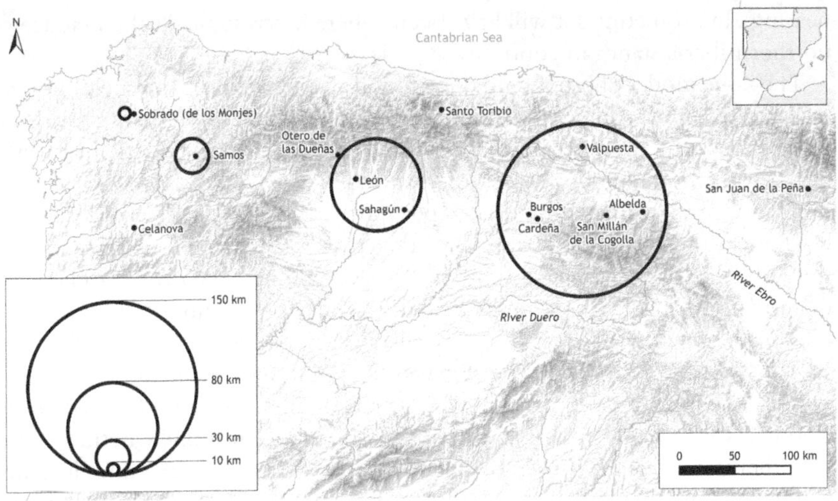

Figure 9.1 Practical demonstration of differences of scale

in Domesday Book and related texts; while taking evidence from a dozen or so jurors per hundred appears to have been normal (an administrative unit of widely varying size, from at least 15 to 60 km^2), it is clear that evidence was also taken, sometimes simultaneously, from jurors from much smaller and much larger units; some of these groups have tenth-century precedents.[47] If the analogy is relevant, it suggests that panels were drawn from small-scale localities and also from much wider regions, a mixed practice, with mixed experience feeding into the process – as indeed the (very imperfect) witness lists would suggest. It seems unlikely that most collective judgment in Europe was made by panels of local people (where 'local' means from within a few kilometres of the site of the

47 See Robin Fleming, *Domesday Book and the Law: Society and Legal Custom in Early Medieval England* (Cambridge, 1998), especially pp. 11–28. Fleming cites six people to provide testimony from each Cambridgeshire vill (a unit smaller than the hundred, most easily envisaged as parish-size, although again in practice there was huge variation), ibid., p. 11, n. 2, as also representatives of groups of hundreds together. She suggests that English practice was distinctive, but see Philippe Depreux, 'La prestation de serment dans le monde franc: formes et fonctions (VIe–IXe siècles)', in Françoise Laurent (ed.), *Serment, promesse et engagement: rituels et modalités au moyen âge* (Montpellier, 2008), pp. 517–32, at pp. 529–30, on oath-helpers in Francia, noting multiples of three and – especially – multiples of 12, up to 72 (p. 519). There are also many vernacular additions to liturgical and other books in England, recording provision of testimony, from eleventh- and twelfth-century contexts, though the provenance of the witnesses is rarely stated. For the corpus, see, for example, David A.E. Pelteret, *Catalogue of English Post-Conquest Vernacular Documents* (Woodbridge, 1990); *The Production and Use of English Manuscripts 1060 to 1220*, ed. Orietta Da Rold, Takako Kato, Mary Swan and Elaine Treharne, updated 2013: http://www.le.ac.uk/ee/em1060to1220/. I am extremely grateful to Professor Julia Crick for providing further comment and many references, following her seminar paper on this, Institute of Historical Research, London, 26 March 2014.

hearing), but sometimes it will have been; where it was so made, the practice of northern Iberia stands in contrast.

The same modes of proof tend to be found all over western Europe, although, as suggested above, different elements were preferenced in different regions, as Italian courts came to prefer writing.[48] In northern Iberia, documentary evidence was required, produced, studied and then accepted or rejected.[49] Asking for it was a normal thing; it was expected that litigants would have charters to support their cases; it was explicit that texts could provide clarification – the judges *intellexerunt omnia* (understood everything) when they studied the documents – and it was known that they could be manipulated, hence the questioning by Iñigo Garcés of Cillanueva's charter in 968.[50] The very fact that so many charters still survive today makes the point that documentary evidence was valued. All this is no different from practice one might find elsewhere in Europe. Now, it could be that an oath was required to determine whether or not documentary evidence should be heeded, as also happened sometimes in other European contexts.[51] In one of the Lugo disputes over control of a church, the contending priest brought his charters to court, whereupon the judges required the production of five witnesses to swear to the truth of the documents;[52] and in the Iñigo Garcés case, which was heard in the court of the regent Elvira, it was the oaths of his monastic adversary that demonstrated that a charter was good.[53] Elsewhere, oaths could at times topple written evidence, as they could in Iberia too.[54]

The oral evidence of witnesses was also used. Although enquiries were occasionally launched to discover local knowledge and past practice from uncommitted parties, use of the inquest is very infrequently recorded in northern Iberia, and appears to have been much less common than it was in other parts of Europe (boundary enquiries were so politically slanted that they cannot fall into the category of objective inquest).[55] But witnesses were frequently

48 In general, see *La preuve*; on Italy, see Wickham, 'Land disputes and their social framework', pp. 240–5; cf. Bougard, *La justice*, pp. 221–9; and for Catalonia, see Salrach, *Justícia i poder*, p. 41.

49 For example: C90 (957); Li144 (941); PMH DC 183 (999); Sam126 (960); C55 (945). See above, pp. 211–13. Cf., for Catalonia, Michel Zimmermann, *Écrire et lire en Catalogne (IXe–XIIe siècle)* (2 vols, Madrid, 2003), vol. 2, pp. 1,340–42.

50 PMH DC 183, Lii410 (see above, p. 211).

51 Paul Barnwell, 'Action, speech and writing in early Frankish legal proceedings', in Mostert and Barnwell (eds), *Medieval Legal Process*, pp. 11–25, at p. 19. Cf., on use of the oath in court cases, Depreux, 'La prestation de serment dans le monde franc', pp. 527–31; Stefan Esders and Thomas Scharff, 'Die Untersuchung der Untersuchung. Methodische Überlegungen zum Studium rechtlicher Befragungs- und Weisungspraktiken in Mittelalter und früher Neuzeit', in Stefan Esders and Thomas Scharff (eds), *Eid und Wahrheitssuche. Studien zu rechtlichen Befragungspraktiken in Mittelalter und früher Neuzeit* (Frankfurt am Main, 1999), pp. 11–47, at pp. 23–8.

52 AHN 1325A–6 (922): 'et iurent per sagro iuramento quia sic illos scriptos in concilio presente quia sic est ueritas'.

53 Lii410.

54 Heidecker, 'Communication by written texts in court cases', pp. 111–13.

55 Sob109 (early 990s), for example; on boundary cases, see further above, pp. 221–6. For a Carolingian inquest into metropolitan rights in Istria, see Stefan Esders, 'Regionale Selbstbehauptung

required and produced by one or other party, in support of that party, in northern Iberia, with the appropriate number of witnesses sometimes specified by the judges.[56] When witnesses were presented, the judges would characteristically select the witnesses of one party to take the oath and direct how many of them should do it. In fact, use of witnesses is noted nearly twice as often as use of documents, although a few charters record the use of both; here, oral evidence tended to be preferenced. Moreover, although the records are framed in a manner which suggests that oaths were about the specifics of particular events – that is, that they were about facts – in effect, the witnesses were swearing in support of the party that had called them. In practice, it is therefore difficult to differentiate between oath-helping and the sworn witness statement and, as has been observed for other areas, we probably should not try to do so.[57] Judicial oaths certainly existed in Francia, as they did in Italy: however, Bougard argues that the oath became ritualized in Italy by the later tenth century – a *banalisation* – just a ritual procedure, in practice disassociated from the specifics of witness evidence.[58] The Iberian emphasis on the oath is striking, and is of course reminiscent of the importance of the oath of loyalty in the Carolingian Empire, although in the latter case the contexts and the functions of the oath are quite different.[59] Overall, although the judicial oath can be found throughout the West, dependence on it appears more prominent and more frequent in Iberia than in many other parts of Europe.

Iberian use of the ordeal before the year 1000 was as rare as it was elsewhere in Europe, but there is a significant difference in its use.[60] With one apparent exception (in which a woman used the ordeal to deny a charge),[61]

zwischen Byzanz und dem Frankenreich. Die *inquisitio* der Rechtsgewohnheiten Istriens durch die Sendboten Karls des Grossen und Pippins von Italien', in Esders and Scharff (eds), *Eid und Wahrheitssuche*, pp. 49–112, and on Carolingian inquest in general, see ibid., pp. 99–103.

56 See above, pp. 211–12.

57 See above, pp. 125, 213. Cf. the comments of Wormald, 'Giving God and king their due', p. 566, and especially Lemesle, *Conflits et justice*, pp. 151–6, on the interdependence of oath and evidence.

58 Bougard, *La justice*, pp. 331–4; François Bougard, 'Rationalité et irrationalité des procédures autour de l'an mil: le duel judiciaire en Italie', in Castan et al. (eds), *La justice en l'an mil*, pp. 93–122, at p. 97.

59 Capitulare missorum (789), *Capitularia Regum Francorum*, vol. 1, ed. Boretius, pp. 66–7. See Janet L. Nelson, 'Liturgy or law: Misconceived alternatives?', in Stephen Baxter, Catherine Karkov, Janet L. Nelson and David Pelteret (eds), *Early Medieval Studies in Memory of Patrick Wormald* (Farnham, 2009), pp. 433–47, at pp. 442–7; cf. Stefan Esders, 'Treueidleistung und Rechtsveränderung im früheren Mittelalter', in Stefan Esders and Christine Reinle (eds), *Rechtsveränderung im politischen und sozialen Kontext mittelalterlicher Rechtsvielfalt* (Münster, 2005), pp. 25–61, for precedents.

60 On its rarity, see: Bougard, *La justice*, p. 229; Dominique Barthélemy, 'Les ordalies de l'an mil', in Castan et al. (eds), *La justice en l'an mil*, pp. 81–92; Lemesle, *Conflits et justice*, pp. 157–8; Salrach, *Justícia i poder*, pp. 37–8 (citing Iglesia's suggestion that maybe its occurrence was a consequence of Frankish influence); cf. Roger Collins, '"Sicut lex Gothorum continet": Law and charters in ninth- and tenth-century León and Catalonia', *English Historical Review*, 100 (1985), pp. 489–512, at pp. 503–4. Aquilino Iglesia Ferreirós, 'El proceso del Conde Bera y el problema de las ordalías', *Anuario de historia del derecho español*, 51 (1981), pp. 1–221. See also n. 85 below.

61 A27 (978).

ordeal was primarily used to test the credibility of witnesses rather than that of the accused. The texts stress that it was an 'innocent' party – unconnected to either protagonist – who had undertaken the ordeal. Procedure in this respect is therefore somewhat distinctive in the European context.[62] There is also no echo of the duelling requirements of Carolingian capitularies nor of the shift to duel which characterized Italian practice after 967.[63] I am only aware of 12 references to ordeal in the Iberian corpus – a tiny proportion both of all charters and of all dispute records – and in five of those references it appears that the ordeal did not take place in the end;[64] of those, the San Millán record is explicit that no ordeal was needed because there was sufficient testimony and guarantee. These five references to ordeals that were not carried out are useful because they suggest that its use must have been on the spectrum of possibilities – it was part of the known repertoire of procedures.[65] Where it is recorded as having taken place, the practical reason for its use is extremely difficult to fathom: only two records give the full detail of witnessing the procedure, and it is particularly unclear why they proceeded to the ordeal in the Sobrado case, since acceptable oaths appear to have been sworn.[66] One has to suppose that there was some element of doubt about the credibility of the oath-taker (people did swear false oaths sometimes[67]) and that a further test was needed. The parts of *Forum Iudicum* which detail procedure for the ordeal make clear that the test should be applied to suspicious persons who presented themselves in court to give testimony against others.[68] Use of the ordeal was clearly very rare in northern Iberia before 1000, as it was elsewhere, but the possibility did

62 Although the Burgundian case of 908 cited by Heidecker, 'Communication by written texts in court cases', pp. 104–5, is similar in much of its practical detail. Cf. the treatment of Collins in '"Sicut lex Gothorum continet"' and Roger Collins, 'Visigothic law and regional custom in disputes in early medieval Spain', in Davies and Fouracre (eds), *Settlement of Disputes*, pp. 85–104, although my reading of OvC26 differs significantly; see above, pp. 62, 136–7.

63 Olivier Guillot, 'Le duel judiciaire: du champ legal (sous Louis le Pieux) au champ de la pratique en France (XIe siècle)', in *La giustizia nell'alto medioevo*, pp. 715–85; Bougard, *La justice*, pp. 334–9; Bougard, 'Rationalité et irrationalité'.

64 Cast1 (927), SM27 (= BG 391) (940), AHN 1325A-9 (973), OD31 (991), Cel252 (1000). See above, pp. 136–9, and Figure 5.4 above.

65 Being on the spectrum of possibilities would also be true of the Carolingian world, for prayers for blessing the hot water and the hot iron survive in a later ninth-century manuscript from northern France, MS München BS 14508: 'Deus iudex iustus fortis et patiens qui es auctor pacis et amator iustitiae qui iudicas aequitatem iudicii domine quod iustum es quia recta iudicia tua sunt . . . tu hanc aquam per ignem feruentem sanctifica . . . tu clementissime presta ut quis innocens in hanc aquam feruentem manum mittat . . . ex hac aqua et inlesam perducas'. I am extremely grateful to Carine van Rhijn for giving me access to her transcript. I have been unable to find anything comparable in the early eleventh-century Iberian liturgical collections, although there are ordeal prayers added to the early eleventh-century Catalan manuscript of *Lex Visigothorum*; see Alturo et al., *Liber iudicum popularis*, pp. 791–9, and pp. 251–5 for discussion.

66 See above, p. 29; OvC26; Sob109: 'Trasuarius presbiter et confessus ubi fidelem fui de parte monasterii Superato, ipsum innocentem ad pena caldaria ingredientem uidi, et in III uel IIII die'.

67 C151 (972), for example.

68 *Leges Visigothorum* II.1.32 (p. 251); see above, pp. 138–9.

exist, and reports of it must have been retrospectively provided by the scribe for the victorious side, to underwrite the quality of its case and the robustness of the outcome, a threat to would-be contesters.[69]

Socio-political context

There are no parallels in the northern Iberian context to the exceptionally articulate approach to justice of Carolingian rulers and their advisers: there are no programmes of reform, of providing justice for all, of establishing regular meetings of court.[70] Nor are there statements of royal responsibility for justice, such as that expressed by Jonas of Orléans in his advice to Louis the Pious and by comparable Irish texts, statements echoed in English legislation of the tenth and eleventh centuries;[71] Iberian charters, although at times making much of the Day of Judgment, hardly utter the word *iustitia*, as one might have expected in royal preambles at least.[72] But the Carolingian activity is so remarkable, its absence in Iberia is hardly surprising. Probably more significant is the fact that there was much less of the state about judicial procedure in Iberia than there appears to have been in many other parts of western Europe, including in Catalonia: in the areas that are the subject of this book, there was no top-down system, run by officers who were appointed by the ruler, or by his or her agents, and recorded by official scribes; rather, it was a public system proceeding on a customary basis, and the records were for the most part made by or for the victorious parties.[73] True, kings did preside at court hearings and had royal judges; there were counts, and they had a strong association with court holding, but there do not seem to have been very many of them and very few seem to have been royal delegates.[74] By contrast, there appear to have been a significant number of landowner courts, those of the territorial *potestates*, operating the public system and using the standard procedures.[75] The strong sense of the public in northern Iberian judicial practice has much to do with public performance, with declaration and with the importance of making things known;[76] and with the fact that the same long-established, standard procedures were used across a

69 The cases are not entirely ecclesiastical, although there appears to have been an underlying ecclesiastical interest even where the protagonists were lay.

70 Ganshof, 'Charlemagne et l'administration de la justice'; François Louis Ganshof, 'Charlemagne et les institutions de la monarchie franque', in Braunfels (ed.), *Karl der Grosse*, vol. 1, pp. 349–93, at pp. 350–54; Innes, 'Charlemagne, justice and written law'.

71 Jonas d'Orléans, *Le metier de roi (De institutione regia)*, ed. and trans. Alain Dubreucq (Paris, 1995), especially pp. 188–93, 212–15; see Janet L. Nelson, 'Kings with justice, kings without justice: An early medieval paradox', in *La giustizia nell'alto medioevo*, pp. 797–823; *Audacht Morainn*, ed. Fergus Kelly (Dublin, 1976); Wormald, 'Giving God and king their due', pp. 555–6.

72 See above, pp. 112–16, for the Day of Judgment; and below, p. 260, for *iustitia*.

73 See above, pp. 202–3. For judges as public appointees and the system as a state system in Catalonia, see Salrach, *Justícia i poder*, pp. 26–8, 40–41.

74 See above, p. 25.

75 See above, pp. 157–8, 198–200, 226–9.

76 See above, p. 228.

very wide area, regardless of the identity of court holders or judges or *saiones*. There was a known, acceptable, way of proceeding. This had little to do with any state imposition; it was simply the way that things were done. Landowners operated the same system as kings and counts, and they did so in a public way. We do not therefore have to suppose that justice was distributed exclusively by the state nor that 'the state was *at the core* of all social order'.[77] If the system was not state-organized, neither was it seigneurial in the sense that court holders had discrete, exclusive zones of jurisdiction which residents were compelled to use – later in the middle ages, the right to choose a lord was indeed one of the distinctive features of Castilian society.[78] Court holding in the greater part of northern Iberia fits neither the state model nor the classic model of the *seigneurie banale*; but it did involve an element of seigneurial power in the capacity of some landowners to hold courts for those who were not their tenants or dependants; this was a looser kind of lordly judicial power to hold a court and take fines. And it is probably in this that the real distinctiveness of the region lies.

Fitting the paradigms

In considering judicial process, the two last generations have seen a major shift from a focus on the development of institutions to a focus on what actually happened in court cases, as well as a shift from a literal reading of early medieval texts to a recognition that many documents cannot be taken at face value – different interpretations are possible and words mean different things to different readers, now as then.[79] One has only to realize that key words like *auctor* and *placitum* meant different things in early medieval Iberian and Italian contexts to appreciate the complexity of trying to place and understand medieval texts. In accordance with these wider trends, the long tradition of the study of institutions by Spanish scholars has given way in the past few decades to a much greater concern with practice, although, to date, less of a concern to question the texts.[80]

There has been much discussion in the transatlantic world on whether or not early medieval judicial process was itself 'normative' or 'processual': was it, on

77 See Humfress, 'Laws' empire', p. 92, whose point is that the state was NOT at the core (citing Marc Galanter, 'Justice in many rooms: Courts, private ordering, and indigenous law', *Journal of Legal Pluralism and Unofficial Law*, 19 (1981), pp. 1–47, who however saw courts as an organ of state, e.g. ibid., p. 34). Salrach, *Justícia i poder*, pp. 82–3, although expressing it in a different way, makes a very similar point about co-existing systems of law in Catalonia.

78 Carlos Estepa Díez, *Las Behetrías castellanas* (2 vols, Valladolid, 2003), vol. 1, pp. 43–7, and *passim*; cf. Julio Escalona Monge, 'Unidades territoriales supralocales: una propuesta sobre los orígenes del señorío de behetría', in Carlos Estepa Díez and Cristina Jular Pérez-Alfaro (co-ords), *Los Señoríos de behetría* (Madrid, 2001), pp. 21–46, at pp. 24–5 (available in translation in Cristina Jular Pérez-Alfaro and Carlos Estepa Díez (eds), *Land, Power, and Society in Medieval Castile: A Study of Behetría Lordship* (Turnhout, 2009)).

79 Cf. White, 'Tenth-century courts at Mâcon', pp. 63–4.

80 See above, pp. 19–20.

the one hand, constrained by the existence of legal norms, generated beyond the particular circumstances of any one case but determining appropriate procedure, or on the other hand, was it subject to the creation of rules by interested parties and the invocation or defiance of such rules to suit the moment?[81] As noted above, records of judicial process in northern Iberia unquestionably make reference to an existing, old body of law, and full law texts were copied in our period.[82] That being the case, we might say that this was certainly a world in which rules existed beyond the circumstances of any particular court session, that there was a widespread awareness of this corpus of written law, and that these rules were evoked relatively frequently. Northern Iberia therefore fits the normative model. On the other hand, the variability of the citations must mean that rules were being used to suit the circumstances, and that some rules were selected and others ignored; it could also mean that not many – if any – scribes and judges knew the entire corpus of law. It would therefore be quite misleading to suppose that this external set of norms was applied comprehensively, systematically and rigorously to all cases. There was inevitably an element of the so-called processual as well. Both characteristics apply, and they are not alternatives – a point now increasingly made in the European discourse.[83]

In reaction to earlier approaches, which had characterized early medieval procedure as fundamentally irrational, there has been plenty of insistence on the intrinsic rationality of what happened in court. Our 1986 book made much of the importance of taking evidence, from documents as well as from witnesses.[84] There is a large historiography on the rational aspects of the ordeal – its use as a system of last resort, as a reflection of community judgment and as, simply, a strategy used or avoided by knowing parties in order to gain an advantage.[85] In northern Iberia there was certainly plenty of ritual in records of the ordeal, an element of ritual about the performance of the oath, as well as the ritual words uttered elsewhere in judicial proceedings – in ritual words of confession and ritual words of agreements.[86] To that extent, practice might

81 Cf. Brown and Górecki, 'What conflict means', p. 7. See Wormald, 'Giving God and king their due', pp. 549–50, for an extreme statement of the processual position.

82 See above, pp. 26–7.

83 Chris Wickham, *Courts and Conflict in Twelfth-century Tuscany* (Oxford, 2003), pp. 303–12; Caroline Humfress, 'Law and custom under Rome', in Rio (ed.), *Law, Custom, and Justice*, pp. 23–47; Innes, 'Charlemagne, justice and written law', especially p. 179, on the 'interpenetration between local "customary" practice and universalising written norms'.

84 Davies and Fouracre (eds), *Settlement of Disputes*, *passim*.

85 Peter Brown, 'Society and the supernatural: A medieval change', *Daedalus*, 104/2 (1975), pp. 133–51; Robert Bartlett, *Trial by Fire and Water: The Medieval Judicial Ordeal* (Oxford, 1986); Dominique Barthélemy, 'Présence de l'aveu dans le déroulement des ordalies (IXe–XIIIe siècle)', in *L'Aveu, Antiquité et Moyen Âge* (Rome, 1986), pp. 191–214; Barthélemy, 'Les ordalies de l'an mil', p. 92 ('Nous pouvons encore les trouver cruelles, mais non pas irrationnelles'); Stephen D. White, 'Proposing the ordeal and avoiding it: Strategy and power in western French litigation, 1050–1110', in Thomas N. Bisson (ed.), *Cultures of Power: Lordship, Status, and Process in Twelfth-century Europe* (Philadelphia, PA, 1995), pp. 89–123.

86 See above, pp. 124–39. Cf. the elaborate rituals recorded in the liturgy, above, pp. 118–19.

be regarded as 'irrational'. However, quite apart from the fact that taking an oath remains an important component of modern court procedures and that it is difficult to conceive of social life without rituals, at any period, these early medieval procedures had more to do with expressions of commitment, with following the correct form and with social pressure than with a direct appeal to irrational or supernatural forces. And although there have been recent warnings about overemphasizing the place of ritual in medieval texts,[87] ritualized words and actions had a practical social function.[88] Rational and irrational no longer seem to be useful categories of classification.[89] In this, Iberian practice was no more nor less rational than that of anywhere else in western Europe, and the classification is no more useful.

Recent writers have also stressed the performance element of court procedure and of tracing boundaries; 'seeing and hearing' could be as important as – or rather, more important than – reading the record.[90] The record could be ancillary to the actions performed, a mere reflection of the performance, where it was the performance that mattered. But documents could in themselves also be part of the story: provision of credible written evidence could be part of the performance – documents were produced, read, studied, pronounced decisive; or they could be declared false, an attempt to mislead; they might therefore – sometimes ritually – be destroyed (by *transpunctio* (piercing) in Italy, or by burning elsewhere).[91] Adding marks to a document could in some circumstances be part of performance too, whether incorporated into the formal act of transfer or separated into a subsequent confirmation.[92] In northern Iberia, the ordeal, especially, is explicitly recorded as performance. In the case of ACO B.1.11, concerning the monastery of Gordón, of 33 witnesses brought by the abbot, three took the initial oath, with at least 11 further (named) witnesses of that oath; then an innocent went to the ordeal, with three further, special, witnesses of this event; another six (four named, together with one party's advocate and one of the ordeal special witnesses) then confirmed the innocent's entry to

87 Philippe Buc, *The Dangers of Ritual: Between Early Medieval Texts and Social Scientific Theory* (Princeton, NJ, 2001), p. 3 and *passim*. Against this, see Charles Insley, 'Rhetoric and ritual in late Anglo-Saxon charters', in Mostert and Barnwell (eds), *Medieval Legal Process*, pp. 109–21, at pp. 110–12, and others cited there.

88 Cf. Jacob, 'Conclusions. Logiques et langages', p. 157.

89 Cf. the comments of Lemesle, *Conflits et justice*, pp. 152–3, and Jacob, 'Conclusions. Logiques et langages', p. 161.

90 See Patrick J. Geary, 'Land, language and memory in Europe 700–1100', *Transactions of the Royal Historical Society*, 6th ser., 9 (1999), pp. 169–84, and Horst Wenzel, *Hören und Sehen, Schrift und Bild: Kultur und Gedächtnis im Mittelalter* (Munich, 1995). See also Mostert and Barnwell (eds), *Medieval Legal Process*; Daniel Lord Smail, *The Consumption of Justice: Emotions, Publicity, and Legal Culture in Marseille, 1264–1423* (Ithaca, NY, 2003).

91 Davies and Fouracre (eds), *Settlement of Disputes*, pp. 57–9 (Nelson), pp. 74–6 (Davies), pp. 114–18 (Wickham); Brown and Górecki, 'Where conflict leads', p. 281.

92 Cf. the comments of Georges Declercq, 'Between legal action and performance: The *firmatio* of charters in the early middle ages', in Mostert and Barnwell (eds), *Medieval Legal Process*, pp. 55–73; and see above, pp. 77, 79–82.

the ordeal; and then another eight (five named, together with the abbot of the disputed monastery and the two judges of the case) witnessed the clean hand three days later.[93] With four differentiated sets of witnesses, we are given to understand that this was a performance, whether it actually happened or not. Walking the bounds and finding the all-important markers look like performances too.[94] Transferring property after the resolution of a case must also have been performance.[95] A good case has been made for much the same in courts elsewhere in Europe.[96] This does not seem to have been intrinsically different in northern Iberia, where seeing and hearing is part of the standard ritual of the oath: after invoking the deity and saints, 'we swear that we have seen with our eyes and heard with our ears and we were present when'.[97]

Another prominent theme of the literature is that of compromise and negotiation. Our 1986 book tended to stress the availability of compromise and the fact, in practice, of lots of negotiation.[98] Settlement mechanisms were available, and used. Since then, the discourse has tended to modify the view of substantial compromise.[99] Successful negotiation could depend on coercion, and records of 'peace made' are seen to signal the defeat of one party, just as recorded 'agreements' are seen to mask the victory of one party.[100] Indeed, some scholars prefer the view that nothing was ever settled – round after round of disputing, any successful outcome simply the starting point for yet another contest.[101] There is some point in this, and the usefulness of the analysis has been well demonstrated in some particular cases – but it certainly did not apply to all areas and all disputes.

Given the nature of the surviving written evidence, what we have most often and in the greatest detail in northern Iberian texts is the perspective of the victor. The prevailing mood of the discourse is confrontational and adversarial, and the texts, especially the Accounts, emphasize the victory of one party. To take all this at face value would imply that there was very little compromise or

93 OvC26 (953). See above, pp. 3, 63, for the witness lists added subsequently.

94 See above, pp. 221–5; and see Geary, 'Land, language and memory', pp. 180–83.

95 See above, pp. 136, 166.

96 Geary, 'Land, language and memory', especially pp. 175, 183; Marco Mostert, 'Introduction', in Mostert and Barnwell (eds), *Medieval Legal Process*, pp. 1–10, at p. 5.

97 'iuramus quia occulis uidimus et aures audiuimus et de presente fuimus . . . quando'; see above, pp. 124–5, and n. 122 below.

98 Davies and Fouracre (eds), *Settlement of Disputes*. Cf. Bourin, 'Les *boni homines*', pp. 64–5, and Régine Le Jan, 'Les transactions et compromis judiciaires autour de l'an mil', in Castan et al. (eds), *La justice en l'an mil*, pp. 67–79.

99 Wormald, 'Giving God and king their due', p. 575, notes that only 40 of 97 'civil' suits in Anglo-Saxon England ended in compromise.

100 Brown and Górecki, 'Where conflict leads', pp. 283–5; but see Wickham, 'Conclusion: Dispute processes and social structures', in Davies and Fouracre (eds), *Settlement of Disputes*, pp. 235–7.

101 William I. Miller, 'Gift, sale, payment, raid: Case studies in the negotiation and classification of exchange in medieval Iceland', *Speculum*, 61 (1986), pp. 18–50; Barbara H. Rosenwein, *To be the Neighbor of Saint Peter: The Social Meaning of Cluny's Property* (Ithaca, NY, 1989), especially pp. 109–43, 202–7.

negotiation. But deals were certainly done: contested properties were swapped for others, just as Lovesindo got another farm (and a payment) when he refused to take the oath to hand over Villa Sotello to the monastery of Guimarães, despite the judges' declaration for Guimarães; and the former king's son Fruela got a large payment in silver and two valuable horses in return for handing over a disputed property to the monastery of Samos.[102] Even in criminal cases, penalties seem to have been regularly reduced in response to petitions. Indeed, in formal court cases, so common is the intervention of *boni homines* to moderate the penalty in the late tenth century that this is almost (or indeed is) a topos; however, this was about reducing penalties, not reaching compromise – someone had usually won.[103] Negotiating for this particular purpose was nevertheless common, and seems to have been expected. It would, however, be ridiculous to suggest that everything was negotiated, and I cannot see anything to suggest that it was; some individuals, and families, clearly lost. One or two expressed defiance, like Lovesindo and like the rebel Gonzalo Menéndez, who refused to give up Vermudo II's servants who had run away to join him.[104] There is no basis for estimating the proportion of negotiation, nor indeed for knowing whether it was the prevailing approach. Given the trend towards acquisition by ecclesiastical bodies, it seems unlikely. So, of course, this is similar to what happened elsewhere in Europe – compromise was a fact – but this does not have to mean that it was dominant.[105]

We see more of the final settlement of cases in northern Iberia and less of cases which go on, cropping up in different generations, although competition for control of the Pardomino hills might be regarded as a continuing case, and control of the church of Santa María of Bonimento (in Présaras) was certainly contested by Count Gutier, and again by his son.[106] The several charters that bear on the lands of the monastery of Pardomino include two Accounts, of which the first is intended as a final settlement (in 944) and the second, of 997, is particular to a very small part of those lands; other Pardomino charters record gifts and an Agreement.[107] There are plenty of examples of the shift of property from one party to another, at all social levels; this is characteristic of the successes of many monastic houses and some bishoprics, as also of some aristocrats, who acquired land from peasant offenders. A few disputes did surface repeatedly, but a shift of property towards the more powerful appears to have been the dominant trend, rather than any ongoing process of circulation.

The detailed records of court cases of Accounts were constructed in order to achieve high-level confirmation of a real or desired outcome.[108] These were

102 PMH DC 183 (999); Sam44 (975).
103 See above, pp. 171–2.
104 SantA57 (993).
105 Cf. Brown and Górecki, 'Where conflict leads', p. 284.
106 See above, p. 218; Sob130 (992).
107 See above, pp. 133–4. Li184, Liii577; Lii290 (955).
108 See above, pp. 39, 148.

tools employed in the high-level politics of property acquisition and control, and they could be used against contesting aristocrats or peasants. They were clearly intended to be the final word, the endpoint in what might have been generations of conflict, although, as just indicated, it is unusual to find repeated cases about the same property.[109] So, in the case of disputed water courses with the monastery of Valdevimbre, the row clearly flared up on several occasions; but we have one final Account (which in fact gave victory to local peasants, but nevertheless secured an advantage for the monastery).[110] The several different Accounts of conflict over the boundaries of properties neighbouring on Pazos, near Verín in southern Galicia, deal with several different properties, and the ultimate objective was to secure further property for the monastery of Celanova.[111] Most of the properties which are the subject of Accounts feature only once in these kinds of text. For the most part they are final, and designed to be final.

The technical issue of the procedure of making a judgment in court has become associated in the historiography with the wider issue of privatization of the public in the central middle ages (or, in White's version, 'personal' and 'moral' versus 'legal' or 'public').[112] Whether or not judgment was collective is not simply a matter of who was involved, for collective judgment has in itself been seen as critical to political change – indeed, so critical that it has been seen to differentiate the early from the central middle ages. To Susan Reynolds, it was central to process in both;[113] to others, particularly the French school, it was characteristically Carolingian, overtaken as private interests came to replace public responsibility in the tenth and eleventh centuries.[114] Chris Wickham's

109 The Castañeda fisheries case seems to have recurred; Cast1 (927) and Cast3 (952).

110 Li128 (938) and Li34 (915) before it; cf. the related Li144 (941).

111 Cel93 (950), Cel94 (987), Cel95 (950, 951); see above, pp. 221–2.

112 White, 'From peace to power', p. 207. See above, pp. 239–40.

113 Reynolds, *Kingdoms and Communities*, pp. 23–34; Susan Reynolds, 'Rationality and collective judgement in the law of western Europe before the twelfth century', *Quaestiones Medii Aevi Novae*, 5 (2000), pp. 3–19.

114 Marc Bloch, *Feudal Society*, trans. Lucy Manyon (London, 1961 [first published 1939–40]), pp. 359–74; Georges Duby, 'Recherches sur l'évolution des institutions judiciaires pendant le Xe et le XIe siècle dans le sud de la Bourgogne', *Le moyen âge*, 52 (1946), pp. 149–94, and Georges Duby, 'Recherches sur l'évolution des institutions judiciaires pendant le Xe et le XIe siècle dans le sud de la Bourgogne', *Le moyen âge*, 53 (1947), pp. 15–38, with much subsequent comment; for a survey of the latter, see White, 'Tenth-century courts at Mâcon'. See also Thomas N. Bisson, 'The "feudal revolution"', *Past and Present*, 142 (1994), pp. 6–42; Dominique Barthélemy and Stephen D. White, 'Debate: The "feudal revolution"', *Past and Present*, 152 (1996), pp. 196–223; Reuter, Wickham and Bisson, 'Debate: The "feudal revolution"'; Reynolds, *Kingdoms and Communities*, pp. 324–5; Susan Reynolds, *Fiefs and Vassals: The Medieval Evidence Reinterpreted* (Oxford, 1994), pp. 25–6, 51–2 and *passim*. For some Spanish discussion of 'privatization', see: Pierre Bonnassie, 'From the Rhône to Galicia: Origins and modalities of the feudal order', in Pierre Bonnassie, *From Slavery to Feudalism in South-western Europe*, trans. Jean Birrell (Cambridge, 1991 [first published 1980]), pp. 104–31; José Ángel García de Cortázar and Esther Peña Bocos, 'Poder condal ¿y "mutación feudal"? en la Castilla del año mil', in María Isabel Loring García (ed.), *Historia social, pensamiento historiográfico y edad media* (Madrid, 1997), pp. 273–98; Josep M. Salrach, 'Les féodalités méridionales: des Alpes à la Galice', in Eric Bournazel and Jean-Pierre Poly (eds), *Les féodalités* (Paris, 1998), pp. 313–88.

refinement of this position – that the size of group involved in judgment changed after the year 1080 in Italy – maintains the idea of significant change, but shifts attention towards the later eleventh century;[115] indeed the weight of recent discussion locates change in the eleventh century, not pre-1000.[116] As discussed above, the public-to-private model does not fit northern Iberia; there were kings, but state interest in the courts was minimal or non-existent, and landowners operated a public system in accordance with standard procedures.[117] In this area, there is no detectable change in the process of making a judgment before the year 1000 and no suggestion that system was in itself unstable. There is therefore no change in collective judgment and no indication that this was symptomatic of deeper political change such as the privatization of judicial process.

★ ★ ★

In all of this, comparison between northern Iberia and other parts of Christian Europe before the year 1000 depends on the attitude of the historian to the dispute settlement process and to records of disputes. It is easier to compare interpretations, and historians, rather than what actually or characteristically happened. One kind of interpretation can make processes look extremely similar; another kind can make them look very different. There are clearly differences between northern Iberia and the rest of the former West Roman Empire in the format of the records and in the availability of a professional notariate. We see more of lay cases in court and more peasant use of the system, as well as greater availability of records of criminal cases in Iberia, all certainly arising because of these differences in recording format and perhaps because of actual differences in practice. There seems to have been a different approach to the transmission of law texts, although citation of written law was more common in Iberia (in this case, including Catalonia) than in other parts. Much, indeed, was clearly very similar about procedure, although there are some differences of emphasis (for example, in the frequency of recourse to written or oral evidence) and some technical differences, like the existence of a dedicated legal officer (also true of Catalonia) We see more landowner courts.[118] Not surprisingly, the role of the state is rather less evident in northern Iberia (unlike Catalonia this time); there is a weaker suggestion of privatization; and the nature of

115 Wickham, 'Public court practice'; Chris Wickham, 'Justice in the kingdom of Italy in the eleventh century', in *La giustizia nell'alto medioevo*, vol. 1, pp. 179–255, at pp. 237–9, especially 249–50; see above, p. 239.

116 Salrach, *Justícia i poder*, pp. 213–34. But Michel Parisse, 'Cadres judiciaires vers l'an mil', in Castan et al. (eds), *La justice en l'an mil*, pp. 15–26, maintains the tenth-century change.

117 See above, pp. 202–3, 245–6. All this, despite the comments of Bonnassie, 'From the Rhône to Galicia'; José María Mínguez, 'Justicia y poder en el marco de la feudalización de la sociedad leonesa', in *La giustizia nell'alto medioevo*, vol. 1, pp. 491–546; Salrach, *Justícia i poder*, pp. 40–43.

118 Salrach, *Justícia i poder*, pp. 26–7, seems to have something similar in mind when he refers to 'private' judges (though his overall interpretation is different).

collective judgment may be rather less rooted in the small-scale locality. The place of Catalonia in this overview is particularly interesting, for it shares many features of Iberian law and procedure, but its judicial practice is framed within a relationship with Frankish kings, at least until the mid-tenth century; it was therefore in many senses pivotal.[119] If we were to look northwards and westwards, however, rather than eastwards to the Carolingian Empire and southern Italy, there is much less evidence of secular court activity in, for example, Wales. In Brittany, there are differences in the use of advocates, in the use of clerics in panels of judges, which is quite common in Iberia, and in the absence of reference to written norms. The prominence of the oath in Spain and Portugal is in contrast with Wales and Brittany, but not so different from what we find in Ireland;[120] here too witnessing (also dependent on seeing and hearing) needed a confirmatory oath;[121] there were also some comparable expert judges and comparable judges' fees.[122] The presence of the state is even less apparent in Ireland than it is in Iberia: while there were secular and ecclesiastical courts across the far west, there is little contemporary evidence to locate these within a ruler-controlled process.

If we compare northern Iberian court procedures with those of other parts of western Europe in the early middle ages, we find many similarities and not so many real differences. If we try to compare interpretations of judicial practice, we have problems, because the available sources are different, because historians take some very different approaches and because we all have our favoured interpretations. It is nevertheless important to try to make the comparison, because the role of courts has been crucial during the last half-century to interpretation of socio-political change in the central middle ages: although questioned by many in recent years, a shift in the practice of court holding and court procedure in the later tenth and eleventh centuries has been seen as symptomatic of a key phase of change, with public assembly and collective

119 Salrach, *Justícia i poder*, pp. 45–63, but 'Carolingian precepts' feature throughout his book, e.g. pp. 34, 79, 84, 103. Cf. Zimmermann, *Écrire et lire*, vol. 2, p. 1,339.

120 See Kelly, *Guide to Early Irish Law*, pp. 198–202; Kathleen Hughes, *Early Christian Ireland: Introduction to the Sources* (London, 1972), pp. 41–61.

121 'It is true that he is no witness who does not see or hear nor appear nor swear to it'; Robin C. Stacey's translation of part of the Old Irish tract on witnessing, 'Córus Fiadnuise', in 'Translation of the Old Irish tract *Berrad Airechta*', in Charles-Edwards, Owen and Walters (eds), *Lawyers and Laymen*, pp. 210–33, at pp. 219–21. See Kelly, *Guide to Early Irish Law*, pp. 202–3, 281.

122 See above, pp. 238–9. See also Wendy Davies, 'Holding court: Judicial presidency in Brittany, Wales and northern Iberia in the early middle ages', in Fiona Edmonds and Paul Russell (eds), *Tome: Studies in Medieval Celtic History and Law in Honour of Thomas Charles-Edwards* (Woodbridge, 2011), pp. 145–54; Wendy Davies, 'Settling disputes in early medieval Spain and Portugal: A contrast with Wales and Brittany?', in Ralph A. Griffiths and Phillipp R. Schofield (eds), *Wales and the Welsh in the Middle Ages: Essays presented to J. Beverley Smith* (Cardiff, 2011), pp. 89–107; Wendy Davies, 'Law and the learned in northern Iberia in the early middle ages: Some comparative thoughts', in Emer Purcell, Paul MacCotter, John Sheehan and Julianne Nyhan (eds), *Clerics, Kings and Vikings: Essays on Medieval Ireland in Honour of Donnchadh Ó Corráin* (Dublin, 2015), pp. 45–54.

judgment disappearing, and a move from a Carolingian world order to one in which 'feudal' lords pursued their entirely personal interests.[123] Although there were clear political changes in northern Iberia in the later tenth century, I do not see change of this type at this time. If procedures in (the non-Carolingian) Iberian courts were similar to those of the Frankish world, this must suggest that the exceptionally articulate Carolingian approach to justice did not entirely determine what happened in court. And if we extend our comparison to place the Iberian system between those of the far west (Ireland, Wales, Brittany) and the Frankish paradigm to the east, then we can see many similarities there too, although origins are likely to have been quite different. This must surely suggest that the state is less significant in determining many elements of judicial procedure in the early middle ages than we are accustomed to suppose.

123 See above, pp. 251–2. Duby, 'Recherches sur l'évolution des institutions judiciaires pendant le Xe et le XIe siècle', certainly located changes in the tenth century. See also Bisson, 'The "feudal revolution"'; Barthélemy and White, 'Debate: The "feudal revolution"'; Reuter, Wickham and Bisson, 'Debate: The "feudal revolution"'; cf. Guy Bois, 'Poder y parentesco en el siglo X en el Mâconnais', in Reyna Pastor (comp.), *Relaciones de poder, de producción y parentesco en la edad media y moderna. Aproximación a su estudio* (Madrid, 1990), pp. 1–12.

10 Where is justice?

> 'That's the figure of justice', said the painter, finally. 'Now I see', said K., 'here's the blindfold and here are the scales. But aren't those wings on her heels, and isn't she moving?' 'Yes', said the painter, 'I had to paint it like that according to the contract. It's actually the figure of justice and the goddess of victory all in one.' 'That is not a good combination', said K. with a smile. 'Justice needs to remain still, otherwise the scales will move about and it won't be possible to make a just verdict.' . . . But around the figure of Justice, apart from some coloration that was barely noticeable, it remained light, and in this brightness the figure seemed to shine forward so that it now looked like neither the God of Justice nor the God of Victory, it seemed now, rather, to be a perfect depiction of the God of the Hunt.[1]

In the surreal, or perhaps all too real, world of Kafka's *Trial*, the image of justice is associated with power, oppression, mystery, confusion. After the encounter with the painter, K. goes on to find a priest who tells him the story of the 'man from the countryside' whose access to the law was barred by the doorkeeper, a doorkeeper of powerful build (one might think of several *saiones* as well as modern-day bouncers[2]); the man from the country was puzzled, because he thought 'the law was supposed to be accessible for anyone at any time', so he sat down to wait until he was allowed to enter; and there he waited till he died.[3] Here there was no fair distribution, with justice impartially balancing the interests of each and every individual, handing out her judgments regardless of the status of the supplicants; rather, Ulpian's famous dictum is interpreted literally, nothing at all being due to the man from the country; the peasant had nothing, and so he had no rights and no deserts.[4]

1 Franz Kafka, *The Trial*, translated by David Wyllie, Project Gutenberg: http://www.gutenberg.org/ebooks/7849, ch. 7.

2 See above, p. 168, for *saiones* who were also *ostiarii*.

3 Kafka, *The Trial*, ch 9.

4 *Iustitia est constans et perpetua uoluntas ius suum cuique tribuendi* (in S.P. Scott's translation, 'Justice is the constant and perpetual desire to give to each one that to which he is entitled'). Cf. Fredric L. Cheyette's agenda-setting paper, '*Suum cuique tribuere*', *French Historical Studies*, 6 (1976), pp. 287–99; Geoffrey Koziol, *Begging Pardon and Favor: Ritual and Political Order in Early Medieval France* (Ithaca, NY, 1992), especially pp. 214–18.

It is not too difficult to make the same case for ninth- and tenth-century northern Iberia. Peasants were punished by the courts, losing property and property rights to court holders and to successful adversaries, such as the many monasteries which benefited from judicial process. Cases involving peasants leave little trace of evidence carefully taken or of friends offering support; penalties for their offences seem to have been assessed in advance of any court hearing; witnesses could be 'too frightened' to take the oath; and not only did several people run away rather than appear in court, it was clearly expected that they would do so, since guarantees for their appearance could be required.[5] Subject to the whim of the landowners who held courts, there was little customary practice within which to channel resistance. So also Catalonia, for which a similar case has been proposed.[6]

And yet. Although there are bound to have been cases of oppression, and although it is quite clear that property shifted from peasants to aristocrats, peasants did use the courts. There was the woman who went to court to complain that her grandfather had sexually assaulted her; there was a man called Guirigo who took another called Osevio to court because, in a previous case, Osevio had made a false accusation which led to Guirigo wrongly paying a fine; there was the woman, Andilo, who stole horses from Munio Ovécoz and had to compensate him with some of her property; and there are many cases of 'action' in court, with consequent penalties, between one lay person and another – like the case of Gemondo, who laid siege to Gonzalo and his wife and family at home.[7] There are also the fleeting references to property which had been acquired by making a claim in court; another Munio and his wife Ermesinda had successfully made such a claim some time before they sold the parcel they had been awarded, on the River Esla, in 952.[8] This was not a simple world of oppression and submission. Relationships were more complicated, and peasants, like aristocrats, clearly used the long-established judicial system to gain advantages in local conflicts.

We can sometimes glimpse a principle of equitable distribution in the search for a 'just price' – in fact, a concept that is more frequently invoked than any abstract notion of justice.[9] Remember the *boni homines* whose assistance was sought to find the price that was fair and to make a fair share of a bequest. Remember too that *boni homines*, and others who did not have this label, intervened in court to reduce penalties and negotiate compromises. This principle of fairness was sometimes articulated in the course of describing the business of an ordinary person and, quite apart from words, there were clearly practices that were intended to alleviate the severity of the law: some people clearly knew

5 See above, pp. 179, 198, 218.

6 See Josep M. Salrach, *Justícia i poder a Catalunya abans de l'any mil* (Vic, 2013), pp. 98–103.

7 Cel368 (p. 530), Cel180 (p. 252), Cel368 (p. 524), Cel197 (p. 276). The properties handed over as penalties in these cases are of very small scale. All are from the very late tenth century.

8 Li243; *uindicauimus per iudicio* – see above, pp. 119–20.

9 See above, pp. 172–3; for 'justice', see below, p. 260.

that the law required adultery to be punished with slavery, but the rule was not in practice applied.[10]

Although these principles can be found from Portugal to Aragón and Santiago to Sahagún, and although there are standard elements of judicial practice and standard elements of recording this are widespread, that does not mean that everywhere was the same. Of course, we are not helped by the uneven survival of records; the fact that there are relatively few records from Navarre and Aragón means that we cannot make a realistic comparison of those regions; and although the surviving records from the Liébana and from Oviedo are extremely important, there are not enough of them to develop a balanced view of practice north of the Cantabrian Mountains. However, for those regions as well as others, there is enough to see that the charter writing habit was of very early – in effect, of Late Antique – origin; so early that pockets of devolved local practice are visible in the ninth and early tenth centuries; as also that there was a broad difference in formulaic habits between the east and west of northern Iberia (see Figure 10.1).[11] There are also differences in the incidence of different types of record, and this does not seem to have been a simple consequence of different scribal habits: the fact that there are disproportionately many Debt records from Galicia reflects the proactive character of some powerful monasteries there; the fact that there are no Fine records from Asturias, Cantabria, Castile and Navarre may be a consequence of different archival practice, but may also suggest that penalties were not so often paid in land in those areas; the fact that there are far more Confiscations from the *meseta* and Galicia almost certainly reflects the greater royal presence in those regions.[12]

Kings do not feature in Accounts from Portugal and Castile; this must mean that kings were not viewed as especially significant players in those regions, and probably reflects their infrequent presence there; just as a king's capacity to act varied from place to place within the single region of the *meseta*, so it varied across the peninsula.[13] Accordingly, we also see more royal judges on the *meseta* than in other parts. In contrast, we have much better evidence of the presence and authority of counts in Castile than elsewhere.[14] The place of Galicia is also interesting: this is an area which kings of León visited and within which they established some powerful aristocratic alliances, but it is also an area which had some distinctive judicial practice.[15] Judging panels were consistently larger, with more members, than panels elsewhere, and the intervention of *boni homines* at

10 Liii561 (994). Interestingly, the alleviation is not here associated with any ruler or other authority, as in so many cultures; see Fernanda Pirie and Judith Scheele, 'Justice, community, and law', in Fernanda Pirie and Judith Scheele (eds), *Legalism: Community and Justice* (Oxford, 2014), pp. 1–24, at p. 4.

11 See above, pp. 99–105.

12 See above, pp. 39–54, for distribution of types of record.

13 See Álvaro Carvajal Castro, 'The monarchy and the elites in early medieval León (ninth–eleventh centuries)', *Journal of Medieval Iberian Studies* (2015): DOI 10.1080/17546559.2015.1065339.

14 See above, p. 24.

15 For Galician politics, see Robert Portass, 'All quiet on the western front: Royal politics in Galicia from *c.* 800 to *c.* 950', *Early Medieval Europe*, 21 (2013), pp. 283–306.

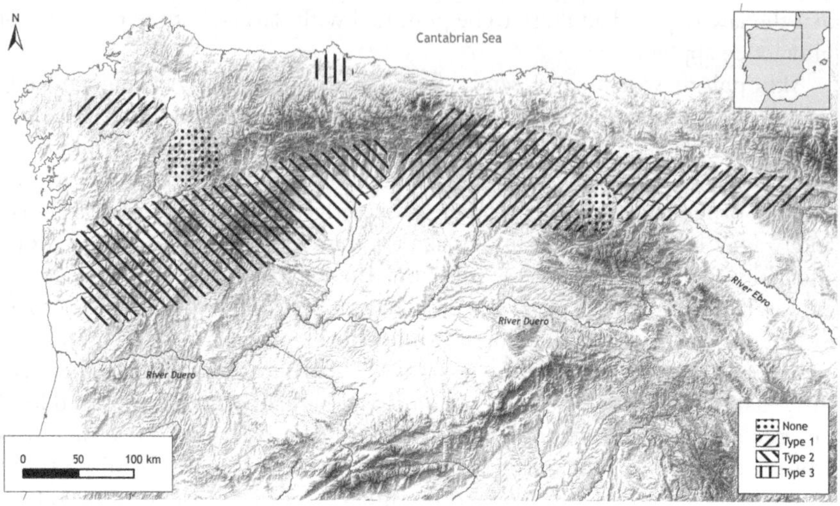

Figure 10.1 Distribution of Types 1–3 of the *cogentis* formula

some stage of a case was more likely to be invoked.[16] Given that there were major differences between regions in climate and physical environment, those differences are to some extent reflected in practice: the judicial practices of Galicia, those of the *meseta* and those of Castile appear to have been distinguishable. This is partly because of subtle differences in recording habits, but partly also because of differences in political structure, and almost certainly differences in social structure too. How far northern Portugal belongs with the Galician orbit is arguable: although there were strong contacts between southern Galicia and northern Portugal through both monastic culture and the spread of aristocratic interests, there are features of Portuguese formulaic writing and also of the Portuguese experience (such as the absence of kings) that distinguish it.

Nor was everywhere the same in the year 1000 as it had been in 800. Some of those formulas of early origin were still used, but clearly not understood, by the ninth and tenth centuries. Many aspects of judicial practice itself appear to have derived from the Visigothic period, given some of the prescriptions of *Forum Iudicum*; but the standard features of records of disputes seem to have a later, post-Visigothic, origin, although earlier than the mid-ninth century.[17] Record-making clearly changed further across the tenth century as the pockets of local practice disappeared, scribal traditions became much more mixed and the influence of large monastic scriptoria extended. Late in the tenth century, the number of references to *boni homines* and the *iudicatum* increased, as also the

16 See above, pp. 205, 171.
17 See above, pp. 144–5.

association of truth, *veritas*, with descriptions of outcomes. These changes seem to reflect changes in attitudes, of which a desire to convey a sense of legitimacy is prominent; but they also reflect changes in practice, with more concern to record the levying of penalties.[18] Quite apart from changes in words and formulas, different types of record predominated at different times. The occurrence of Oaths, Confessions and Agreements in ninth-century contexts harks back to the much earlier judicial practice from which their formats derived; it suggests a long background of use. The fact that the late tenth century produced more Fines and Incidental records, at a time when overall numbers of records declined, reflects the greater activity of court holders and their increasing rate of acquisition of property. Indeed, the late tenth century is precisely the period when one can see kings creating stronger alliances with particular aristocratic families, as one can also see some aristocrats exercising both more extensive and more intensive powers. The later tenth century is the time when a royal power to command begins to be well evidenced and when kings can be seen to delegate – a trend which continued and intensified in the early eleventh century.[19] At the end of the tenth century, we start to see more people take the title of count, and we see them exercising authority – again, a trend which intensified through the eleventh century. As noted above, almost a quarter of all the references to *saiones* in our period fall in the 990s; this is quite disproportionate, for it is a decade in which the number of surviving records declines sharply. Notice of *saiones*, and of their increasingly proactive character, also increased, rapidly, in the eleventh century.

It is a commonplace to note monastic drafting of judicial records. These texts provide plenty of examples of deliberate drafting to achieve monastic ends, such as that of the many disputed boundary cases.[20] These records were tools used in the strategies of high-level politics, emphasizing victory and seeking confirmation from more and more kings. The Incidental records that briefly mention a case here, a penalty there shed light on events, on things that actually happened, of which we would otherwise know nothing. Without the Incidental records, we would not know that a priest pursued property cases in both a count's and a bishop's court; that a man who raped a relation was pursued through the courts; that a peasant who hid a thief was culpable.[21] Nor would we have the priceless information that if families did not receive the assessed compensation for the killing of one of their members, they were entitled to pursue the perpetrator to death, and the equally priceless information that ordinary people could seize a suspected thief and take him to a court of their choice.[22] Taking note of this incidental information allows us to adjust the

18 See above, pp. 123–4.

19 See above, p. 25.

20 See above, pp. 221–6.

21 LaC50 (947), OD33 (992), T41 (932) – the first two on single sheets. Cf. also the cases of lay use of courts to pursue their interests in n. 7 above.

22 PMH DC 53 (943), Lii378 (964) – both on single sheets.

picture traditionally derived from the retrospective constructions of narrative Accounts, adjusting the balance between royal courts and landowners' courts, the balance between use of courts by monasteries and by lay persons, and the volume of criminal cases. Some of what we see is what certain monastic bodies wanted us to see, deftly controlling the record; but some of it, undeveloped, drops – as it were, accidentally – into the record. Contrast too the tortuous and very repetitive narrative of what happened in the Gordón case of ACO B.1.11 with the snappy precision of the closer-to-court documents appended to it; the latter make it clear that the formal concession of the property was to happen at Erias, a place that does not even feature in the rambling account.[23]

There are, of course, many things that we do not and cannot know, but the framing of the records determines the kinds of window available as we look at procedures and process after a thousand years. While the notion of judgment seems to pervade ecclesiastical written culture, justice, *iustitia*, is rarely evoked in these texts about court practice, and when it does feature, it is largely in the monastic framing of the Account. 'Injustice' was intrusion onto monastic land;[24] and 'justice' is the word occasionally chosen to summarize the final resolution of a case: all the council acknowledged or saw justice, what was just.[25] 'Truth' is in fact more common in these contexts, but the import of both is the same: evoking 'truth' and 'justice' means that the right answer was found, just as 'everyone said that you have the truth' (*cuncti dixerunt quia uestra est ueritas*) in the reconstructed confession of Cel94.[26] It is another way of saying 'you have won'; in both cases, the word might as well have been 'victory' as 'justice' or 'truth'.

But the practical experience was different. Lay people, including peasants, could and did pursue their interests through judicial court process. Not only was going to court part of the customary culture, people went to and through the formal court to get the compensations that had already been assessed. This can only be because they wanted what they believed was their due. If they were attacked, assaulted, wounded, it was surely a sense of personal outrage, some innate sense of justice, that drove them. Justice, then, did not lie in any set of external procedures; rather in an interior sense of what was right.

23 See above, pp. 1–4, 60–3, 146–7.

24 Cel93 (950): 'homines ipsi episcopo similem iniustitiam faciebant'.

25 See C22 (932), Li144 (941), Li256 (952) – *agnoscentes ueritatem et iustitiam.*

26 See above, pp. 46–7, 123.

Bibliography and abbreviations

Charters are cited by number of the edition in which they are published, and in the case of archives by number within a *carpeta* (folder).

ACL	Archivo de la catedral de León
ACLu	Archivo de la catedral de Lugo
ACO	Archivo de la catedral de Oviedo
AHDE	Anuario de Historia del Derecho Español
AHDL	Archivo histórico diocesano de León
AHDS	Archivo histórico diocesano de Santiago de Compostela
AHN	Archivo histórico nacional
AHUS	Archivo histórico universitario de Santiago de Compostela
ARG	Archivo del reino de Galicia
ASV	Archivo del monasterio de San Vicente

Editions of Charters

A *Cartulario de Albelda*, ed. Antonio Ubieto Arteta, València, 1960.

Ar *Cartulario de San Pedro de Arlanza, antiguo monasterio benedictino*, ed. Luciano Serrano, Madrid, 1925.

Ast *Colección documental de la catedral de Astorga (646–1126)*, I, ed. Gregoria Cavero Domínguez and Encarnación Martín López, León, 1999.

BG 'Becerro Galicano de San Millán de la Cogolla', online edition (2013): http://www.ehu.es/galicano/?l=es. See also SM.

C *Colección documental del monasterio de San Pedro de Cardeña*, ed. Gonzalo Martínez Díez, Burgos, 1998.

Cañ Ventura Cañizares del Rey, *Colección diplomática (569–1463)*, ed. Manuel Rodríguez Sánchez and Óscar González Murado, Lugo, 2012.

Cast *El Tumbo del monasterio de San Martín de Castañeda*, ed. Ángel Rodríguez González, León, 1973.

Cel *O Tombo de Celanova: estudio introductorio, edición e índices (ss. IX–XII)*, ed. José Miguel Andrade Cernadas with Marta Díaz Tie and Francisco J. Pérez Rodríguez, 2 vols, Santiago de Compostela, 1995.

Dueñas *El monasterio de San Isidro de Dueñas en la edad media. Un priorato cluniacense hispano (911–1478). Estudio y colección documental*, ed. Carlos M. Reglero de la Fuente, León, 2005.

E *Colección documental del monasterio de San Pedro de Eslonza (912–1300)*, vol. 1, ed. José Manuel Ruiz Asencio and Irene Ruiz Albi, León, 2007.

Flor Antonio Cristino Floriano Cumbreño, *Diplomática española del periodo astur: estudio de las fuentes documentales del reino de Asturias (718–910)*, 2 vols, Oviedo, 1949–51.

Jaca Roger Collins, 'Visigothic law and regional custom in disputes in early medieval Spain', in Wendy Davies and Paul Fouracre (eds), *The Settlement of Disputes in Early Medieval Europe*, Cambridge, 1986, pp. 85–104, 252–6, at pp. 255–6 (English translation at p. 98).

Li, Lii, Liii *Colección documental del archivo de la catedral de León (775–1230)*, vol. 1 (775–952), ed. Emilio Sáez; vol. 2 (953–985), ed. Emilio Sáez and Carlos Sáez; vol. 3 (986–1031), ed. José Manuel Ruiz Asencio, León, 1987, 1990, 1987.

LaC *La Coruña. Fondo Antiguo (788–1065)*, ed. Carlos Sáez and María del Val González de la Peña, 2 vols, Alcalá, 2003–2004.

Leire *Documentación medieval de Leire (siglos IX a XII)*, ed. Ángel J. Martín Duque, Pamplona, 1983.

Lor *Liber testamentorum coenobii Laurbanensis*, 2 vols, León, 2008.

OD *Colección documental del monasterio de Santa María de Otero de las Dueñas (854–1108)*, ed. José Antonio Fernández Flórez and Marta Herrero de la Fuente, vol. 1, León, 1999.

Oña *Colección diplomática de San Salvador de Oña*, ed. Juan del Alamo, vol. 1, Madrid, 1950.

Ov *Colección diplomática del monasterio de San Vicente de Oviedo (años 781–1200)*, ed. Pedro Floriano Llorente, Oviedo, 1968.

OvC *Colección de documentos de la catedral de Oviedo*, ed. Santos García Larragueta, Oviedo, 1962.

PMH DC *Portugaliae Monumenta Historica a saeculo octavo post Christum usque ad quintumdecimum, Diplomata et Chartae*, vol. 1, ed. Alexandre Herculano de Carvalho e Araujo and Joaquim José da Silva Mendes Leal, Lisbon, 1867–73.

S *Colección diplomática del monasterio de Sahagún (857–1230), I (siglos IX y X)*, ed. José María Mínguez Fernández, León, 1976.

Sii *Colección diplomática del monasterio de Sahagún, II (1000–1073)*, ed. Marta Herrero de la Fuente, León, 1988.

Sam *El Tumbo de San Julián de Samos (siglos VIII–XII)*, ed. Manuel Lucas Álvarez, Santiago de Compostela, 1986.

San Pedro *Tumbo Viejo de San Pedro de Montes*, ed. Augusto Quintana Prieto, León, 1971.

SantA *La documentación del Tumbo A de la catedral de Santiago de Compostela: estudio y edición*, ed. Manuel Lucas Álvarez, León, 1997.

SJP *Cartulario de San Juan de la Peña*, ed. Antonio Ubieto Arteta, 2 vols, València, 1962–63.

SM *Cartulario de San Millán de la Cogolla (759–1076)*, ed. Antonio Ubieto Arteta, València, 1976; see also BG and Fernando García Andreva, *El Becerro Galicano de San Millán de la Cogolla. Edición y estudio*, Logroño, 2010.

SMdelP 'Cartulario de la iglesia de Santa María del Puerto (Santoña)', ed. Manuel Serrano y Sanz, *Boletín de la Real Academia Historia*, 73 (1928), pp. 420–42 (Edición digital: Biblioteca Virtual Miguel de Cervantes, Alicante, 2009).

Sob *Tumbos del monasterio de Sobrado de los Monjes,* ed. Pilar Loscertales de García de Valdeavellano, 2 vols, Madrid, 1976.

T *Cartulario de Santo Toribio de Liébana,* ed. Luis Sánchez Belda, Madrid, 1948.

TV 'Tumbo Viejo de Lugo (transcripción completa)', ed. José Luis López Sangil and Manuel Vidán Torreira, *Estudios Mindonienses,* 27 (2011), pp. 11–373.

V *Los becerros gótico y galicano de Valpuesta,* ed. José Manuel Ruiz Asencio, Irene Ruiz Albi, Mauricio Herrero Jiménez, 2 vols, Burgos, 2010.

Other Primary Sources

Antiphonary of León (ACL MS 8): *Antifonario visigótico mozarabe de la catedral de León,* ed. Louis Brou and José Vives, Barcelona and Madrid, 1959.

Alturo, Jesús, Joan Bellès, Josep M. Font i Rius, Yolanda García and Anscari M. Mundó, *Liber iudicum popularis. Ordenat pel jutge Bonsom de Barcelona,* Barcelona, 2003.

Audacht Morainn, ed. Fergus Kelly, Dublin, 1976.

Authorised version of the Bible.

Capitularia Regum Francorum, vol. 1, ed. Alfred Boretius, MGH Legum Sectio II, Hanover, 1883.

Capitularia Regum Francorum, vol. 2, ed. Alfred Boretius and Victor Krause, MGH Legum Sectio II, Hanover, 1897.

Cartulaire de l'Abbaye de Redon en Bretagne, ed. Aurélien de Courson, Paris, 1863.

Cassiodori Senatoris Variae, ed. Theodor Mommsen, Ludwig Traube, Berlin, 1894.

Concilios visigóticos e hispano-romanos, ed. José Vives, with Tomás Marín Martínez and Gonzalo Martínez Díez, Barcelona, 1963.

Corpus Iuris Hibernici, ad fidem codicum manuscriptorum recognovit, ed. Daniel A. Binchy, 6 vols, Dublin, 1978.

Crónicas Asturianas, ed. and trans. Juan Gil Fernández, José L. Moralejo and Juan Ignacio Ruiz de la Peña, Oviedo, 1985.

The Digest of Justinian, ed. Theodor Mommsen and Paul Krueger, with English translation by Alan Watson, 4 vols, Philadelphia, PA, 1985.

Formulae Merowingici et Karolini Aevi, ed. Karl Zeumer, MGH Legum Sectio v, Formulae, Hanover, 1882–86.

'Formulae Wisigothicae', ed. Juan Gil, in Juan Gil (ed.), *Miscellanea Wisigothica,* Seville, 1972, pp. 70–112.

Die Gesetze der Angelsachsen, ed. Felix Liebermann, 3 vols, Halle, 1898–1916.

Jonas d'Orléans, *Le metier de roi (De institutione regia),* ed. and trans. Alain Dubreucq, Paris, 1995.

Leges Visigothorum, ed. Karl Zeumer, MGH Leges nationum Germanicarum, sectio I.1, Hanover, 1902.

Liber fidei sanctae bracarensis ecclesiae, ed. Avelino de Jesus da Costa, 3 vols, Braga, 1965, 1978, 1990.

Liber Ordinum Episcopal (Cod. Silos, Arch Monástico, 4), Studia Silensia, 15, ed. José Janini, Silos, 1991.

Liber Ordinum Sacerdotal (Cod. Silos, Arch. Monástico, 3), Studia Silensia, 7, ed. José Janini, Silos, 1981.

Livro Preto. Cartulário da Sé de Coimbra, ed. Manuel Augusto Rodrigues, Coimbra, 1999.

Martianus Capella, ed. James Willis, Leipzig, 1983.

Martín, José Carlos, 'Los *Annales Castellani Antiquiores* y *Annales Castellani Recentiores*: edición y traducción anotada', *Territorio, Sociedad y Poder,* 4 (2009), pp. 203–26.

Njal's Saga, trans. Magnus Magnusson and Hermann Pálsson, Harmondsworth, 1960.

Pérez de Urbel, Justo, *Sampiro. Su crónica y la monarquía leonesa en el siglo X*, Madrid, 1952.

Rodríguez Fernández, Justiniano, *Los fueros del reino de León*, 2 vols, León, 1981.

Sánchez-Albornoz, Claudio, 'Documentos para el estudio del procedimiento judicial en el reino asturleonés', in *Homenaje a Don Agustín Millares Carlo*, 2 vols, Gran Canaria, 1975, vol. 2, pp. 145–56.

Die Urkunden Pippins, Karlmanns und Karls des Grossen, ed. Engelbert Mühlbacher et al., MGH Diplomata Karolinorum I, Hanover, 1906.

Urkundenbuch der Abtei Sanct Gallen, ed. Hermann Wartmann, 6 vols, Zurich, 1863–1955.

'*La Vita Froilanis episcopi Legionensis* (BHL 3180) (s. X): introducción, edición crítica y particularidades lingüísticas', by José Carlos Martín, in Monique Goullet (ed.), *Parva pro magnis munera. Études de littérature tardo-antique et médiévale offertes à François Dolbeau par ses élèves*, Instrumenta Patristica et Mediaevalia, 51, Turnhout, 2009, pp. 561–84.

Zimmermann, Michel 'Un formulaire du xème siècle conservé à Ripoll', *Faventia*, 4/2 (1982), pp. 25–86.

Secondary Works

Agúndez San Miguel, Leticia, 'Memoria, escritura y control social: la construcción de la memoria histórica en el monasterio de Sahagún (siglos X–XIII)', Universidad de Cantabria, Tesis Doctoral, 2011.

Alfonso, Isabel, 'Litigios por la tierra y "malfetrías" entre la nobleza medieval castellanoleonesa', *Hispania*, 57/3 (1997), pp. 917–55.

———, 'Judicial rhetoric and political legitimation in medieval León-Castile', in Isabel Alfonso, Hugh Kennedy and Julio Escalona (eds), *Building Legitimacy: Political Discourses and Forms of Legitimacy in Medieval Societies*, Leiden, 2004, pp. 51–87.

———, 'Memoria e identidad en las pesquisas judiciales en el área castellano-leonesa medieval', in José Antonio Jara Fuente, Georges Martín and Isabel Alfonso Antón (eds), *Construir la identidad en la edad media. Poder y memoria en la Castilla de los siglos VII a XV*, Cuenca, 2010, pp. 249–79.

———, 'El formato de la información judicial en la alta edad media peninsular', in Julio Escalona and Hélène Sirantoine (eds), *Chartes et cartulaires comme instruments de pouvoir. Espagne et Occident chrétien (VIIIe–XIIe siècles)*, Toulouse, 2013, pp. 191–218.

———, in Andrew Reynolds, Jane Carroll, Barbara Yorke (eds), *Power and Place in Later Roman and Early Medieval Europe*, forthcoming.

Alfonso Antón, Isabel, 'Resolución de disputas y prácticas judiciales en el Burgos medieval', in Juan José García González, Francisco Javier Peña Pérez and Luis Martínez García (eds), *Burgos en la plena edad media*, Burgos, 1994, pp. 211–43.

Alturo Perucho, Jesús, Miquel Torras Cortina and Ainoa Castro Correa (eds), *La escritura visigótica en la Península Ibérica: nuevas aportaciones*, Barcelona, 2012.

Álvarez Borge, Ignacio, 'Estructuras de poder en Castilla en la alta edad media: señores, siervos, vasallos', in *Señores, siervos, vasallos en la alta edad media. XXVIII Semana de estudios medievales, Estella, 16 a 20 de julio de 2001*, Pamplona, 2002, pp. 269–308.

Álvarez Palenzuela, Vicente Ángel, 'La nobleza del reino de León en la alta edad media', in *El reino de León en la alta edad media, VII, Estudios*, León, 1995, pp. 149–329.

Amory, Patrick, *People and Identity in Ostrogothic Italy, 489–554*, Cambridge, 1997.

Andrade Cernadas, José Miguel, 'Villas regias y asambleas judiciales entre los siglos X y XI: el caso de Larín', *Revista Signum*, 12 (2011), pp. 18–35.

Andrés Sanz, María Adelaida, Carmen Codoñer, Salvador Iranzo Abellán, José Carlos Martín and David Paniagua, *La Hispania visigótica y mozárabe. Dos épocas en su literatura*, co-ord. Carmen Codoñer, Salamanca, 2010.

Arvizu y Galarraga, Fernando de, *La disposición 'mortis causa' en el derecho español de la alta edad media*, Pamplona, 1977.

Ayala Martínez, Carlos de, *Sacerdocio y reino en la España altomedieval. Iglesia y poder en el Occidente peninsular, siglos VII–XII*, Madrid, 2008.

Barbero, Abilio, and Marcelo Vigil, *La formación del feudalismo en la Península Ibérica* (Barcelona, 1978).

Barnwell, Paul, 'Action, speech and writing in early Frankish legal proceedings', in Mostert and Barnwell (eds), *Medieval Legal Process*, pp. 11–25.

Barrow, Julia, *The Clergy in the Medieval World: Secular Clerics, Their Families and Careers in North-Western Europe, c.800–c.1200*, Cambridge, 2015.

Barthélemy, Dominique, 'Présence de l'aveu dans le déroulement des ordalies (IXe–XIIIe siècle)', in *L'Aveu, Antiquité et Moyen Âge*, Collection de l'école française de Rome, 88, Rome, 1986, pp. 191–214.

———, 'Les ordalies de l'an mil', in Castan et al. (eds), *La justice en l'an mil*, pp. 81–92.

———, and Stephen D. White, 'Debate: The "feudal revolution"', *Past and Present*, 152 (1996), pp. 196–223.

Bartlett, Robert, *Trial by Fire and Water: The Medieval Judicial Ordeal*, Oxford, 1986.

Barton, Simon, and Robert Portass (eds), *Beyond the Reconquista: Essays on the Politics, Society and Culture of Medieval Iberia, 800–1200*, Liverpool, forthcoming.

Bedos-Rezak, Brigitte, 'Towards an archaeology of the medieval charter: Textual production and reproduction in northern French *chartriers*', in Adam J. Kosto and Anders Winroth (eds), *Charters, Cartularies, and Archives: the Preservation and Transmission of Documents in the Medieval West*, Papers in Mediaeval Studies, 17, Toronto, 2002, pp. 43–60.

———, *When Ego was Imago: Signs of Identity in the Middle Ages*, Leiden, 2011.

Binchy, Daniel A., 'Distraint in Irish law', *Celtica*, 10 (1973), pp. 22–71.

Bishko, Charles J., 'Salvus of Albelda and frontier monasticism in tenth-century Navarre', *Speculum*, 23 (1948), pp. 559–90.

Bisson, Thomas N., 'The "feudal revolution"', *Past and Present*, 142 (1994), pp. 6–42.

Bloch, Marc, *Feudal Society*, trans. Lucy Manyon, London, 1961 [first published 1939–40].

Bois, Guy, 'Poder y parentesco en el siglo X en el Mâconnais', in Reyna Pastor (comp.), *Relaciones de poder, de producción y parentesco en la edad media y moderna. Aproximación a su estudio*, Madrid, 1990, pp. 1–12.

———, *The Transformation of the Year One Thousand: The Village of Lournand from Antiquity to Feudalism*, trans. Jean Birrell, Manchester, 1992 [first published 1989].

Bonnassie, Pierre, *La Catalogne du milieu du Xe à la fin du XIe siècle: croissance et mutations d'une société*, 2 vols, Toulouse, 1975–76.

———, *La Catalogne au tournant de l'an mil. Croissance et mutations d'une société*, Paris, 1990.

———, 'From the Rhône to Galicia: Origins and modalities of the feudal order', in Pierre Bonnassie, *From Slavery to Feudalism in South-western Europe*, trans Jean Birrell, Cambridge, 1991, pp. 104–31 [first published 1980].

Bougard, François, *La justice dans le royaume d'Italie de la fin du VIIIe siècle au début du XIe siècle*, Bibliothèque des écoles françaises d'Athènes et de Rome, 291, Rome, 1995.

———, 'Rationalité et irrationalité des procédures autour de l'an mil: le duel judiciaire en Italie', in Castan et al. (eds), *La justice en l'an mil*, pp. 93–122.

Bourin, Monique, 'Les *boni homines* de l'an mil', in Castan et al. (eds), *La justice en l'an mil*, pp. 53–65.

Bowman, Jeffrey A., *Shifting Landmarks: Property, Proof, and Dispute in Catalonia around the Year 1000*, Ithaca, NY, 2004.

Boye, Fritz, 'Über die Poenformeln in den Urkunden des früheren Mittelalters', *Archiv für Urkundenforschung*, 6 (1918), pp. 77–148.

Bresslau, Harry, *Handbuch der Urkundenlehre für Deutschland und Italien*, 2nd edn, 2 vols, Leipzig, 1912–31.

Brown, Peter, 'Society and the supernatural: A medieval change', *Daedalus*, 104/2 (1975), pp. 133–51.

Brown, Warren C., *Unjust Seizure: Conflict, Interest, and Authority in an Early Medieval Society*, Ithaca, NY, 2001.

———, *Violence in Medieval Europe*, Harlow, 2011.

———, and Piotr Górecki, 'What conflict means: The making of medieval conflict studies in the United States, 1970–2000', in Warren C. Brown and Piotr Górecki (eds), *Conflict in Medieval Europe: Changing Perspectives on Society and Culture*, Aldershot, 2003, pp. 1–35.

———, and Piotr Górecki, 'Where conflict leads: On the present and future of medieval conflict studies in the United States', in Brown and Górecki (eds), *Conflict in Medieval Europe*, pp. 265–85.

———, Marios Costambeys, Matthew Innes and Adam J. Kosto (eds), *Documentary Culture and the Laity in the Early Middle Ages*, Cambridge, 2013.

Brunner, Heinrich, *Deutsche Rechtsgeschichte*, 1st edn, 2 vols, Leipzig, 1887–92.

Buc, Philippe, *The Dangers of Ritual: Between Early Medieval Texts and Social Scientific Theory*, Princeton, NJ, 2001.

Cabezas Fontanilla, Susana, 'De la *invocatio* en los documentos altomedievales (718–910)', in *VIII Jornadas cientificas sobre documentación de la Hispania altomedieval (siglo VI–X)*, Madrid, 2009, pp. 43–78.

Calleja Puerta, Miguel, 'Cartularios y construcción de la memoria monástica en los reinos de León y Castilla durante el siglo XII', in Véronique Lamazou-Duplan and Eloísa Ramírez Vaquero (eds), *Les cartulaires médiévaux. Écrire et conserver la mémoire du pouvoir, le pouvoir de la mémoire*, Pau, 2013, pp. 187–97.

———, 'Ecos de las *Fórmulas visigóticas* en la documentación altomedieval astur-leonesa', in *Les formulaires. Compilation et circulation des modèles d'actes dans l'Europe médiévale et moderne*, Paris, forthcoming.

Canellas López, Ángel, *Diplomática hispano-visigoda*, Zaragoza, 1979.

Carbajo Serrano, María José, *El monasterio de los santos Cosme y Damián de Abellar*, León, 1988.

Carlé, María del Carmen, '*Boni homines* y hombres buenos', *Cuadernos de Historia de España*, 39/40 (1964), pp. 133–68.

Carvajal Castro, Álvaro, 'La construcción de la monarquía asturleonesa en la meseta del Duero. Estudio de los procesos de integración territorial (s. IX–XI)', Universidad de Salamanca, Tesis Doctoral, 2013.

———, 'Sociedad y territorio en el norte de León: Valdoré, los Flaínez y el entorno del Alto Esla (siglos IX–XI)', *Studia Histórica. Historia Medieval*, 31 (2013), pp. 105–31.

———, 'The monarchy and the elites in early medieval León (ninth–eleventh centuries)', *Journal of Medieval Iberian Studies* (2015): DOI 10.1080/17546559.2015.1065339.

Castan, Nicole, et al. (eds), *La justice en l'an mil*, Collection histoire de la justice, 15, Paris, 2003.

Castro, Ainoa, *Colección diplomática altomedieval de Galicia I: Documentación editada en escritura visigótica (662–1234)*, A Coruña, 2011.

Chalmeta Gendrón, Pedro, *Invasión e islamización: la sumisión de Hispania y la formación de al-Andalus*, Colección al-Andalus, 10, Madrid, 1994.

Charles-Edwards, Thomas M., 'Early Irish law', in Dáibhí Ó Cróinín (ed.), *A New History of Ireland, Volume I: Prehistoric and Early Ireland*, Oxford, 2005, pp. 331–70.

———, Morfydd E. Owen and Dafydd B. Walters (eds), *Lawyers and Laymen: Studies in the History of Law Presented to Professor Dafydd Jenkins on His Seventy-fifth Birthday, Gŵyl Ddewi 1986*, Cardiff, 1986.

Cheyette, Fredric L., '*Suum cuique tribuere*', *French Historical Studies*, 6 (1970), pp. 287–99.

Collins, Roger, '"Sicut lex Gothorum continet": Law and charters in ninth- and tenth-century León and Catalonia', *English Historical Review*, 100 (1985), pp. 489–512.

———, 'Visigothic law and regional custom in disputes in early medieval Spain', in Davies and Fouracre (eds), *The Settlement of Disputes in Early Medieval Europe*, pp. 85–104.

———, 'The Spanish kingdoms', in Timothy Reuter (ed.), *The New Cambridge Medieval History, Volume III: c. 900–c. 1024*, Cambridge, 1999, pp. 670–91.

Comaroff, John, and Simon Roberts, *Rules and Processes: The Cultural Logic of Dispute in an African Context*, London, 1981.

Davies, Wendy, 'Disputes, their conduct and their settlement in the village communities of eastern Brittany in the ninth century', *History and Anthropology*, 1 (1985), pp. 289–312.

———, 'People and places in dispute in ninth-century Brittany', in Davies and Fouracre (eds), *The Settlement of Disputes in Early Medieval Europe*, pp. 65–84.

———, *Small Worlds: The Village Community in Early Medieval Brittany*, London, 1988.

———, 'The composition of the Redon cartulary', *Francia*, 17 (1990), pp. 69–90.

———, 'Anger and the Celtic saint', in Barbara H. Rosenwein (ed.), *Anger's Past: The Social Uses of an Emotion in the Middle Ages*, Ithaca, NY, 1998, pp. 191–202.

———, 'Sale, price and valuation in Galicia and Castile-León in the tenth century', *Early Medieval Europe*, 11 (2002), pp. 149–74.

———, *Acts of Giving: Individual, Community, and Church in Tenth-century Christian Spain*, Oxford, 2007.

———, 'Judges and judging: Truth and justice in northern Iberia on the eve of the millennium', *Journal of Medieval History*, 36/3 (2010), pp. 193–203.

———, 'Summary justice and seigneurial justice in northern Iberia on the eve of the millennium', *Haskins Society Journal*, 22 (2010 [2012]), pp. 43–58.

———, 'When gift is sale: Reciprocities and commodities in tenth-century Christian Iberia', in Wendy Davies and Paul Fouracre (eds), *The Languages of Gift in the Early Middle Ages*, Cambridge, 2010, pp. 217–37.

———, 'Holding court: Judicial presidency in Brittany, Wales and northern Iberia in the early middle ages', in Fiona Edmonds and Paul Russell (eds), *Tome: Studies in Medieval Celtic History and Law in Honour of Thomas Charles-Edwards*, Woodbridge, 2011, pp. 145–54.

———, 'On suretyship in tenth-century northern Iberia', in Julio Escalona and Andrew Reynolds (eds), *Scale and Scale Change in the Early Middle Ages: Exploring Landscape, Local Society, and the World Beyond*, The Medieval Countryside, 6, Turnhout, 2011, pp. 133–52.

———, 'Settling disputes in early medieval Spain and Portugal: A contrast with Wales and Brittany?', in Ralph A. Griffiths and Phillipp R. Schofield (eds), *Wales and the Welsh in the Middle Ages: Essays Presented to J. Beverley Smith*, Cardiff, 2011, pp. 89–107.

———, 'Local priests and the writing of charters in northern Iberia in the tenth century', in Escalona and Sirantoine (eds), *Chartes et cartulaires comme instruments de pouvoir*, pp. 29–43.

———, 'Law and the learned in northern Iberia in the early middle ages: Some comparative thoughts', in Emer Purcell, Paul MacCotter, John Sheehan and Julianne Nyhan (eds), *Clerics, Kings and Vikings: Essays on Medieval Ireland in Honour of Donnchadh Ó Corráin*, Dublin, 2015, pp. 45–54.

———, 'Local priests in northern Iberia', in Steffen Patzold and Carine van Rhijn (eds), *Men in the Middle: Local Priests in Early Medieval Europe*, Berlin, forthcoming.

———, 'The language of justice in northern Iberia before AD 1000', in Andrew Reynolds, Jane Carroll and Barbara Yorke (eds), *Power and Place in Later Roman and Early Medieval Europe*, forthcoming.

———, 'Regions and micro-regions of scribal practice', in Stuart Brookes, Julio Escalona and Orri Vesteinsson (eds), *Polity and Neighbourhood in Early Medieval Europe*, Turnhout, forthcoming.

———, and Paul Fouracre (eds), *The Settlement of Disputes in Early Medieval Europe*, Cambridge, 1986.

Declercq, Georges, 'Between legal action and performance: The *firmatio* of charters in the early middle ages', in Mostert and Barnwell (eds), *Medieval Legal Process*, pp. 55–73.

Delogu, Paolo, 'La giustizia nell'Italia meridionale longobarda', in *La giustizia nell'alto medioevo*, vol. 1, pp. 257–308.

Depreux, Philippe, 'La prestation de serment dans le monde franc: formes et fonctions (VIe–IXe siècles)', in Françoise Laurent (ed.), *Serment, promesse et engagement: rituels et modalités au moyen âge*, Montpellier, 2008, pp. 517–32.

Díaz y Díaz, Manuel Cecilio, *Index Scriptorum Latinorum Medii Aevi Hispanorum*, Madrid, 1959.

———, 'La Lex Visigothorum y sus manuscritos. Un Ensayo de reinterpretación', *Anuario de historia del derecho español*, 46 (1976), pp. 163–224.

———, *Libros y librerías en la Rioja altomedieval*, Logroño, 1979.

———, *Códices visigóticos en la monarquía leonesa*, León, 1983.

Duby, Georges, 'Recherches sur l'évolution des institutions judiciaires pendant le Xe et le XIe siècle dans le sud de la Bourgogne', *Le moyen âge*, 52 (1946), pp. 149–94.

———, 'Recherches sur l'évolution des institutions judiciaires pendant le Xe et le XIe siècle dans le sud de la Bourgogne', *Le moyen âge*, 53 (1947), pp. 15–38.

———, *La société aux XIe et XIIe siècles dans la région mâconnaise*, Paris, 1953.

Eisenlohr, Erika, 'Monogramme und Invokationszeichnen in iberischen und fränkischen Urkunden', *Signo*, 1 (1994), pp. 35–50.

———, 'Von ligierten zu symbolischen Invokations- und Subskriptionszeichen in frühmittelalterlichen Urkunden', in Rück (ed.), *Graphische Symbole*, pp. 167–262.

Erhart, Peter, and Julia Kleindinst, *Urkundenlandschaft Rätien*, Forschungen zur Geschichte des Mittelalters, 7, Vienna, 2004.

Escalona Monge, Julio, 'De "señores y campesinos" a "poderes feudales y comunidades". Elementos para definir la articulación entre territorio y clases sociales en la alta edad media castellana', in Ignacio Álvarez Borge (ed.), *Comunidades locales y poderes feudales en la edad media*, Logroño, 2001, pp. 115–55.

———, 'Unidades territoriales supralocales: una propuesta sobre los orígenes del señorío de behetría', in Carlos Estepa Díez and Cristina Jular Pérez-Alfaro (co-ords), *Los Señoríos de behetría*, Madrid, 2001, pp. 20–46.

———, 'Mapping scale change: Hierarchization and fission in Castilian rural communities during the tenth and eleventh centuries', in Wendy Davies, Guy Halsall and Andrew Reynolds (eds), *People and Space in the Middle Ages, 300–1300*, Turnhout, 2006, pp. 143–66.

Escalona, Julio, 'Scale change on the border: The county of Castile in the tenth century', in Escalona and Reynolds (eds), *Scale and Scale Change*, pp. 153–83.

———, 'In the name of a distant king: Representing royal authority in the county of Castile, ca. 900–1038', in *Early Medieval Europe*, 24 (2016), pp. 74–102.

———, and Andrew Reynolds (eds), *Scale and Scale Change in the Early Middle Ages: Exploring Landscape, Local Society, and the World Beyond*, The Medieval Countryside, 6, Turnhout, 2011.

———, and Hélène Sirantoine (eds), *Chartes et cartulaires comme instruments de pouvoir. Espagne et Occident chrétien (VIIIe–XIIe siècles)*, Toulouse, 2013.

———, and Iñaki Martín Viso, 'Los *palatia*, puntos de centralización de rentas en la meseta del Duero (siglos IX–XI)', in Alfonso Vigil-Escalera Guirado, Giovanna Bianchi and Juan Antonio Quirós (eds), *Horrea, Barns and Silos: Storage and Incomes in Early Medieval Europe*, Vitoria, 2013, pp. 103–26.

———, Isabel Velázquez Soriano and Paloma Juárez Benitez, 'Identification of the sole extant original charter issued by Fernán González, count of Castile (932–970)', *Journal of Medieval Iberian Studies*, 4 (2012), pp. 259–88.

Esders, Stefan, 'Regionale Selbstbehauptung zwischen Byzanz und dem Frankenreich. Die *inquisitio* der Rechtsgewohnheiten Istriens durch die Sendboten Karls des Grossen und Pippins von Italien', in Stefan Esders and Thomas Scharff (eds), *Eid und Wahrheitssuche. Studien zu rechtlichen Befragungspraktiken in Mittelalter und früher Neuzeit*, Frankfurt am Main, 1999, pp. 49–112.

———, 'Treueidleistung und Rechtsveränderung im früheren Mittelalter', in Stefan Esders and Christine Reinle (eds), *Rechtsveränderung im politischen und sozialen Kontext mittelalterlicher Rechtsvielfalt*, Neue Aspekte der europäischen Mittelalterforschung, 5, Münster, 2005, pp. 25–61.

———, and Søren Kaschke, '*Ut sub fideiussoribus ad nostrum palatium veniat*. Gestellungsbürgschaft und Letztentscheidung des Hofgerichtes unter Ludwig dem Frommen', forthcoming.

———, and Thomas Scharff, 'Die Untersuchung der Untersuchung. Methodische Überlegungen zum Studium rechtlicher Befragungs- und Weisungspraktiken in Mittelalter und früher Neuzeit', in Stefan Esders and Thomas Scharff (eds), *Eid und Wahrheitssuche. Studien zu rechtlichen Befragungspraktiken in Mittelalter und früher Neuzeit*, Frankfurt am Main, 1999, pp. 11–47.

Estepa Díez, Carlos, *Estructura social de la ciudad de León (siglos XI–XIII)*, Fuentes y estudios de historia leonesa, 19, León, 1977.

———, 'Formación y consolidación del feudalismo en Castilla y León', in *En torno al feudalismo hispánico. I congreso de estudios medievales*, Ávila, 1989, pp. 157–256.

———, 'Poder y propiedad feudales en el período astur: las mandaciones de los Flaínez en la montaña leonesa', in *Miscel·lània en homenatge al P. Agustí Altisent*, Tarragona, 1991, pp. 285–327.

———, 'Configuración y primera expansión del reino astur. Siglos VIII y IX', in Francisco Javier Lomas and Federico Devís (eds), *De Constantino a Carlomagno. Disidentes, heterodoxos, marginados*, Cádiz, 1992, pp. 179–95.

———, *Las Behetrías castellanas*, 2 vols, Valladolid, 2003.

———, 'En torno a propiedad dominical, dominio señorial, y señorío jurisdiccional', in Gregorio del Ser Quijano and Iñaki Martín Viso (eds), *Espacios de poder y formas sociales en la edad media: estudios dedicados a Ángel Barrios*, Salamanca, 2007, pp. 67–76.

———, 'La Castilla primitiva (750–931): condes, territorios y villas', in *Territorio, Sociedad y Poder*, 2 (2009), pp. 261–78.

———, 'Los confirmantes en los diplomas de Alfonso VIII (1158–1214)', in Escalona and Sirantoine (eds), *Chartes et cartulaires comme instruments de pouvoir*, pp. 45–69.

Falk Moore, Sally, *Law as Process: An Anthropological Approach*, London, 1978.

Fees, Irmgard, 'Tauschurkunden in Venedig und im Veneto', in Irmgard Fees and Philippe Depreux (eds), *Tauschgeschäft und Tauschurkunde vom 8. bis zum 12. Jahrhundert. L'acte d'échange, du VIIIe au XIIe siècle*, Köln, 2013, pp. 99–128.

Fernández Flórez, José Antonio, 'El fondo documental del monasterio de Sahagún y sus *scriptores* (siglos IX–X)', in Juan Ignacio Ruiz de la Peña Solar (ed.), *El monacato en los reinos de León y Castilla (Siglos VII–XIII). X Congreso de Estudios Medievales, 2005*, Ávila, 2007, pp. 125–46.

———, 'Los documentos y sus *scriptores*', in *Monarquía y sociedad en el reino de León de Alfonso III a Alfonso VII*, 2 vols, León, 2007, vol. 2, pp. 97–139.

———, and Marta Herrero de la Fuente, 'Libertades de las copistas en la confección de cartularios: el caso del Becerro Gótico de Sahagún', in Emma Condello and Guiseppe de Gregorio (eds), *Scribi e colofoni. Le sottoscrizioni di copisti dalle origini all' avvento della stampa*, Spoleto, 1995, pp. 301–19.

Fichtenau, Heinrich, 'Monarchische Propaganda in Urkunden', in *Beiträge zur Mediävistik*, 3 vols, Stuttgart, 1977, vol. 2, pp. 18–36.

Filippov, Igor, 'Bible and the Roman law: The notions of law, custom and justice in the Vulgate', in *Lex et religio: XL incontro di studiosi dell'antichità cristiana (Roma, 10–12 maggio 2012)*, Studia ephemeridis Augustinianum, 135, Rome, 2013, pp. 105–41.

Firey, Abigail, 'Canon law in the Carolingian era', in John C. Wei and Anders Winroth (eds), *Cambridge History of Medieval Canon Law*, Cambridge, forthcoming.

Fleming, Robin, *Domesday Book and the Law: Society and Legal Custom in Early Medieval England*, Cambridge, 1998.

Fouracre, Paul, '"Placita" and the settlement of disputes in later Merovingian Francia', in Davies and Fouracre (eds), *Settlement of Disputes*, pp. 23–43.

Galanter, Marc, 'Justice in many rooms: Courts, private ordering, and indigenous law', *Journal of Legal Pluralism and Unofficial Law*, 19 (1981), pp. 1–47.

Gambra, Andrés, *Alfonso VI. Cancillería, curia e imperio, I: Estudio*, León, 1997.

Ganshof, François Louis, 'Charlemagne et l'administration de la justice dans la monarchie franque', in Helmut Beumann (ed.), *Persönlichkeit und Geschichte* = vol. 1 of Wolfgang Braunfels (ed.), *Karl der Grosse: Lebenswerk und Nachleben*, 5 vols, Düsseldorf, 1965, pp. 394–419.

———, 'Charlemagne et les institutions de la monarchie franque', in Braunfels (ed.), *Karl der Grosse*, vol. 1, pp. 349–93.

García de Cortázar, José Ángel, 'La formación de la sociedad feudal en el cuadrante noroccidental de la península ibérica en los siglos viii a xii', *Initium*, 4 (1999), pp. 57–121.

———, and Esther Peña Bocos, 'Poder condal ¿y "mutación feudal"? en la Castilla del año mil', in María Isabel Loring García (ed.), *Historia social, pensamiento historiográfico y edad media*, Madrid, 1997, pp. 273–98.

García de Cortázar y Ruiz de Aguirre, José Ángel, *El dominio del monasterio de San Millán de la Cogolla (siglos X a XIII). Introducción a la historia rural de Castilla altomedieval*, Acta Salmanticensia, Filosofía y Letras, 59, Salamanca, 1969.

García de Valdeavellano, Luis, 'La cuota de libre disposición en el derecho hereditario de León y Castilla en la alta edad media (Notas y documentos)', *Anuario de Historia del Derecho Español*, 9 (1932), pp. 129–76.

———, 'Escodriñamiento y otorificación (contribución al estudio de la reivindicación mobiliaria en el derecho español medieval)', in *Centenario de la ley del notariado. Sección primera: estudios históricos*, 2 vols, Madrid, 1965, vol. 2, pp. 125–335.

———, *Curso de historia de las instituciones españolas. De los orígenes al final de la edad media*, Madrid, 1968.

García Leal, Alfonso, 'Los condes Fruela Muñoz y Pedro Flaínez: la formación de un patrimonio señorial', *Anuario de estudios medievales*, 36/1 (2006), pp. 1–110.

García Turza, Claudio (co-ord.), *Los manuscritos visigóticos: estudio paleográfico y codicológico. I. Códices riojanos datados*, Logroño, 2002.

García-Gallo, Alfonso, 'El fuero de León. Su historia, textos y redacciones', *Anuario de Historia del Derecho Español*, 39 (1969), pp. 5–171.

Geary, Patrick J., 'Vivre en conflit dans une France sans état: typologie des mécanismes de règlement des conflits (1050–1200)', *Annales ESC*, 41 (1986), pp. 1,107–33.

———, 'Land, language and memory in Europe 700–1100', *Transactions of the Royal Historical Society*, 6th ser., 9 (1999), pp. 169–84.

Giry, Arthur, *Manuel de Diplomatique*, 2nd edn, Paris, 1925.

Guillot, Olivier, 'Le duel judiciaire: du champ legal (sous Louis le Pieux) au champ de la pratique en France (XIe siècle)', in *La giustizia nell'alto medioevo*, vol. 2, pp. 715–85.

Guyotjeannin, Olivier, and Laurent Morelle, 'Tradition et réception de l'acte médiéval: Jalons pour un bilan des recherches', *Archiv für Diplomatik*, 53 (2007), pp. 367–403.

———, Laurent Morelle and Michel Parisse (eds), *Les cartulaires. Actes de la Table ronde*, Mémoires et documents de l'école des chartes, 39, Paris, 1993.

La giustizia nell'alto medioevo (secoli IX–XI), Settimane di studio del centro italiano di studi sull'alto medioevo, 44, 2 vols, Spoleto, 1997.

Hammer, Carl I., 'Land sales in eighth- and ninth-century Bavaria: Legal, economic and social aspects', *Early Medieval Europe*, 6 (1997), pp. 47–76.

Härtel, Reinhard, 'Zu Transformation und Bedeutungswandel graphischer Symbole in Unterfertigungen', in Rück (ed.), *Graphische Symbole*, pp. 121–41.

Harvey, Sally, *Domesday: Book of Judgment*, Oxford, 2014.

Heidecker, Karl, 'Communication by written texts in court cases: Some charter evidence (*ca.*800–*ca.*1100)', in Marco Mostert (ed.), *New Approaches to Medieval Communication*, Utrecht Studies in Medieval Literacy, 1, Turnhout, 1999, pp. 101–26.

———, 'Les actes privés de la période carolingienne dans les archives de Saint-Gall', *Annuaire de l'école pratique des hautes études, Section des sciences historiques et philologiques*, 139 (2008), pp. 372–77.

Herrero de la Fuente, Marta, 'Cartularios leoneses. Del *Becerro Gótico de Sahagún* al *Tumbo Legionense* y al *Libro de las Estampas*', in Rodríguez Díaz and García Martínez (eds), *La escritura de la memoria*, pp. 111–52.

Hornby, Emma, and Rebecca Maloy, *Music and Meaning in Old Hispanic Lenten Chants: Psalmi, Threni and the Easter Vigil Canticles*, Woodbridge, 2013.

Hughes, Kathleen, *Early Christian Ireland: Introduction to the Sources*, London, 1972.

Humfress, Caroline, 'Law and custom under Rome', in Rio (ed.), *Law, Custom, and Justice*, pp. 23–47.

———, 'Laws' empire: Roman universalism and legal practice', in Paul J. du Plessis (ed.), *New frontiers: Law and Society in the Roman World*, Edinburgh, 2013, pp. 73–101.

Iglesia Ferreirós, Aquilino, 'La creación del derecho en Cataluña', *Anuario de Historia del Derecho Español*, 47 (1977), pp. 99–423.

———, 'El proceso del Conde Bera y el problema de las ordalías', *Anuario de Historia del Derecho Español*, 51 (1981), pp. 1–221.

Innes, Matthew, *State and Society in the Early Middle Ages: The Middle Rhine Valley, 400–1000*, Cambridge Studies in Medieval Life and Thought, 47, Cambridge, 2000.

———, 'Charlemagne, justice and written law', in Rio (ed.), *Law, Custom, and Justice*, pp. 155–203.

Insley, Charles, 'Rhetoric and ritual in late Anglo-Saxon charters', in Mostert and Barnwell (eds), *Medieval Legal Process*, pp. 109–21.

Isla Frez, Amancio, *La sociedad gallega en la alta edad media*, Biblioteca de historia, 12, Madrid, 1992.

———, *Realezas hispánicas del año mil*, A Coruña, 1999.

———, *La alta edad media. Siglos VIII–XI*, Madrid, 2002.

Jacob, Robert, 'Conclusions. Logiques et langages du procès autour de l'an mil', in Castan et al. (eds), *La justice en l'an mil*, pp. 149–67.

Jarrett, Jonathan, *Rulers and Ruled in Frontier Catalonia, 880–1010: Pathways of Power*, Woodbridge, 2010.

———, 'Comparing the earliest documentary culture in Carolingian Catalonia', in Jonathan Jarrett and Allan Scott McKinley (eds), *Problems and Possibilities of Early Medieval Charters*, International Medieval Research, 19, Turnhout, 2013, pp. 89–126.

Jenkins, Dafydd, and Morfydd Owen, 'The Welsh marginalia in the Lichfield Gospels, Part 2,' *Cambridge Medieval Celtic Studies*, 7 (1984), pp. 91–120.

Kaiser, Wolfgang, *Die Epitome Iuliani: Beiträge zum römischen Recht im frühen Mittelalter und zum byzantinischen Rechtsunterricht*, Frankfurt, 2004.

Kelly, Fergus, *A Guide to Early Irish Law*, Early Irish Law Series, III, Dublin, 1988.

Kennedy, Hugh, *Muslim Spain and Portugal: A Political History of al-Andalus*, London, 1996.

Kosto, Adam J., *Making Agreements in Medieval Catalonia: Power, Order, and the Written Word, 1000–1200*, Cambridge, 2001.

———, 'Reasons for assembly in Catalonia and Aragón, 900–1200', in Paul S. Barnwell and Marco Mostert (eds), *Political Assemblies in the Earlier Middle Ages*, Turnhout, 2003, pp. 133–49.

———, '*Sicut mos esse solet*: Documentary practices in Christian Iberia, *c.* 700–1000', in Brown, Costambeys, Innes and Kosto (eds), *Documentary Culture and the Laity in the Early Middle Ages*, pp. 259–82.

Koziol, Geoffrey, *Begging Pardon and Favor: Ritual and Political Order in Early Medieval France*, Ithaca, NY, 1992.

Lambert, Tom, 'Theft, homicide and crime in late Anglo-Saxon law', *Past and Present*, 214 (2012), pp. 3–43.

Larrea, Juan José, 'La documentación de San Martín de Cillas. Un Ensayo de crítica de las fuentes altomedievales', *Revista de Historia Jerónimo Zurita*, 61–2 (1990), pp. 7–44.

———, *La Navarre du IVe au XIIe siècle*, Paris and Brussels, 1998.

Larrea Conde, Juan José, 'Construir iglesias, construir territorio: las dos fases altomedievales de San Román de Tobillas (Álava)', in Jorge López Quiroga, Artemio M. Martínez Tejera and Jorge Morín de Pablos (eds), *Monasteria et territoria. Elites, edilicia y territorio en el Mediterráneo medieval (siglos V–XI)*, BAR International Series, S1720, Oxford, 2007, pp. 321–36.

Le Jan, Régine, 'Justice royale et pratiques sociales dans le royaume franc au IXe siècle', in *La giustizia nell'alto medioevo*, vol. 1, pp. 47–85.

———, 'Les transactions et compromis judiciaires autour de l'an mil', in Castan et al. (eds), *La justice en l'an mil*, pp. 67–79.

Lemesle, Bruno, *Conflits et justice au moyen âge. Normes, loi et résolution des conflits en Anjou aux XIe et XIIe siècles*, Paris, 2008.

Leyser, Karl J., *Rule and Conflict in an Early Medieval Society: Ottonian Saxony*, London, 1979.

Liebs, Detlef, *Römische Jurisprudenz in Gallien (2. bis 8. Jahrhundert)*, Berlin, 2002.

Little, Lester K. *Benedictine Maledictions: Liturgical Cursing in Romanesque France*, Ithaca, NY, 1993.

———, 'Anger in monastic curses', in Barbara H. Rosenwein (ed.), *Anger's Past: The Social Uses of an Emotion in the Middle Ages*, Ithaca, NY, 1998, pp. 9–35.

López Alsina, Fernando, *La ciudad de Santiago de Compostela en la alta edad media*, Santiago de Compostela, 1988.

Loring García, María Isabel, 'Nobleza e iglesias propias en la Cantabria altomedieval', *Studia Histórica, Historia Medieval*, 5 (1987), pp. 89–123.

Lucas Álvarez, Manuel, 'La colección diplomática del monasterio de San Lorenzo de Carboeiro', *Compostellanum*, 3 (1958), pp. 221–308, 547–638.

———, *El reino de León en la alta edad media. VIII. La Documentación real astur-leonesa (718–1072)*, León, 1995.

———, *El archivo del monasterio de San Martiño de Fóra o Pinario de Santiago de Compostela*, 2 vols, A Coruña, 1999.

Luis Corral, Fernando, 'Lugares de reunión, *boni homines* y presbíteros en Valdevimbre y Ardón en la alta edad media', forthcoming.

Maloy, Rebecca, *Inside the Offertory: Aspects of Chronology and Transmission*, Oxford, 2010.

Manzano Moreno, Eduardo, *Conquistadores, emires y califas. Los omeyas y la formación de al-Andalus*, Barcelona, 2006.

Martín, Iñaki, 'The memory of the "holy men" in Hispanic monasticism: The case of the Bierzo region', *Imago Temporis. Medium Aevum*, 6 (2012), pp. 165–90.

Martín Viso, Iñaki, *Fragmentos del Leviatán. La articulación política del espacio zamorano en la alta edad media*, Zamora, 2002.

———, 'Poder político y estructura social en la Castilla altomedieval: el condado de Lantarón (siglos VIII–XI)', in José Ignacio de la Iglesia Duarte (co-ord.), *Los espacios de poder en la España medieval. XII semana de estudios medievales Nájera 2001*, Logroño, 2002, pp. 533–52.

———, 'Monasterios y redes sociales en el Bierzo altomedieval', *Hispania*, 71/237 (2011), pp. 9–38.

Martínez Díez, Gonzalo, 'Las instituciones del reino astur a través de los diplomas (718–910)', *AHDE*, 35 (1965), pp. 59–167.

———, 'Terminología jurídica en la documentación del reino de León. Siglos IX–XI', in *Orígenes de las lenguas romances en el reino de León, Siglos IX–XII*, 2 vols, León, 2004, vol. 1, pp. 229–72.

———, *El condado de Castilla (711–1038): la historia frente a la leyenda*, 2 vols, Valladolid, 2005.

Martínez Peñín, Raquel, 'La secuencia altomedieval de la iglesia paleocristiana de Marialba de la Ribera (León)', *Estudios Humanísticos. Historia*, 6 (2007), pp. 47–64.

Martínez Sopena, Pascual, *La Tierra de Campos Occidental. Poblamiento, poder y comunidad del siglo X al XIII*, Valladolid, 1985.

———, 'El conde Rodrigo de León y los suyos. Herencia y expectativa de poder entre los siglos X y XII', in Reyna Pastor (comp.), *Relaciones de poder, de producción y parentesco en la edad media y moderna*, Madrid, 1990, pp. 51–84.

———, 'La justicia en la época asturleonesa: entre el *Liber* y los mediadores sociales', in Ana Rodríguez (ed.), *El lugar del campesino. En torno a la obra de Reyna Pastor*, València, 2007, pp. 239–60.

———, 'Reyes y nobles en León (ca. 860–1160)', in José María Fernández Catón (co-ord.), *Monarquía y sociedad en el reino de León. De Alfonso III a Alfonso VII*, Fuentes y estudios de historia leonesa, 117, 2 vols, León, 2007, vol. 1, pp. 149–200.

———, 'La aristocracia hispánica. Castilla y León (siglos X–XIII)', *Bulletin du centre d'études médiévales d'Auxerre*, Hors-série 2 (2008): http://cem.revues.org/10052.

Mattoso, José, 'Sanctio (875–1100)', *Revista portuguesa de história*, 13 (1971), pp. 299–338.

———, *A nobreza medieval portuguesa: a família e o poder*, 4th edn, Lisbon, 1994 [1st edn 1980].

McKitterick, Rosamond, *The Carolingians and the Written Word*, Cambridge, 1989.

Mendo Carmona, Concepción, 'La suscripción altomedieval', *Signo*, 4 (1997), pp. 207–29.

———, 'La escritura de los documentos leoneses en el siglo X', *Signo*, 8 (2001), pp. 179–210.

Menéndez Pidal, Ramón, 'Repoblación y tradición en la cuenca del Duero', in Manuel Alvar, Antonio María Badía Margarit, Rafael de Balbín and Luís Felipe Lindley Cintra (eds), *Enciclopedia Lingüística Hispánica*, 2 vols, Madrid, 1960–67, vol. 1, pp. xxix–lvii.

Milagros Cárcel Ortí, María (ed.), *Vocabulaire international de la Diplomatique*, Commission Internationale de Diplomatique, València, 1994.

Millares Carlo, Agustín, *Tratado de paleografía española*, 3rd edn, 3 vols, Madrid, 1983.

———, *Corpus de códices visigóticos*, prep. Manuel Cecilio Díaz y Díaz, Anscari M. Mundó, José Manuel Ruiz Asencio, Blas Casado Quintanilla and E. Lecuona Ribot, 2 vols, Las Palmas de Gran Canaria, 1999.

Miller, William I., 'Gift, sale, payment, raid: Case studies in the negotiation and classification of exchange in medieval Iceland', *Speculum*, 61 (1986), pp. 18–50.

Mínguez, José María, 'Justicia y poder en el marco de la feudalización de la sociedad leonesa', in *La giustizia nell'alto medioevo*, vol. 1, pp. 491–546.

———, 'Pervivencia y transformaciones de la concepción y práctica del poder en el reino de León', *Studia Histórica. Historia Medieval*, 25 (2007), pp. 15–65.

Mostert, Marco, and Paul S. Barnwell (eds), *Medieval Legal Process: Physical, Spoken and Written Performance in the Middle Ages*, Utrecht Studies in Medieval Literacy, 22, Turnhout, 2011.

Nehlsen-von Stryk, Karin, *Die Boni Homines des frühen Mittelalters unter besonderer Berücksichtigung der fränkischen Quellen*, Freiburger Rechtsgeschichtliche Abhandlungen, n.s. 2, Berlin, 1981.

Nelson, Janet L., 'Kings with justice, kings without justice: An early medieval paradox', in *La giustizia nell'alto medioevo*, vol. 2, pp. 797–823.

———, 'Liturgy or law: Misconceived alternatives?', in Stephen Baxter, Catherine Karkov, Janet L. Nelson and David Pelteret (eds), *Early Medieval Studies in Memory of Patrick Wormald*, Farnham, 2009, pp. 433–47.

Niermeyer, Jan Frederik, *Mediae Latinitatis Lexicon Minus*, 2nd edn, Leiden, 1984.

Ostolaza, María Isabel, 'La validación en los documentos del occidente hispánico (s. X–XII). Del signum crucis al signum manus', in Rück (ed.), *Graphische Symbole*, pp. 453–62.

Pallares, María del Carmen, and Ermelindo Portela, 'El lugar de los campesinos. De repobladores a repoblados', in Ana Rodríguez (ed.), *El lugar del campesino. En torno a la obra de Reyna Pastor* (València, 2007), pp. 61–87.

Pallares Méndez, María del Carmen, *El monasterio de Sobrado: un ejemplo de protagonismo monástico en la Galicia medieval*, A Coruña, 1979.

———, *Ilduara, una aristócrata del siglo X*, A Coruña, 1998.

Parisse, Michel, 'Cadres judiciaires vers l'an mil', in Castan et al. (eds), *La justice en l'an mil*, pp. 15–26.

Pastor, Reyna, *Resistencias y luchas campesinas en la época del crecimiento y consolidación de la formación feudal. Castilla y León, siglos X–XIII*, 2nd edn, Madrid, 1990 [1st edn 1980].

———, 'Sur la genèse du féodalisme en Castille et dans le León, Xe–XIIe siècles. Point de départ pour une histoire comparative', in Hartmut Atsma and André Burguière (eds), *Marc Bloch aujourd'hui. Histoire comparée et sciences sociales*, Paris, 1990, pp. 259–70.

Pelteret, David A.E., *Catalogue of English Post-Conquest Vernacular Documents*, Woodbridge, 1990.

Pérez, Mariel, '*Rebelles, infideles, traditores*. Insumisión política y poder aristocrático en el reino de León', *Historia, instituciones, documentos*, 38 (2011), pp. 361–82.

———, 'El control de lo sagrado como instrumento de poder: los monasterios particulares de la aristocracia altomedieval leonesa', *Anuario de Estudios Medievales*, 42 (2012), pp. 799–822.

Pérez de Urbel, Justo, *Historia del condado de Castilla*, 3 vols, Madrid, 1945.

Peterson, David, *Frontera y lengua en el alto Ebro, siglos VIII–XI*, Logroño, 2009.

———, 'Reescribiendo el pasado. El *Becerro Galicano* como reconstrucción de la historia institucional de San Millán de la Cogolla', *Hispania*, 69 (2009), pp. 653–82.

———, 'El *Becerro Gótico* de San Millán. Reconstrucción de un cartulario perdido', *Studia Histórica. Historia Medieval*, 29 (2011), pp. 147–73.

Pirie, Fernanda, and Judith Scheele, 'Justice, community, and law', in Fernanda Pirie and Judith Scheele (eds), *Legalism: Community and Justice*, Oxford, 2014, pp. 1–24.

Pollock, Frederick, and Frederic William Maitland, *The History of English Law before the Time of Edward I*, 2 vols, Cambridge, 1895.

Portass, Robert, 'The contours and contexts of public power in the tenth-century Liébana', *Journal of Medieval History*, 38 (2012), pp. 389–407.

———, 'All quiet on the western front: Royal politics in Galicia from *c.* 800 to *c.* 950', *Early Medieval Europe*, 21 (2013), pp. 283–306.

———, *Society, Community and Power in Early Medieval Christian Spain*, Woodbridge, forthcoming.

Portela Silva, Ermelindo, 'Galicia y la monarquía leonesa', in *El reino de León en la alta edad media, VII, Estudios*, León, 1995, pp. 9–70.

———, and María del Carmen Pallares Méndez, 'Elementos para el análisis de la aristocracia altomedieval de Galicia: parentesco y patrimonio', *Studia Histórica, Historia Medieval*, 5 (1987), pp. 17–32.

La preuve. Deuxième partie: moyen âge et temps modernes, Recueils de la Société Jean Bodin pour l'histoire comparative des institutions, 17 (1965).

Prieto Morera, Agustín, 'El proceso en el reino de León a la luz de los diplomas', in *El reino de León en la alta edad media, II: Ordenamiento jurídico del reino*, León, 1992, pp. 381–518.

Prieto Prieto, Alfonso, 'La potestad judicial de los reyes de León', in *El reino de León en la alta edad media, II: Ordenamiento jurídico del reino*, León, 1992, pp. 519–64.

The Production and Use of English Manuscripts 1060 to 1220, ed. Orietta Da Rold, Takako Kato, Mary Swan and Elaine Treharne, updated 2013: http://www.le.ac.uk/ee/em1060to1220/.

Quirós Castillo, Juan Antonio, and Belén Bengoetxea Rementeria, *Arqueología (III) (Arqueología Postclásica)*, Madrid, 2006.

Radding, Charles M., and Antonio Ciaralli, *The Corpus Iuris Civilis in the Middle Ages: Manuscripts and Transmission from the Sixth Century to the Juristic Revival*, Brill's Studies in Intellectual History, 147, Leiden, 2006.

Reuter, Timothy, Chris Wickham and Thomas Bisson, 'Debate: The "feudal revolution"', *Past and Present*, 155 (1997), pp. 177–225.

Reynolds, Susan, *Kingdoms and Communities in Western Europe, 900–1300*, Oxford, 1984.

———, *Fiefs and Vassals: The Medieval Evidence Reinterpreted*, Oxford, 1994.

———, 'Rationality and collective judgement in the law of western Europe before the twelfth century', *Quaestiones Medii Aevi Novae*, 5 (2000), pp. 3–19.

Ribeiro Guerra, António Joaquim, *Os diplomas privados em Portugal dos séculos IX a XII*, Lisbon, 2003.

Rio, Alice, *Legal Practice and the Written Word in the Early Middle Ages: Frankish Formulae, c. 500–1000*, Cambridge, 2009.

——— (ed.), *Law, Custom, and Justice in Late Antiquity and the Early Middle Ages*, London, 2011.

Ripoll, Gisela, and Isabel Velázquez, 'Origen y desarrollo de las *parrochiae* en la *Hispania* de la antigüedad tardía', in Philippe Pergola and Palmira Maria Barbini (eds), *Alle origini della parrocchia rurale (IV–VIII sec.)*, Sussidi allo Studio delle Antichità Cristiane, 12, Città del Vaticano, 1999, pp. 101–65.

Roberts, Simon, *Order and Dispute: An Introduction to Legal Anthropology*, Harmondsworth, 1979.

Rodríguez, Justiniano, *Ordoño III*, León, 1982.

Rodríguez Díaz, Elena E., and Antonio Claret García Martínez (eds), *La escritura de la memoria. Los cartularios*, Huelva, 2011.

Rosenwein, Barbara H., *To be the Neighbor of Saint Peter: The Social Meaning of Cluny's Property, 909–1049*, Ithaca, NY, 1989.

Rubio, José-Antonio, '"Donationes post obitum" y "donationes reservato usufructo" en la alta edad media de León y Castilla', *Anuario de Historia del Derecho Español*, 9 (1932), pp. 1–32.

Rück, Peter (ed.), *Graphische Symbole in mittelalterlichen. Urkunden Beiträge zur diplomatischen Semiotik*, Sigmaringen, 1996.

Ruiz Asencio, José Manuel, 'Rebeliones leonesas contra Vermudo II', *Archivos Leoneses*, 45–6 (1969), pp. 215–41.

———, 'Notas sobre la escritura y monogramas regios en la documentación real asturleonesa', in José María Fernández Catón (co-ord.), *Monarquía y sociedad en el reino de León. De Alfonso III a Alfonso VII*, 2 vols, León, 2007, vol. 1, pp. 265–312.

Sáez, Carlos (ed), *Libros y Documentos en la alta edad media. Los libros de derecho. Los archivos familiares* = vol. 2 of Carlos Sáez and Antonio Castillo Gómez (eds), *Actas del VI Congreso Internacional de Historia de la Cultura Escrita*, 2 vols, Madrid, 2002.

Sáez Sánchez, Carlos, 'Crismones en la documentación particular de la catedral de León del periodo astur (864–910)', in Rück (ed.), *Graphische Symbole*, pp. 439–42.

Salrach, Josep M., 'Prácticas judiciales, transformación social y acción política en Cataluña (siglos IX–XIII)', *Hispania*, 57/3 (1997), pp. 1,009–48.

———, 'Les féodalités méridionales: des Alpes à la Galice', in Eric Bournazel and Jean-Pierre Poly (eds), *Les féodalités*, Paris, 1998, pp. 313–88.

———, *Justícia i poder a Catalunya abans de l'any mil*, Vic, 2013.

Sánchez-Albornoz, Claudio, 'Las behetrías: la encomendación en Asturias, León y Castilla', *Anuario de Historia del Derecho Español*, 1 (1924), pp. 158–336 [reprinted in his *Viejos y nuevos estudios*, vol. 1, pp. 15–191].

———, *Estampas de la vida en León durante el siglo X*, Madrid, 1924 [republished as *Una ciudad de la España cristiana hace mil años: estampas de la vida en León*, 5th edn, Madrid, 1966].

———, *Despoblación y repoblación del valle del Duero*, Buenos Aires, 1966.

———, 'Pequeños propietarios libres en el reino Asturleonés. Su realidad histórica', in *Agricoltura e mondo rurale in occidente nell'alto medioevo*, Settimane di studio del centro italiano di studi sull'alto medioevo, 13 (1966), pp. 183–222.

———, '*Homines mandationis* y *iuniores*', in Sánchez-Albornoz, *Viejos y nuevos estudios*, vol. 1, pp. 365–577.

———, 'El régimen de la tierra en el reino asturleonés hace mil años', in *Viejos y nuevos estudios*, vol. 3, pp. 1,313–521.

———, *Viejos y nuevos estudios sobre las instituciones medievales españolas*, 3 vols, Madrid, 1976–80.

———, 'Rebeliones en Galicia', in *Estudios sobre Galicia en la temprana edad media*, A Coruña, 1981, pp. 159–82.

Sánchez Badiola, Juan José, *El territorio de León en la edad media. Poblamiento, organización del espacio y estructura social (siglos IX–XIII)*, 2 vols, León, 2004.

Sanz Fuentes, María Josefa, 'El lenguaje de los documentos falsos', in *Orígenes de las lenguas romances en el reino de León, siglos IX–XII*, 2 vols, León, 2004, vol. 1, pp. 119–58.

Schulz, Fritz, *Principles of Roman Law*, Oxford, 1936.

Scragg, Donald, *A Conspectus of Scribal Hands Writing English, 960–1100*, Cambridge, 2012.

Ser Quijano, Gregorio del, 'Movilidad y promoción del grupo eclesiástico y su vinculación con la aristocracia. La diócesis de León en el período asturleonés', *Hispania*, 53/185 (1993), pp. 1,053–67.

Smail, Daniel Lord, *The Consumption of Justice: Emotions, Publicity, and Legal Culture in Marseille, 1264–1423*, Ithaca, NY, 2003.

Stacey, Robin C., 'Translation of the Old Irish tract *Berrad Airechta*', in Charles-Edwards, Owen and Walters (eds), *Lawyers and Laymen*, pp. 210–33.

———, *The Road to Judgment: From Custom to Court in Medieval Ireland and Wales*, Philadelphia, PA, 1994.

Taviani-Carozzi, Huguette, *La principauté lombarde de Salerne. IXe–XIe siècle. Pouvoir et société en Italie lombarde méridionale*, 2 vols, Rome, 1991.

Tock, Benoît-Michel, *Scribes, souscripteurs et témoins dans les actes privés en France (VIIe–début du XIIe siècle)*, Turnhout, 2005.

Torres Sevilla-Quiñones de León, Margarita, *Linajes nobiliarios en León y Castilla (siglos IX–XIII)*, Valladolid, 1999.

Van Caenegem, Raoul Charles, 'La preuve dans le droit du moyen âge occidental. Rapport de synthèse', in *La preuve. Deuxième partie: moyen âge et temps modernes*, Recueils de la Société Jean Bodin pour l'histoire comparative des institutions, 17 (Brussels, 1965), pp. 691–753.

Velázquez Soriano, Isabel, *Las pizarras visigodas (Entre el latín y su disgregación. La lengua hablada en Hispania, siglos VI–VIII)*, Salamanca, 2004.

Vives, José, 'El oracional mozárabe de Silos. British Museum, ms. Addit. 30852', *Analecta Sacra Tarraconensia*, 18 (1945), pp. 1–25.

von Savigny, Friedrich Carl, *Geschichte des römischen Rechts im Mittelalter*, 6 vols, Heidelberg, 1815–31.

Walters, Dafydd, 'From Benedict to Gratian: The Code in medieval ecclesiastical authors', in Jill Harries and Ian Wood (eds), *The Theodosian Code: Studies in the Imperial Law of Late Antiquity*, London, 1993, pp. 200–216.

Wenzel, Horst, *Hören und Sehen, Schrift und Bild: Kultur und Gedächtnis im Mittelalter*, Munich, 1995.

White, Stephen D., '*Pactum . . . legem vincit et amor judicium*: The settlement of disputes by compromise in eleventh-century western France', *American Journal of Legal History*, 22 (1978), pp. 281–308.

———, 'Proposing the ordeal and avoiding it: Strategy and power in western French litigation, 1050–1110', in Thomas Noël Bisson (ed.), *Cultures of Power: Lordship, Status, and Process in Twelfth-century Europe*, Philadelphia, PA, 1995, pp. 89–123.

———, 'From peace to power: The study of disputes in medieval France', in Esther Cohen and Mayke B. de Jong (eds), *Medieval Transformations: Texts, Power, and Gifts in Context*, Leiden, 2001, pp. 203–18

———, 'Tenth-century courts at Mâcon and the perils of structuralist history: Re-reading Burgundian judicial institutions', in Warren C. Brown and Piotr Górecki (eds), *Conflict in Medieval Europe: Changing Perspectives on Society and Culture*, Aldershot, 2003, pp. 37–68.

———, *Feuding and Peace-making in Eleventh-century France*, Aldershot, 2005.

Wickham, Chris, 'Conclusion: Dispute processes and social structures', in Davies and Fouracre (eds), *The Settlement of Disputes in Early Medieval Europe*, pp. 228–40.

———, 'Land disputes and their social framework in Lombard-Carolingian Italy, 700–900', in *Land and Power: Studies in Italian and European Social History, 400–1200*, London, 1994, pp. 229–56.

———, 'Justice in the kingdom of Italy in the eleventh century', in *La giustizia nell'alto medioevo*, vol. 1, pp. 179–250.

———, *Courts and Conflict in Twelfth-century Tuscany*, Oxford, 2003.

———, 'Public court practice: The eighth and twelfth centuries compared', in Stefan Esders (ed.), *Rechtsverständnis und Konfliktbewältigung. Gerichtliche und aussergerichtliche Strategien im Mittelalter*, Köln, 2007, pp. 17–30.

Wood, Susan, *The Proprietary Church in the Medieval West*, Oxford, 2006.

Wormald, Patrick, 'A handlist of Anglo-Saxon law-suits', *Anglo-Saxon England*, 17 (1988), pp. 247–81.

———, 'Giving God and king their due: Conflict and its regulation in the early English state', in *La giustizia nell'alto medioevo*, vol. 1, pp. 549–83.

———, *The Making of English Law: King Alfred to the Twelfth Century, Volume I: Legislation and its Limits*, Oxford, 1999; vol. 2 published as Patrick Wormald, *Papers Preparatory to the Making of English Law: King Alfred to the Twelfth Century, Volume II: From God's Law to Common Law*, ed. Stephen Baxter and John Hudson, London, 2014: http://www.earlyenglishlaws.ac.uk/reference/wormald/.

Zeller, Bernhard, 'Writing charters as a public activity: The example of the Carolingian charters of Saint Gall', in Mostert and Barnwell (eds), *Medieval Legal Process*, pp. 27–37.

Zimmermann, Michel, *Écrire et lire en Catalogne (IXe–XIIe siècle)*, Bibliothèque de la Casa de Velázquez, 23, 2 vols, Madrid, 2003.

Index of dispute texts

★ indicates single sheet, some of which are copies; F = *falso*; **bold** = figure; 137n = see footnote(s) on p. 137

Accounts	*Incidental*	*Confessions*	*Agreements*	*Oaths*	*Fines*	*Implied*	*Mixed*	*Debts*	*Confiscations*
1325A6	1325A5	Ar18	1325A11	Cast1	Ast26	Cel509	A27	Cel180	Cel104
1325A9	Ast84	C151	Ast25	Li34	Cel169	DC113	Cel265	Cel197-3	Li123
Ast5	C54	C35	C103	SMdelP2	Cel180-4	DC115	Li192	Cel204-3	Li253
Ast71	C59	C90	Cast5	V10	Cel189	DC167	Lii508	Cel229	Lii411
C129	Cañ49	Cel94	Cel204	V11	Cel190	DC17	OvC26	Cel353	Lii442
C22	Cañ69-8	Flor74	Cel446		Cel191	LaC71	S276	Cel368-6	Lii479
C55	Cel144	Li191	Cel507		Cel197	Ov3		Cel409	Lii482
Cañ41	Cel161	OD38	DC144		Cel204-3	S101		Cel411	Lii507
Cañ65	Cel165	S261	Flor73		Cel368-11	SMdelP4		DC81	Liii541
Cast3	Cel205	SMdelP1	Flor75		Cel393	V43		DC91	Liii567
Cel215	Cel210	Sob75	Li94		Cel456			LaC58	Liii581
Cel252	Cel228	T17	Lii290		Cel72			Lii457	S287
Cel502	Cel233	T30	Lii330		DC58			Lii465	S322
Cel93	Cel338	T66A	Lii400		Li138			Liii564	S84
Cel95	Cel511	V33	Lii437		Lii458			OD14	SantA13
DC13	Cel527		Lii477		Lii463			OD41	SantA15
DC163	Cel84		Liii597		Lii473			Ov23	SantA16
DC183	DC160		Lor35		Liii556			S198	SantA5
DC42	DC179		OD39		Liii561			Sob14	TV15
Jaca	DC39		OD4		Liii578			Sob98	
LaC59	DC43		OD43		Liii590			Sob99	
LaC65	DC53		S33		OD34				
LaC95	E30		S372		OD37				
Li128	LaC102		Sam247		OD40				
Li144	LaC50-2		SantA28		OD44				
Li184	LaC61		SJP31		S218				
Li256	LaC87		SMdelP3						
Li89	Li116		T62						
Li99	Li141		T66B						
Lii312	Li148								
Lii410	Li243								
Lii452	Li71								
Liii559	Lii278								
Liii577	Lii355								
Oña3	Lii360								
OvC24	Lii378								
S159	Lii405								
S295	Lii432								
S356	Lii450								
Sam126	Lii474								
Sam35	OD27								
Sam44	OD29								
Sam46	OD31								
Sam5-9	OD32								
SantA24	OD33								
SantA42	S133								
SantA58	S180								
SJP13	S221								
SJP14	S358								
SJP18	Sam156								
SM23	Sam16								
SM27	Sam239								
SM50	Sam6								
SM98	SantA57								
Sob103	Sob122								
Sob109	Sob21								
Sob129	Sob23								
Sob130	Sob24								
TV135	Sob29								
	Sob31								
	Sob32								
	Sob43								
	Sob46								
	Sob54								
	Sob6								
	T41								

Index

For Product Safety Concerns and Information please contact our EU representative GPSR@taylorandfrancis.com Taylor & Francis Verlag GmbH, Kaufingerstraße 24, 80331 München, Germany